THE MYTHOLOGY OF ALL RACES

VOLUME II
EDDIC

PLATE I

WAYLAND SMITH'S CAVE OR FORGE

Wayland Smith is the Volund of the Eddic poem *Volundarkvitha*. The Volund story had its origin among the Saxon tribes, but spread all over the Teutonic area. It was known to the Anglo-Saxons, and 'Wēlandes Smiththan' is mentioned in a document dating from a few years before the Norman Conquest. The name had been given to the remains of a chambered tumulus or 'Long Barrow' (or, as some regard it, a chambered dolmen) at Ashbury, Berkshire. For the legend connected with this, see p. 271, and Sir W. Scott's *Kenilworth*, chapter xiii and note 2. The Anglo-Saxon poem, *Deor's Lament*, refers to the Volund story, and in a document of the year 903 A.D. mention is made of a place in Buckinghamshire called 'Wēlandes Stocc.' The phrase 'Wēlandes geweorc' was also used by the Anglo-Saxons to denote weapons and ornaments of exceptional value.

THE MYTHOLOGY
OF ALL RACES

IN THIRTEEN VOLUMES

CANON JOHN ARNOTT MacCULLOCH, D.D., Editor

GEORGE FOOT MOORE, A.M., D.D., LL.D., Consulting Editor

EDDIC

BY

JOHN ARNOTT MacCULLOCH

HON. D.D., ST. ANDREWS

VOLUME II

NEW YORK

COOPER SQUARE PUBLISHERS, INC.

1964

Printed in U.S.A. by
NOBLE OFFSET PRINTERS, INC.
NEW YORK 3, N. Y.

TO MY WIFE

CONTENTS

CONTENTS

ILLUSTRATIONS

ix

PREFACE

WHEN this Series was first projected, Professor Axel Olrik, Ph. D., of the University of Copenhagen, was asked to write the volume on Eddic Mythology, and no one more competent than he could have been chosen. He agreed to undertake the work, but his lamented death occurred before he had done more than sketch a plan and write a small part of it.

Ultimately it was decided that I should write the volume, and the result is now before the reader.

Throughout the book, the names of gods, heroes, and places are generally given without accents, which are meaningless to most readers, and the spelling of such names is mainly that which accords most nearly with the Old Norse pronunciation. 'Odin,' however, is preferred to the less usual 'Othin,' and so with a few other familiar names, the spelling of which is now stereotyped in English.

Several of the illustrations are from material which had been collected by Professor Olrik, with which the publisher supplied me. The coloured illustrations and those in pen and ink drawing are by my daughter. I have to thank the authorities of the British Museum for permission to use their photographs of the Franks' Casket and of Anglo-Saxon draughtsmen; the Director of the Universitetets Oldsaksamling, Oslo, for photographs of the Oseberg Ship; Mr. W. G. Collingwood, F.S.A., for permission to reproduce his sketches of Borg and Helga-fell; and Professor G. Baldwin Brown, LL.D., of the Chair of Fine Art, University of Edinburgh, for photographs of the Dearham, Bewcastle, and Ruthwell Crosses.

J. A. MacCULLOCH

THE BRIDGE OF ALLAN
SCOTLAND
October 8, 1929

EDDIC MYTHOLOGY

BY

JOHN ARNOTT MacCULLOCH

INTRODUCTION

THE Teutonic peoples in the early centuries of our era were found over a considerable part of central Europe, north of the Rhine and the Danube. They also stretched farther northwards and had occupied Denmark and a great part of the Scandinavian peninsula from prehistoric times. In the fifth century began those movements of the Teutonic tribes which led to their occupation of the Roman empire. Ethnology divides the Teutons into three groups — the High Germans in middle and upper Germany, Switzerland, and Austria; the Low Germans, including the North Germans, Flemings, Dutch, Frisians, and Anglo-Saxons; and the Scandinavians of Denmark, Sweden, Norway and Iceland.

The religious beliefs of this widespread people are known to us imperfectly, and while all of them must have had a common religious heritage, one of the chief problems of religion and mythology is to decide how far all the various tribes had the same deities, the same beliefs and customs, the same myths. Very different views are advocated as solutions of this problem. What is known from classical observers regarding Teutonic religion, from archæological remains, from notices in the lives and writings of Christian missionaries, from survivals in folk-custom and folk-belief, from ecclesiastical laws, is of the highest importance. From these sources we gather that, on many matters, there was much similarity of belief and practice, but there are many others on which it is impossible to come to a definite conclusion.

While we may speak within limits of Teutonic mythology, strict exactitude should rather speak of Eddic mythology — the myths found in the *Eddas*, for detailed myths can hardly be said to have survived elsewhere. These myths belong to Iceland and Norway, possibly also to Sweden and Denmark. How far any of them belonged to other branches of the Teutonic people is a matter of conjecture. Here and there we have certain lines of evidence which suggest a common heritage of myth. Certain myths, however, belong solely to the Scandinavian regions where the Eddic material was native, just as do also the beliefs in certain gods and goddesses.

The purpose of this book is to give an account of Eddic mythology, showing wherever possible its connexions with that of other branches of the Teutonic stock.

What, then, are the *Eddas,* and where and when were they composed?

According to one manuscript of a work composed by Snorri Sturluson (1178–1241), which came into possession of Brynjolf Sveinsson, bishop of Skálholt in the seventeenth century, the work itself is called ' *Edda.*' It deals, as we shall see, with Norse mythology. Sveinsson was also owner of a manuscript containing poems, many of which were cited by Snorri and used by him in compiling his work. From this connexion these poems now came to be called *Edda* or ' the Elder *Edda,*' in distinction from the prose work which was styled ' the Younger *Edda.*' The collection of poems was also called *Sæmundar Edda,* from the belief that they were the work of Sæmund the Wise, an Icelandic priest and collector of old poetry, who lived in the second half of the eleventh century and died in 1133 A.D. It is now generally known as ' the Poetic *Edda.*'

Different derivations of the word *Edda* have been suggested. By many scholars it is now conceded that the word is the genitive of ' *Oddi,*' the name of a homestead in Iceland, which was a seat of learning, and where Snorri was educated and lived for many years, and where Sæmund had also dwelt for some time, if tradition speaks true. Hence Snorri's book would be ' of Oddi ' or ' the book of Oddi.' Another derivation much favoured is that *Edda* is from *oþr,* ' song,' ' poem,' and that the title, as given to Snorri's work, signified its contents and their purpose, viz., ' Poetics ' or ' treatise of Poetics.'

Snorri Sturluson was one of the most learned men of his time — a historian, a lover of poetry, of antiquities, of the traditions of the past, an able and gifted writer. His position in Iceland was one of great influence, and eventually he became chief judge and president of the legislative assembly there. He wrote or composed the *Heimskringla* — a series of sagas or stories of the lives of the kings of Norway down to 1177. The first part of the work, the *Ynglinga-saga*, is based on the old poem *Ynglinga-tal*, and shows how Odin and other deities were kings and chiefs, and how the Norwegian kings were descended from the Ynglings at Upsala. Snorri's *Edda* is justly styled ' a manual of Poetics.' There had developed in the North not only special rules for the composition of poetry but a special poetic language. In the latter innumerable periphrases or ' kennings ' (*kenningur*) had come into use, and without them poetry was now little thought of. Fortunately the poems of the Poetic *Edda* are remarkably free of such kennings, and in many other ways differ from the poetry of the skalds or court poets. The following examples of kennings may be given — battle was ' storm of Odin '; a ship was ' steed of the billows '; the earth was ' flesh of Ymir '; gold was ' Sif's hair.' Thousands of such kennings, many of them even more elaborate than these, and mostly based on the old pagan mythology, were in use in the composition of verse. Obviously a knowledge of kennings demanded much study and implied a wide acquaintance with mythology. To give to young poets a full account of the old myths and to illustrate the kennings enumerated from the verses of other skalds, was Snorri's purpose in compiling his *Edda*.

It consists of three parts. The first of these, *Gylfaginning*, ' Beguiling of Gylfi,' is a methodical account of the old gods and goddesses, the myths in which some of them figure, the cosmogony, and the final Doom of the gods. It is written with much liveliness, spirit, humour, and pathos, and it is a wonderful monument of medieval literature. The name of this section of the work is due to the framework in which it is set. Gylfi was king of Sweden, wise and skilled in cunning and magic. He wondered whether the Æsir or gods were so cunning by nature or whether this was a gift from the powers which they worshipped. It should be observed that here and elsewhere in Snorri's *Edda*, though not uniformly, as also in a Prologue to the work, he adopts the euhemeristic theory of the gods — they were mortal kings, magicians and the like. Gylfi, in the form of an old man called Gangleri, set out for Asgard, the seat of the gods. The Æsir, knowing who he really was and foreseeing his coming, prepared deceptions for him. He arrived and was well received, and was presented to three lords who sat on as many seats, one above the other. Their names were Har, 'High,' Jafnhar, 'Equally High,' and Thridi, 'Third' — all forms of Odin. Gylfi now began his questions. The answers are the myths of which *Gylfaginning* is full. When all had been recounted, Gylfi heard great noises, and, looking round, found himself out of doors on a level plain. Hall and castle and Æsir had vanished. He had been deceived by glamour.

In this part of his book Snorri uses some of the Eddic poems — *Voluspa, Grimnismal, Vafthrudnismal,* with occasional use of four others. These he sometimes expands in reducing them to prose. He also uses poems of an Eddic character now lost, save for fragments quoted by him, poems by the court poets, and, in all likelihood, much oral tradition. The result is a full and systematic account of Norse mythology as it was possible to reconstruct it in Snorri's day.

The second part, the *Skaldskaparmal,* 'Poetry of skalds,' is preceded by the *Bragarœdur* — an account of the origin of the poetic mead, told by Bragi to Ægir, also a visitor to Asgard and the Æsir. In the *Skaldskaparmal,* by means of innumerable quotations from skaldic verse, the use of kennings for many subjects is shown. Much of it deals with the gods and several myths are told. An example of the method used may be cited. 'How should one periphrase Njord? By calling him God of the Vanir, Kinsman of the Vanir, Van, Father of Frey and Freyja, God of wealth-giving.' Then follows a verse by a skald illustrating some of these kennings.

The third part, the *Hattatal*, ' Enumeration of Metres,' contains three songs of praise in which each of over a hundred stanzas is in a different metre, the oldest kinds being given last. Between them are definitions, comments and notes.

It may seem strange that, in a Christian age, Snorri should have composed a work full of pagan myths, regarded from a fairly tolerant point of view. But his enthusiasm as a lover of the past, an antiquary, a folk-lorist, and a poet, explains much. If there were objectors to this telling of heathen lore, the purpose of it — the guidance of youthful poets and the preservation of the glories of poetic tradition — would serve as its best apology in a cultured age.

The manuscript of the Poetic *Edda* owned by Sveinsson had been written *c.* 1300. It is now known as Codex Regius and is in the Royal Library at Copenhagen. It contains twenty-nine poems. Another manuscript in the Arnamagnæan collection at Copenhagen has six of the poems of Codex Regius and a seventh, *Baldrs Draumar,* which the latter lacks. Other manuscripts contain four poems now included in the Eddic collection — *Rigsthula, Hyndluljod,* and *Svipdagsmal,* which consists of two poems, *Grougaldr* and *Fjolsvinnsmal.* Another poem, *Grottasongr,* given in Snorri's *Edda,* is usually joined with these. Thus the Poetic *Edda* consists of thirty-four poems. Almost certainly many other poems of a similar kind and differing from the poetry current in Norway must have existed, but are now lost. A few fragments of such poems are found in Snorri's *Edda.* What we do possess is a collection of mythical and heroic poems, which, taken together with Snorri's work, give us a connected though far from complete view of Norse mythology and heroic legend. Such collections of poems as are found in the *Edda* must have been made previous to 1300 A.D. and most probably in Iceland.

Iceland had been colonized from Norway in the ninth century as a result of Harold the Fair-haired's victory over the Norse nobles, which gave him rule over the whole land. In Iceland there grew up a vigorous civilization and intellectual life, which was abundantly fostered by the links with the world overseas, through the roving habits of the Icelanders. This manifold life was enhanced by the coming of Christianity to Iceland. The Scandinavian peoples had remained outside the Christian fold long after the conversion of the other Teutonic peoples, though not unaffected by currents from Christian civilization. Denmark received Christianity in the tenth century; from there it passed to Sweden and by 1075 was firmly established there. Norway was Christianized during the tenth and eleventh centuries, and in the same period Iceland also became Christian.

Very different opinions are held regarding the date and place of composition of the Eddic poems. Probably many of them belong to the pagan period, i.e., before 1000 A.D. None of them were composed before 800 A.D., and only a few belong to so late a time as the twelfth century. The bulk of the mythological poems, i.e., those dealing with the divinities, were composed before 1000 A.D. Some scholars believe that the poems were written by Norsemen in the Western Isles of Britain and under Celtic influences, or, like Sophus Bugge, that the bulk of them are based on tales and poems heard by the Norsemen from Irishmen and Englishmen, and that these poems and tales were in turn based on Graeco-Roman myths and Jewish-Christian legends.[1] Others hold that Norway was their place of origin. Others, again, maintain that they were Icelandic, part of the product of the busy intellectual life of that island. It is quite possible that both Norway and Iceland shared in their production. Two of the heroic poems, *Atlamal* and *Atlakvitha* were ascribed to Greenland in the thirteenth century manuscript. The authors of the Eddic poems are quite unknown.

The poems are divided into two groups, mythological (stories in which the divinities are the chief personages) and heroic. The former are almost certainly based on native traditions regarding the gods. On the other hand the material of the heroic poems is not Scandinavian, but was carried to Norway from Denmark and Germany, and freely worked upon by the poets. One peculiarity of the Eddic poems is that they are not descriptive: only here and there a prose insertion explains the situation. Mostly they are in dialogue form, and the narrative is mirrored in the speeches of the protagonists. Many explanations of this have been put forward. The most recent is that of Miss B. S. Phillpotts who maintains that many of the poems were folk-dramas, the action of the actors serving instead of explanatory narrative, while knowledge of the story of the drama would be presupposed.[2]

Of the mythological poems *Voluspa* stands first. It is spoken by a Volva or seeress, perhaps one raised from the dead for that purpose by Odin, whom she seems to address. She gives an account of the origin of the world, of men, of dwarfs; of the early days of the gods; and then passes on to a prophecy of the Doom of the gods, preceded by the death of Balder. The poem is impressive, though its meaning is occasionally obscure, and it seems probable that a much shorter original poem was added to and edited at different times.[3]

In certain poems Odin figures prominently. *Vafthrudnismal* tells of his questions to the giant Vafthrudnir, the answers forming a kind of cosmogonic encyclopaedia. *Grimnismal* is of the same character, though here Odin himself as Grimnir, set between two fires by king Geirrod, gives the information to Geirrod's son, Agnar, and in the end vanishes, while king Geirrod dies on his own sword. In *Baldrs Draumar* (' Balder's Dreams '), we see Odin descending to the Underworld to rouse a dead sibyl in order that she may explain Balder's evil dreams. *Havamal* is a compound of several poems, in two of which ethical advice or proverbial wisdom is given, presumably by

Odin. The poem also tells of Odin and the daughter of Billing, of his obtaining the poetic mead from Gunnlod, a giant's daughter, and of his gaining runes.

In other poems Thor is the chief protagonist. *Hymiskvitha* tells how he sought a huge kettle from the giant Hymir, and how he caught the Midgard-serpent when fishing with the giant. In *Thrymskvitha* Thor, disguised as Freyja, whom the giant Thrym desires as his wife, deceives the giant and slays him with his hammer, which the giant had stolen. *Alvissmal* tells how the dwarf Alviss desired Thor's daughter as his wife. Thor demanded that he should recite the various names given to different objects by gods, elves, giants, dwarfs, men, etc., and thus kept him talking till sunrise which is fatal to dwarfs. In *Lokasenna*, though Loki is the chief speaker, Thor appears towards the end of the poem and forces him to cease his slanders against the gods and goddesses.

Both Thor and Odin (as Harbard) figure in *Harbardsljod*. The poem is a ' flyting ' or abusive dialogue between the gods, who boast of their exploits and threaten each other, Thor being ignorant that his opponent is Odin.[4]

Skirnismal is the story of Frey's passion for the giantess Gerd and tells how his servant Skirnir was sent to seek her for the god.

In *Hyndluljod* Freyja, mounted on a boar (her lover Ottarr in disguise), seeks the wisdom of the seeress Hyndla to learn the descent of Ottarr. This poem contains a fragment of a cosmogonic poem known as ' the short *Voluspa*.'

Rigsthula tells how the god Heimdall or Rig came to earth and begat the first thrall, the first karl or peasant, and the first jarl or warrior-noble. From the last there ultimately comes one who is a future king. The poem is thus one in praise of kingship, and for that reason is probably of Norwegian origin, though composed by one who had picked up much Celtic speech and culture.

Svipdagsmal consists of two parts — *Grougaldr* or ' Groa's spell,' and *Fjolsvinnsmal*. In the first, Svipdag rouses his dead mother in order that she may aid him in his quest of Menglod, set him by his hostile step-mother. In the second we follow him on the quest and listen to the dialogue between him and the giant guardian of Menglod's dwelling. In this there is much mythological information.

The heroic poems, with the exception of *Volundarkvitha* and the three Helgi poems, are concerned with the Volsungs and particularly with Sigurd, the German Siegfried.

Volundarkvitha consists of two poems about Volund joined together. The first is a Swan-maiden story; the second deals with Volund in the power of King Nithud and his escape and revenge. Volund is Weyland the smith of English tradition, and the subject of the poem is of German origin. The stories must have passed from the Saxon region to Scandinavia.

The Helgi poems are based on Danish originals, Helgi having been a Danish hero. In *Helgakvitha Hjorvardssonar* Helgi is regarded as a different personage from the Helgi of the two *Helgakvitha Hundingsbana* poems. Both, however, are the same traditional personage, and the prose annotation of the poems makes one a rebirth apparently of the other. The poems tell the adventures of the heroes, chiefly in avenging their fathers, and their love of Valkyries who are also daughters of men (Svava, Sigrun).

The remainder of the poems, sixteen in number, are devoted to various episodes of the story of the Volsungs.

Some of the poems of the skalds of the ninth and tenth centuries deal with mythological subjects and contain references to the deities or to myths about them. The authors of these poems, as distinct from the Eddic poems, are known to us by name. A convenient collection of these, with text and translation, will be found in the *Corpus Poeticum Boreale* of G. Vigfusson and Frederick York Powell.

From the Icelandic Sagas much information regarding religion and folk-lore is derived. These Sagas are stories of a historical or biographical kind, though history and biography are often fictitious. Before they assumed written form from the mid-twelfth century onwards, Sagas had formed a favourite entertainment at festive gatherings, told orally by a skilled story-teller.[5]

Another source of information is the *Gesta Danorum* or *Historia Danica* of Saxo Grammaticus, especially the first nine books. Saxo was a Danish scholar living in the twelfth century, and he has incorporated in his work both Danish and Norse materials — sagas, history, poems, and myths. Where myths of the gods are concerned, Saxo regards these deities from a euhemeristic point of view, as we shall see presently.

For Teutonic religion in general the sources are wider, but contain little regarding mythology. The classical writers, especially Tacitus in his *Germania* and *Annales*, are first. Inscriptions with names of deities from altars and other monuments in the Romano-German area supply some information. There are also many scattered notices in ecclesiastical and other writings, Lives of Saints, and Histories, e.g., those of Bede or Gregory of Tours. Laws, secular and ecclesiastical, canons of Councils and Synods, the Penitentials, as well as passages of sermons, yield abundant evidence regarding surviving pagan customs and beliefs. Place and personal names, names of plants and the like, have also been found significant. And, in general, folk-customs, folk-lore, and folk-stories, if critically regarded, can be used as sources of information regarding the distant past.

Although the chief if not the only source for mythology is contained in the *Eddas*, it is impossible to treat the subject without reference to what is known or can be deduced regarding the beliefs of the Teutonic people outside Scandinavia. Taking the myths themselves, some are nature myths, and the meaning of a few, at least, lies on the surface. Many writers on the subject of Eddic mythology have been tempted to give elaborate explanations of all the myths in terms of natural phenomena. Each writer treats a myth according to his own predilections. We cannot be certain that the old myths had any of the meanings assigned to them, certainly they could not have had all of these, and such writers do not seem to have seen that they themselves are modern mythologizers, elaborating a complicated mythology of their own upon the stories of the past.

EDDIC MYTHOLOGY

CHAPTER I

THE GODS: A GENERAL SURVEY

A STANZA of the short *Voluspa* in *Hyndluljod* (30) says that eleven of the gods remained when Balder's corpse was laid on the funeral pyre. Snorri also says that the number of the gods is twelve,[1] but this is merely a round figure, not borne out by other references in his work. Thus, in the account of the gods which follows this statement, fourteen are named. These are Odin, Thor, Balder, Njord, Frey, Tyr, Bragi, Heimdall, Hod, Vidarr, Vali, Ull, Forseti, and Loki.

At the beginning of the *Bragarœdur* Snorri enumerates the gods present at a banquet, and, including Odin, names thirteen of them. Balder is omitted, and Hœnir appears in place of Hod.

The prose introduction to *Lokasenna* names Odin, Thor, Bragi, Tyr, Njord, Frey, Vidarr, and Loki. In *Grimnismal* Odin, Ull, Frey, Balder, Heimdall, Forseti, Njord, Vidarr, and Thor are named. In other poems the other gods are mentioned.

With these gods are also several goddesses, some of whom are little more than names or hypostases of a greater goddess. Their names are Frigg, consort of Odin, Freyja, sister of Frey, Saga, Eir, Gefjun, Fulla, Hnoss, Sjofn, Lofn, Var, Syn, Hlin, Snotra, Gna, Idunn, Nanna, Sif. Besides these, two local goddesses, Thorgerd Hölgabrud and her sister Irpa, are mentioned in *Skaldskaparmal* and in some of the Sagas.

Other more or less divine beings are mentioned occasionally. Vili and Ve are brothers of Odin, and form a kind of creative

triad with him. A similar triad is that of Odin, Hœnir, and
Lodur. There are also subordinate gods, regarded as servants
of the higher deities, e.g., Skirnir and Hermod. Ægir, not
counted among the gods, is yet a god of the sea; a giant, however, rather than a god. Ran is his consort. Then, again, Hel
is a somewhat vague female personification of the Underworld.

Some of the gods are married to giantesses, who, as their
consorts, are reckoned with the deities — Frey to Gerd, Njord
to Skadi, Odin to Jord (Earth), co-wife with Frigg. Such
nature objects as the sun, personified as Sol, and one of the two
beings who follow the moon in the sky, i.e., Bil, are also reckoned among the goddesses by Snorri.[2]

We do not know that all these deities were worshipped
together in Norway and Iceland, indeed for many of them no
evidence of a cult exists. Some may have been local divinities:
some are regarded as creations of the skalds. Among them all
Odin, Thor, and Frey are pre-eminent, but, as we shall see, the
precise significance of Odin's position in relation to Thor requires elucidation. In Snorri's *Edda* Odin is head of a court or
assembly of divinities. Their common home is Asgard, but most
of them have a separate abode, as appears from *Grimnismal*,
here followed by Snorri.

We now enquire whether any of these deities were known in
other parts of the Germanic area outside Norway and Iceland.

For Denmark and Sweden we depend mainly on Saxo Grammaticus and Adam of Bremen, the eleventh century historian.
Saxo may be assumed to speak for the pagan past of Denmark,
though he uses Icelandic sources to some extent in his curious
account of the legendary history of that country. He has a
conception of the gods as gods, though he generally tends to
visualize them from a euhemeristic standpoint, as kings, magicians, and the like. He mentions Othinus (Odin), chief of the
gods, whose rule, with that of the other gods, extended over
Denmark, Sweden, and Norway, but who used to sojourn more
continually at Upsala. Odin is also called Uggerus (Norse

Ygg).   Other deities named are Frey, 'satrap of the gods,' whose seat was at Upsala; Thor, Balder, Hotherus (Hod), Ollerus (Ull), Freya (Frigg), and Nanna.   Loki may be represented by Ugarthilocus (Utgard-Loki).   Proserpina may stand for Hel.[3]   Adam of Bremen describes a sanctuary at Upsala, with images of Thor, Woden, and Fricco (Frey).[4]   The other Eddic deities are not mentioned by these or other writers about the Danes and Swedes, though Procopius speaks of Ares as a Scandinavian deity, i.e., Odin or Tyr.[5]

For the Germanic tribes, apart from place or personal names, there are few references to the gods of the pagan period.   Tacitus gives Roman names to native gods — Mars (Ziu or Tyr), Mercury (Wodan), Hercules (perhaps Thor).   He also mentions a native name of a goddess Nerthus and describes her cult. Two brothers called Alcis are compared to Castor and Pollux, and are said to have been worshipped in a grove as deities by one tribe.   He also speaks of the grove of Baduhenna among the Frisians and the temple of Tamfana among the Marsi.   The first part of the name Baduhenna is connected with AS *beadu*, OHG *batu-*, ON *boþ*, 'war,' and the second part with OHG *winna*, ' quarrel,' MHG *winnen*, ' to rage,' Gothic *winno*, ' passion,' showing that Baduhenna was a War-goddess, 'the war-mad one.'   A division of the Suebi worshipped Isis, whose symbol was a ship.   This cult Tacitus considers of foreign origin, but it is doubtless that of a native goddess whose name is concealed in that of Isis.

Several names of deities are mentioned in inscriptions on altars and other monuments, mainly in Romano-German territory, but the names of these, doubtless more or less local deities, have nothing in common with those of Scandinavia.

More to the purpose are the two Merseburg charms found in a tenth century manuscript in the library of the cathedral at Merseburg, and probably of earlier date.   Both charms refer to mythical actions of the deities, and by recounting these similar results are expected to follow.   Such charms as these are met with in ancient times and are of widespread occurrence. The first charm concerns a group of beings called Idisi, a name resembling that of the Norse female spirits called Disir and including Valkyries and Norns. To the functions of the Valkyries those of the Idisi in the charm correspond — binding or loosing fetters on prisoners of war and keeping back the enemy.

The other charm relates that while Phol and Uuodan (Wodan) rode to the wood, the foot of Balder's colt was wrenched. Sinthgunt charmed it and her sister Sunna; then Frîa charmed it and Volla her sister. Then Uuodan charmed it, as he well knew how to do. The implication is that the goddesses could not heal the foot by their magic, while Wodan's magic succeeded. As we shall see later various explanations of ' Phol ' have been suggested, while ' Balder ' has been regarded as not a proper name here, but an appellative for ' prince,' and referring to Odin himself, Phol being then explained as the name of Odin's horse. Of the four goddesses Frîa is Frigg; Volla suggests the Norse Fulla; Sunna may be a personification of the sun. Sinthgunt is unexplained. Some scholars think that two goddesses only are mentioned in the charm as present; it should then read: ' Sinthgunt, Sunna's sister,' and ' Frîa, Volla's sister.' [6]

Wodan and Frija (Frigg) were also known to the Lombards, as a legend concerning them shows.[7]

The next piece of evidence is derived from German names of the days of the week. These show that Wodan was known in North-west Germany and Holland; Frîa (Frigg) over a wider area; Donar (Thor) all over Germany, Tiu (Tyr) in the South-west.

A formula of renunciation used at the baptism of Saxon converts in Charlemagne's time names three gods — Woden, Thunaer (Thor), and Saxnot, as well as other *Unholden,* divinities or spirits regarded from a Christian point of view as demons.[8] Saxnot, ' Sword companion,' is the Seaxneat of

Anglo-Saxon genealogies, and is regarded as a form of the god Tyr.

Another god of a local kind is Fosite, mentioned in Alcuin's *Life of S. Willibrord,* as worshipped on an island named after him. According to Adam of Bremen this island was Helgoland.[9] It is not certain that Fosite is the Eddic Forseti.

Turning now to the Anglo-Saxons, the only available evidence is that of names of the days of the week, genealogical lists, and place-names. The first of these gives Tiw or Tyr (Tuesday), Woden (Wednesday), Thunor or Thor (Thursday), Fri or Frigg (Friday). The genealogical lists of the royal families trace descent back to Woden. In those of Bernicia and Wessex Bældæg (Balder) succeeds Woden. In that of Essex Seaxneat is his son.[10] Thor's name occurs in place-names.

The evidence from these different regions shows that there was a certain number of deities known locally and objects of a local or tribal cult. Few names of these have been preserved. The wide acceptance of Roman deities by the Celts had no parallel among the Teutons. Nor does the rich variety of native Celtic local deities, whether equated or not with Roman deities, meet us in Teutonic lands. Inscriptions with names of local deities are few and generally enigmatic.[11] On the other hand there are some deities known more or less over the whole area — Wodan or Woden or Odin, Thunor or Thor, Tiu or Tyr, and Frija, Frîa, or Frigg. Hence these have been called 'pan-Teutonic deities,' who 'must have come down from a period when the Teutons were still an undivided people.'[12] Nevertheless this statement of Mogk's requires some modification, since, as is suggested by various lines of evidence and as he himself admits, the cult of Wodan migrated from Germany by way of Denmark to Scandinavia, where it tended to supersede that of Thor.

The divinities of Norse mythology are called Æsir (singular Áss). The original meaning of the word is uncertain. Mogk and others, however, regard it as connected etymologically with

Sanskrit *anas*, ' breath,' ' wind.' Hence the Æsir were originally animistic beings or souls. Odin, as leader of the host of
the dead, belonged to the Æsir, but as his rank became higher
and more divine so the word Áss as applied to him assumed the
meaning of ' god,' and all gods associated with Odin were known
as Æsir, Odin being *oztr asa*, ' mightiest of the Æsir.' [13] This
theory gains some support from the fact that the corresponding
Gothic word *ansis* was used as the title of dead ancestral chiefs
in the sense of *semi-deos*, according to Jordanes, the historian
of the Goths. The *Bardar-saga* relates that, after his death,
Bardar, as guardian spirit of the region about Snaefell was
known as ' Snaefells-áss.' [14] The corresponding Anglo-Saxon
word is *ēsa* (singular *ós*), used in the phrase *esa gescot, ylfa
gescot*, ' the shot of *ēsa* and elves.' *Ēsa* here apparently meant
supernatural beings hostile to men, rather than gods, but
the word may have once meant ' gods,' and Æsir and
Alfar (' elves ') are frequently coupled together in Eddic
poetry. In other branches of Teutonic speech a corresponding word is found as part of personal names — OHG *ans* in
Anso, Anshelm, and the like, Saxon and AS *os* in Oswald, Oslaf,
Osdag.

Among the Æsir were included certain deities, Njord, Frey,
Freyja, and possibly others, called collectively Vanir. These
were once opposed to the Æsir, according to certain myths.
They were deities of wealth, fruitfulness, trade, and prosperity,
and their name may be connected with words meaning ' bright,'
' shining.'

The gods are also known by the general neuter name *goþ*,
' gods,' with the epithet ' holy,' ' blessed,' this corresponding to
Gothic *guþ;* AS and OS *god*. Under Christian influence the
word became masculine. Other names applied to the gods are
regen, the word signifying ' decreeing ' and ' deciding,' hence
perhaps ' counsellors.' *Voluspa* speaks of all the *regen* assem-
bling at the seat of judgment to take counsel. In *Havamal,
Alvissmal,* and *Hymiskvitha* occurs the word *ginn-regen*, ' the

high *or* holy gods,' and in *Alvissmal up-regen* is used with the meaning 'the gods above.' In the two passages of *Alvissmal* where *ginn-regen* occurs the word may signify the Vanir.[15]

Still another term for gods is *tivar*, 'shining ones,' related to Sanskrit *devas*. It occurs in some of the Eddic poems. The forms *sig-tivar*, *val-tivar*, 'battle-gods,' also occur.[16] For some reason not quite clear gods are described as *hopt ok bond*, 'fastenings and bands' or 'fetters.'

Goddesses are included in the term Æsir, but a specific name for them is Asynjur (singular Asynja).

Generally speaking the gods of Eddic mythology are conceived under anthropomorphic forms, yet distinguished from men in different ways. Noble or princely men were sometimes regarded as gods. The sons of Hjalti, as they came to the assembly in Iceland, looked so magnificent and well-equipped that the people thought they were Æsir. Of Sigurd in his magnificent war-gear, riding a splendid horse, as he entered Gjuki's town, it was said: 'Surely here comes one of the gods!'[17] The birth of some of the gods is related; their human passions or weaknesses are described; they grow old; eventually they must die.

Some of the gods are described in striking language. They are white or shining, like Balder or Heimdall. The goddess Sif is famed for her luxuriant gold hair. On the other hand, if they have not the numerous hands and arms of Hindu gods, some are deformed. Odin is one-eyed, Tyr has only one hand, Hod is blind. Probably most of the gods were regarded as larger than men: this is true of Thor in particular. Some are thought of as older, some younger. Odin is grey-bearded, yet has none of the weakness of age. Thor is as a man in his prime. Balder is a youth, attractive and graceful. Some of the gods waxed in size and strength as soon as born. Vali, son of Odin, avenged Balder's death when he was one night old. Magni, son of Thor, when three nights old, could lift the giant Hrungnir's foot off his father, though all the Æsir together could not do this, and said that he would have slain him with his fist had not Thor killed him.

The gods eat and drink, and much is told of their banquets and ale or mead drinking. To Odin alone wine suffices for meat and drink. Thor is a gluttonous eater and drinker, whose gigantic meals are described. Though the gods are longer-lived than men, they are not absolutely immortal, and their long age or renewed youth depends upon eating the apples of immortality guarded by Idunn. To give immortal youth may originally have been the purpose of Odrörir, the magic mead of poesy.[18] Yet the gods are doomed to destruction, and the death of Balder is recounted. Meanwhile they are subject to wounds, and Frey falls sick of love.

The gods have preternatural powers, knowledge, and strength, but sometimes this strength seems to depend on certain possessions, e.g., Thor's hammer, girdle of strength, and gloves. Odin can overlook the worlds, but only when he sits on his Heaven-throne. *Skirnismal* shows that when Frey sat thereon, he had the same far vision. Magical powers were inherent in the gods: vanishing suddenly, transformation into other forms, human or animal, the production of glamour, and the like. Though they can move quickly from place to place, swift flight depends on a falcon's plumage or feather-dress (*fiadr-hamr*), which belongs to Freyja or Frigg, but is put on by others, e.g., Loki.

They are often described as riding, and their horses are famous steeds. They ride through air and sea and on land, or daily to their place of judgment. Earth shakes when they ride. Freyja rides on a boar, but she has also her wagon drawn by cats. Thor is famed for his wagon drawn by goats.

Like mortals the gods are subject to passions. They are mild or blithe. Their laughter is mentioned. They are joyous. But sometimes they are angry, and then their wrath is terrible, and especially is this true of Thor.[19] They are subject to the passion of love, and, besides their consorts, Odin and Thor have other wives or mistresses.

In many other ways the life of the gods reflects that of men. As described by Snorri, Odin, as chief of the gods, has a court which resembles that of earthly kings. The gods meet for counsel and judgment in the Thing, the Scandinavian assembly for the discussion of important matters and for the making of laws and giving of decisions. Snorri describes their riding daily over Bifrost, the rainbow-bridge, to the well of Urd, where they hold a tribunal. In the stanza which he quotes from *Grimnismal* and which seems to refer to this, Thor is said to walk when he goes to give dooms at the ash Yggdrasil, beneath one of the roots of which is Urd's well. The gods delight in banquets and feasting, in song and games of skill. They are fond of fighting and some of them follow the chase. The goddesses spin and weave; one of them, Gefjun, ploughs. They have servants, messengers, and cup-bearers.

The Æsir dwell in Asgard as the Vanir dwell in Vanaheim, the Alfar in Alfheim, the giants in Jötunheim. Asgard is the heavenly home of the gods, but in Snorri's euhemeristic account, it is in the centre of the earth, perhaps on a mountain, its top reaching to the heavens. Gods also dwell on mountains. The poetic account in *Grimnismal* of the separate abodes of individual gods is probably due to skaldic fiction rather than to popular belief.

The rank and functions of the gods vary, but these will be discussed in dealing with them separately. It should be noted, however, that, in describing some of the gods, Snorri uses a kind of formula. He tells what phenomena of nature or department of life each one rules over, and for what things it is good for men to call upon them.[20]

There is a tendency to group certain gods together. Besides the larger groups of Æsir and Vanir, we find certain gods associated, usually three in number. For purposes of cult this was true of Odin, Thor, and Frey. But myths associate Odin,

Hœnir, and Lodur (Loki) in the work of creation and in other actions, or, again, Odin and his brothers, Vili and Ve.[21] Snorri tells how Gylfi was received by three lords of ascending rank, and their names Har, Jafnhar, and Thridi seem to be poetic names for Odin, as all three are given in the list of his names in *Grimnismal*. There may here have been some conscious imitation of the Christian Trinity by Snorri in this otherwise inexplicable triad.

The older grouping of the chief Germanic gods was that of Wodan, Donar and Ziu (Tyr), and it was connected, as doubtless the other threefold groupings were, with the sacredness of the number three. It appears again in the Germanic theogony as reported by Tacitus in speaking of the progenitors of gods and men, the third member of the triad being a group of three — Tuisto, Mannus, and the three sons of Mannus. Corresponding to these in Eddic mythology are Buri, Borr, and Borr's three sons, Odin, Vili and Ve. The same threefold grouping is seen in the three Norns, three Swan-maidens (as in the Volund story), three groups of Idisi in the Merseburg charm, and three groups of Valkyries, as in *Helgakvitha Hjorvardssonar*.[22]

The relation of gods and men is generally that of interest and help on the one hand, and of dependence, exhibited by prayer and sacrifice, on the other. Certain offences or kinds of conduct seem to have been regarded as punishable by the gods. Myths speak of their coming and going among men, to help them or to take part in their affairs, as Odin does in battle. This was symbolized in ritual — the procession of a divine image in a wagon (Frey, Nerthus), in which, as Tacitus says, the actual deity was believed to be present.

CHAPTER II

THE VANIR

THOUGH associated in cult with the Æsir or even included among them in the *Eddas*, the Vanir are a small but distinct group of gods. They dwell in Vanaheim, not Asgard, and include Njord, Frey, and Freyja, possibly also Heimdall, who is guardian of Frey and is said to be 'like the Vanir' in knowing the future well. This forethought is not elsewhere attributed to the Vanir, but they are called 'wise.'[1] They are also 'warlike,' just as Frey is 'battle-bold.'[2] Their general functions seem to be those of nature deities, rulers of the fruitful earth and of prosperity. They are connected with sea-faring, commerce, and hunting, with peace (Frey), and with love (Freyja). *Vafthrudnismal* seems to regard them as a larger group than those specifically named, for it says that 'the wise powers' (*vis regen*) in Vanaheim created Njord, and that having been given as a pledge to the Æsir, at the Doom of the world he will return home to the Vanir. Other references to the Vanir suggest a numerous body, though this may be a result of the process of euhemerization, which is apt to make a group of deities into a whole people. Njord is called 'god of the Vanir,' 'kinsman of the Vanir,' with other epithets, applied also to his son Frey. His daughter Freyja is 'goddess of the Vanir,' 'lady of the Vanir,' 'bride of the Vanir.'[3] Yet all three are included among the Æsir. The poem *Alvissmal*, like other Eddic references, however, shows clearly their separate identity, by telling what names they, as distinct from Æsir, Alfar, etc., use for different things. *Sigrdrifumal* also distinguishes them from the Æsir, when it says that runes were given to Æsir, Vanir, Alfar, and men.

This distinction is upheld also in the different and mostly euhemerized accounts of the war between the Æsir and the Vanir. Of this Snorri gives two accounts. In his *Edda*, Bragi, recounting to Ægir the origins of poetry, says that the gods had a dispute with the people called Vanir. The cause or nature of the dispute is not mentioned. A peace-meeting was appointed, and peace was established by each and all spitting into a vat. When they parted, the gods would not let this token perish, but from it created a man, Kvasir. His story will be told later.[4] A different account of the settlement is given in a previous chapter of the *Edda*. Njord, reared in Vanaheim, was delivered as hostage to the Æsir, Hœnir being taken in exchange by the Vanir. He became an atonement between the two groups. This statement is copied from *Vafthrudnismal*.[5]

The euhemeristic account of the war and final agreement is fuller in Snorri's *Ynglinga-saga*. Odin and his host attacked the Vanir, who defended their land. Now one, now the other, prevailed: each harried the land of the other, until, tiring of this, they held a meeting of truce, made peace, and delivered hostages to each other. The Vanir gave their noblest — Njord the wealthy and his son Frey. The Æsir gave Hœnir, and said that he was meet to be lord, big and goodly as he was. With him they gave Mimir, wisest of men, the Vanir giving for him one of their best wits, Kvasir. Hœnir was made lord at Vanaheim (here said to be situated at the mouth of the Tanais, at the Black Sea), and Mimir taught him good counsel. Hœnir's stupidity was soon discovered by the Vanir when, at meetings of the Thing, Mimir not being present, Hœnir would say: ' Let others give rule,' whenever any hard matter was brought up. They saw that the Æsir had over-reached them, and, having cut Mimir's throat, sent his head to the Æsir. Odin made Njord and Frey temple-priests or Diar (from Irish *día*, ' god '). Njord's daughter Freyja first taught spell-craft (*seidr*) according to the custom of the Vanir among the Æsir (i.e., some special form of magic). Frey and Freyja, though brother and sister, were married, also in accordance with Vanir custom.[6] Vanaheim, thus made a district on earth's surface, is one of the nine worlds mentioned in *Alvissmal*.

A less euhemeristic account of this war and its origin is found in *Voluspa*. The seeress remembers the first war in the world. The Æsir had smitten Gollveig with spears and burned her in Odin's hall. Three times they burned her, yet ever she lives. They called her Heid, a Volva, a magic-wielder, who practised mind-disturbing magic and sorcery, and was the desire of evil women. All the gods held council whether the Æsir should give tribute, i.e., to the Vanir, or all gods (Æsir and Vanir) should share the sacrifices. Odin threw his spear over the host — this happened in the first world-war; now the Vanir trod the field, and the wall of Asgard was broken down.

The order of the stanzas telling this myth varies in different manuscripts, and the account of Odin's throwing his spear and the subsequent fight should probably precede the account of the council of Æsir and Vanir. The meaning seems to be that Gollveig, who may be Freyja, came among the Æsir and was shamefully treated, perhaps for her skill in magic. This led to the war, in which the citadel of the Æsir was broken down and the Vanir were triumphant. A council was then held. From the prose sources we gather that a compromise was arrived at — the sharing of the cult by both groups and an exchange of hostages. The latter is known to the author of *Vafthrudnismal*, and must have been part of the original myth.

Gollveig, 'Gold-might,' who is burned and comes alive again, is thought to embody the power of gold and its refining by fire. Whether she is the same as Heid, or whether the stanza about Heid is in its wrong place and refers to the Volva who utters the whole poem, is a moot point. If Gollveig and Heid are identical, both have some connexion with Freyja. Freyja's tears are said to be red gold, and gold is called Freyja's tears.[7] Freyja is described as a sorceress who introduced magic or a special kind of magic among the Æsir. Gollveig-Heid would

thus be Freyja, and the ill-treatment of this Vanir goddess would be the cause of the war. Unfortunately the myth in
Voluspa is too enigmatic and the stories given by Snorri are too
much euhemerized, to tell exactly what the primitive form of
the myth was. Whether, as asserted by Müllenhoff, it meant
that by gold the gods were corrupted or endangered, like heroes
of Sagas, is problematical. Gollveig may, however, have some
connexion with the introduction of gold among the Northern
people.

This myth of a war between groups of gods or of these regarded more or less as mortals, seems to reflect the opposition of
rival cults and their upholders — one recently introduced and
gaining popularity, but opposed by the supporters of the other.
At last, after violent conflict, a compromise was effected and
both cults now existed side by side. The groups of deities are
linked together, but their separate origin is never quite forgotten. Which group of gods was first in the field, and where
was the scene of this cult war? Opinions vary. Njord is closely
linked to the goddess Nerthus whose cult on an island, probably
Seeland, is described by Tacitus. Frey, sometimes called
Yngvi-Frey, would then have been, like Nerthus, a divinity
of the Teutonic amphictyony known as the Ingvæones, whose
habitat was North-west Germany. The Vanir group would thus
be indigenous in that region: did it there come in contact with
an incoming cult of Odin, with the result of a cult war, the
legends of which were carried to Scandinavia with the passing
of the cult to that region?

On the other hand, the Vanir cult, passing to Sweden, where
the worship of Frey obtained great prominence and was carried
thence to Norway and Iceland, would come in conflict with the
cult of Odin recently introduced into Sweden, and Sweden
would thus be the scene of a cult war. It will be observed that
Odin is the chief protagonist on the side of the Æsir in the
myth.[8]

Others think that the cult of Frey, the Svia-god, or Sweden-

god, or the *blot* or ' sacrifice ' god of Sweden, though introduced
to Sweden from without, was now firmly rooted there. The
cult of Odin, the Saxa-god or Saxon-god, was introduced later,
c. 800 A.D., and aroused a strong national counter-current of
opposition. This is the view of Golther, and Chadwick says:
' That the two cults of Odin and Frey were originally quite distinct, and that the latter was the earlier of the two, there can
hardly be any serious doubt.' [9]

Whatever be the truth regarding this cult war, it is clear that
some fusion occurred, and that now the temples, altars, and
images of Æsir and Vanir stood side by side. This is seen from
historical notices of cult, and from the grouping of Odin, Thor,
and Frey.

Golther also finds a trace of this cult war in another chapter
of the *Ynglinga-saga*. After Odin heard that good land was
to be found in Gylfi's country or Sweden, he journeyed there.
Gylfi had no power to withstand the Æsir folk. Peace was
made, and Odin and Gylfi had many dealings in cunning tricks
and illusion. Odin erected a temple with blood-offerings according to the custom of the Æsir at Sigtun. Frey's seat was at
Upsala.[10] Here, instead of the Vanir, the Swedish king opposes
Odin, and the latter succeeds in establishing a cult. The
Swedish kings, who regarded themselves as descendants of
Frey, would naturally oppose the cult of Odin.

Though the cult of Odin does not strike one as other than
that of a barbaric people, that of the Vanir was not necessarily
more enlightened, and it has some primitive traits — the
brother-sister marriages of Njord and of Frey, and the phallic
aspect of the latter.

There are traces also of the opposition between gods of light,
fertility, merchandise, and prosperity, such as the Vanir were,
and gods of war, like Odin — the gods of people with contrasted cultures, but later coalescing and sharing cult and
sacrifice. This appears in the statement of *Voluspa* about Æsir
and Vanir sharing sacrifices, and of the *Ynglinga-saga*, that the

Æsir had blood-offerings, while Odin gave sites to the 'temple-priests,' i.e., the gods Njord, Frey, etc.[11]

A similar view of a war between divinities is found in the euhemerized accounts of Celtic mythology in Ireland. The Tuatha Dé Danann fought with Firbolgs and Fomorians. Yet both intermarried or were in friendly relations with each other. There is an echo here of the strife of friendly and hostile nature powers, or, more likely, of the conquest of aboriginal people and their deities by an incoming race and their gods, with subsequent union between the two.[12]

CHAPTER III

EUHEMERISM

THE theory of the Greek Euhemerus (fourth century B.C.) that the gods were deified men, played an important part in the later Christian interpretation of the deities of different lands. Along with the beliefs that the gods were really devils, this theory that they had been men who, usually by demoniac aid or magic craft, dominated the minds of their fellows and caused them to worship them, was the stock argument against paganism for many centuries. We need not be surprised, therefore, to find it used as an explanation of the origin of the Scandinavian deities, even by the mythographer Snorri himself, who has preserved so much of the old mythology.

Snorri was an enthusiast for the traditions of the past as well as for the poetic art and its fitting expression, but he was a Christian, and therefore could not believe in the truth of these traditions nor in the gods themselves. Hence he says, addressing his audience of youthful skalds, that while they should not forget nor discredit the traditions by removing from poetry the ancient metaphors which originated out of them, yet, on the other hand, Christian men could not believe in pagan gods nor in the truth of the myths about them except in the sense set forth in the beginning of the book.[1]

The beginning of the book of which he speaks is the Prologue to the *Edda*, which, because it is written from the euhemeristic point of view in greater or less contradiction to the standpoint of the book itself, has sometimes been regarded as by another hand. On the contrary, Snorri's definition of his position shows that this Prologue and the traditions or myths of the book are quite in keeping with each other.

The Prologue begins with a notice of the Creation, of Noah and the Flood, and of the races descended from him, and their thoughts about all that they saw around them. The world is divided into three parts — Africa, Europe, and Asia. The centre of the earth, Troy or Turkland, is in Asia, 'best of homes and haunts.' Here we notice the influence of the classical tradition of Troy, as distinct from the general medieval view, as in Dante, that Jerusalem was the centre of the earth. In Troy were twelve kingdoms and one high king. In the stronghold were twelve chieftains, and one of these, Munon (Agamemnon), had a son Tror or Thor, by Troan, daughter of Priam. At twelve years old he had attained his full strength, and went forth over all the earth, slaying berserks, giants, dragons, and beasts. He married the prophetess Sibil, 'whom we call Sif.' From him, strangely enough, and certainly in contradiction to what is said in the *Edda*, through a long line of descendants, came Voden, 'whom we call Odin,' a man famed for wisdom and every accomplishment. His wife was Frigida (Frigg).

Odin and Frigg had second sight, and thus he knew that his name would be exalted in the northern regions. With a great multitude he journeyed out of Turkland, wandering over many lands, where he and his people seemed more like gods than men. At last they came to Saxland, where Odin abode long, taking possession of the land. In it he set three of his sons to rule — Vegdeg, Beldeg (Balder), and Sigi from whom came the Volsungs. Odin now made his way northwards to Reidgothland (Jutland), where he set his son Skjold, ancestor of the Skjoldings or kings of the Danes.

Going still farther north, Odin came to Sweden, then ruled by Gylfi. When Gylfi heard of the coming of these Æsir, or 'men of Asia,' he met them, offering Odin such power in his kingdom as he himself wielded. Learned medieval etymology thus connected the Æsir with Asia. Snorri says that well-being, good seasons, and peace followed on the footsteps of Odin and

the Æsir. Men believed that these were caused by them. The
Æsir were unlike all other men in fairness and wisdom.

In this region Odin founded a city called Sigtun, and established chieftains there as in Troy, with twelve doomsmen to
judge. He now went to Norway and set his son Sæming to
rule there. Another of his sons, Yngvi, was king in Sweden
after him, and from him are descended the Ynglings.

Snorri stops short here, without explaining how Odin and his
sons came to be worshipped as gods, but it is clear that, in his
mind, the gods had once been heroic men. This is more definitely shown in the earlier chapters of the *Ynglinga-saga,* which
forms the first part of his *Heimskringla.*

Here it is said that a great river, Tanais, flows from the North
over Sweden to the Black Sea, dividing Europe and Asia. To
the East of it is Asaheim, the land of the Æsir; its chief city is
Asgard (the Troy of the Prologue to the *Edda*). Here a great
chieftain, Odin, dwelt. It was a place of blood-offerings, with
twelve temple-priests, who ruled the sacrifices and judged between men. They were called Diar or Drotnar, and all men
were bound to their service.

Odin was a great warrior and far-travelled, who conquered
many realms and was always victorious. He went West and
South, even to Saxland, where he set his sons to rule. Thence
he journeyed North to an island called now Odin's island
in Fion. Afterwards he went to Gylfi's land and made
peace with him. Gylfi knew that he could not withstand the
Æsir, who were mightier than he, especially in magic. Odin
abode at the Low and made there a great temple. This he
called Sigtun, and here he gave their abodes to the temple-
priests. Njord dwelt at Noatun, Frey at Upsala, Heimdall at
Himinbjorg, Thor at Thrudvang, Balder at Breidablik.

Having told how Odin and the Diar taught crafts to the
North countries, Snorri gives details of Odin's superiority in
many things, especially magic, an account of which will be given
in Chapter IV. Hence he grew famous. He taught much of

his cunning to the temple-priests, who were now next to him in magic and craft. Others got knowledge of this magic, and so it spread far and wide and lasted long.

To Odin and these twelve lords men now offered sacrifice and called them gods, and named their children after them — a clear statement of the euhemeristic point of view.

Odin settled laws and arranged how the dead were to be burned with their goods, so that they might come to Valhall. All over Sweden men paid Odin tribute, but he was bound to keep their land from war, and to sacrifice for them for a good year. At last he died in his bed in Sweden, but was marked with a spear-point, claiming as his own all who died by weapons. He said that he would go his way to Godheim and there welcome all his friends. The Swedes thought that he had gone to the Asgard of old days, there to live for ever. So began anew the worship of Odin and vowing of vows to him. The Swedes believed that he showed himself to them in dreams before a battle. To some he gave victory; others he bade come to him; and either lot was held to be good.

To Odin succeeded Njord, and to him Frey, and a similar euhemeristic account is given of these.[2]

The notices of the deities given by Saxo Grammaticus in his *Gesta Danorum* show that he also adopted the euhemeristic theory, probably from Icelandic writers who preceded him and from whom he borrowed. But he differs from Snorri in his incisive and contemptuous way of referring to the gods. He has none of Snorri's irony or wit or delight in the humour of a story, none of his interest in preserving traditions intact. To him the gods were mortal deceivers and magicians. There had been in old days three races of such magicians. The first was that of the giants. Following them was a race skilled in divination, and surpassing the giants in mental power as these surpassed them in bodily condition. Constant wars for supremacy were waged between them, till the second race subdued the first, and gained not merely rule but also the repute of being divine. Both races were skilled in the art of delusion and in appearing to change their form or that of others. The third race, springing from the union of the two others, had neither the bodily size nor the skill in magic of their parents, yet they gained credit as gods with those deluded by their magic.[3]

The second race is apparently the Æsir, but the third is more obscure, and perhaps Vanir, or Alfar, or Dwarfs are intended. The passage, however, is far from clear, and is not connected with what is presently said of Odin and other deities.

According to Saxo the gods first dwelt in Byzantium, which here stands for Asgard, in a *senatus divinus* or *collegium*. This resembles Snorri's account of the temple-priests. Odin was reckoned to be chief of the gods. He was believed all over Europe to have the honour of divinity, which was false. He used to dwell much at Upsala, and the kings of the North, anxious to worship his deity, made an image of him, which they sent to Byzantium. Frey, the regent (*satrapa*) of the gods, also took up his abode at Upsala.[4]

These scattered statements are followed by a more definite notice of Saxo's opinion. In former days there were men who excelled in sorcery — Thor, Odin, and many others. They were cunning in contriving magical tricks, and thus, gaining the minds of the simple, they began to claim the rank of gods. They ensnared Norway, Sweden, and Denmark in the vainest credulity, and by moving these lands to worship them, infected them with their imposture. The effect of this spread far and wide, and men adored a sort of divine power in them, and, supposing them to be gods or in league with gods, they offered up prayers to them. Hence days are called by their names, and Saxo here enters into a short discussion of their equivalence with Roman deities. He concludes by telling his readers that they will now know to what kind of worship their country once bowed the knee.[5]

Saxo is sometimes satirical towards these deified impostors. When Odin seeks advice from diviners and prophets regarding vengeance on Balder, he adds this comment: ' Godhead that is incomplete is often in need of human help.' [6]

According to the theories set forth by Snorri and Saxo, the gods had once been kings or priests or men possessed of profound magical powers, and because of their superiority or their cunning, caused credulous people to worship them as deities both before and after their deaths.

CHAPTER IV

THE GREATER GODS — ODIN

IN one form or another Odin or Wodan was known to many
of the Teutonic peoples, for, since he is undoubtedly the god
whom the *interpretatio Romana* identified with Mercury, the
existence of a word formed from his name for the title of the
fourth day of the week, corresponding to *Dies Mercurius,* was
widespread. This was in OS Wodanes dag, in AS Wodenes
daeg (English Wednesday), OF Wonsdei, ON Odensdagr
(Swedish and Danish Onsdag), MHG Wodenesdach, Gudens-
dag.[1]

Among the tribes of Upper Germany (Alemanni, Bavarians,
Suabians), the name of Wodan for the fourth day of the week
is unknown, the word *mittawecha,* ' mid-week,' taking its place,
and suggesting that Wodan was unknown to them, or did not
occupy a high place when the Roman names for the days of the
week were introduced on Teutonic ground, and rendered in
terms of the names of native gods. Place-, plant-, and star-
names formed from Wodan are also lacking in this region.[2]

Tacitus says that the Germans, i.e., the Rhineland tribes,
chiefly worship Mercury, to whom on certain days they think it
lawful to offer human sacrifice.[3] The Batavians dedicated
votive tablets to Mercury, either alone (one of these is to
Mercurio Regi) or with Hercules (the native Donar) and·
Mars (Tiu). An altar to *Mercurio Channini* has been found
in the upper Ahr region. Mercury here stands for Wodan.
Jonas of Bobbio speaks of the god Vodan as Mercury, and Paulus
Diaconus says that Gwoden is called Mercury by the Romans.[4]
Wodan is thus probably the Mercury mentioned with Jupiter
in the eighth century *Indiculus Superstitionum* (c. 8) as gods to

whom sacrifices were offered and whose festivals were observed by the Saxons even in Christian times.

The cult of Wodan was thus found over a wide area, but it is generally believed that it spread outward from one central region — Lower Germany, or that, if in most places indigenous, it grew in importance through influences from that central region. The Saxons, Frisians, and Franks gave Wodan a high place. When the Saxons entered England in the fifth century, Woden was their principal god, from whom chiefs and kings claimed descent.[5] He was still the god whom the Saxons in their native region were forced to renounce at baptism in the eighth century, along with other gods.[6]

An interesting legend regarding the Lombards, who had been neighbours of the Saxons, is preserved by Paulus Diaconus, and relates to the time of their southward migration in the fifth century. Paulus calls them Vinili, and says that when they encountered the Vandals, the latter implored victory from Godan (Wodan), who replied that he would give it to those whom he saw first at sunrise. Gambara, mother of the Lombard leaders, now approached Wodan's consort, Frea, and begged her for victory. Frea gave the advice that the Lombard women should join the men with their hair hanging over their faces, in order to give them a bearded appearance. Wodan, looking from his windows towards the East, would see them. This advice was followed, and Wodan, seeing the Lombards, asked: ' Who are these Longobardi? ' (Longbeards, Lombards). Frea replied that he ought to grant victory to those on whom he had conferred a name, and this Wodan did. According to Paulus, Wodan was worshipped by all the German tribes. This legend is related by earlier writers with variations. Wodan's seat is in the sky, just as in the *Eddas* he looks over the world from his seat Hlidskjalf, and is giver of victory.[7]

The Alemanni were influenced by the Franks in religious matters. S. Columbanus found them sacrificing to Wuotan, and the Merseburg charm, found in Alemannic territory, shows that

Wodan, as a god of healing or of magic, was known to one of
their tribes, possibly the Thuringians.[8]

Saxo relates myths of Othinus among the Danes and represents him as their chief god.   How far a cult of Wodan was
indigenous in Denmark is uncertain, for Saxo's sources are in
part Norwegian and Icelandic as well as Danish.

In the Scandinavian region, as is seen from the native literature, Odin appears as chief god, head of a pantheon which, in
Snorri's *Edda,* seems to be imitated from classical sources.
There is some evidence that this position was given to him in
the Viking age, from the eighth century onwards, and mainly
in royal and aristocratic circles, and that he was much less god
of the folk, with whom Thor had a higher place.   In Adam of
Bremen's account of the Swedish deities, Wodan, god of war,
has a lower place than Thor.[9]   The accounts in Snorri and
Saxo of Odin's coming to Scandinavia from Saxland, where he
had reigned for a long time, may contain a kernel of truth —
the cult of the high god Wodan (Odin), the Saxa-god, god of
the Saxons' land, coming from there to Scandinavia.[10]

The *interpretatio Romana* of Wodan as Mercury is not clear,
but Cæsar had regarded the chief god of the Gauls as equivalent
to Mercury.   That god was described by him as ' the inventor
of arts, guide of travellers, and possessing great influence over
bargains and commerce.'[11]   Tacitus and later writers may have
regarded Wodan in the light of what they knew of the Gaulish
god.   Tacitus does in fact mention Mars in close connexion with
the German Mercury, as if the latter were also a War-god.   If
his functions resembled those of the Gaulish Mercury, these
find a certain parallel in what is said of Odin in *Hyndluljod*
by Freyja.   He gives gold to his followers, weapons and armour
to heroes, triumph to some, treasure to others, to many wisdom
and skill in words, fair winds to sailors, to the poet his art, to
heroes valour.   In other Eddic attributes of Odin there is a
further resemblance — his skill in arts, his mastery in magic,
his description as a traveller.   Like Mercury he was a god or

leader of the dead. Both gods were depicted with hat and staff. In spite of this, the identification with Mercury still remains a problem, especially when we consider the warlike aspect of Odin. As he appears in the *Eddas*, Odin is on the one hand a War-god who gives victory or defeat. On the other hand, he is concerned with wisdom, magic, cunning, and poetry, of which he was creator, according to the skalds.

Snorri says that the Swedes believed that Odin appeared in dreams before great battles, giving victory to some or inviting some to himself, and either lot was thought good. We may compare with this Adam of Bremen's account of Odin as worshipped by the Swedes at Upsala. ' Wodan carries on wars, and gives courage to men against their foes.' He also says that his image resembled that of the Roman Mars. Obviously Odin's functions as a War-god had become prominent, and he had taken the place of the god Tyr, if this deity was a god of war. Tyr's place is quite subordinate in the *Eddas*.

The name Wodan (OHG Wuotan, OS Wodan, AS Woden, ON O þenn) is found in the OHG personal name Wuotunc and in the appellative *wôtan*, glossed *tyrannus*. Wode, Wude, Wute, and the like, names of the leader of the Furious Host, Wudes Heer, are probably dialect forms of Wodan. The Furious Host was the storm personified as a host of spirits rushing through the air with their leader, who had many local names. The derivations of the name Wodan vary. It has been connected with a root *wōd*, found in Old Teutonic *wōdo*, ' mad,' ' furious,' and ON *oþ-r*, ' poetic frenzy ' (cf. Irish *fáith*, Latin *vates*). This would refer the name to the god's attributes in connexion with poetry and poetic inspiration. With this derivation may be noted Adam of Bremen's explanation: ' *Wodan, id est furor.*' Another suggested derivation is that which connects Wodan with Indo-Germanic *wâ*, ' to blow,' with the idea that the god in his earliest form was a spirit or god of the wind, and, as the spirits of the dead were supposed to wander in the wind, a spirit or god of the dead. The traditions of the Furious Host, spread all over the Germanic area and traced back to medieval times, are held to prove that Wodan had once been known to all Germanic peoples in the aspect of the leader of the Furious Host. With some of the groups he attained a much higher position, ultimately becoming the chief god. Before the evidence for this is set forth, it is well to consider that medieval tradition is somewhat doubtful as an index of belief in the pagan period. The leadership of the Furious Host was apt to be given now to this, now to that personage, and often to one with a bad reputation.[12] As all pagan gods were regarded in Christian times as sinister and demoniac, is it not possible that Wodan, as a discredited deity, was popularly made leader of what was known to be a demoniac host, and that he had not been so regarded in pagan times?

The name ' daz wuetunde Her ' or ' wûtendes Heer,' ' Furious Host,' is found in the thirteenth century, and is connected etymologically with 'Wuotes Heer,' 'Wuotunges Heer,' 'Wodan's Host,' mentioned in fourteenth century writings.[13] German tradition still preserves the memory of Wodan's Host. When the Host is heard by the Mecklenburg peasant, he cries ' de Wode tût,' ' Wode passes,' or, as in Pomerania and Holstein, ' Wode jaget,' ' Wode hunts.' A furious tempest is called ' Wudes Heer ' in the Eifel.[14] ' Wutes ' or ' Mutes Heer ' is known in Suabia as is ' Wuetes Heer ' in Bavaria. Wotn hunts in Austria, and the belief in ' das wütende Heer ' is widespread, the Host being led by different personages.[15] In Swedish folk-tradition (Småland) ' Oden's jagt ' is known, and in storms the folk say, ' Oden far förbi ' or ' Odin jäger.' Here Odin rides, wearing a broad-brimmed hat, with two or more hounds. Elsewhere in Scandinavia howling wind is thought to be caused by the rolling of Odin's wagon.[16]

The main aspects of the Furious Host are found in the leader, often wearing a cloak and a broad hat, and riding a white or black horse, with a number of hounds, and in his train of followers, among whom are sometimes souls — those not good enough for Heaven nor bad enough for Hell, or the unbaptized, suicides, and the like, these probably taking the place of an earlier more general throng of the dead.   The Host rushes along with noise and shouting, hunting animals or the Moss-wives, the Wood-wife, the Mer-woman, or other female elfins. It appears in autumn or spring, but generally in the Twelve Nights, from Christmas to Epiphany.   Generally the Host presages evil or works harm, but sometimes when it is heard as soft music, it betokens a good harvest.   In order to escape injury from it, one should fall on one's face, or keep the middle of the road, or run to a wayside cross, or to the cross-roads.   Many stories are told of adventures of wayfarers with the Host, and it has often a hellish aspect.[17]   The leader often bears some form of the name Hackelberg, the equivalent of Hakel-berend, ' the Mantle-wearer.'   Another name for him is Breit-hut or ' Broad Hat.'

In some degree corresponding to this in Norse mythology, and perhaps pointing to Odin as god of the wind, are the names given to him.   He is called Vafud, Vegtam (' Wanderer '), Gangler (' Traveller '), Ómi (' Noisy one '), Vidforull (' Far-traveller '), or, as in Saxo, *viator indefessus*, ' unwearied travel-ler,' or in Snorri's *Heimskringla*, ' the far travelled.'   He says in *Vafthrudnismal* ' much have I travelled,' or ' long have I travelled.'[18]   We hear in *Harbardsljod* of his journeys, and in a story of his appearing to king Olaf, he tells him of his travels. Whether all this denotes that Odin was an earlier god of the wind may be doubted, but it suggests that, as traveller, he is akin to the Gaulish Mercury, god of travellers, as well as to the classic god Mercury.

One of the magic runes which Odin knows points to his power over the wind.   If there is need to shelter his ship, he calms the wind and makes the waves sleep by its means.   He gives fair winds to sailors, as Freyja says in *Hyndluljod*.   The storm subsides when Odin, the man from the mountain, goes on board Sigurd's ship.[19]   Odin, as god of cargoes, Farma-tyr, may have been so called because he gave fair winds, and was thus a god worshipped by sailors.[20]

To the appearance of the leader of the Host corresponds that of Odin with his cloak, under which he conveys his *protégés* through the air,[21] his broad-brimmed hat, and his long grey beard, giving rise to his names Sidhottr ('with broad hat'), Harbard ('grey beard'), and Skidskegg ('long beard'). He also rides through sea and air the famous grey, eight-legged steed, Sleipnir, 'best of all horses,' born of Loki in the form of a mare to the giant's stallion Svadilfari.[22] *Baldrs Draumar* gives a picture of Odin saddling Sleipnir and riding down to Niflhel to consult the Volva about Balder's baleful dreams, On Sleipnir he rides daily to Urd's well to the divine tribunal, and, after Balder's death, Odin's son, Hermod, rode Sleipnir to Hel to offer a ransom for Balder.[23] Snorri depicts Odin riding forth with gold helmet, birnie, and his spear Gungnir, to fight at the end of all things.[24] The name of the world-tree, Yggdrasil, means 'Ygg's horse,' Ygg ('the Terrible') being a name of Odin's.[25] The true name of the tree is Askr Yggdrasils ('the ash of Yggdrasil' or 'of Odin's steed').[26] The gallows is also called Odin's steed, and he is *galga valdyr* ('lord of the gallows') and *hanga-tyr* ('god of the hanged'). The gallows was a steed ridden by the hanged, and Odin himself had hung on a tree (whether Yggdrasil or another) for nine nights, as is told in *Havamal*. Later legend knew of a smith in Nesjar in 1208 A.D. to whom came a rider asking him to shoe his horse. The smith had never seen such large horseshoes nor heard of such journeys as the stranger told him he had undertaken in a brief space of time. Then the stranger revealed himself as Odin and bade the smith watch how he would leap his horse over a hedge seven ells high. Having done this, horse and rider vanished. Four nights later a great battle was fought.[27] In the same way the Furious Host was sometimes a precursor of battle, but it must be confessed that, apart from the rather forced suggestions of Odin as a rider and the like, the *Eddas* do not sup-

port the theory of the god's origin in a leader of the Furious
Host.

As the wind was believed to rest in a hill in calm weather and
to come forth in a storm, so the Furious Host sometimes comes
from a hill and goes to a hill. If we regard the dead as following in the train of the Host or of Wodan, then we may conceive
of them as dwelling in a hollow hill ruled over by the god. To
this corresponds the numerous mountain names such as
Wôdenesberg, Wodnesbeorh (*mons Wodeni*), Othensberg,
Odensberg, Gudenesberg.[28] When Regin and Sigurd were in
a storm at sea, a man was seen standing on a mountain. As the
ship passed he asked who they were, and when Regin told him
and demanded his name, he replied that he was called Hnikar,
' Thruster,' but now they must call him *Karl af berge*, ' the man
of the mountain.' He was Odin. Gudrun speaks of Sigtyr's
(' the Victory-god's) mountain in *Atlakvitha*.[29] In this conception of Odin or Wodan as god of a mountain and of the
mountain as a place of the dead, may be seen the germ of the
Valhall myth as developed in the Viking age (see p. 315).
To die was ' to journey to Odin ' (*til Odins fara*), or ' to be a
guest with Odin,' or ' to visit Odin,' and similar phrases with
the same meaning were used of Valhall. Saxo tells how Odin,
as a man of amazing height called Rostarus, cured Siward's
wounds on condition of his consecrating to him the souls of all
slain by him in battle. So the *Landnama-bok* tells how Helgi
said, when Thorgrim was slain: ' I gave Asmod's heir to
Odin.' [30]

Epithets of Odin's show his connexion with the dead. He is
drauga drottinn, ' lord of the ghosts '; *hanga drottinn*, ' lord of
the hanged '; *hanga tyr* and *hanga-god*, ' god of the hanged ';
galga valdr, ' lord of the gallows '; *valgautr*, ' god of the
slain.' [31] Souls of those slain by violence go in the Furious
Host, and souls of heroes go to Odin in Valhall. Hence, too, he
was called *val-fadir*, ' father of the slain,' because, as Snorri says,
' all that fall in battle are sons of his adoption ' (*oski synir*).[32]

Valkjosandi, 'chooser of the slain,' is one of Odin's titles in *Kormaks-saga*.

According to *Grimnismal* Odin in Gladsheim, 'the world of joy,' where the wide, gold-shining Valhall lies, chooses daily those who are to fall in strife. For them, says Snorri, he appoints Valhall, 'Hall of the slain,' and Vingolf, 'friendly Floor.' Hence 'the way of the slain' is the way to Valhall.[33] The Valkyries, 'Choosers of the slain,' were sent by Odin to every battle; they determined men's feyness and awarded victory and took the slain.[34] They were called Wish-maidens, because they fulfilled Odin's wishes about the slain.[35] On one occasion Odin, as god of the dead, acted as ferryman of the dead to the Other World. Sinfjotli's body was carried by Sigmund to a fjord, where was a boat with a man in it, who offered to take Sigmund across. But when he had carried the body into the boat there was no place for Sigmund, and the man disappeared with the body. He was Odin,[36] and the incident illustrates the belief in the dead being ferried over to the region of the dead. In *Harbardsljod* Odin, as Harbard, appears as a ferryman.

Although Odin's lofty character is emphasized by Snorri and in the court poetry of the skalds, both in his *Edda* and still more in the Eddic poems Odin appears in lower aspects. Indeed, in these poems Odin is hardly at all the lofty War-god and the creator who appears in skaldic verse, much less the supreme god of a pantheon. Especially is his connexion with magic emphasized. He is *aldenn gautr*, 'the enchanter old'; *galdrs fadir*, 'father of magic,' and he spoke magic and mighty charms to the dead Volva whom he had raised, yet required to seek knowledge of Balder's fate from her.[37] Loki accused Odin of having once worked charms like witches in Samsey, disguising himself as a witch and going thus among men.[38] Saxo tells how Odin disguised himself as a soldier and struck Rinda with a piece of bark on which were written charms (runes), thus driving her to frenzy. This was already referred to by the skald Kormak in

the line ' Odin wrought charms on Rind.' [39]   From Hlebard the
giant Odin got a magic wand (*gambantein*) and then stole away
his understanding; and Odin admits that he learned scornful
language from the dead in their hills.   Both incidents occur in
Harbardsljod.[40]   As in the Merseburg charm where Odin is
found curing a lame horse by a charm or magic rune, so in
Havamal he describes the power of the magic songs known to
him.   They bring help in sickness and sorrow, and in witchcraft;
they produce fetters and blunt an enemy's weapons; they break
fetters; they stop the swiftest arrows; they neutralize the danger of a root on which magic runes are written and turn the
danger against the sender; they quench fire, remove hatred,
calm the wind, work on House-riders or witches, aid friends in
fight, make a hanged man talk to him, give knowledge of the
gods and elves, and win love.   One of these had been sung by
the dwarf Thjodrörir, who sang ' strength to the Æsir, success
to the Alfar, and wisdom to Hroptatyr ' (Odin).[41]

When Mimir's head was sent by the Vanir to the Æsir, Odin
embalmed it and spoke magic runes over it, so that it might
impart wisdom to him at any time.   It told him tidings from
other worlds.   *Voluspa* refers to this when, before the Doom of
the gods, Odin is said to give heed to the head of Mimir, and in
Sigrdrifumal he is depicted with sword and helmet, standing
on a mountain and consulting Mimir's head.[42]   Elsewhere it is
Mimir himself whom Odin consults.   This recalls Celtic myth
and custom about heads.   Those of enemies were offered to
divinities.   Bodies or heads of warriors had a powerful influence,
and the head of the Brythonic god Bran, when cut off, preserved
the land from invasion, and, in its presence, time passed as a
dream.[43]   Odin, called Hropt, is said to have arranged thought-
runes out of the draught which dropped from the head of Heith-
draupnir and the horn of Hoddrofnir, both probably names of
Mimir.   To Odin Loddfafnir owes his magic knowledge.[44]

As a result of his magic powers Odin takes different forms,
that of a ferryman, a servant or peasant, a snake, an eagle, as

in myths presently to be given.   Hence he is called Fjolnir,
' the many-shaped.' [45]

To this corresponds Snorri's euhemerized account of Odin in
his *Ynglinga-saga*.   He was far-seeing and wise in wizardry.
He waked the dead and would sit under hanged men, to obtain
knowledge from them.   By words alone he slaked fire or stilled
the sea, and would turn the wind in whatever way he desired.
He knew the fate of men and things in the future, or how to
work ill or to take strength and wit from men and give these
to others.   Of all buried treasure did he know, as well as runes to
open the earth, mountains, rocks, and mounds, and how to bind
their inmates with words.   Then he would go in and take what
he wished.   He would change his shape, and while his body
lay as if asleep or dead, he himself was in a bird or wild beast,
a fish or worm, and he would go in the twinkling of an eye on his
own errands or those of others.[46]   All this is merely the current belief in magical practices and assumed possible actions reflected back on Odin, who in this aspect resembles a shaman.

In this aspect, also, so prominent in the Eddic poems as compared with those of the court poets, we see a somewhat different
Odin from Odin the supreme god of a pantheon and god of
war.   He is altogether on a lower level, and perhaps we may
suppose that this was the popular view of him, as contrasted with
that of the aristocracy, the warriors and skalds.

This lower aspect of Odin is seen in what is said of his
amours, of which he boasts, and we hear how he sometimes made
women or giantesses his victims by means of magic runes.   He
wrought charms on Rind the giantess, who bore him a son Vali
or Ali, the avenger of Balder.[47]   This is much elaborated in
Saxo.   Rind, called by Saxo Rinda, is in this account daughter
of the king of the Ruthenians.   After Balder's death Odin,
though chief of the gods, enquired of prophets and diviners
how to avenge his son, and one of these, a Finn, said that a
son must be born to him by Rinda.   Odin, as a soldier, gained
her father's favour, but Rinda would have nothing to say to

him. Next year as one skilled in smith-craft, he made many
wonderful things for the king and for Rinda, who still refused
him. Again as a soldier he sought to win her and tried to kiss
her, but she repelled him. He now touched her with a piece of
bark on which runes were written, and she became like one in
frenzy. Then as a maiden with skill in leechcraft, he said that
he would cure Rinda. So he gained access to her, and now
accomplished his desires. The child born was called Bous, not
Vali, as in the *Eddas*.[48]

In *Harbardsljod* Odin boasts of overcoming seven sisters,
and of working much love-craft with the Night-riders or
witches, alluring them by stealth from their husbands. He
had also an amour with a ' linen-white ' maid, and with Grid,
mother of Vidarr.[49]

Two stories, both put in Odin's mouth, show little reverence
for him and are told from a humorous point of view. Both are
found in *Havamal*, and a verse stating that lacking the desired
joy is worse than sickness, precedes the first story, that of Billing's daughter. Odin lay in the reeds awaiting her who was
dear to him as his life. He entered the house; she was asleep
on her bed, bright as the sun for beauty. She bade him come
at evening in secret, but when he did so, a band of warriors with
torches prevented his entering. He returned at early morning
when all were asleep, only to find a dog tied to her bed. So he
draws the moral: ' many fair maids are found fickle.' [50]

The same poem gives briefly the story of Odin's acquiring
the poetic mead and his love affair with Gunnlod, daughter of
the giant Suttung. This is prefaced by the saying that good
memory and eloquence are needful to the sage, as Odin found in
the hall of the old giant Suttung, over-reaching Gunnlod ' with
many words.' With the snout of Rati he penetrated the rocks
and so entered the place. Gunnlod gave him a draught of the
mead from her golden seat: poor was his recompense to her.
He got the mead Odrörir as well as Gunnlod's favours. Had
he not won her, hardly would he have returned from the giants'

halls. Next day the Frost-giants came to ask about Hor (Odin) in his hall. They asked whether Bolverk had returned to the gods, or had Suttung slain him — Bolverk being the name under which Odin had passed. The episode ends by saying that Odin had forsworn himself: how can he be trusted? He defrauded Suttung of the mead and left Gunnlod in grief. This myth is also mentioned in earlier stanzas of *Havamal*, where Odin speaks of being overcome with beer, ' fettered with the feathers of the bird of forgetfulness (the heron) in Gunnlod's abode, very drunk in the house of wise Fjallar ' (Suttung).[51]

Miss Martin Clarke has compared these two stories with each other and with that of Odin and Rinda, and has suggested that all three may be versions of the poetic mead myth, mutilated in the Billing's daughter and Rinda stories. In all three there are a hero, a reluctant lady, a wooing, a crafty disguise or stealth, a definite purpose, and a final success in the Gunnlod and Rinda stories, a rebuff in the third tale. But, interesting as the suggestion is, the Rinda story has a purpose quite distinct from that of the mead story, viz., to obtain a son who will avenge Balder's death.

Odin was not always victorious. With Loki and Hœnir he was overcome by Hreidmar after killing Otter, and forced to pay wergild or be slain.[52] In *Lokasenna* Odin shows himself frightened for Loki, and it is Thor, not Odin, who silences him.

In spite of his wide knowledge, if not omniscience, Odin requires to seek knowledge, especially of the future. This he obtains from the Volva, who recites the drama of the last things, or from a dead seeress who tells of Balder's fate. Again he obtains knowledge from the giant Suttung's mead, from the giant Vafthrudnir, from the dead or spirits or dwarfs, and from Mimir.[53] Odin is called ' friend of Mimir,' who is perhaps a water-spirit, with his well beneath one of the roots of Yggdrasil; in this well wisdom and understanding are stored. Hence Mimir himself is full of wisdom and drinks of the well from

the Gjallar-horn.   To him came Odin and desired a drink of
the well, but Mimir withheld it until he had given his eye in
pledge.   Now the eye is hidden in the well, and Mimir is said
to drink every morning from this pledge, perhaps regarded as
some kind of vessel, or out of it is poured water for the tree.
The picture of Mimir drinking from Odin's eye is perhaps the
mistake of a later redactor of the poem, as Boer has shown.[54]
Odin consults Mimir, as when he rides to his well to take
counsel with him before the Doom of the gods, but elsewhere,
as has been seen, he consults Mimir's head.[55]

Another picture is given of Odin with the goddess Saga, daily
drinking in gladness from golden cups out of the cool waves of
her abode, Sokkvabekk ('sinking stream,' 'torrent').   Saga
has been regarded by Gering as a form of Frigg, Odin's consort, or by Grimm as Odin's daughter or wife, but Snorri mentions her separately from Frigg as second of the goddesses,
and he describes Sokkvabekk as 'a great abode.'   Golther
considers Saga to be a female water-elfin, dwelling in
the stream, and visited by Odin to obtain knowledge, which
is thus again connected with the water, or to carry on a love
affair.[56]

Odin is the possessor of magic runes, or even their creator,
according to *Havamal*.   He, 'the chief of singers,' coloured
them — an allusion to the practice of reddening the engraved
runes, e.g., with blood; and he as 'ruler' or 'speaker' of the
gods wrote or carved them.   Another section of *Havamal* tells
in an obscure manner how Odin came to possess magic runes: —

> 'I know that I hung
>   On the wind-stirred tree
>   Nine nights long,
>   Wounded by spear,
>   Consecrated to Odin,
>   Myself to myself;
>   On the mighty tree
>   Of which no man knows
>   Out of what root it springs.

No one refreshed me
With horn or bread;
I looked downward.
I took up the runes,
Shrieking I took them,
Then I fell to the ground.

Bestla's brother,
Son of Bolthorn,
Taught me nine mighty songs;
And a drink I obtained
Of the choice mead
Out of Odrörir.

Then I began to thrive
And gained wisdom.
I grew and felt well;
One word led to another,
One deed to another.' [57]

These lines and their meaning have been much discussed, and it is not certain that all the stanzas belong together. They may be fragments from different poems. The third stanza suggests an interpolation from a poetic form of the myth of the mead stolen from Suttung, ' of which,' says Snorri, ' he who drinks becomes a skald.' Three myths of the gaining of runes or wisdom seem to be conjoined as a narrative in three acts, as shown by Boer. These are (1) a myth of Odin's acquiring runes by hanging on a tree and wounded by a spear, an offering to himself. He bows his head and looks down, perhaps into the deep, and takes up the runes, falling now from the tree to the ground. How he took up runes while hanging is not clear: perhaps a magical act is intended. The tree is taken to be Yggdrasil by most commentators, but is it? The whole passage is puzzling, and no other evidence exists to support this view of the tree.

(2) The second rune myth refers to Odin's learning magic songs from the son of Bolthorn who is father of Bestla, Odin's mother. If the son of Bolthorn dwells at the foot of the tree, he might be Mimir, who also has such an abode, and who is thus Odin's uncle.

(3) The third rune myth tells how Odin obtained a draught of the mead out of Odrörir, possibly through use of these magic songs.[58]

Whether Odin's hanging on the tree is to be connected with the idea that Yggdrasil is Odin's gallows is uncertain. Bugge supposed that the lines are a reflexion from Christian belief regarding the Crucifixion, yet even so, some older Odin myth may underlie them. There is perhaps some link with human sacrifice to Odin by hanging the victim on a tree and stabbing him. Odin himself, regarded as a king in Snorri's euhemerized account, died in bed but was yet marked with a spear-point, and claimed as his own all who died by weapons.[59] A mythic story of such a sacrifice is told in the *Gautreks-saga*. The ships of king Vikar had encountered a great storm and the sacrificial chips had indicated that it was necessary to propitiate Odin by a human victim. The lot fell on the king himself, and all were now in such fear that it was resolved to defer the sacrifice till next day. Meanwhile Odin desired his foster-son, the hero Starkad, to bring about Vikar's death, in return for his favours to him. He told him what he must do. Next day, when the counsellors suggested that a mere mock sacrifice of Vikar should be made, Starkad gave directions how this should be done. Vikar was made to stand on the stump of a tree and a noose made of the entrails of a newly slaughtered calf was placed round his neck and attached to a branch, which Starkad held down. Then he thrust at Vikar with a reed which Odin had given him and which now became a spear, at the same time letting go the branch. The noose became a strong rope: the stump was overturned; and thus Vikar was both hung and stabbed. As these changes occurred, Starkad said: ' Now I give you to Odin.' [60]

A fuller version of the Odrörir myth is given by Snorri in the *Bragarœdur* as an explanation of the origin of the art of poetry.

Here it is connected with the war between Æsir and Vanir. To establish a pledge of peace between the two parties, both of them spat into a vessel. This is doubtless derived from some folk-custom, of which there are examples from other regions, showing that the saliva-rite is analogous to the blood-covenant.[61] This saliva now becomes the subject of a further myth, for, as is obvious, if the saliva of men is important in folk-belief, that of gods must have greater virtues. The Æsir took the contents of the vessel and out of the saliva formed the being Kvasir, who was so wise that to every question about anything he could give the right answer. He went everywhere instructing men, until the dwarfs Fjalar and Galarr slew him, and collected his blood in the kettle Odrörir and in the vats Son and Bodn. They blended honey with the blood, and so formed the mead of which whoso drinks becomes a skald. These dwarfs, having drowned the giant Gilling and slain his wife, were set on a reef by Suttung, the son of the giant pair. Over this reef the waters poured at high tide, and to save themselves they offered him the precious mead as a satisfaction. Suttung hid it in the rock Hnitbjorg, and set his daughter Gunnlod to watch it.

The story then goes on to tell how the Æsir came into possession of the mead. Odin set out and came to a place where nine thralls were mowing. He took out a hone from his belt and sharpened their scythes so that they cut better than ever before. As they wished to possess the hone, he threw it up in the air, and when they rushed to catch it, each struck his scythe against the other's neck. Odin now went to the giant Baugi, Suttung's brother, to seek a night's lodging. Baugi was bewailing the loss of his thralls, and Odin, calling himself Bolverk, offered to do their work, asking as wage a draught of Suttung's mead. Baugi said that he had no control over it, but nevertheless went with Odin to Suttung when harvest was over. When Suttung heard of the bargain, he refused to grant a drop of the mead. Odin, as Bolverk, now suggested certain wiles to Baugi, who agreed to them. He drew out the auger Rati,

' Gnawer,' and bade Baugi pierce the rock with it. When the hole was made, Bolverk changed himself into a serpent and crawled through it. Baugi, who had tried to deceive him in boring the hole, thrust at him with the auger but missed him. Bolverk now went to the place where Gunnlod was and slept with her for three nights. Then she gave him three draughts of the mead. With the first draught he emptied Odrörir; with the second Bodn, with the third Son, and thus gained all the mead. Turning himself into an eagle, he flew off swiftly. Suttung saw the eagle in flight, and himself as an eagle pursued it. When the Æsir saw Odin approach, they set out vats, and Odin, entering Asgard, spat out the mead into these. But he was so nearly caught by Suttung that he sent some mead backwards. No heed was taken of it; whosoever would might have it: it is called the poetaster's part. Odin gave the mead to the Æsir and to those men who have the ability of composition.

In this tale and in one of the *Havamal* passages the vessel containing the mead is called Odrörir; in the other *Havamal* passage it is the mead itself that is so called. The myth has some likeness to the Indian Soma myth. Soma is medicinal and immortal; it has to do with poetry and stimulates speech. It was acquired through a Soma plant having been brought from the mountains by an eagle, and Indra on one occasion is called an eagle in connexion with Soma.[62] The story has some relation to the numerous folk-tales in which the wife or daughter of a giant or monster aids a hero who escapes with the giant's treasure.

The poetic mead is now in possession of Odin, but it was first, like all wisdom, as *Vafthrudnismal* suggests, in the possession of giants. Hence Odin gives wisdom to many, and to the poets their art. Egil, though resenting his being deprived of his sons by Odin, says that Mimir's friend has given him a recompense in the gift of the poetic art. The hero Starkad obtained from Odin the art of poetry or the composing of spells. A poet called himself ' Ygg's (Odin's) ale-bearer,' and poetry is styled 'gift,' 'find,' 'drink,' 'booty' of Odin, or 'Odin's mead,' 'Odin's kettle-liquor,' as well as 'liquid of the dwarfs,' 'Gunnlod's liquor,' 'Kvasir's blood,' 'Suttung's mead,' and the like, with reference to this story.[63] Odin was thus god of the skalds, to whom he gave their gift of verse.

The *Havamal* or 'words of the High One' (Odin) sets forth a long array of wise sayings applicable to the incidents and conduct of daily life. Then follows the Odrörir story; a series of counsels addressed to Loddfafnir; the story of Odin and the runes; and a list of runes or rather of the effects of such runes. The whole seems to be intended as a kind of summary of Odin's wisdom due, as we may suppose, to the actions recorded in the myths. That Odin should be god of poetry at a time when poetry had been so highly developed in the North, may be a development of his being lord of magic runes, which were in verse form. 'All his craft he taught by runes,' says Snorri in the *Ynglinga-saga,* and again: 'In measures did he speak all things, even such as skald-craft now uses.'[64] Save for the Odrörir myth, it is Odin's invention or possession of magic runes which is emphasized in the Eddic poems, thus laying stress on his character as a master of magic, winner and user of runes. According to *Havamal* Odin made runes for the Æsir, as Dainn did for the Alfar, Dvalinn for the dwarfs, and Asvid for the giants.[65]

Odin's position as god of war is not prominent in the Eddic poems. Even in *Harbardsljod,* where he boasts of his exploits, he does not speak much of warlike deeds. That he became god of war is undoubted. Though Tacitus equates Wodan with Mercury, the human sacrifices offered to him can hardly be explained otherwise than as sacrifices to a War-god. Odin caused the first war, that between Æsir (of whom Odin alone is named) and Vanir. As *Voluspa* says: 'He hurled his spear on the host, and war then came first into the world.' According to *Harbardsljod* and *Helgi Hundingsbana,* he causes war, makes princes angry, brings peace never, and raises strife even between kindred

by means of spiteful runes, and is guilty of all ill.[96]   This is
corroborated by the old pagan proverb: ' Odin sets kings war-
ring '; and by Saxo, who tells how the god, disguised as Brun,
Harald's counsellor, shook the union of the kings by his treachery, and sowed strife so guilefully that he caused hatred among
men bound by friendship and kin, which seemed unappeasable
save by war.[67]   In *Harbardsljod* Odin speaks of his presence
with the host; in *Lokasenna* he is charged by Loki with partial-
ity, giving victory to those who do not deserve it.   He is angry
when victory is given against his will, as by the Valkyrie Brynhild to Agnar, and for this he casts her into a magic sleep by
means of a sleep-thorn.[68]   He takes part in the battles of men
and helps his favourites to victory.   Hence men entreat his
favour and he promises victory.[69]   To his favourites he gives
weapons.   Dag, son of Hogni, sacrificed to Odin in order to be
avenged of his father's death.   Odin gave him his spear, which
made victory sure.   Freyja in *Hyndluljod* says that to his
followers he gives gold, to Hermod helm and coat of mail, to
Sigmund a sword, and triumph to some.[70]   A curious statement
in *Helgi Hundingsbana* says that Odin gave to Helgi co-rule
with himself when he came to Valhall.[71]

Saxo shows how Odin is patron of heroes and kings.   When
Hadding was passing Norway with his fleet, an old man on the
shore signed to him with his mantle to put ashore.   In spite of
opposition, Hadding did this, took him on board, and was taught
how to order his army in the wedge formation attributed to
Odin.   When the army was thus disposed, the old man stood
behind it and shot ten arrows at the enemy, and also overcame
the rain-storm caused by their spells, driving it back and causing
a mist.   Before leaving, he told Hadding that he would die
by his own hand, and bade him prefer glorious to obscure wars,
and those with remote rather than with neighbouring people.
The old man was Odin.   A later passage tells how he was the
discoverer and imparter of the wedge-shaped formation.   In
the likeness of Brun, he set Harald's army in this array, but the

army of Ring, Harald's opponent, was also found to be in the
same formation, doubtless also taught them by Odin.   Already
Odin, as a one-eyed old man, of great height, in a hairy mantle,
had appeared to Harald, revealing to him that he was Odin,
versed in the practice of war, and instructing him regarding this
wedge formation.[72]

Odin went forth with the host to battle, and, in Saxo, we see
him not only provoking war between Harald and Ring, but in
the form of Brun taking part in the battle.   Harald besought
him to give victory to the Danes, promising to dedicate to him
the spirits of all who fell.   Odin remained unmoved, thrust the
king out of his chariot, and slew him with his own weapon.[73]
This personal share of the god in battle in order to secure victims, occurs elsewhere.   His desire was to fill Valhall with
chosen warriors, *einherjar*, who would aid the gods in time of
need.   Hence he caused death to his favourites, even in the
hour of victory, or they were foredoomed to slay themselves,
like Hadding, or their death was brought about by Odin at the
hands of another, as Vikar's by Starkad.[74]   The clearest statement of this is found in *Eiriksmal*.   Sigmund asked Odin why
he robbed Eirik of life, seeing that Odin regarded him as a
mighty warrior.   Odin answered that it was because none knew
when the grey wolf would come to the seat of the gods.[75]

The Valkyries were sent to battle-fields to choose those who
were to die.   As these helmeted maids rode forth, their corselets
were besprinkled with blood, and from their spears sparks flew
forth.[76]

Sacrifices, even of human victims, were offered to Odin for
victory, and also after a victory, when prisoners were sacrificed,
though such sacrifices may have been less common in Norway
than in Denmark and Sweden.   Hence we hear of a leader devoting the enemy to Odin, or shouting to the opposing army:
'Odin has you all.'   Reflexions of this are found in some of
Saxo's references to Odin, as when he cured Siward's wounds,
on condition of his devoting the slain to him, or when Harald

offered him the souls of the slain. Earlier in his life Harald had vowed to Odin all souls cast forth from their bodies by his sword, because of Odin's boon to him. He received such favours from Odin, whose oracle was supposed to be the cause of his birth, that steel could not injure him, and shafts which wounded others could do him no harm.[77]

Snorri's euhemerized account of Odin speaks of him as a great warrior, who made many realms his own and always gained the victory. His men held that of his own nature he would always be victorious. Before sending them to war, he laid his hands on them and blessed them, and they believed they would fare well thereby. In sore straits by sea or land they called on him, and deemed that they gained help. In battle their foes were made blind, deaf, or terror-stricken, and their weapons rendered useless. His men went without birnies, and were mad as dogs or wolves, bit on their shields, and were strong as bears or bulls — a reminiscence of the *berserkr-gangr*, or 'berserker-rage.' In Snorri's Prologue to the *Edda*, Odin, as a king, goes from land to land, occupying them and making them his own. So Saxo calls Odin 'the mighty in battle,' and Mars 'the war-waging god,' and he is said to have a white shield and a great horse.[78] On a helmet found in a grave at Vendel, in Sweden, of the Iron Age period, a warrior on horseback, armed, with helmet, shield, and spear, is believed to represent Odin, as two birds in flight, one on each side of the head, are most probably his ravens.[79]

Odin's names or titles bear witness to his functions as god of war. He is Sigfadir, 'Father of victory'; Sigtyr, 'god of victory.' Oaths were sworn by 'Sigtyr's mountain.' His city was Sigtun. Other names are Hertyr, 'god of hosts'; Heryan, 'Leader of hosts'; Herfadir, 'Father of hosts'; Valfadir, 'Father of the slain.' He is Hnikarr, 'Spear-lord'; Biflindi, 'Spear-brandisher'; he is 'the weapon-decked' god. Hence many kennings for battle connect it with Odin. It is his 'grimness' or 'fury,' 'the storm of Odin,' 'the storm-wind of the

Valkyries '; the sword is ' Odin's fire.' ' Weapons and arms should be periphrased in figures of battle and with reference to Odin and the Valkyries,' says Snorri in *Skaldskaparmal*. We may also recall what Adam of Bremen said of Odin as god of war.[80]

While generally, though not invariably, Odin is more prominent than Thor in the myths, this prominence is much less obvious in historical documents. There must have been a time when Odin was unknown in Scandinavia, or on a much lower level than that which he ultimately attained. Odin as Wodan was certainly prominent at an earlier time in Germany, especially in its southern region. The presumption, therefore, is that the cult of Odin as a higher god, possibly with that of others, passed first to Denmark and then to Sweden, where he gained popularity. Perhaps he was first worshipped, or his cult first came to prominence, in Gautland or Götland, in South Sweden, for he was called Gaut, Gautatyr, ' god of the Gauts,' and also ' friend of the Gauts.' [81] From Sweden his cult passed to Norway, where, however, it never overthrew that of the indigenous Thor. In the Sagas relating to the families of Iceland, the cult of Odin is never mentioned. It is only in those which concern the legendary period that he is prominent.

This migration of cult may be indicated in the migration legend, as told by Snorri, that Odin and others came from the South-east to Denmark and Sweden, as well as in the fact that Adam of Bremen still knows Odin at Upsala as Wodenus, a Saxon form of the name, while Danish documents know him as Wodhen. Significant, too, is his name Saxagod, ' god of the Saxons.' [82]

The growing supremacy of Odin was one aspect of the growth of a new culture in the Viking age and the rise of a splendid courtly life through the power of the great kings. The art of war was cultivated for itself: the art of poetry was fostered by kings, and skalds became a definite class in this new and vigorous stage of history. Odin was associated with both war and poetry. He became important and necessary to kings, nobles, and court poets, and those aspects of his personality connected with war and poetry were ever the more emphasized. Odin's seat was a royal court: he himself a supreme divine ruler.

Yet even in the Eddic poems there are hints of the earlier stages when Odin was not so prominent, just as they emphasize lower aspects of his personality, as we have seen. We see Frey seated on Odin's Hlidskjalf, looking over the world, possessed of a magic horse, sword, and the ring Draupnir, and called *folkvaldi goda*, ' chief of the gods,' in *Skirnismal*. Frigg and Gefjun share foreknowledge with Odin in *Lokasenna*, and Freyja shares the slain with him, according to *Grimnismal*. Thor, who had been chief god in Norway, remained chief god of the people, in contradistinction to the aristocracy, and he was especially prominent in Iceland, where kingship did not exist and few of the emigrants were of royal blood. This seems to be hinted at in *Harbardsljod* where the nobles who fall in battle are said to be Odin's, but the peasants belong to Thor, the rough, homely, peasant-like god.[83] Odin, as a god of knowledge, is contrasted with Thor, the embodiment of physical force. Even Odin's spear, the warrior's weapon, suggests a higher stage of culture than Thor's hammer. Odin drinks wine, which is meat and drink to him: Thor drinks ale and is a mighty eater. Snorri, it is true, speaks of the first toast drunk at festivals as one consecrated to Odin, ' for victory and power to the king,' but this cannot override the more general evidence regarding Thor, nor the fact that the *Islendinga Sögur* never speak of temples, images, or priests of Odin in Iceland.

Odin's growing cult, on the whole, however, affected the more popular cults of Thor and Frey, and in the later Scandinavian literature he has achieved the highest position as head of a pantheon. To him were assimilated many lesser and local gods, whose individual functions corresponded to some of Odin's. Many of the names given to him must be the last traces of such local deities, just as the Ollerus and Mit-othin stories, presently to be given, suggest that he had absorbed the personality and cult of other gods.

'Of all the gods Odin is the greatest,' and, according to Snorri, he is foremost and oldest of the gods, or, as in *Voluspa,* ruler of the gods. 'He lives through all ages and rules all realms, and directs all things, small and great.' He is Alda-fadir, 'father of men,' 'because he is father of all the gods and men,' and, as in the Lombard story, he is depicted as sitting in the high seat, Hlidskjalf, looking out over the world and seeing every man's deeds.[84] *Grimnismal* shows Odin and Frigg sit-ting on this seat and viewing the whole world, and from it Odin looked forth and saw where Loki had hidden himself. Hlid-skjalf is in Valaskjalf, one of the heavenly abodes, made by the gods and thatched with silver, and possibly the same as Valhall.[85]

The other gods or Æsir are Odin's people. He is highest and eldest of these; he rules all things, and, mighty as are the others, all serve him as children obey a father. With Vili and Ve, or Hœnir and Loki, Odin is creator or fashioner of the world, of the first man and woman, to whom he gave soul. But Snorri, apart from the myths which tell of this, says that Odin 'fashioned Heaven and earth and air, and all things in them: he made man and gave him the immortal spirit.'[86] As chief god Odin grants to men their wishes, and he has knowledge of all things, though this is not necessarily innate to him, but gained in different ways. We see him displaying his cosmogonic knowl-edge to Agnar in *Grimnismal.* Frigg had said that his fosterling, king Geirrod, was miserly and tortured his guests if too many of these came to him. Odin denied this and set off to prove it. Meanwhile Frigg sent Fulla to Geirrod to tell him that he must beware of a magician who is coming to him, and whom he will know by the sign that the fiercest dog will not leap at him. Odin, calling himself Grimnir, 'the hooded one,' arrived, clad in a dark blue mantle, and would not speak when questioned.

Geirrod tortured him by setting him between two fires for eight nights. Geirrod's young son, Agnar, had pity on him and brought him a horn of ale. Odin praised him and then went on to tell of the different divine abodes, of Yggdrasil, of creation, lastly reciting his various names and disclosing himself as Odin. When Geirrod heard this he ran to take him from the fire, but stumbled and fell on his sword. Odin now vanished. Agnar ruled long as king.

In *Vafthrudnismal* Odin desires to match his knowledge with that of the giant Vafthrudnir. Frigg would fain keep him at home, because Vafthrudnir is such a mighty giant. Odin proclaims his intention of going to seek him, and now Frigg bids him a safe journey and trusts that his wit will avail him. He sets out and reaches the giant's hall. Vafthrudnir says that he will never go forth again unless he proves himself wiser than the giant. Each questions the other, and the answers form a stock of mythological knowledge. In the end Odin, who has all through called himself Gagnrath and is unknown to the giant, asks him what words Odin spoke in the ear of Balder on his pyre. Now Vafthrudnir knows the god, and admits that he is the wiser. As the two had wagered their heads on the result of the contest, it is to be presumed that the giant, who speaks in the last verse of his ' fated mouth,' now loses his head, though the poem does not say so.

In the *Nornagests-thattr*, having taken the form of Gestumblindi, ' Gest the blind,' Odin enters King Heidrik's hall at Yule, and propounds to him riddles, because the king is famous at guessing these. One of the riddles is: ' Who are the two that have ten feet, three eyes, and one tail? ' The answer is: ' The one-eyed Odin, riding Sleipnir, his eight-legged steed.' Heidrik answered all the riddles, save that one which baffled Vafthrudnir: ' What did Odin speak into Balder's ear before he was burned on the pyre? ' By this Heidrik recognized Odin, and threw his magic sword Tyrfing at him, but he escaped as a falcon. Odin, however, was angry at Heidrik, and that night he was slain by his slaves, or, according to a Faroese ballad-version of this story, Odin burned him in his hall.[87]

This high position ascribed to Odin, chiefly by the skalds and in Snorri's *Edda*, is a later development of the personality and functions of the god, though traces of it are found elsewhere, as in the Lombard saga. Possibly some Christian influences may have affected the description of Odin's might, as when he is called ' All-father.'

We turn now to Odin's descent and relationships. Snorri says that the mythic cow Audhumla gave origin out of an ice-block to Buri, fair of feature, mighty and great. His son was Borr, who married Bestla, daughter of the giant Bolthorn. To them were born Odin, Vili, and Ve. How Buri procreated Borr is not told. Giants are thus already in existence. Some of these personages are referred to in the poems: Borr's sons in *Voluspa;* ' Borr's heir ' (Odin) in *Hyndluljod;* Bestla's brother, son of Bolthorn, who taught Odin songs, in *Havamal.*[88]

Odin's wife is Frigg, and in *Lokasenna* Loki reminds her of her amours with Vili and Ve — the only passage in the Poetic *Edda* where these two are mentioned. This incident is spoken of in the *Ynglinga-saga.* Odin's brothers ruled the realm in his absence. Once, when he was away, the Æsir thought that he would never return. So Vili and Ve shared his goods and his consort Frigg. Soon after Odin returned and took his wife once more.[89] Whether Vili and Ve are shadowy reflections of Odin or actual deities alternating in cult with him — a view favoured by recent research — is not clear.

Two stories, relics of older myths, are given by Saxo. Frigg had offended Odin, and he went into exile. Now Mit-othin, famous for jugglery, seized the opportunity of feigning to be a god and led the people to worship him. He said that the wrath of the gods could never be expiated by mixed sacrifices, and he appointed to each of the gods his special drink-offering. After a time Odin returned, and Mit-othin fled to Finland, where the inhabitants slew him. All who approached his barrow died and pestilence spread from his body, until it was taken out, beheaded and impaled in vampire fashion. Meanwhile the death of Odin's wife revived the splendours of his name, and he forced all those who had misused his absence by usurping divine honours to renounce them, and scattered the sorcerers.[90]

The other story is that after Odin's amour with Rinda, the gods banished him and stripped him of honour, lest the worshippers should forsake them. Ollerus was put in his place and was called Odin. For ten years he was president of the divine court, until the gods pitied Odin's exile and recalled him. Some judged that he was still unworthy: others said that he had bribed the gods. ' If you ask how much he paid, enquire of those who have found out what is the price of a godhead,' is Saxo's comment. Ollerus was driven out, and retired to Sweden where the Danes slew him. He was said to be a wizard, who used a bone marked with spells to cross the sea. By it he passed over the waters as quickly as by rowing.[91]

Ollerus is the Ull of the *Eddas*. Mit-othin, or Mjotudr-inn, is connected with ON *mjötudr*, AS *meotod*, ' fate ' or ' the power which metes out,' and may mean ' judge.' Others explain the name as ' co-Odin ' or ' contra-Odin,' and as the latter he is regarded as Loki, for, like Loki, he is *celiber praestigiis*. The two stories may be variants of one myth, referring to the introduction of the new cult of Odin in certain regions of the North where another god had been supreme. There are reminiscences of a cult war. The rule of the earlier god, in the eyes of the upholders of the new cult, could only have been possible by cunning and fraud. The theory of a prehistoric cult of alternating twin gods, who share a consort, succeeding each other in her possession, has also been suggested here. Such twin gods are held to be found in the two brother-gods called Alcis, mentioned by Tacitus as worshipped in a grove of the Nahanarvali, an East German tribe, and served by a priest in woman's clothing.[92] Possibly the myths point to Odin as a god whose power waned in winter, when another god took his place, and also his consort.

By Frigg Odin had a son, Balder. Thor is said to be his son by Jord, 'Earth'; Vali was his son by the giantess Rind. Hod, Bragi, Vidarr, and Heimdall are also called sons of Odin.[93] Kings and chiefs traced descent from Odin, e.g., the Skjoldings from his son Skjold.[94]

Certain possessions are ascribed to Odin. His ravens Huginn, 'Thought,' and Muninn, 'Memory,' sit on his shoulders and whisper to him all they see or hear. He sends them forth at day-break to fly about the world, and they return at evening with their budget of news. Hence Odin is Hrafna-god, 'Raven-god.' These birds are also called his hawks. 'For Huginn I fear lest he return not home, but I am more anxious for Muninn,' says Odin in *Grimnismal*, as if he feared they might not return from their flight.[95] The ravens which haunt battle-fields were naturally connected with Odin as War-god, but there is also a suggestion in this raven myth of his superior knowledge, inasmuch as he understands the language of birds. The presence of two ravens flying past when Earl Hakon offered a great sacrifice was a sign to him that Odin had taken his offering and that he would have a happy day of fighting. Ravens are mentioned as Odin's birds in the *Havardar-saga:* 'There is a flight of ravens, Odin's messengers, on the left hand.' Thus all ravens are the birds of Odin.[96]

Odin has two wolves, Geri, 'the Ravener,' and Freki, 'the Glutton,' to whom he gives his food, for wine is to him meat and drink. They are called his hounds.[97] Wolves, like ravens, visiting battle-fields and eating the slain, were appropriate to a War-god and a god of the dead.

Sleipnir is Odin's horse, born of Loki, grey, eight-legged, perhaps a symbol of speed. It is the 'best of all horses' among gods and men. On it Odin rides over land and sea, into Jötunheim and down to Hel, as did Hermod when he went to seek Balder's deliverance. On one occasion, Odin rode Sleipnir into

Jötunheim and visited the giant Hrungnir, 'Blusterer.' Hrungnir asked who this might be, riding through air and water on
such a good steed. Odin wagered his head that there was no
such steed in Jötunheim. Hrungnir said that his horse, Gull-
faxi, ' Golden-mane,' was better, and, growing angry, leaped on
it and rode after Odin, who went so furiously that he was on
the top of the next hill first. Hrungnir, overcome with giants'
frenzy, rode after him into Asgard where, in the sequel, he was
dealt with by Thor.[98]

The spear Gungnir was made by dwarfs and given to
Odin by Loki. He lent it to heroes. Against it all other
weapons were useless, e.g., Sigmund's sword. On Gungnir's
point and Sleipnir's teeth, the head of Mimir bade runes to be
written.[99]

Odin's ring, Draupnir, ' Dropper,' made by the dwarf Sindri
and given by his brother to Odin, was so called because eight
rings of the same weight dropped from it every ninth night.
Odin laid it on Balder's pyre, and Balder sent it back to him
from Hel as a token of remembrance. In *Skirnismal* the ring is
Frey's and is offered by Skirnir to Gerd as a means of inducing
her to accept Frey's love. Balder is also called ' possessor of
Draupnir.' [100] If, as is thought, this ring is a symbol of fruitfulness, it would naturally belong to Frey, the god of fruitfulness,
afterwards passing into Odin's possession.

Odin was still remembered in Christian times, and appears in
different stories, as well as in folk-belief. Out of several tales
in which he appears before Christian kings may be cited that of
his coming to king Olaf Tryggvason, as he was keeping Easter.
He appeared as an old man, one-eyed, of sombre aspect, wearing
a broad-brimmed hat, and wise of speech. Olaf was entranced
with his conversation, for he told him of all lands and all times.
Hardly would the king go to bed, even when his bishop reminded him of the lateness of the hour. When he was in bed,
the stranger came and held further converse with him, until
the bishop told Olaf that he must sleep. When he awoke, the

THE GREATER GODS — ODIN

guest was gone, but not before telling the cook that the meat which he was preparing was bad, and giving him two sides of an ox in its stead.   Hearing this, the king ordered the meat to be burned and thrown into the sea, for the stranger could have been no other than Odin in whom the heathen had believed.[101]

CHAPTER V

THE GREATER GODS—THOR

THE name of the god Thor (ON þórr) of the *Eddas* occurs elsewhere in the following forms — OHG Donar, OS Thunaer, AS Thunor, and, in the speech of the Normans, Thur. These are from an earlier Thunaraz, and the root is connected with Indo-Germanic (*s*)*ten*, 'to boom,' 'to roar.' Donar-Thor is thus the Loud-sounder, the Thunderer, the Thunder-god — the earliest aspect of this deity.

His widespread cult is attested by the equally widespread name of the fifth day of the week over the Teutonic area — OHG Donarestag or Toniristag; AS Thunoresdaeg; OE Thunresdaeg, hence Thursday; Swedish Thorsday, Danish Torsdag. The names were equivalents of the Roman *Dies Jovis*, and this suggests that Donar was regarded as the Teutonic Jupiter. In the early part of the eighth century S. Boniface found the Hessians at Geismar revering a huge sacred oak, *robur Jovis*, which he began to cut down, when the wind completed his efforts.[1] Boniface denounced the cult of such demons as Jupiter and spoke of Christian priests who sacrificed to Jupiter, feasting on the sacrifice.[2] Jupiter is undoubtedly Thor. The *Indiculus Superstitionum* (eighth century) speaks of the Saxon *sacra Jovis* and *feriae Jovis*, and Thunaer was one of the gods whom Saxons renounced at baptism.[3] The eighth century *Homilia de Sacrilegiis*, probably written by a priest of the northern part of the Frankish kingdom, says that no work was done on the day of Jupiter, and earlier notices of this ritual idleness occur in Cæsarius of Arles (fifth century) and Eligius of Troyes (588 to 659 A.D.), both referring to customs of the Germanic inhabitants of these regions.[4] The German Peni-

tential bearing the names ' Corrector ' and ' Medicus' which
forms the nineteenth Book of the collection of decrees made by
Burchard of Worms, c. 1000 A.D., and which was itself compiled in the early tenth century, also speaks of the observance
of the fifth day in honour of Jupiter.[5]

Saxo had difficulty in accepting the equivalence of Thor as
Jupiter and Odin as Mercury, for this would make Jupiter son
of Mercury, since Thor was Odin's son. He concludes that, if
Jupiter was father of Mercury, Thor could not be Jupiter nor
Odin Mercury.[6]

The identification of Thor with Jupiter was apparently sub-
sequent to his equivalence with Hercules as the *interpretatio
Romana*. Tacitus places Hercules next to Mercury among the
German tribes, and Hercules with his club is plainly the
same as Thor with his hammer. Both were strong, both fought
against evil powers. Hercules also occurs in inscriptions in
Batavian territory — Hercules Magusanus, and in the lower
Rhine region, where dedications to a Germanic Hercules occur.
Magusanus, ' the strong,' from an old German *magan*, ' to be
strong,' is connected with the name of Thor's son Magni, and
corresponds to a Norse epithet of Thor's, *hin rammi*, ' the
strong.' A Hercules Deusoniensis, named on coins, is presumed
to be a native German god, the name appearing in such place-
names as Duisberg. Hercules Barbatus on Rhenish inscriptions
is also Donar, whose beard is often mentioned in Norse literature. Hercules Malliator, in an inscription at Obernburg,
refers to Donar with his hammer.

Tacitus speaks of the Germanic Hercules and Mars being
placated with the permissible animal victims. ' They tell how
Hercules appeared among them, and on the eve of battle they
hymn the first of all brave men.' Arminius convened the tribes
in a wood sacred to Hercules — a cult-centre of the Cherusci
and other tribes, east of the Weser.[7]

Donar-Thor, the Thunder-god, thus corresponds to Jupiter,
in whose hands are thunder and lightning; and, as the strongest

of the gods with his hammer, to Hercules, the strong hero with his club. If the Teutons known to the Romans told myths about Donar conquering giants and monsters, like the Norse Thor, the equivalence with Hercules is intelligible.

Apart from the occurrence of Donar's name in that of the fifth day of the week, we find it on the Nordendorf brooch, discovered in Alemannic territory and belonging to the seventh century, joined with that of Odin in a runic inscription. The meaning of this seems to be that Thonar and Wodan are asked to consecrate a marriage. Donar the mighty is named in a twelfth century manuscript in a charm against epilepsy.[8] The witness of mountain names in Germany is significant — Donnersberg (Thoneresberg), Thuneresberg, and others, like the Thorsbiörg in Norway.[9] Among the Anglo-Saxons the name Thunor does not occur in the royal genealogies as does that of Woden, but its frequent appearance in English place-names points to his cult.[10]

Saxo speaks of Thor among the Danes as a god ' to the greatness of whose force nothing human or divine could fitly be compared.' He, Odin, and many others, ' being once men skilled in magic, claimed the rank of gods, and ensnared the people of Norway, Sweden, and Denmark.' [11] For Thor's cult and popularity in Sweden we have the witness of Adam of Bremen who equates Thor with the sceptre with Jupiter, and describes him as ' most powerful of the gods ' there. He is ' ruler of the air, controls lightning and thunder, winds, rain-storms, fine weather and crops.' Saxo also speaks of him as ' the great Thor ' of Sweden.[12] Above all, Norway was the region where the cult of Thor was most popular and long existent.

In Norway and in Iceland after its colonization, and to some extent in Sweden, Thor appears as the chief god, whose sovereignty Odin had taken. His cult was popular; his images are often mentioned. Where his image stood beside those of other deities, it had the most prominent place or was most richly decked. At Throndhjem, in the chief temple, Thor sat in the midst as the most honourable, his image large and decked with gold and silver. He sat in his wagon, very magnificent, drawn by two goats carved in wood, with horns covered with silver. The whole was mounted on wheels.[13] His image with his hammer was carved on the pillars of high-seats belonging to heads of families, or on the backs of chairs, or on the sterns of ships.[14] Carved in bone, it was used as a protective amulet. Men carried his images with them, made of silver or ivory. Many temples of Thor existed in Norway and Iceland, and are mentioned in the Sagas and other writings. No other god had so many temples there as Thor.

Thor's name was common in personal- and place- names in Scandinavia — Thordis, Thorkell, Thorgerd, Thorstein, and innumerable others, and the proportion is large compared with those of other deities, Odin's name occurring seldom in Norse names. Among the Icelandic colonists of the ninth and tenth centuries names compounded of Thor are fifty-one as compared with three of Frey and none of Odin. On monuments with runes Thor is besought to consecrate these, and they sometimes have the form of his hammer.[15] The Thing or assembly was opened on Thor's day, in a place consecrated to Thor, showing that he was associated with law and justice. His superiority is seen in epithets bestowed upon him — *ásabragr,* 'first of the Æsir'; *landás,* 'god of the country'; *hofdingi allra goda,* 'chief of all gods'; *mest tignadhr,* 'most honoured.' He is 'Midgard's warder'; 'the mighty one of the gods.' At law-business oaths were taken with the words: 'so help me Frey and Njord and the almighty god,' viz., Thor.[16] It is significant that Odin's name does not occur in this formula.

The reasons for Odin's later supremacy have already been discussed. Thor's supremacy, however, was never forgotten, and to the end he remained chief god to the peasants and yeomen. The Icelandic colonists believed that they were under his protection and guided by him to their new abodes, which they called after him. The images of Thor and Frey are often mentioned in Iceland: Odin's but once. Apart from the king's sacrifice to Odin, sacrifices were made only to Thor and Frey. Thor consecrates runes, not Odin; and the Thing met on his day, not Odin's. The lines already cited from *Harbardsljod* show that the warrior aristocracy went to Odin at death, the folk to Thor, and the statement is significant of the relative position of the two gods at the time when the poem was composed (tenth century). The poem might be viewed as an attempt of its author to emphasize Odin's greatness at the expense of Thor's. While this is possible, yet the poem illustrates the lower aspects of Odin, his amours and magic, and it might equally be regarded as the comment of a mocking half-believer upon the gods. The poem is a contest of wits between Thor and Odin, disguised as a ferryman, Harbard. Thor appears as a peasant, with a basket on his back, coming back from a journey to the East. He asks Harbard to bring his boat over, but Harbard enquires what sort of peasant is this and twits him with his lowly position, not even possessing the usual peasant's farm, barefoot, and in a peasant's dress. What is his name? 'I am Odin's son, the strong one of the gods,' Thor replies, and threatens Harbard for his mockery. The two then relate their adventures: each bidding the other tell what he was doing at the time. Thor's adventures are the slaying of the giants Hrungnir and Thjazi, and of evil giant-women; his compelling the sons of Svarang to sue for peace; his slaying the evil brides of the berserkers. Odin recounts his love-affairs and his causing of wars, and taunts Thor with cowardice, betraying troth, slaying women, and with Sif's infidelity. Thor reproaches Harbard with repaying good gifts with evil mind, calls him ' womanish,' utters foul speech against him, and threatens him with death if he could cross the water to him. Harbard still refuses to ferry him over, and adds that he never thought that Asa-Thor, Thor of the Æsir, would be hindered by a ferryman. Finally he bids him take his way on foot and directs him how to go. Thor says that Harbard is speaking in mockery and then the latter tells him to go hence where every evil thing will harm him.

Odin's contempt for Thor in this poem mirrors the relation of the higher classes with their cult of Odin to the people outside the courtly and aristocratic circles to whom Thor was still the chief god.

Thor's supremacy is attested in *Lokasenna*, for he alone of the gods can silence Loki. He saves the gods from the vengeance of giants according to other myths, or, as the poet Thorbjorn sings: 'Bravely fought Thor for Asgard and the followers of Odin.' [17]

The opposition between Thor and Odin appears in an episode of the life of the ideal Danish and Norse hero, Starkad. He had been nourished by Odin, called Hrosshars-grani, 'Horse-hair-beard.' Becoming one of king Vikar's companions, he was with him when his fleet was stayed by a storm, and when the lots showed that Vikar himself must be sacrificed to Odin. That night Odin called Starkad and took him to a wood where, in a clearing, eleven men were sitting on as many seats. The twelfth seat was empty. Odin sat on it and was hailed by the others as Odin. The occasion had now come for Starkad's fate to be pronounced. Thor said that as his mother had chosen a giant for his father instead of Thor, Starkad would have neither son nor daughter. Odin then said that he would live for three generations. In each, Thor said, he would do a dastard's deed. Odin announced that he would have the best of weapons and armour. Thor replied that he would have neither lands nor heritage. Odin promised him many possessions. Thor asserted that still he would always long for more. Odin promised him victory in every fight. Thor said that he would always receive terrible wounds. Odin announced that he would give him such a gift of poetry that verse would flow from his lips like common speech. Thor said that he would forget all his poems. Odin declared that the bravest and noblest would honour him; Thor said that the common people would hate him. These

different fates were endorsed by the others. Odin finally
said that Starkad must repay him by slaying Vikar, and
gave him instructions how to effect this, as has already been
told.[18]

Thor appears in this story as opponent of the aristocratic
warrior class dear to Odin, and of their ideals, turning every
gift of Odin's into a curse or neutralizing it, and thus acting the
part of the third Norn in some tales.

In the *Eddas* Thor is regarded as son of Odin, but this could
only have been a mythic convention resulting from Odin's
growing supremacy and the desire to bring all other deities into
relation with him. This mythic relationship is asserted in the
old English homily written by Ælfric, who says that the Danes
held Jupiter, whom they call Thor, to be son of Mercury, called
by them Odin. This he regards as erroneous according to
Roman mythology. Saxo, as has been seen, was also puzzled
by the equation.

Thor's mother is Jord, 'Earth.' His wife is Sif, 'the fair-
haired goddess,' with hair like gold, who was accused by Loki
and by Odin of unfaithfulness to him. Thor himself was not
faithful to her. Their daughter is Thrud, 'might,' promised
by the gods to Alviss in Thor's absence. Thor is sometimes
described as 'Thrud's father': hence she may be regarded as
a personification of his might. He himself is Thrudugr, 'the
Mighty,' and Thrudvald, 'strong Protector'; his hammer is
Thrudhamarr, 'mighty Hammer'; his dwelling Thrudheim
and Thrudvang, 'Strength-home,' 'Strong field.' The giant
Hrungnir is called 'thief of Thrud' in allusion to some unre-
corded abduction of her.[19]

Thor's sons are Magni (his mother Jarnsaxa) and Modi,
who survive the Doom of the gods and inherit his hammer.
They are personifications of his might (Magni) and wrath
(Modi). When Magni was three days old he lifted the giant
Hrungnir's foot off Thor, a feat which none of the Æsir could
do.[20] Thor's brother is Meili, of whom nothing is known. His

servants are Thjalfi and Roskva, children of a husbandman, according to a story presently to be told.[21] His relationship to Jord is seen in the epithet given to him, *burr Jarthar*, 'son of Earth,' in *Lokasenna* and *Thrymskvitha*.[22]

Thor's names and epithets throw light on his character and functions. He is *thrudvaldr goda*, 'the strong one of the gods'; *veorr Midgards*, 'Warder of earth'; *vinr verlidha*, 'the Friend of man'; Vingnir, 'the Hurler'; Vingthor, 'Thor the Hurler'; Hlorrithi, 'the Noisy one'; *orms ein-bani*, 'Serpent's destroyer'; *Thurs radbani*, 'Giant-killer.' These show him as the champion of the gods, the Thunder-god, the destroyer of obnoxious powers and beings, the helper of men. Though in origin a Thunder-god, he has other aspects, mostly of a beneficent kind, as summed up in Adam of Bremen's account, cited above. As Thunder-god his functions show that the thunder-storm was regarded in a beneficent aspect as furthering fertility. Sacrifices were made and prayers offered to Thor by the Swedes and Norsemen in times of famine and sickness, as Adam of Bremen and a passage in the *Eiriks-saga* show. Thorkill prayed to Thor, the red-bearded god, for food, and he sent a whale to the shore.[23] Thor helped to make the ground arable, and protected men against rocks and cliffs.[24] To sea-farers he was helpful, giving them favourable winds. The Norman Vikings offered him human victims before setting sail, and animal and food offerings were made to him by voyagers to Iceland.[25] Helgi the Thin asked him where he should land in Iceland, and he was advised to go to Eyjafjord. Helgi was a Christian, but was still so inclined to the old faith that he sought Thor's help in all sea-faring and difficult journeys.[26] Kraoko Hreidarr and his party sailed to Iceland, and he made vows to Thor in order that he should point out a site for his possession. Though the land to which he was directed belonged to another, Kraoko maintained that Thor had sent him to it and intended him to settle there.[27] Settlers in Iceland dedicated their land to Thor and called it by his name.[28] Hence the great number of place-names which bear witness to the cult of Thor.

Several accounts in the Sagas show how prominent this cult was in the lives of the Norse settlers in Iceland. Rolf, who was called Thorolf, had been guardian of Thor's temple on the island of Most near the Norwegian coast. He was called 'a great friend' of Thor's, and, when he quarrelled with king Harald, he made a great sacrifice and enquired of 'his beloved friend' Thor whether he should make peace with the king or leave Norway. The answer was that he should go to Iceland. He now took the temple to pieces and removed the timbers and earth from the spot where Thor's image had rested. On drawing near Iceland, he threw overboard the pillars carved with Thor's image, believing that by them he would be guided to a landing-place. They drifted ashore at a place afterwards called Thorsness, and there Thorolf landed and built a temple.[29] Other examples of this use of pillars are given in the *Land-náma-bók*, as well as of taking down a temple before migrating.[30] The *Kjalnesinga-saga* tells of a great sacrificer called Thorgrim, grandson of Ingolf, the first settler in Iceland. He had a large temple to which all his men had to pay toll. He held Thor in highest honour, and in the temple his image was in the centre, with those of other deities on either hand.[31] The dedication of sons to the service of Thor is also spoken of in the Sagas. Thorolf, himself dedicated to Thor, gave his son Stein to the god as Thorstein. His son in turn, Grim called Thorgrim, was also dedicated to Thor in order that he should be a temple-priest. The naming of lands or places or persons after Thor is prominent in stories of the settlement of Iceland.

Thor's power over the winds and storms is also seen in the fact that he caused shipwreck to those who forsook their allegiance to him by turning to Christianity. In the *Njals-saga* Thangbrand, a Christian, was asked by Steinvora, mother of Ref the skald, if he had heard that Thor challenged Christ to single combat and that He dared not accept the challenge. He replied that he had heard that Thor was but dust and ashes, if God had not willed that he should live. Then she asked him if he knew how he had been shipwrecked, and told him that Thor had done this. 'Little good was Christ when Thor shattered ships to pieces. . . . A storm roused by Thor dashed the bark to splinters small.'[32] An Icelander named Thorgisl became a Christian, and in dreams was threatened by Thor if he did not return to his allegiance. The ship on which he was sailing encountered a great storm, caused by Thor. The god asked him in one dream to pay him what he had vowed to him. On awaking he recalled that this was a calf which was now an old ox. He threw it overboard, as this was the reason that Thor was haunting the ship.[33]

Thor's aid was also sought in war. Styrbjorn prayed to him for victory over king Eirik, who prayed to Odin, and because he was mightier than Thor, Eirik was victorious.[34]

At banquets a cup of wine, consecrated by the sign of Thor's hammer, was drunk to him. At a certain banquet Earl Sigund signed the first cup to Odin. King Hakon, a Christian, took it and signed it with the Cross, whereupon Sigund said that he was signing it to Thor with the hammer sign.[35]

Before discussing Thor's possessions a passage from Snorri's *Edda* describing him may be quoted. ' He is strongest of gods and men. His realm is in Thrudvang; his hall is Bilskirnir, and in it are five hundred and forty rooms. That is the greatest house known to men.' Here Snorri quotes a verse of *Grimnismal* in which Odin describes his son's hall and says that it is the greatest of all houses, i.e., greater even than his own Valhall. The stanza is an interpolation, but it may be a reminiscence of Thor's supreme place among the gods, and it is significant also that, in describing the various seats of the gods, Odin begins, not with his own, but with Thor's. Snorri then speaks of Thor's chariot and goats, and his three precious possessions — hammer, girdle, and iron gloves.[36]

Thor has two he-goats called Tanngnjost, ' Tooth-gnasher,'

and Tanngrisnir, ' Tooth-gritter,' and a chariot in which he
drives, drawn by them. Hence he is called Öku-Thor,
' Wagon-Thor.' Snorri also quotes the poet Kormak who said:
' In his wagon Thor sitteth.' The wagon is ' the car of Hrungnir's slayer,' on which runes were bidden to be written by
Mimir.[37] In thunder-storms a god or supernatural being is
often supposed to be on a journey through the sky, and this
was true of Thor. A thunder-clap was *reidar thruma*, the rumbling noise of chariot wheels. In Sweden the people said during thunder: *godgubben åker; gofar åker*, ' the good old fellow' or ' the gaffer drives.' In Gothland thunder is *Thors
akan*, ' Thor's driving,' and in Schleswig-Holstein the noise of
thunder is attributed to the rumbling of a wagon through the
air, i.e., Thor's wagon. Hence his name Öku-Thor or such
epithets as Valdi Kjöla, ' ruler of the wagon,' Reidartyr, ' god
of the wagon,' Vagna verr, ' wagon-man.' [38] From the goats
which drew the wagon Thor was called Hafra drottin, ' lord of
the goats.' [39] One of the myths of Thor told by Snorri begins:
' Öku-Thor drove out with his he-goats and his chariot,' and in
the *Haustlong* of Thjodolf of Hvin we see the goats driving the
god in his wagon to fight with giants. Hail beats down, earth
is rent, rocks shake, crags are shivered, the sky burns, as he rolls
along — the description of a thunder-storm. *Thrymskvitha*
describes how the mountains were rent and earth burned with
fire, as the goats drove Thor's wagon to Jötunheim.[40]

Besides going in his wagon Thor is depicted walking, while
other gods ride. Thus he walks to the daily Thing or perhaps
to the final catastrophe, wading through many rivers according
to an obscure passage in *Grimnismal*.[41]

' The hammer Mjöllnir which is known to the Frost-giants
and Hill-giants, when it is raised aloft; and little wonder, for it
has smashed many a skull of their fathers or kinsfolk.' This
' mighty ' or ' murder-greedy ' hammer was made by the dwarf
Sindri and was deemed by the gods to be best of all precious
works. It could be wielded by Thor only when he wore his

iron gloves. However hard he smote, it would not fail him:
if he threw it, it would never miss nor fly so far as not to return
to his hands. If he desired, it could become so small that he
could keep it under his shirt. The only flaw in it was the short-
ness of its haft.[42] With his hammer Thor slew monsters and
giants, and forced Loki to keep silence by threatening him with
it. Thunder and lightning sometimes preceded its stroke.[43]
Hence it is most easily explained as the thunderbolt, which, in
German superstition, was an essential part of the lightning-flash,
and believed to be a black wedge which buried itself in the
earth, but at each succeeding thunder-storm rose towards the
surface, which it reached in seven years.[44] Does this belief correspond to the statement that Thor's hammer returned to his
hand after being thrown? The superstition is echoed in
Thrymskvitha in which the giant Thrym steals the hammer and
buries it eight miles deep in the earth. In many regions flint
weapons found in the earth are believed to be thunderbolts,
and the myth of Thor's hammer is doubtless connected with this
belief. They are generally used as amulets or for magical
purposes.

The hammer was a sacred symbol, and the sign of the hammer was used in consecrations and blessings. This custom is
reflected in certain passages of the *Eddas*. The giant Thrym,
believing the disguised Thor to be Freyja, the bride demanded
by him, said:

> ' Bring now the hammer, to bless the bride,
>   Lay Mjöllnir in the maiden's bosom,
>   That our bond may be consecrated in Vor's name.' [45]

Thor himself hallowed the hides and bones of his dead goats
with his hammer, so that they lived again. With it he also hallowed Balder's pyre. The sign of the hammer, as in Christian
circles the sign of the Cross, was made over cups of liquor, especially in sacrifices. As a divine symbol the hammer was used
for many purposes. Sickness was healed by it, demons kept

at a distance, marriages consecrated. According to Norse custom, when a newly born child had been accepted by its father and so permitted to live, it was washed and signed with Thor's hammer, i.e., a symbol of that mythic weapon, and thus received into the family.[46] The hammer carved on a tombstone showed that the dead man was dedicated to Thor. Small hammers were used as amulets, and specimens of these have been found in Denmark and Sweden. 'Thor's hammers' were used by the island-men in their ancient faith, according to Saxo, who calls them *malleos joviales*. The men of old thought that thunder was caused by such hammers, and they apparently used them in thunder-storms. In c. 1123 A.D. Magnus Nicholasson the Dane spoiled Thor's temple in Sweden of these tokens of the god's, and the Swedes considered him guilty of sacrilege.[47] All this points to the connexion of Thor's hammer both with the mythic powers attributed to weapons and with the superstitious use of stone weapons regarded as supernatural. Thor's hammer became the possession of Magni and Modi, his sons, in the renewed world.[48]

When Thor clasps his girdle around him 'his divine strength is increased by half.' In his iron gloves, his third precious possession, there is also much virtue.[49]

Thor is red-bearded, though whether this redness alludes to the fiery appearance of lightning, as Grimm supposed, is doubtful. He shakes his beard when roused; when he speaks into it, every one quails. His anger is described by his bristling hair and tossing beard, or he lets his brows sink down below his eyes, so that whoso looks at him must fall down before his glance alone. Flame flashes from his eyes. When Thor met king Olaf at a time when Christianity was encroaching on his cult, ' he blew hard into his beard, and raised his beard's voice,' with the result that a storm arose.[50] He is seen travelling on foot like a peasant, carrying a basket on his back — an appropriate appearance for a god of the peasants and the folk. He visits a peasant's house for a night's lodging, and from such a house he took his servants Thjalfi and Roskva. Thjalfi, the swift-runner, is so swift that only Hugi or thought can beat him. Hence he may be a personification of lightning. Peasant-like, too, is Thor in his wordy flyting with Odin in *Harbardsljod.*[51]

At the Doom of the gods Thor fights with the Midgard-serpent, which he slays, but falls dead through its venom.[52]

Thor is often described as journeying to the East to fight giants or trolls. The *Eddas* contain several myths of these expeditions and combats. Indeed no other Eddic god has so many myths told of him as Thor. Several of his titles refer to his power over giants and monsters: 'adversary and slayer of giants and troll-women,' 'smiter of Hrungnir, of Geirrod, of Thrivaldi,' 'foe of the Midgard-serpent,' 'hewer in sunder of the nine heads of Thrivaldi,' 'merciless destroyer of giantesses.' Hence also he is 'the defender of Asgard and of Midgard.'[53] In his aspect as queller of giants, Thor, the Thunder-god, represents the folk-belief that thunder is obnoxious to giants, trolls, and other demoniac beings.[54]

The myths in which Thor plays a part will now be given, beginning with that of the giant Hrungnir. After Odin's visit to Hrungnir (p. 66), the giant pursued him into Asgard. The Æsir gave Hrungnir drink out of Thor's flagons, and when drunk, the giant boasted that he would carry Valhall into Jötunheim and kill all the deities, save Sif and Freyja. Freyja alone dared pour ale for him, and now, as his insolence increased, the gods called for Thor. Thor, swinging his hammer, asked why Hrungnir was drinking here and who had given him safe-conduct, and, hearing from him that it was Odin, Thor said that he would repent of his presence there. Hrungnir protested that Thor would have no fame for killing a defenceless giant, and offered to fight him on the borders of Grjotunagard. He then rode back to Jötunheim, and news of the duel was spread among the giants, who feared for themselves lest Thor should win. They made a giant of clay, nine miles high and three broad, and gave him a mare's heart. Hrungnir had a stone heart with three corners; of stone also were his head and shield. His weapon was a whetstone. Beside him stood the clay giant, Mökkurkálfi, in great terror.

Thor and Thjalfi went to the meeting, and Thjalfi ran forward and advised the giant to stand on his shield for Thor would come up through the earth to him. This he did. Now arose thunder and lightnings, and Thor in divine fury (*ásmodi*), swung his hammer and cast it at Hrungnir, who meanwhile threw his whetstone. The weapons crashed together, and part of the whetstone fell to earth, forming all the whinstone rocks, part of it burst on Thor's head, so that he fell forward. The hammer, however, broke Hrungnir's head in pieces, and he fell with his foot on Thor's neck. Thjalfi struck the clay giant down. He tried to raise Hrungnir's foot from Thor's neck, but could not, neither could any of the Æsir when they arrived. None could succeed but Magni, Thor's three days' old son by the giantess Jarnsaxa. ' Sad it is,' he said, ' father, that I came so late, for I would have slain this giant with my fist, had I come sooner.' Thor praised him and gave him Hrungnir's horse, which Odin said should have been given to him.

The whetstone fragment remained in Thor's head. The wise woman Groa, wife of Aurvandil the Valiant, sang spells over Thor until the stone was loosened. Thor told her how he had waded from the north over Elivagar, ' Icy Stream,' bearing Aurvandil in a basket on his back from Jötunheim. As one of his toes stuck out of the basket, he broke it off and cast it up to the sky, where it is now the star called ' Aurvandil's toe.' He also said that soon Aurvandil would be home, and in her joy Groa forgot her incantations, and the stone remained in Thor's head. Hence a stone should not be cast across the floor, for the stone is then stirred in his head.[55]

A poem by Thjodolf of Hvin (tenth century) deals with this myth as depicted on a shield, and gives a vivid description of the rending of earth, the beating down of hail, and the shaking of the rocks, as Thor drives forth in his wagon to the fight.[56]

There are occasional references to the myth in the Eddic and other poems. Thor calls Mjöllnir ' Hrungnir's slayer,' and he himself is ' Hrungnir's killer,' ' smiter of Hrungnir,' ' skull-splitter of Hrungnir.' The stone shield is ' blade of Hrungnir's foot-soles ' according to a kenning, because the giant stood on it.[57] The fullest reference is in *Harbardsljod*. Harbard said to Thor that he would await his attack and that since Hrungnir died no stouter opponent has faced him. Thor replied:

> ' Thou now remindest me
> How I with Hrungnir fought,
> The insolent Jötun,
> Whose head was all of stone;
> Yet I made him fall,
> And sink before me.' [58]

While the foundation of this myth may be the effect of a thunder-storm in the mountains, the further modern interpretations of details in it can only be regarded as highly problematical. The story of the part of the whetstone which stuck in Thor's head is possibly an ætiological myth originating as an explanation of images of the god Thor which, as among the Lapps, had an iron nail with a piece of flint stuck in the head, ' as if Thor should strike out fire.' The purpose of this iron and flint was probably to produce the sacrificial fire. On the high-seat pillars of the Norsemen the image of Thor was carved and in the head was set the *reginnagli*. In earlier times flint may have been used instead of iron in these images.[59]

Aurvandil, ' the Sea-wanderer,' is the hero Orendil still sung in an epic of the twelfth century, and possibly the Horvendillus of Saxo, father of Amleth (Hamlet). The constellation Earendel was also known to the Anglo-Saxons.[60] This constellation is thought to be Orion.

Another giant adventure of Thor's is that in Geirrod's land, related by Snorri. Loki, flying in Frigg's hawk-plumage, went to Geirrod's court where he was shut up in a chest for three months. In order to get free, he told Geirrod that he would induce Thor to come there without his hammer or girdle. Thor, having been persuaded, went off with Loki and spent the night with the giantess Grid, mother of Vidarr, who told him of Geirrod's craft and lent him a pair of iron gloves, a girdle of might, and a staff called ' Grid's staff ' (*Gridar völr*). By aid of the staff Thor crossed Vimur, greatest of rivers, Loki holding on to the girdle of might. When they were in mid-stream Gjalp, daughter of Geirrod, caused the waters to increase. Thor sang: ' Swell not, O Vimur, I must wade through thee to the giants' garth. If thou swellest, so will swell my divine strength in me up to Heaven.' Going forward he saw how Gjalp caused the swelling of the stream, and caused her to retire by throwing a stone at her. Then taking hold of a rowan-tree on the bank, he pulled himself out: hence the rowan is called ' Thor's deliverance.' Reaching Geirrod's court, Thor was given a seat which moved under him to the roof. Thrusting his staff against the rafters, he pushed back the chair, which now crashed on Gjalp and her sister Greip, breaking their backs. Geirrod called him to play games in a hall where great fires burned, and taking with the tongs a white hot iron bar from the fire, he threw it at Thor, who caught it with his iron gloves. Seeing him about to throw it at him, Geirrod leaped behind an iron pillar, through which the bar passed, as well as through Geirrod and the wall into the earth.[61]

This myth is the subject of a poem by Eilif Gudrunarson (*c.* 976 A.D.), in which, not Loki, but Thjalfi accompanies Thor.[62] Saxo Grammaticus, in his account of King Gorm's visit to the land of Geruthus (Geirrod), refers to the hurt done by Thor to him and his daughters, here three in number. Geirrod's land is full of treasure. The way to it across the ocean is beset with peril. Sun and stars are left behind and the journey is taken down to chaos, to a land of darkness and horror, and here the story is probably coloured by visions of Hell. ' Long ago the god Thor had been provoked by the insolence of the giants to drive red-hot irons through the vitals of

Geirrod, who strove with him. The iron slid farther, tore up the mountain, and battered through its side. The women were stricken by the might of his thunderbolts, and were punished for their attempt on Thor, by having their backs broken.' [63]

The myth of Hymir is told by Snorri and also in the Eddic poem *Hymiskvitha*. Snorri says that Thor went from Midgard on foot and in haste disguised as a youth, and arrived at the giant Hymir's abode. Next morning he wished to aid Hymir in fishing, but Hymir said he was so small that he would freeze. Thor's anger was great, but he restrained himself from attacking Hymir, as he had another purpose to fulfil. To obtain bait he struck off the head of Hymir's largest ox, Himinbrjot. He aided Hymir in rowing to the usual fishing-banks, and beyond them, in spite of the giant's fear of the Midgard-serpent. Thor prepared a strong line with a large hook, on which he fixed the ox's head. Then he cast it overboard, intending to beguile the Midgard-serpent. The monster snapped at the bait and was caught by the hook, dashing off so quickly that Thor's fists crashed against the gunwale. Thor's divine anger came upon him: he braced his feet so firmly that they dashed through the planking and struck the bottom of the ship. Then he drew the serpent up, flashing fiery glances at it, while it glared at him and blew venom. The giant was in terror and, while Thor clutched his hammer, he fumbled for his knife and hacked the line, so that the serpent fell back into the sea. Thor hurled his hammer after it, and ' men say that he struck off its head,' but ' I think it were true to tell thee that the serpent still lives and lies in the encompassing sea.' Then Thor struck Hymir with his fist and sent him overboard, and he himself waded ashore.[64]

Snorri makes this adventure one taken in revenge for Thor's outwitting by Utgard-Loki, of which we shall hear presently. The *Hymiskvitha* gives a somewhat different version of the myth, showing that Snorri must have used other sources, and it is the subject of several poems, verses of which are quoted by him in *Skaldskaparmal*.[65]

The *Hymiskvitha*, which is based on earlier lays, consists of three incidents — the obtaining of a kettle for the gods' banquet, the Hymir story, and the tale of Thor's goats. The third has no real connexion with the rest of the poem, the two incidents of which are much more welded together.

The gods were feasting and not satisfied, so they used divining-twigs to discover where more drink could be obtained. They learned that there was plenty in the hall of the giant or sea-god Ægir, and to him they went, bidding him prepare a feast for them. The giant sought revenge and bade Thor bring a kettle in which to brew ale. The gods did not know where to seek it, until Tyr, who here calls Hymir his father, said that Hymir had a mighty kettle, a mile deep. Thor and Tyr set out to the east of Elivagar at the end of Heaven, where Hymir dwelt, first going to Egil's house, where Thor left his goats. At Hymir's abode Tyr found his grandmother, who had nine hundred heads, and his bright-browed mother, who brought them ale. She hid them beneath the kettle, for Hymir was often hostile to guests. Late returned the giant from hunting, icicles rattling on his beard. His wife told him that Thor and their son Tyr, long waited for, had come, and were sitting under the gable, behind the beam. The giant looked at the gable: it gave way and eight kettles fell, of which all but one — that under which the gods were hiding — broke. The giant saw them, and, though enraged, could not forget the duty of hospitality. Three oxen were slaughtered and their flesh boiled: of these Thor ate two, to Hymir's amazement. The poem now passes suddenly to the fishing incident. Hymir bids Thor go and get bait from the oxen. On this expedition Hymir caught two whales, while Thor was still preparing his hook with great cunning. Having cast it he drew up the serpent, and struck at its ' hill of hair ' (head) with his hammer, and it sank into the sea.

Thor and Hymir returned to the giant's house.   Hymir
would reckon no one strong who could not break his glass cup.
Thor struck the stone pillars with it: they broke, but not the
cup.   Now Hymir's wife told Thor to strike the giant's head
with the cup, for that was harder than the glass.   Hymir bewailed his treasure, and said that now they might take the kettle
if they could move it.   Tyr tried in vain: Thor raised it to his
head and set off.   The giant with other many-headed ones out
of caves pursued.   Thor put down the kettle, swung his hammer
and slew the giants.   Thus the kettle was brought to the gods.
After the killing of the giants, one of Thor's goats was found
with its leg hurt — this evil Loki had done.   Nothing further
is said of this in the poem, and the goat incident is told by Snorri
in another connexion.

This lay consists mainly of a widespread folk-tale, to which
the episode of the Midgard-serpent has been attached, unlike
the prose account.   Heroes come to a giant's abode to seek some
coveted possession.   In the adventure they are aided by the
giant's wife or daughter, and so overcome him and obtain the desired object.   Thor and Tyr are here made the heroes of the
tale.   The cup is suggestive of the giant's Life-token, containing
his soul, but contrary to usual custom, though it is broken, the
giant does not immediately die.   Such folk-tales usually tell
how the pursuers are stopped by transformed objects thrown
down by the pursued.   This is lacking in the lay.   That the
kettle signifies the sea, frozen in winter, i.e., in the power of the
Frost-giant, and freed by the first thunder-storm in spring,
seems a forced and unnatural explanation of the tale.[66]   A
gigantic vessel would rather be the rock basin or shores containing the sea, not the sea itself.

The adventure with the Midgard-serpent prefigures the
coming time when, at the Doom of the gods, Thor will have to
engage with it.   But this adventure may have given rise to the
conception of that final combat with the monster.   The suggestion of both prose and poetic narrative is that the serpent is slain

or receives a severe wound. The poem called *Bragi's Shield-lay* and the *Húsdrápa* both describe the adventure, and in the latter Thor struck the serpent a deadly blow and smote off its head as it rose from the sea.[67]

One of the finest Eddic poems, *Thrymskvitha* or 'Lay of Thrym,' composed about 900 A.D., has, as its subject, the recovery of Thor's hammer from the giant Thrym, who had stolen it. Ving-Thor awoke to find his hammer missing. Great was his rage — hair bristling, beard shaking — as he sought it. Loki was told of his loss, and together they sought Freyja and borrowed her feather-dress. In this Loki flew to Jötunheim (as he had flown to Geirrod's realm), where Thrym, lord of the giants, sat on a mound, making golden leashes for his dogs and stroking the manes of his steeds. ' How fares it with gods and elves: why comest thou alone to Jötunheim? ' he cried to Loki. ' Ill fares it with gods and elves,' replied Loki, ' hast thou hidden Hlorrithi's hammer? ' Thrym said it was hidden eight miles deep: none would win it back, unless Freyja was given him as a bride. Back flew Loki to Thor with the tidings, and again they sought Freyja, Loki bidding her bind on the bridal veil and haste to Jötunheim with him. So great was Freyja's anger that the gods' dwelling was shaken and her necklace, Brisinga-men, broke. The gods met in council. How was the hammer to be recovered? Heimdall advised that Thor, disguised as Freyja, should go to Thrym. Thor refused such unmanly conduct, but Loki bade him be silent, for if the advice were not followed, and he did not recover his hammer, the giants would soon dwell in Asgard — a significant statement.

So the bridal-veil was put on Thor, with a woman's dress, keys at her girdle, a woman's head-gear, and the necklace and other gems. Loki attended him as a maidservant, and in the goats' chariot they sped to Jötunheim, while the mountains burst and blazed with fire. Thrym bade a great feast to be prepared. To his amazement Thor ate an ox, eight salmon, and all the dainties provided for the women, and drank three huge vessels of mead. Loki said that the bride had been fasting for eight nights, in her longing for Jötunheim. Thrym, eager to kiss the bride, lifted her veil, but at sight of the fiery eyes, leaped back the length of the hall. Loki explained that for eight nights the bride had not slept, in her longing for Jötunheim. Now came the giant's sister, asking the bridal fee — rings of gold from the bride's hand, if she would gain her love and favour. Then Thrym commanded that the hammer be brought to hallow the bride, and placed on her knees, that the hand of Vor, goddess of vows, might bless them both. Thor laughed inwardly and, seizing the hammer, slew Thrym and all the giants and his sister.

Some dualistic conceptions may lie behind this myth. The giant wishes to gain the power of the gods, and steals its symbol and medium, the hammer Mjöllnir. But what precisely the giant represents, whether a primitive thunder-deity or demon or the force of winter, is problematical. Thor, whose strength is quiescent apart from his hammer, may represent here a nature god whose power wanes in winter, but waxes in spring. If this is the mythic foundation, the story is built upon it without itself having any significance in nature phenomena. It is well told, with much humour, and Thor excellently sustains the part of the bride. The story is remembered in Norse folk-tales.[68]

Here, there is a quest by Thor for his own property, as in *Hymiskvitha* for that of another, in Jötunheim. In both tales he eats in a gluttonish manner, and in both he ends by slaying the giants.

Still another exploit of Thor's against a giant is found in the tale of the building of a citadel for the gods, which would be proof against the Hill-giants and Frost-giants. This was done by a giant craftsman (*smidr*) on condition that he should have Freyja and the sun and moon. The occasion of the building was after the attack on Asgard by the Vanir. The gods said that the giant must complete it in one season, and that he would lose his reward if it were not done by the first day of summer.

The bargain was sealed with many oaths, since it was unsafe
for the giant to be in Asgard without truce, should Thor, who
was in the East fighting trolls, return. The giant asked permission for the help of his stallion Svadilfari. He began on the
first day of winter, and the gods were amazed to see the horse
drawing such huge stones. Within three days of summer, the
work was nearly done. The gods were inclined to evade their
promise, asking who had advised handing over Freyja or so
destroying air and sky as to propose taking sun and moon from
them. All agreed that Loki must have advised this. He de-
served death, if he could not devise means of outwitting the
giant. Accordingly, in the form of a mare he met Svadilfari,
who snapped his traces and rushed after the mare. The giant
fell into frenzy, knowing that the work would not now be
finished. The gods sent for Thor who came and struck the
giant into fragments with his hammer. Loki gave birth to a
foal with eight feet, Odin's horse Sleipnir.[69]

This bargain and Thor's deliverance of the gods are referred
to in *Voluspa,* quoted also by Snorri:

> ' Then went the powers to their judgment seats,
> The all-holy gods, and thereon held council
> Who had all the air with venom mingled
> Or given Od's maid to the giant race.
>
> Then alone was Thor with anger swollen,
> He seldom sits when the like he hears.
> Oaths were broken, words and pledges,
> The mighty bonds between them made.'

Behind this myth as applied to the gods and their citadel is the
traditional belief that large buildings of unknown origin must
have been the work of giants. Some German and Scandinavian
folk-tales closely resemble this story, though the method of
outwitting giant, troll, or devil is different.[70]

Thor here appears as guardian and helper of the gods, as in
the Hrungnir myth. So *Lokasenna* shows his coming in to the

banquet-hall where Loki has been slandering the deities, and bidding him be silent or he will close his mouth. So the skald Thorbjorn sang:

> 'Bravely fought Thor for Asgard
> And the followers of Odin.' [71]

Other adventures of Thor with giants are mentioned in the *Eddas*. *Harbardsljod* and the skald Bragi attribute to him the destruction of Thjazi, 'the Thick,' and the casting of his eyes to Heaven. The former deed, however, is ascribed to the gods generally by Snorri and in *Lokasenna*; the latter to Odin by Snorri.[72] Thor slew the nine-headed Thrivaldi, broke the leg of Leikn, and slew giantesses.[73] 'Eastward I fared and felled the giants' ill-working women,' says Thor in *Harbardsljod*, and again, 'When I was in the East, guarding the river, the sons of Svarang sought me and assailed me with stones. But little joy was theirs: they were first to sue for peace.' He also slew the brides of the berserkers in Hlesey, who were like she-wolves rather than women. They crushed his ship and threatened him with iron clubs, and drove off Thjalfi. In *Hyndluljod* Thor is said by Freyja to love little the brides of the giants. Of the tales here referred to or in the epithet 'slayer of Hrod' nothing is known.[74]

In these myths Thor is a boisterous, undaunted being, opponent of the forces which are inimical to the rule of the gods and, therefore, presumably, to the welfare of men. These forces, personified as giants, are the wild, harsh, sinister aspects of nature, all in nature that is opposed to the kindly forces of growth and fertility.

Another long story, related by Snorri, may have less mythical significance than some are disposed to discover in it. It rather suggests the inventive imagination of one well-versed in folk-tale formulae than a myth proper, though the first incident belongs to Thor-mythology.

Thor and Loki stayed for the night at a peasant's house,

where the god slew his goats as a meal for his host and his family and guests. He bade them lay the bones on the hides, but Thjalfi, the peasant's son, split a thigh-bone to extract the marrow. Next morning Thor resuscitated the goats by swinging his hammer, and, discovering that one was lame, was angry and so terrified the peasant that he and his family offered all they had as a recompense. Thor therefore took his son Thjalfi and his daughter Roskva as his servants.

All four journeyed towards Jötunheim, and at night reached a great forest, where they found a huge hall in which they lay for the night. At midnight an earthquake caused them to seek shelter in a side-chamber. Thor kept watch with his hammer at its entrance. In the morning he went out and found a huge man sleeping and snoring. He would have struck him with his hammer, but for the first time his heart failed him. The giant recognized him as Asa-Thor and, telling him that his name was Skrymir, asked why he had dragged away his glove. Then Thor saw that the hall with the inner chamber where they had slept was Skrymir's glove with its thumb. All now joined forces and shared their food, but next night Thor was unable to open the provision-bag, try as he might. Skrymir was asleep. Seizing his hammer, he dealt him three successive blows on the head. After each blow Skrymir said that a leaf had fallen on him, then an acorn, then some bird-droppings. Next morning he left the others after directing them to Utgard, and bidding them not boast before its lord, Utgard-Loki.

Arrived at the castle of Utgard, its lord spoke of Thor as a toddler, and asked what accomplishments he and the others could show. Loki said that no one could eat food more rapidly than he. A trough of food was set out and one Logi (Fire) was set to eat against him, and ate meat, bones, and trough also. The swift Thjalfi was beaten in a race by the lad Hugi. Thor boasted of his drinking-feats, but could not do more in three prodigious draughts than take a little from a horn which was given him. Then he attempted to lift Utgard-Loki's cat, but could do no more than raise one of its feet from the ground. Lastly he attempted to wrestle and throw Utgard-Loki's nurse Elli, but was himself brought to one knee. Now Utgard-Loki bade them spend the night in feasting.

Next morning Thor admitted that he must be called a man of little might, but Utgard-Loki said that he would never have received him, had he known he was so strong. He himself was Skrymir and had prepared ' eye-illusions ' to outwit him. The provision-bag was bound with iron, hence Thor could not undo its apparent knots. He had struck three terrific blows, which would have been fatal had not Skrymir placed a hill between himself and them, and the hill was now deeply indented. Logi was Fire and thus could consume meat, bones, and trough so quickly. Hugi was Thought and Thjalfi could not outrun him. The end of the horn was in the sea, so Thor could not empty it, yet he had diminished the sea, and this is the cause of ebb-tides. The cat was the Midgard-serpent, and Thor had raised it nearly to Heaven. Elli was Old Age, and it was a marvel that Thor had withstood her so long. Hearing all this, Thor clutched his hammer and was about to strike, when he found that Utgard-Loki had vanished, and where the castle stood was a wide plain. Hence Thor resolved to encounter the Midgard-serpent again, if he could.[75]

The goat-episode is referred to in *Hymiskvitha*, as has been seen. In *Harbardsljod* Harbard taunts Thor with cowardice in creeping into the glove of Skrymir, here called Fjalar; and in *Lokasenna* Loki sneers at him for the same act and for believing that he was no longer Thor, and for failing to open Skrymir's provision-bag.[76]

How far the episodes of this story are to be interpreted in terms of natural phenomena, or what these may be, is difficult to say, in spite of many attempts in this direction. Some of the mythical conceptions of the North are here — Thor in his contest with giant or unearthly powers; the region of these powers; Utgard, Outside Land; the power of Thor's hammer, penetrat-

ing a hill; the might of fire; the Midgard-serpent; the idea
that a god is superior to old age, yet not immortal; the mythic
explanation of the origin of ebb-tide. But, on the whole, the
story — the longest in Snorri — is perhaps no more than a
skilful weaving of episodes and ideas into one tale, utilizing
Märchen formulae — deception and glamour, by which even
gods are deceived, and the futility of a race with Thought or
of defeating Old Age. The episode of the restoration of Thor's
goats to life has many folk-tale parallels, in which dead or dis-
membered persons or animals are restored. A near parallel is
found in Celtic mythology. One of the swine of the god
Manannan is slain and cooked, and afterwards restored to life,
in a story where the god and his wife are hosts to the adventurer
Cormac. Manannan's swine were immortal, and myth said
of them that, killed one day, they came alive next day, and with
their flesh the gods were made immortal.[77]

By some, Utgard-Loki is regarded as a form of Loki himself,
partly because the Midgard-serpent, his offspring, appears in
the story. But as Loki himself shares in the adventure, this is
unlikely, and he may be regarded as an abstraction of giant
power, against which, for once, Thor sets himself in vain. A
distorted form of Utgard-Loki, with traits of the medieval
devil, appears in Ugarthilocus whom Saxo describes as a being
or deity to whom sacrifices are paid. King Gorm was perplexed
about immortality. Some of his courtiers told him that the
gods should be consulted and suggested that Thorkill should
be sent on this mission. Thorkill sailed to a sunless region and
reached a place where he entered a foul cavern, at the entrance
to which were two huge men, swart, with beaked noses. One of
them told Thorkill that he had a dangerous journey before him
in his desire to visit a strange god. After four days roving in
darkness he would reach a dark land and discover Ugarthilocus
in his grisly caves. When Thorkill and his party reached these
caves they saw seats covered with serpents, and beyond this
another cave with a foul room where Ugarthilocus was bound

with chains. Each of his hairs was as large as a spear of cornel.
Thorkill plucked one from his beard as a token, and straightway
a foul stench nearly choked the visitors. Only five escaped with
Thorkill, pursued by demons. Eventually he reached Germany
and became a Christian. King Gorm was so affected by his
description of Ugarthilocus that he died. Many of the by-
standers perished of the smell from the hair when he produced it.[78] Gorm himself, after visiting Geirrod's realm, on the
return journey had obtained fair weather by vows and peace-
offerings to Ugarthilocus.[79] In this narrative, Ugarthilocus is
rather a blending of Loki chained by the gods and the medieval
Satan bound in Hell, than the Utgard-Loki of Snorri's story.

Another story, the subject of *Alvissmal*, shows how Thor
tricked a dwarf and caused his destruction. The narrative part
of this Eddic poem is slight: most of it consists of questions put
by Thor to the dwarf Alviss about the different names, mainly
fanciful, given to earth, Heaven, moon, sun, clouds, wind, calm,
sea, etc., by men, gods, Vanir, giants, dwarfs, and elves. These
different synonyms resemble the artificial kennings of the
scalds, but more recent investigation shows that some, at least,
are circumlocutions used e.g., at sea, to avoid the real names,
which were dangerous and tabu.[80] Alviss has come by night to
claim Thor's daughter, Thrud, who had been promised him by
the gods in Thor's absence. Thor confronts Alviss and asks
who he is and why he is so pale of face, as if he had been lying
with the dead. Alviss says that his home is under the earth,
beneath the rocks. He has come to speak with the Wagon-
man (Vagna-verr) and trusts that the gods will keep their word.
Thor says that he will break it, for, as father, he has foremost
right over the bride, nor was he present when the promise was
made. Alviss pretends to take Thor for a wandering man, such
is his appearance. ' I am Ving-Thor, the wide-wanderer, Long-
beard's (Sidgrani's, Odin's) son, and against my will shall
thou take the maid,' cries Thor. Alviss says he would fain gain
her through good will, and Thor says that he will not keep her

from a guest so wise, if only he will tell about every world of which he asks him. Then follow the questions and answers; at the end of them Thor says he has never known such wealth of knowledge in a single breast, but he has detained Alviss by craft and betrayed him. ' The day has caught thee, O dwarf; the sun (deceiver of Dvalin) shines in the hall.' The dwarf is destroyed by daylight, fatal to underearth beings, and Thor thus overcomes him by craft, as he overcomes giants by strength. Thor's *rôle* of seeker after wisdom is unusual, and rather suggests that of Odin in *Voluspa, Vafthrudnismal,* etc.

If Miss Phillpotts is right in her theory that many of the Eddic poems are folk-dramas, there is a distinct group in which, as she points out, a god causes the death of his opponent. Odin slays Vafthrudnir, Freyja destroys the giantess Hyndla by fire, but the *rôle* of destroyer is mainly Thor's, the great champion of gods and men against all dangerous forces and especially the Frost-giants. The power of frost was feared by the Northern people, and a mighty winter was expected to destroy all life in the future, as will be seen later. Such folk-dramas were not performed merely with a view to entertainment. Hence when Thor was represented destroying giants, the purpose was to secure his victory in actual fights against these forces. The dramas were, in fact, a kind of mimetic magic, intended to bring about the result which was enacted. The time of the action-drama may have been the winter festival of Yule, when evil powers were in the ascendant. Then it was necessary to strengthen the hands of the guardian of Midgard, the champion of gods and men. Miss Phillpotts also makes the interesting suggestion that if the lost poem on which Snorri founded his story of Thor and Hrungnir was a folk-drama, then an effigy probably represented Hrungnir. This effigy, after the dramatic tradition was lost, was regarded as an accessory to Hrungnir, and called Mökkurkálfi.[81]

CHAPTER VI

THE GREATER GODS—TYR

THE Eddic god Tyr was known to other Teutonic tribes as Zio or Ziu (OHG), Tyw or Tiw (AS). These names are deduced from the Teutonic names of the third day of the week — OHG Ziestag, AS Tiwesdaeg (English Tuesday), ON Tyrsdagr and Tysdagr. The prevalence of these names in the Rhine region, Upper Germany, North Germany, Saxony, and Scandinavia, shows that this god was widely known. The primitive form of the name was *Tiwaz, which has been regarded as the equivalent of the Vedic Dyaus, Greek Zeus, Latin Diespiter (Jupiter). Others connect *Tiwaz rather with a primitive *deivos (= deus), Sanskrit devas, Latin divus, cf. Norse tivar, 'gods,' probably a plural of tyr, 'god.' This would agree with the Norse use of tyr in the general sense of 'god,' as in Sigtyr, Veratyr, Hangatyr, etc.

The former derivation would point to *Tiwaz as an early Teutonic Sky-god. But the occurrence of the various forms of the name in the titles of the third day of the week as equivalents of dies Martis, suggests that this Sky-god had become a god of war, or that greater emphasis had been laid on some of his functions,[1] the result of the growing place of war as a business of life among the Teutons.

Tacitus says that Mars had a high place with certain tribes or groups of tribes. The Tencteri on the east side of the Rhine regarded Mars as chief of the gods. The god who had a highly sacred grove among the Semnones, a branch of the Suevi, and to whom human sacrifices were offered, is supposed to have been Zio. He is not named, but he is called regnator omnium.[2] In the sixth century Jordanes says of the Goths that they sacrificed

their prisoners of war to Mars as the best means of placating
him.³ Procopius similarly relates of the Scandinavians in the
sixth century that they regarded human victims as the best offering. They sacrificed them to Mars (Ares), whom they regarded as the greatest god.⁴ The place of Tyr as War-god must
have decreased before the growing power of Odin. Yet in the
late Middle Ages an Icelander could translate *in templo Martis*
by *í týs hofi*, showing that Tyr's place had not been forgotten.⁵
It is also significant of the pre-eminence of Tiwaz that in inscriptions which give Roman equivalents of the three great Teutonic
gods, Mars is often first. The Wessobrunner gloss (eighth
century), which speaks of the Suabian descendants of the Semnones of that time, speaks of them as Cyuuari, ' Worshippers of
Ziu.'⁶ In the region of this people their chief town Augsburg
was called Ciesburc, ' Ziu's town.'

Another name or epithet of the god is seen in the Thingsus
(Mars Thingsus) to whom Frisian soldiers from Twenthe (in
the territory of the Salic Franks) dedicated altars with figures in relief. These were brought to light at Housesteads on
the line of Hadrian's wall in 1883. The names of the two
Alaisiagae, Bede and Fimmilene, are joined with that of Mars
Thingsus. The god is represented as a warrior, at his right
hand a swan or goose. Female figures, the Alaisiagae, hover
in the receding sides of the semi-circular reliefs, with sword or
staff in one hand, and a wreath in the other. Thingsus is regarded as a name of Ziu in his capacity as tutelary god of the
Thing or assembly, i.e., the Frisian cohort regarded as a unit or
Thing. The same divine name appears in Dinsdag, Dingsdach
(Tuesday). Thingsus has also been explained as meaning
' Warrior.' The explanations of the names and functions of
the two goddesses are numerous. They may possibly be equivalents of Valkyries.⁷

In the *Eddas* Tyr has a subordinate place and, if he was once
a Heaven-god, Odin had ousted him. He was called Odin's
son, and even as War-god he had fallen into the background

through Odin's supremacy. Snorri says of him: 'He is most daring and stout-hearted, and has chief authority over victory in battle. It is good that brave men should invoke him.' 'A Tyr-valiant man' is one who surpasses others in stoutness of heart. Another proverbial saying, illustrating Tyr's wisdom, was to call the wisest man 'Tyr-prudent.' 'Tyr cannot be called a reconciler of men.'[8] Runes for victory were written on swords, Tyr being invoked in the process.[9] Scaldic kennings for Tyr were 'god of battles,' 'son of Odin,' 'the one-handed god,' and 'fosterer of the wolf.'[10] Famous chiefs were known as Tyr's offspring, and Tyr occurs in personal names and in place-names.

The myths told of Tyr are few in number. Loki's offspring, the Fenris-wolf, was brought up by the Æsir, of whom Tyr alone ventured to give him meat. When the gods saw how he grew, and recalled the prophecies which told how the Wolf would be their destruction, they resolved to bind him. Two fetters in turn were tried, but these were broken in pieces. Then the gods sent to the dwarfs, who made the fetter Gleipnir out of six things — the noise of a cat in walking, a woman's beard, the roots of a rock, the sinews of a bear, the breath of a fish, and the spittle of a bird (all non-existent things). The fetter was soft and smooth, yet strong and sure. The gods then held debate with the Wolf about submitting to have this fetter put on him. He finally agreed, provided that one of them put his hand in his mouth. None of the Æsir was willing to part with a hand, until Tyr stretched out his and put it in the Wolf's mouth. The more the monster lashed out, the firmer became the fetter, but Tyr's hand was bitten off. Then the Wolf was chained to a great rock, and there he is bound until the Doom of the gods.[11] Much ingenuity has been expended in inventing explanations of this myth. Beyond suggesting that Tyr is in conflict with dark and demoniac powers, it does not explain itself further. That Tyr, as god of war, should have lost a hand, may reflect what often happened to warriors in battle. Similar

myths are told of gods elsewhere, e.g., the Irish Nuadu, whose
hand, struck off by an opponent, was replaced by one of silver;
Zeus, who lost his tendons; the Vedic Vispala, whose leg was
cut off in battle and replaced by one of iron.[12]

When Tyr was present at Ægir's feast, and spoke in defence
of Frey, Loki bade him be silent, for he could never fashion
friendship between men, and then taunted him with the loss
of his hand. Tyr replied that it boded ill for Loki's Wolf, now
awaiting in chains the great battle. Loki retaliated by saying
that Tyr's wife — mentioned for the first and only time — had
a son by him, and that Tyr never got a penny in compensation
for the wrong done to him.[13]

The *Hymiskvitha*, which tells how Thor and Tyr, at the
latter's advice, sought the mighty cauldron of the giant Hymir,
makes this giant father of Tyr by ' the white eye-browed one,'
with golden hair, who welcomes Tyr at Hymir's abode, and who
may have been a goddess, not a giantess. A nine-hundred-
headed giantess, also present, is Tyr's grandmother, whom he
loathed. Hence Tyr is called ' kinsman of giants.' Tyr takes
no further part in the action, save that he twice tries to move
the kettle, but cannot, and then, when Thor has raised it, re-
turns with him to the Æsir.

The meaning of this myth as well as of Tyr's relationship to
the giant Hymir has been the occasion of much debate. While
it is in keeping with mythology that an important god should
be related to a giant, it is possible that ' Tyr ' in this poem means
not the War-god, but is used merely in the sense of ' the god.'
This god might be Loki, for at the end of the poem we hear that
Thor on his return found his goats lame, and this was Loki's
doing. Snorri gives an incident of the laming of Thor's goat in
another connexion, when he and Loki were on a journey.[14]

The only other reference to Tyr in the *Eddas* is the notice
of his conflict with the dog Garm at the Doom of the gods, when
each slew the other.[15]

CHAPTER VII

THE VANIR GROUP—NJORD

ACCORDING to Snorri, Njord (ON Njǫrþr) is third of the Æsir, though not of their race, for he was reared in the land of the Vanir and given by them as a hostage to the Æsir.[1] This agrees with other passages in Snorri and in the Poetic *Edda,* where Njord appears among the Æsir, e.g., at Ægir's banquet. It is based on passages in *Vafthrudnismal* and *Lokasenna.* In the former Odin says:

> 'Tell me . . .
> Whence Njord came among the Æsir's sons?
> O'er fanes and shrines he rules by hundreds,
> Yet was not among the Æsir born.'

Vafthrudnir answers:

> 'In Vanaheim wise powers created him,
> And to the gods a hostage gave.
> At the Doom of the gods he will return
> To the wise Vanir.'

In the latter Loki addresses Njord and tells him that he was sent eastward and given to the gods as a hostage.[2] Hence he is 'god of the Vanir,' 'kinsman of the Vanir,' or simply 'the Van.'[3] His dwelling is in Noatun, 'Ship-place' or 'Haven.'

> 'There Njord built himself the high hall,
> Where the faultless ruler of men
> Sits in his high-timbered fane.'[4]

Njord's wife is Skadi, daughter of the giant Thjazi, but apparently before he came among the Æsir, he had two children

by his unnamed sister, Frey and Freyja. With this Loki
taunted him at Ægir's banquet:

> ' I will no longer keep secret what I heard,
>   With thy sister thou hadst a son
>   Hardly worse than thyself.' [5]

Njord rules the course of the wind and stills the sea, storm,
and fire. Men call on him in sea-faring and hunting. So rich
and abundant in goods is he, that he can give plenty of lands or
gear; hence men invoke him for such things. Thus he is ' god
of wealth-bestowal,' and, according to *Vafthrudnismal* he is
rich in altars and shrines.[6] Njord has thus two distinct divine
attributes — he is a Sea-god and a god of wealth and prosperity,
' a Sea-god of riches.' [7]

His sister-wife was perhaps the goddess Nerthus of whom
Tacitus speaks as worshipped by seven tribes in North-east Germany, and whose name exactly corresponds to that of Njord,
from * *nerthuz*. Golther says: ' the general German word
nertu, " good will," as a name denoting character, was extended
to persons. * *Nerthuz* means the beneficent, friendly divinity,
and may thus be used either of a god or a goddess.' [8]

Tacitus says of Nerthus: ' The Reudingi, Aviones, Anglii,
Varini, Eudoses, Suardones, Nuithones (tribes of the Ingae-
vones) unite in worshipping Nerthus, that is Mother Earth, and
think that she mingles in the affairs of men and visits the na-
tions. There is a sacred grove on an island in the ocean (probably Seeland), and in it stands a wagon covered with a cloth.
The priest alone may touch it. He becomes aware of the presence of the goddess in the innermost place, and follows her with
the greatest reverence as she is drawn about by cows. Then are
there joyful days, places of festivity, wheresoever the goddess
comes as a guest. They do not engage in wars nor take up arms.
Weapons are closed. Peace and quiet alone are then named and
loved, until the same priest restores to her temple the goddess,
satisfied with the intercourse of mortals. Thereupon the vehicle

and its covering and, if it be credible, the goddess, are washed in a secret lake. Slaves do this service, and the lake immediately swallows them up.' [9]

All this suggests rites of fertility and a festival which would most naturally occur in spring. Nerthus is akin to Njord in functions, though different in sex. In spite of Tacitus' assertion some, like Mannhardt, think that Nerthus was a male divinity; others, e.g., A. Kock, that Njord, a male god, had taken the place of a female.[10] But it is quite possible that a pair of deities, regarded as brother and sister, and bearing similar names, were worshipped together, along with a third, their son Frey, part of whose ritual, as we shall see, resembled that of Nerthus. Another theory is that originally Njord was a goddess (Nerthus), not a god, and that Skadi, regarded as a female in the *Eddas*, was a god.[11]

From Seeland, where it was indigenous, this cult passed to Sweden and Norway, and there, apart from the witness of the *Eddas*, many places bear the name of Njord, showing that his cult was widespread. Thence the cult passed to Iceland. In literary sources, Njord and Frey are constantly mentioned together — 'so help me Frey and Njord and Thor.' Together they dispense riches.[12] Hence an old Icelandic phrase, 'as rich as Njord.'

In an interesting myth Snorri makes Skadi the wife of Njord. The giant Thjazi had been slain by the Æsir, and in panoply of war his daughter Skadi went to Asgard to avenge him. The Æsir offered her atonement, viz., to choose a husband from their number, but to choose him by the feet only, for she would see no more than these in making her selection. Her choice fell on him whom she thought to be Balder, but the chosen one was Njord. In the bond of reconciliation it was also agreed that the gods must make her laugh, which she deemed impossible. Loki accomplished this, however, by an act which suggests cruelty and obscenity rather than humour.[13]

In Saxo's account of the mythic Hadding an incident resembling this method of choice occurs. A giant had taken in troth Ragnhild, daughter of Hakon, king of the Nitheri. Hadding overcame him, but was wounded. Ragnhild tended him, not knowing who he was, and, in order not to forget him, enclosed a ring in his wound. At a later time, her father gave her permission to choose a husband, and when the suitors were assembled, she felt their bodies and recognized Hadding by means of the ring.[14]

The identification *motif* in Saxo is a form of a folk-tale formula, but the naked foot incident of the *Edda* has been connected with marriage rites in which only the foot of the future spouse is seen, and with fertility rites in which bare feet play a part. Schröder thinks that Nerthus-Njord is to be explained as ' dancer ' (cf. Sanskrit *nart*, ' to dance '), and that the priest and priestess who represented this pair of fertility deities carried out the ritual with bare feet.[15]

Skadi wished to dwell in her father's abode in the mountains, Thrymheim, ' Home of noise,' of which *Grimnismal* says that here Thjazi, the all-powerful Jötun, dwelt, but Skadi, bright bride of the gods, now inhabits the old dwelling of her father. Njord wished to dwell near the sea. They made a compact to dwell nine nights in Thrymheim and three at Noatun. When Njord came back from the mountains to Noatun he sang:

> ' I love not the mountains, I dwelt not long in them,
>   Nine nights only;
>   Sweeter is to me the song of the swan
>   Than the wild wolf's howl.'

To this Skadi replied:

> ' My sleep was troubled on the shore of the sea
>   By the screaming of sea-birds.
>   Every morning the sea-mew wakens me
>   Returning from the deep.'

These verses, quoted by Snorri, are from a lost Eddic poem. Skadi then went up to the mountains and dwelt in Thrymheim.

She goes on snow-shoes and shoots wild creatures with her bow and arrows. Hence she is called 'goddess' or 'lady of the snow-shoes.'[16] Skadi's departure from Njord is referred to by the skald Thord Sjareksson who speaks of her 'grieving at the Van's side.'[17]

Saxo relates a similar story of Hadding and Ragnhild, quoting in Latin verses which correspond to those cited by Snorri. After years spent in disuse of arms, Hadding reproached himself with dwelling in the hills and not following sea-faring. The cry of the wolves, the howl of beasts, keep him from sleep. The ridges and hills are dreary to one who loves the sea. Far better to ply the oar and revel in sea-fights than to dwell in rough lands, winding woodlands, and barren glades. Ragnhild sang of the shrill bird vexing her as she stayed by the sea, and the noise of the sea-mew keeping her from sleep. Safer and sweeter is the enjoyment of the woods. Hence it has been supposed that Hadding is identical with Njord, or his rebirth, but it is likely that Saxo merely transferred the Eddic poem to the story of Hadding.[18]

In spite of Skadi's separation from Njord, as told by Snorri, she appears with him at Ægir's banquet in *Lokasenna* and also in the Introduction to *Skirnismal*. In the former poem she tells Loki how he will be punished, i.e., by being bound by the gods on the rocks with bowels torn from his 'ice-cold son.' Loki replies that he was first and last at the fight when her father was slain. Skadi says that even so from her dwellings and fields shall ever come forth cold counsels for him. Loki then reminds her that she spoke more mildly when she invited him to her bed. Snorri connects Skadi with the myth of Loki's punishment. She fastened a venomous serpent above him, where he was bound, and its poison dropped on his face.[19]

The explanation given by some scholars of the nine nights' stay in Thrymheim and three at Noatun, is that 'nights' signifies 'months,' and that the sea in the extreme North is open only for three months for ship-faring. For the other nine it is sealed by ice and winter-storms.[20]

Snorri's *Heimskringla,* following the *Ynglinga-tal,* gives a different version of this myth. Njord wedded a woman Skadi, but she would have nothing of him, and hence was wedded to Odin, and had to him many sons, one of whom was Sœming. A poem by Eyvind is cited in support of this, which says that Sœming was begotten by Odin on a giant-maiden when they dwelt in Mannheim. To Sœming Norway traced her line of kings, or more strictly speaking the rulers of Halogaland.[21] The theory of alternating twin gods sharing one mate has been applied here, but Skadi is regarded as the god and Njord the goddess, shared by Odin and Skadi.[22]

Skadi has been held to be a representative of the Finns and Lapps who peopled the north of Norway. She may have been one of their goddesses, regarded as a giant's daughter, because the inhospitable Northern region was akin to or identical with Jötunheim. How she came to be associated with Njord and Odin is far from clear. But a cult war may have been considered mythically as a war of Scandinavian and Finnish deities, ending in a pact and marriage. R. M. Meyer sees in the disputed residence incident of Skadi and Njord an ikonic myth, i.e., a myth based on the history of an image of Skadi which had been carried off to Noatun, and, after a war, shared a residence with Norsemen and Finns.[23]

The euhemeristic notices of Njord in the *Ynglinga-saga* confirm the Eddic account of him as a god of prosperity. He became ruler after Odin's death. The Swedes call him lord and he took tribute of them. In his days there was peace, and hence the Swedes thought that he swayed the year's plenty and men's prosperity. He died in his bed and was marked for Odin ere he died.[24]

The cult of Njord was associated with that of Frey, for the two deities are mentioned together both in taking oaths and in drinking toasts at feasts. First came Odin's toast for victory

and power, second Njord's, and third Frey's for good seasons and peace.[25]   Egil speaks of Njord and Frey as wealth-
givers, and prays that both gods may be angry with king Eirik.[26]
Little light, however, is thrown upon the personality of this god
as a figure of popular worship and esteem, beyond the reference
to his many shrines in *Vafthrudnismal*.   We may suppose that
this god of earth's fruitfulness and of prosperity, when his cult
passed among sea-farers and fishermen, became also a god of
the riches of the sea.

CHAPTER VIII

THE VANIR GROUP—FREY

FREY (ON Freyr), son of Njord, probably by his sister, is like him one of the Vanir but reckoned among the Æsir. He is 'the bold son of Njord'; his 'mighty son'; his 'noble son.'[1] Among the Æsir he is 'the most renowned,' 'foremost of the gods,' 'whom no man hateth,' 'the first of all the heroes in the gods' house.'[2] His name, which corresponds to Gothic *frauja*, OHG *frô*, and AS *fréa*, means 'lord,' and was thus at first a title. Snorri says of him that, like his sister Freyja, he is fair of face and mighty. He rules over rain and sunshine and also over the increase of the earth. Good is it to call on him for fruitful seasons and peace, for he can give peace and prosperity to men. He is god of the fruitful season and of the gifts of wealth. Thus Frey is closely akin to Njord in his functions. It is also said of him that 'he harms not maids, nor men's wives, and frees the bound from their fetters.' He is also 'the battle-bold Frey.'[3]

Frey's seat is in Alfheim, the land of the Alfar or elves, given him by the gods as a 'tooth-gift' in ancient times, i.e., a present to a child on cutting its first tooth. 'As the elves are especially connected with the furthering of vegetable life (the places on the turf where they have danced betray themselves by the rich-ness of the grass), so the god of fruitfulness is naturally their overlord.'[4]

His possessions are Skidbladnir, 'swiftest and best of ships,' and made with great skill of craftsmanship by dwarfs. It was given to Frey, perhaps because he, one of the Vanir, had to do with ship-faring. It is the ideal magic ship, so large that all the gods may man it with their weapons and armaments.

As soon as its sails are hoisted, wherever it is going it has a fair wind, like certain ships in the Sagas. When not in use it can be folded up and put in the pouch.[5] Possibly this ship betokens the clouds. Frey's sword fights of itself or if a worthy hero wields it.[6] His horse, Blodughofi, can go through ' the dark and flickering flames.'[7] To him also is ascribed the ring Draupnir which multiplies itself — a symbol of fertility appropriate to Frey.[8] His chariot, in which he drives at Balder's funeral, is drawn by the boar Gullinbursti, 'Gold bristles,' or Slidrugtanni, ' Fearful tusk,' or, according to the *Husdrapa* of Ulf Uggason, Frey rode on the boar itself. This boar was made by dwarfs and could run through air and water better than any horse; the glow from its mane and bristles was so great that, wherever the boar was, no matter how dark the night, there would be sufficient light. It is also called Hildisvini, ' Battle swine,' ' which shines with bristles of gold.'[9]

Frey's boar is undoubtedly connected with the offering to him of boars in sacrifice, especially the *sónargöltr*, ' atonement boar,' on the eve of the Yule festival. The largest boar was given to Frey, and it was so holy that when it was led into the hall, oaths were sworn and vows made while the hand was laid over its bristles. The purpose of the sacrifice was to cause the god to be favourable to the New Year. According to the *Hervarar-saga* king Heidrek offered the boar to Frey, but an earlier reference does not connect the *sónargöltr* with Frey.[10] A survival of the sacrifice is found in the cakes baked in Sweden at Yule in the form of a boar. Whether all the references to the boar in Teutonic folk-custom or story collected by Grimm are connected with the cult of Frey is doubtful. The ceremonial bringing-in of a boar's head at Christmas banquets in England, still surviving at Queen's College, Oxford, cannot be definitely shown to point to a cult of Frey among the Saxons.[11] According to Tacitus the Aestii worshipped the *Mater deum*, and wore as an emblem of that superstition the forms of boars, which took the place of arms or other protection and guaranteed victory.[12]

Some have seen in this native goddess Freyja who, in *Hyndlu-ljod*, rides a boar with golden bristles. The custom of wearing a boar's image or helmets in that form as protectives was common among the Anglo-Saxons, as their poetry shows, as well as in Germany. It need not necessarily point to a cult of Frey, but to a wider belief in the swine as a sacred or magic animal.[13]

Frey's servants are Skirnir, prominent in *Skirnismal*, and Byggvir and his wife Beyla, both of whom opposed Loki at Ægir's banquet and were addressed contemptuously by him.

At the Doom of the gods Frey contends with Surt and falls, because he lacks his sword which he had given to Skirnir.[14] Reference is made to Frey's slaying of Beli, not with his sword, but with his fist or the horn of a hart. Hence he is called ' adversary of Beli,' ' Beli's hater,' or ' fair slayer.' Beli may be the brother of Gerd, of whom Frey was enamoured, for she speaks of him as her brother's murderer.[15]

Like Njord, Frey is accused by Loki of having a sister-wife, Freyja, the only reference to this save in the *Ynglinga-saga*.[16] Both *Skirnismal* and Snorri give the story of his love for the giant's daughter Gerd, called his wife in *Hyndluljod*: ' Gerd, Frey's spouse, was Gymir's daughter; Orboda bore her to the old giant.' [17] Orboda was one of the Hill-giants' race. Snorri calls Gymir a man, but he was certainly a giant. His daughter was fairest of women. One day Frey sat himself on Hlidskjalf and looked over the worlds, even to Jötunheim, where he saw a woman raising her hands to open the door of a house. Brightness gleamed from her arms over sea, sky, and all worlds. Frey was filled with melancholy, represented by Snorri as a punishment for sitting in Odin's seat, but in *Skirnismal* there is no word of this, and perhaps this seat was Frey's originally, not Odin's. Skadi (or Njord, according to an emendation of the text and also in Snorri's version) sent for Skirnir and bade him ask Frey for whose sake he was so melancholy. Skirnir feared that he would get evil answers from him, but he questioned him

boldly and learned the cause. He was deeply in love with
Gerd, yet ' none of the Æsir or Alfar will grant that we may
live together.' He asked Skirnir to go and woo her for him and
bring her to him. Skirnir asked for Frey's horse and magic
sword, and with these set off. He spoke to the horse, saying
that it was dark and now it was time to travel across the wild
fells, over the giants' land. Either they would return together
or the powerful giant would take them. Then he reached
Jötunheim and Gymir's dwelling, guarded by dogs. On a hill
sat a herdsman who, when Skirnir asked for speech with Gerd,
said that this could never be. Meanwhile within the dwelling
Gerd heard a noise, and learned from her servant that a man
had dismounted at the gate. She bade the servant bring him in,
though she feared that he was her brother's slayer. When he
entered, she asked him if he was one of the Alfar, of the Æsir's
sons, or of the wise Vanir, since he had come through the flickering flame to her abode. He said that he was none of these, and
offered her golden apples if she would say that Frey was dearest
to her. She refused them, saying that she would never be
Frey's. He offered her the ring Draupnir: this also she refused.
Then he threatened to behead her, but she was unmoved and
told him that he might fight Gymir if he liked. Skirnir replied
that the sword would kill her father, and threatened her with
the magic power of his staff and with curses. She will go where
men will nevermore see her. On the eagle's hill she will sit,
facing Hel, and her meat will be loathsome to her. Even the
Frost-giant Hrimnir will stare at her and she will become better
known than Heimdall. Grief and terror will afflict her in the
giants' land, and she will dwell with a three-headed giant.
Odin is angry with her; Frey will hate her; the gods' wrath
will be upon her. Skirnir bade all Jötuns, all Frost-giants, the
sons of Suttung, and the Æsir hear how he forbade her ever to
know the joy of love. Hrimgrimnir is the giant who will have
her beneath near the doors of Hel, and to the Frost-giants' halls
she will daily crawl in misery. Then he wrote four runes, by

which she would know unquenched desire, though he would cut them out again if she relented.

As a result of these curses Gerd yielded, though she said that she had never thought to love one of the Vanir. She bade Skirnir tell Frey to meet her nine nights hence in the secret wood called Barri, where she will be his. On hearing this from Skirnir Frey said: 'One night is long, two are longer, how can I bear three? Often has a month seemed less to me than half a night of longing now.'

Gerd is included among the Asynjur by Snorri, and Loki taunts Frey at Ægir's banquet with buying her with gold, selling his sword at the same time. Hence when Muspell's sons come riding he will have no sword.[18] The 'flickering flame,' *vafrlogi*, by which Gerd's abode is surrounded, is a magic defence against intrusion, and only by magic or supernatural means can a hero go through it. It is found thrice in the Eddic poems. The second reference to it is in *Svipdagsmal* where it surrounds the hall where Menglod is secured. Svipdag makes his way through it to her, his destined bride. The third reference is in *Sigrdrifumal*, where Brynhild is held in a magic sleep imposed by Odin, in a hall on a mountain surrounded by fire. Through it Sigurd makes his way.

Frey was sometimes called Ingvi-Frey or Ingunar-Frey, a name connected with that of Ingw, the tribal ancestor or eponymous hero of the Ingvaeones, the group of tribes dwelling in Schleswig-Holstein, from whom sprang the Saxons, Anglo-Saxons, and Frisians. Ingunar is either a distorted form of Ingvi or the genitive of a feminine Ingun, possibly Frey's unnamed mother or his consort. The name would mean 'Frey of Ingun' or 'Lord (Husband) of Ingun.' The Ynglings, the earliest race of the kings of Sweden, regarded themselves as descendants of Frey, called Yngvi in the *Ynglinga-saga*. 'They were kindred of the god Frey' or 'held him to be the founder of their race,' says Saxo, speaking of Swedish heroes.[19] Yngvi's people were the Swedes. There are, however, two genealogies. One is that of the Saga, which begins with Njord, then Frey or Yngvi. The other is that of the *Islendinga-bók*, which begins with Yngvi, who is followed by Njord, Frey, etc. Whether Yngvi and Frey were actually different mythic personages, and if so, why they became merged in each other, cannot be determined. Perhaps the connexion lay in the fact that the king of the Ingwines or East Danes was called Frea Ingwina; their tribal ancestor was Ing. Ing first dwelt with the East Danes, and then crossed the sea, his wagon following him.[20] Ing is the same as Yngvi, and as Frey means ' lord,' Yngvi may have been the personal name of the god. The Ingvaeones of Tacitus, who dwelt in the coast region between the North Sea and the Baltic, are to be traced back to Yngvi or Frey, their tribal deity. Their region was also the seat of the Nerthus cult. Thus the cult of Yngvi-Frey passed thence to Sweden, where its chief seat was Upsala.

In his account of the Hadding saga, Saxo says that this mythic hero was attacked on one occasion by a sea-monster which he slew. But as he was exulting in his deed, a woman appeared who said that he would suffer the wrath of the gods, for his sacrilegious hands had slain one of them in disguised form. So Hadding, ' slayer of a benignant god,' in order to appease the deities, sacrificed dusky victims to Frey at an annual feast, which he left posterity to follow. This rite was called by the Swedes Fröblot, ' sacrifice to Frey.' Saxo also says that Frey, ' satrap of the gods,' took up his abode not far from Upsala, where he exchanged for a ghastly and infamous sin-offering the old custom of prayer by sacrifice which had been used for many generations. He paid to the gods abominable offerings by beginning to sacrifice human victims.[21] The *Hakonar-saga* also says that Frey raised a great temple at Upsala and set his capital there, endowing it with all his revenues, lands, and movables.[22]

The *Ynglinga-saga* calls Frey a rich and generous lord under whom peace and fruitfulness abounded. He took the realm after Njord and was ' lord of the Swedes.' The ' Peace of

Frodi ' began in his time and good years in all lands, which the Swedes ascribe to Frey. He raised a temple at Upsala and was held dearer than the other gods, because the people were wealthier in his days. Gerd was his wife, and he was called Yngvi and his kindred were the Ynglings. When he died he was put in a barrow with a door and three windows, and the Swedes were told that he was still alive. He was guarded there for three winters, and gold was put through one of the windows, silver through the second, and copper through the third. Peace reigned during these three years. When at last the Swedes learned that he was dead, they would not burn him, but called him ' god of the world ' and sacrificed to him for plenteous years, thinking that while his body was in Sweden, peace and plenty would abound.[23]

The ' Peace of Frodi ' is often spoken of in Northern literature. Frodi was an early Danish king, more mythic than real, and in his time this Peace began — a kind of golden age. Snorri says that during it no man injured another, even if that other were his brother's or father's slayer. No thief or robber was known, and a gold ring lay long untouched on Jalang's heath. This was at the time when Augustus reigned at Rome. The Peace came to an end when two giant maids, Fenja and Menja, ground out of a magic mill a host against Frodi, who was slain. They did this because he forced them to grind out gold. This myth of a golden age was doubtless connected with the cult and person of Frey, whose name is to be found in that of Snorri's king Frodi and the several kings of that name in Saxo.[24]

Behind all these euhemeristic notices of Frey lies the evidence that his cult had been carried into Sweden from elsewhere, and that there this god, who is said to have himself introduced the cult and arranged the sacrifices, had a prominent place. He was called *blotgud Svia*, ' the sacrificial god of Sweden,' and *Sviagod*, ' god of the Swedes.' It is clear also that Frey was regarded as a god of fertility and that human sacrifices were offered in his cult. As in other fertility cults, that of Frey was connected with generation. Adam of Bremen says that at Upsala the image of Fricco (Frey), who bestowed peace and joy on men, stood beside those of Odin and Thor, and was invested with *ingenti priapo* — an obvious symbol of the god's influence on fertility. He also says that, at the nine years' festival, unseemly songs were sung during the sacrifices.[25] We do not know that this was a Frey festival, but if so, the notice would correspond to what Saxo says of the sacrifices at Upsala, that Starkad, who had lived for seven years with the sons of Frey, left that place because he was so disgusted with the effeminate gestures, the play of the mimes, and the ringing of bells. Saxo also declares that the legendary Fro, king of Sweden, put the wives of Siward's kinsfolk in a brothel and delivered them to public outrage. If Fro is Frey, this might be a memory of the erotic aspects of his cult.[26] The only myth of Frey reported in the *Eddas* — his love-sickness for Gerd and his strong desire for her — points to the nature of his personality and worship.

Frey's image was taken in a wagon through the land at the close of winter, under the care of a priestess, who was regarded as his wife and was set over his sacred place. From Upsala the procession traversed the land, and was everywhere received with joy and with sacrifices, in expectation of a fruitful year. A curious story is told of this in the *Olafs-saga Tryggvasonar* by a Christian saga-man. Gunnar Helming had fled from Norway to escape the consequences of a suspected crime. In those days there were great sacrifices to the gods, and Frey had long received more than the others. His image was so enchanted that he used to speak to the people out of it. Gunnar, having come to Sweden, placed himself under Frey's protection. The priestess received him, though the god did not seem favourable to him, and, at the time of the procession, she bade Gunnar come and feast with Frey and her. Gunnar went with the servants of the god, who abandoned the wagon during a snow-storm in the hills. Gunnar led it, but, feeling tired, climbed into it.

After a time the priestess bade him go and lead the wagon, for Frey was against him. He obeyed, but soon after resumed his seat, saying that he would risk standing up against Frey if he opposed him. He wrestled with the god, and, being nearly overcome, he thought that if he conquered, he would return to Norway and accept the Christian faith. The evil spirit which, according to the narrative, was in the image, now abandoned it. Gunnar broke the image and himself personated the god. At the place where a feast was prepared in expectation of the visit, the people marvelled that the god and his priestess should have come through the storm, still more that he should come among them and drink like men! The time was spent in feasting, but the counterfeit Frey would accept no offerings save those of gold, silver, and fine garments. In time the priestess became pregnant, and this, with the fine weather, was regarded as a good omen for a fruitful year. The news of the power of the Swedish god spread far and wide. King Olaf of Norway heard of it, and, suspecting the truth, sent Gunnar's brother to Sweden. He found Gunnar who, with priestess and treasure, returned to Norway and was baptized.[27]

The resemblance of this procession to that of Nerthus and her priest, as recorded eight centuries before by Tacitus, is striking, and suggests the connexion of Frey and Nerthus as deities of fertility, Nerthus, perhaps, being wife or mother of Frey. Not improbably priest and goddess or god and priestess were believed to celebrate the ' sacred marriage ' during this festival time in order to promote fertility. In the Nerthus rite a woman would represent the goddess; in the Frey rite a man would represent the god. In the story, Gunnar acts as the god and as husband of the priestess. The story would thus be reminiscent of actual custom, with priest and priestess as god and goddess. Evidence of such a ritual in prehistoric times in Norway has been collected by Prof. Magnus Olsen, the rite surviving in folk-custom and being represented on engraved gold plates which had been buried in the earth. Such a ritual may lie be-

hind the story in *Skirnismal.* Skirnir is by some regarded as
merely Frey himself, whether or not he is to be taken as the
surviving memory of the mortal who took the part of the god
in the folk-drama, the god himself being also represented by an
effigy for which ' the *rôle* of Gerd's seeker was too active.' [28]
Frey's priestess is called a ' temple-priestess,' but he had also
priests. [29]

Like Njord, Frey was besought to give fair winds to voyagers, and he was frequently named with him and with Thor,
e.g., in taking an oath: ' So help me Frey, Njord, and the
almighty god ' (Thor). [30] Frey was thus a god of many functions — light, sunshine, fertility, fruitfulness, and fair winds.
Sagas speak of sacrifices of bulls to Frey. Libations were also
offered or toasts drunk to him along with those to other gods —
Odin or Thor, and Njord, Frey's and Njord's being for fruitful
seasons and peace. Thorkel, who had been driven out by
Glum, went to Frey's temple at Eyafjord in Iceland with a
full-grown ox, saying to the god that he had long been his chief
toast and had many gifts from him, and that he had repaid
them well. Now he gave Frey the ox, asking him to drive out
Glum and desiring a token of acceptance of the gift. The ox
bellowed and fell dead, and this was regarded by Thorkel as a
good sign. [31] Some time after, Glum dreamed that a great company came to see Frey, and it seemed to him that he saw the god
sitting in their midst. Glum asked the company who they
were, and learned that they were his dead kinsmen who were
praying to Frey that Glum should not be driven out. Their
prayer did not prevail, for Frey was answering them shortly and
angrily, and was mindful of Thorkel's gift. Glum was never
Frey's good friend after that. [32]

Not only were there large images of Frey, smaller ones were
used as amulets. Heid the Volva prophesied to Ingimund
about his settlement in an undiscovered western land. He said
that he would not go, but she declared that he would, and, as a
token, his silver image of Frey would be lost out of his purse

and found when he dug a place in that land for his high-seat pillars. The image was discovered to be missing, and Ingimund sent two Finns to Iceland to discover it. They found it, but could not remove it, for it went from one place to another and they could not take it. So Ingimund was forced to go himself, and when he had set up his pillars, he found the image. It had belonged to a petty Norse king, and had been given to Ingimund by king Harald about 872 A.D.[33]

Sacred horses were kept in Frey's temple at Throndhjem, and a curious story is told of a horse, a half-share of which was dedicated to Frey by its owner, Hrafnkell, who migrated to Iceland in the time of Harald. He revered no god more than Frey and dedicated a temple to him. Hence he was called 'Frey's priest,' *Freys-godi*. He vowed to slay any one who rode this horse. In order to look for sheep, his shepherd Einar mounted it, and by its loud neighings this was made known to Hrafnkell, who slew Einar. The result was a feud between Einar's people and Hrafnkell, who was banished. His enemies cast the horse, whose name was Freyfaxi, into a stream from a cliff, afterwards known as Freyfaxi's Cliff. They burned the temple and robbed the images of their decorations. On hearing this, Hrafnkell said: 'I think it folly to believe in the gods,' and from that day forward offered no sacrifices.[34] We hear of another horse with a white mane called Freyfaxi, belonging to Brand. It was a splendid horse for fighting, and men believed that Brand put his trust in it and worshipped it: hence he was known as Faxabrand.[35]

The cult of Frey seems to have passed from Sweden, with its centre at Upsala, to Norway. There was an important temple of the god at Throndhjem where the people prayed to him for peace and fruitfulness, and looked for announcements about future events from him.[36] When King Olaf commanded the people at Throndhjem in 998 A.D. to break Frey's image, they refused on the ground that they had served him long and that he had done well by them, giving them peace and plenty and revealing the future to them.[37]

From Norway Frey's cult passed to Iceland with the emigrants in the ninth century, and there they placed themselves under his protection and that of Thor. The story of Ingimund offers an interesting illustration of this, and of the god's desire for the spread of his cult, which was strongest in the north of the island. Many temples of Frey are mentioned in the Sagas, some of them peculiarly sacred. In *Viga-Glums-saga* it is told that Glum harboured outlaws at Frey's temple at Eyafjord. This made the god angry: he withdrew his protection from Glum, and now his luck turned.[38]

Not only did groups of men or peoples trace descent from Frey, calling themselves his kin or his offspring,[39] but individuals regarded themselves as his friends or they were dear to him. The *Gisla-saga* tells how no snow lodged on the south side of Thorgrim's barrow, in the north-west of Iceland, nor did it freeze there. So men guessed that this was because Thorgrim had been so dear to Frey that he would not suffer the snow to come between them. Or, as Gisli said: 'Frey warms his servant's grave.' Before his death it was said of Thorgrim that he had intended to hold a festival at the beginning of winter, to greet the winter and to sacrifice to Frey.[40]

Frey's high position is seen in his epithets — Veraldar-god, 'god of the world'; Folkvaldi-god, 'Foremost of the gods.'[41] His occupancy of Hlidskjalf in *Skirnismal* and his possession of the ring Draupnir, elsewhere ascribed to Odin, point to a time when Odin had not yet taken a higher place than Frey in Scandinavia.

CHAPTER IX

THE VANIR GROUP—FREYJA

FREYJA or 'the Lady,' as daughter of Njord and sister of Frey, was one of the Vanir, and was called Vanabrudr, 'Bride of the Vanir'; Vanadis, 'Lady of the Vanir'; and Vanagod, 'Vanir goddess.'[1] Like the other members of the group, she is reckoned among the Æsir, and is 'the most renowned of the goddesses' and 'most gently born.'[2] In Heaven she has the dwelling Folkvang, 'Folk-plain,' and her hall, great and fair, is Sessrumnir, 'Rich in seats.' Here she assigns seats to the heroes who fall in battle, for half of these she shares with Odin. Hence she is 'the Possessor of the Slain.'[3] She drives forth in a chariot drawn by cats, and in this manner she came to Balder's funeral.[4] Her most famous possession is the necklace Brisinga-men, which Loki stole and Heimdall recovered.[5] She has also a hawk's plumage or feather-dress which enables her to fly, and is sometimes borrowed by Loki.[6] She rides the boar Hildisvini, 'Battle-swine,' with golden bristles, which she desires to pass off as Frey's boar. In reality it is her lover Ottarr in that form.[7]

Freyja's husband is Od; hence she is Ods-mær, 'Bride of Od.' Their daughter is Hnoss, 'Jewel,' 'so fair that precious things are called after her, *hnóssir*.' According to the *Ynglinga-saga* she had two daughters, Hross and Gersimi, 'after whom all things dearest to have are named.'[8]

Freyja is willing to help when men call upon her, especially in love affairs, and she is thus called 'goddess of love.' Songs of love were a delight to her.[9] In the euhemerized account of Freyja in the *Ynglinga-saga*, she is said to have introduced evil magic, *seidr*, among the Æsir, its use being already common among the Vanir, perhaps a memory of the use of magic in her cult.[10] From her name noble women had the name of honour *freyjur*.[11]

Freyja is known only in Norway and mainly in Icelandic poetry. Hence it has been asserted that she was a creation of the skalds as a counterpart to Frey. This is unlikely, and she is one of the few goddesses whose cult is definitely mentioned in Northern literature. In *Oddrunargratr*, one of the heroic poems of the *Edda*, occurs the following appeal:

> ' So may the holy Powers grant thee help,
> Frigg and Freyja and full many gods,
> As thou hast saved me from fear and misery.'

And in *Hyndluljod* Freyja says of Ottarr that he had made her a *hörg* (a cairn or altar) piled up with stones, which the sacrificial fires had fused into glass, and that it was often reddened with the blood of animal victims, for Ottarr trusted in the goddesses.[12] To Freyja, with Thor, Odin, and the Æsir, peasants of Throndhjem offered toasts at the beginning of winter in their feasts and sacrifices.[13] In the *Hálfs-saga* she is called upon for aid. King Alfrek determined to keep that one of his two wives, Signy and Geirhild, who should brew the best beer. Signy asked Freyja's aid, Geirhild that of Odin (Hótt, ' he with the hat '). He gave her his spittle in place of yeast, so her beer was the best. For this, she had to give Odin her son Wikar.

If, however, Freyja was an independent goddess, there seems to have been frequent confusion between her and Frigg, Odin's consort, or perhaps she tended to take the place of Frigg. When she is said to share the slain with Odin, one would naturally suppose that this would have been Frigg's privilege. In the *Egils-saga* it is women whom Freyja receives after death.[14] Both goddesses possess hawk's plumage, and Loki borrows it from both.[15] Some have held that the famous Brisinga-men was originally Frigg's possession. In later poetry Freyja is actually called Fjolnir's (Odin's) wife, as Frigg was. The

Christian Hjallti Skeggjason was outlawed at the Thing in Iceland in *c.* 999, because of his blasphemous verses against Odin and Freyja:

> ' Ever will I gods blaspheme,
> Freyja methinks a bitch does seem,
> Freyja a bitch? Aye, let them be
> Both dogs together, Odin and she.' [16]

This suggests that she was regarded as Odin's consort, taking the place of Frigg. Freyja and Frigg may have been both developed out of one original goddess, spouse of the old Heaven-god, to be ultimately confused with each other when the cult of Odin was increasing in the North.

On the other hand, that Freyja could be held to share the slain with Odin suggests her lofty position. Her abode is depicted as a kind of Valhall, and it might be identified with Vingolf, a seat of goddesses and also of the slain.[17] Freyja might also be regarded as chief of the Valkyries, riding forth to the strife, as Snorri depicts her — ' wheresoever she rides forth to the battle, she has half of the slain '; and, in this light, her fearless pouring out of ale for the giant Hrungnir when he invaded Asgard, would be significant, for the Valkyries poured out liquor in Valhall for heroes.[18] As chief of the Valkyries she would have an interest in the slain. If the names of her abodes have reference to their being abodes of the dead, ' Folk-plain ' and ' Rich in seats,' then a wider conception of her rule over the dead might be indicated. The passage in *Egils-saga* points to this. Thorgerd, daughter of Egil, who intends to die with her father, says that she has taken no food and will take none, for she hopes to feast that night with Freyja, just as heroes hoped to be Odin's guests. But there may be a survival in this passage of an older belief that women, not heroes, went to her abode at death.

The myths about Freyja are to some extent in keeping with her position as goddess of love, possibly also of fertility. Some of them suggest her desirableness as a beautiful and voluptuous goddess. She is coveted by giants — by him who rebuilt the citadel of the Æsir, by Hrungnir, and by Thrym. When Thrym sought her as his bride, her indignation was intense, her anger shook the dwelling of the gods, and her necklace broke on her heaving bosom. ' Maddest for men might I be called, did I travel with thee to Jötunheim.' [19] These giants, representing the power of winter, might be regarded as trying to overcome a goddess of fertility.

Similarly she was forced by four dwarfs to surrender herself to them ere they would give her Brisinga-men. This is the subject of a story in the *Sorla-tháttr* (fourteenth century). Freyja is here Odin's mistress. One day, looking into the rock-dwelling of four dwarfs, she saw them fashioning a wonderful necklace. Offering to purchase it, she was told that she would have it only if she yielded herself to the dwarfs. To this she submitted and became possessor of the famous necklace Brisinga-men. Loki heard of this and told Odin, who bade him get the necklace — a difficult task, for no one could enter Freyja's abode without her consent. Loki transformed himself into a fly and sought some opening, but in vain. At last he crept through a tiny hole in the roof. The inmates of the hall were asleep, Freyja lying with the clasp of the necklace under her neck. Transformed now into a flea, Loki bit her cheek. She woke and turned over on her other side. Then, assuming his own form, Loki unclasped the necklace, opened the door, and went with it to Odin. Freyja regained it from Odin only by consenting to incite two mighty kings, Hedin and Hilde, to an unending conflict.[20] This story is probably based on an earlier poem now lost. In the *Eddas* Freyja is the possessor of the necklace, and it so distinguishes her that when Thor disguised himself as the goddess, he wore this necklace. On another occasion or in another myth, the necklace, stolen by Loki, was recovered by Heimdall.

This necklace, ' the necklace of the Brisings,' who must be its artificers, or ' of Brising,' is alluded to as the *brosinga mene* in *Beowulf*, carried off by Hama from Eormanric. Here it forms part of a hoard.[21] The necklace itself is explained by modern mythologists as the rainbow, the moon, the morning or evening star, the red dawn, etc. Some have regarded it as the sun setting in the sea, and of which Freyja, regarded as the Heaven-goddess, is thus dispossessed. The word has also been connected with *brisingr*, ' fire,' a name still given to bonfires in Norway — an allusion to its gleaming quality, the jewel which sparkles like fire.[22] Menglod, ' Necklace-glad,' whom the hero Svipdag is compelled to seek by his stepmother, is so called after this mythic ornament, and is thus held to be a form of Freyja. Svipdag called up his dead mother Groa from the grave, and was given by her several charms to guard him in his difficult quest. He reached the hall of the giants, surrounded by fire, where Menglod was. The giant Fjolsvid sat before it, and held parley with Svipdag. In the course of their dialogue much mythic information is given. At last the giant says that no one is destined to have Menglod save Svipdag, who now reveals himself, and is welcomed by her as bridegroom. The evidence that Menglod is a form of Freyja is slender, and the tale rather suggests a folk-story than a myth. Attempts to explain the necklace in terms of natural phenomena are unsatisfactory, and it seems better to regard it as the reflexion in the divine sphere of such a precious human possession as a valuable necklace.

Freyja's lubricity is emphasized in the *Eddas*. In *Loka-senna* Loki attacks her, in common with other goddesses, for lewdness. She has just repelled his slander of Frigg, when Loki says:

> ' Be silent, Freyja, well I know thee,
>   Thou art not free of faults;
>   All the Æsir and Alfar who now are here
>   Hast thou in turn made happy.'

Freyja denies this, and, ' evil witch,' is then charged by Loki with having been found in her brother's bed by the Æsir.[23]

When Loki says of Thor, disguised as Freyja, that she (he) has eaten nothing nor closed an eye for eight nights, so hot is her desire for the giant's home, there may be a suggestion of Freyja's character.[24]   In *Hyndluljod* Freyja riding on a boar seeks the wise giantess Hyndla in order to learn from her the story of her favourite Ottarr's descent.   She wishes Hyndla to ride with her to Valhall on a wolf.   Hyndla knows her to be Freyja, and says that the boar is her lover Ottarr.   After telling the story of his descent, Hyndla dismisses Freyja with the caustic words: ' In the night-time like the she-goat Heidrun thou leapest after the goats.'   She says also:

> ' To Od didst thou run, ever lusty,
>   And many have stolen under thy girdle,'

and she frequently calls Ottarr Freyja's lover.   Frey admits that the boar is Ottarr and compels Hyndla to bring him the memory-beer, which will help him to recall the genealogy which she has just related.   If Hyndla does not swiftly bring it, she will raise flames around her and burn her alive.   Hyndla brings the drink, but mingled with the venom of an evil fate. Freyja says that this malediction will work no ill.   Ottarr will find a delicious drink when she begs the favour of the gods. Perhaps we may assume that Freyja causes the death of Hyndla, after having forced her to give the desired information.

Thor is called ' Freyja's friend ' in a poem by Eilif Gudrun-arson, and this may refer to some love affair with her.[25]   We should note also her association with Frey, a priapic god of fer-tility, and the glossing of her name in Christian times as Venus.[26]

Od, Freyja's husband, was not a deity but ' the man called Od.'   He ' goes forth into far lands, but Freyja remains behind in tears, and her tears are red gold.   Freyja has many names, because as she went among strange folk seeking Od, she called herself by different names — Mardoll, Horn, Gefn, Syr.'   In this passage Snorri does not explain how Freyja both remains at home and wanders in search of Od.   The account itself has given occasion to the most varied mythologizing interpretations, and, if it is based on natural phenomena, what these are cannot now be determined. With reference to her weeping, one of the goddess's titles is *gratfagra god*, ' goddess beautiful in tears,' and gold is called ' tears of Freyja.' [27] In folk-tales the gift of weeping tears which become pearls is a well-known incident, and tears of gold are wept by a maiden in an Icelandic story.[28] Her name Mœrthöll is a form of Mardoll, and if the latter means ' shining over the sea,' then she might be the Sun-goddess sinking to rest in the sea, the golden shimmer on the waters suggesting her tears as gold.[29] Others, like Gering, see in Freyja the bestower of the fructifying summer rain. She hovers over the earth in a feather-dress (the clouds); hence she is the goddess beautiful in tears. Her tears change to gold — the golden corn-seeds.[30] It should be noted that, as Od leaves Freyja, so Odin leaves Frigg in Saxo's story — another suggestion of the oneness of Freyja and Frigg.

To some degree Freyja is a counterpart of her brother Frey. Both are fair of face. Both are deities of love and that in its more sensual aspects. Both are associated with the boar on which they ride or are driven by it. If Nerthus was once of more importance than her male counterpart Njord, this was probably true also of Freyja in comparison with Frey. We have seen that Frey's name, Ingunar-Frey, means ' Frey of Ingun,' or ' Lord (Husband) of Ingun.' If Ingun here stands for Freyja, this would mean that she had once been more prominent than her consort — an earlier Fertility-goddess, possibly a form of Mother Earth. Prof. Chadwick has argued that the name Yngvi was that not only of Frey, but of the members of the royal house at Upsala.[31] If these were regarded as representatives of Frey, they would each in turn be looked on as consorts of the goddess, and Frey himself may have been originally no more than their eponymous ancestor. These, however, are highly speculative suggestions.

CHAPTER X

BALDER

THE references to Balder (ON Baldr) in the Poetic *Edda* are comparatively few and occur in six of the poems. From these we learn the following facts about him. He is son of Odin and Frigg.[1] According to *Grimnismal* his heavenly dwelling is Breidablik, ' Wide-shining,' which he built for himself, a place free from all crimes.[2] He was troubled by evil dreams: the gods took counsel over this, and Odin rode down to Hel to consult the dead seeress, raised up by his spells, and, calling himself Vegtam, forced her to reply to his questions. She answered first that a place is prepared in Hel for Balder and that hope is gone from the gods. Hod will be Balder's bane, bringing to Hel the hero whom he will deprive of life. But Balder will be avenged: Rind bears Vali in Vestrsalir, ' Western Hall,' to Odin. When one night old, he will fight, and bring Balder's slayer to the pyre. ' What maidens are those who weep for this and toss to the sky the tops of the sails?' asked Odin.[3] This enigmatic question revealed to the seeress who her questioner really was. Odin says that she is no Volva nor prophetess: rather is she the mother of three giants (Thursar). She bids Odin ride home. None will see her again till Loki is free of his bonds and the Doom of the gods arrives. This story is the subject of *Baldrs Draumar*.

Voluspa also refers to the death of *Balder*. The seeress says:

> ' I saw for Balder, Odin's son,
>   The soft-hearted god, destiny set;
>   Full grown on the fields,
>   Slender and fair,
>   The mistletoe stood.

> From this tree was made,
> Which seemed so slender,
> A deadly shaft, which Hod shot.'

Then follow the lines from *Baldrs Draumar* about Vali, and
the seeress resumes:

> ' In Fensalir Frigg weeps sore,
> For Valhall's woe,
> Would ye know yet more? ' [4]

The Short *Voluspa* in *Hyndluljod* refers to Balder's death,
and says that the gods were eleven in number when he bowed
his head on the hill of death. Vali was swift to avenge this,
slaying quickly his brother's slayer.[5]

Skirnismal speaks of the ring Draupnir as that which was
laid on Balder's pyre. In *Vafthrudnismal* Odin asks the giant
what words Odin spoke in the ear of Balder on his pyre. In
Lokasenna Loki tells Frigg that he is the cause of Balder's
death.[6]

In these notices we learn that Hod was Balder's slayer. Only
in *Lokasenna* is it hinted that Loki was to blame for his death.
The long prose narrative compiled by Snorri from these and
other sources shows that Hod was the unwitting cause of the
slaying, because of Loki's action. The original myth may thus
have had no place for Loki, who was later introduced into the
story.

Finally, in *Voluspa* Balder is said to come back to the renewed world after the Doom of the gods, and with Hod he
lives in Hropt's (Odin's) battle-hall.[7]

The *Husdrapa* of Ulf Uggason (tenth century) describes
pictures painted on the wainscot and roof of a hall in Iceland.
Among these were scenes from Balder's funeral. Frey rides his
boar, Heimdall his horse; Odin follows, then the Valkyries and
the ravens. Another scene depicted the giantess Hyrokkin
launching the ship on which the pyre is set, while Odin's
champions follow the wolf on which she rode.[8] The tenth

century skalds, Kormak and Vetrlidhi, also refer to the Balder myth.

We now turn to Snorri's later prose narrative. Balder the good is Odin's second son, and good things are to be said of him. He is the best god, praised by all. So beautiful and fair is he that light shines forth from him. A certain herb is so white that it is called ' Balder's eyelash,' *Baldersbraa.* This shows how fair his hair and body are. He is wisest of the Æsir, most fair of speech and gracious, yet none may gainsay his judgments. He dwells in Breidablik, where nothing impure can be found. Nanna, daughter of Nep, is his wife: their son is Forseti.[9]

In several chapters Snorri describes Balder's death and funeral. He dreamed evil dreams, and the Æsir resolved to ask safety for him from all kinds of dangers. Frigg took oaths from fire, water, metals, stones, trees, animals, etc., that none of these should hurt him. Now it became a sport of the gods to shoot or hew or beat Balder; nothing could do him harm. When Loki saw this, he was displeased and went to Fensalir in woman's form to ask Frigg why this was done. Then he learned that she had taken oaths of all things save a tree-sprout called mistletoe, growing to the west of Valhall, which had seemed to her too young to take an oath of. Loki went and pulled up the mistletoe by the root, and, going to the Thing, spoke to Hod who was standing outside the ring, because he was blind. He asked him why he did not shoot at Balder and was told that he could not see where Balder was and, besides, he was weaponless. Loki then put the mistletoe in his hand and bade him be guided by him and throw the rod at Balder. This he did and Balder fell dead.

The Æsir looked at each other in silence: none could there take vengeance, so great a sanctuary was that place. They wept, but Odin was of all most grieved, knowing the harm that would befall the Æsir. Frigg then asked who would go down to Hel and offer her a ransom to release Balder. Hermod, the son of

Odin, undertook this, and mounting Sleipnir, rode away. He went for nine nights through dark valleys to the river Gjoll and on to the Gjoll-bridge, thatched with gold, and guarded by the maiden Módgud. She asked his name and race and said that on the previous day Balder and five hundred dead men (his servants?) had crossed, but the bridge thundered less with their tread than with his alone. Why did he ride on Hel-way? To seek out Balder: had she seen him? ' Yes: Balder rode over the bridge, and Hel-way lies down and to the north.'

Hermod rode on to Hel-gate, over which his horse leaped. Now he entered the hall, where Balder sat in the high seat. Next morning he besought Hel to let him go; she would only release him if all things, quick or dead, wept for him. Balder now let Hermod out of the hall. Nanna sent to Frigg a kerchief and to Fulla a gold ring. Hermod rode back to Asgard and told his tidings.

Meanwhile Balder's funeral had been celebrated. The Æsir brought his corpse to the sea and set it on Hringhorni, greatest of all ships. They would have launched it and set his pyre upon it, but it would not stir. A message was sent to Jötunheim to the giantess Hyrrokin. She came, riding a wolf bridled by a snake. Leaping off her steed, which Odin bade four berserkers tend, though they could not hold it till they had felled it, she pushed the boat so that fire burst from its rollers as it was thrust into the sea, and earth trembled. Thor, in his rage, would have broken her head with his hammer, had not the gods calmed him.[10]

The corpse was now laid on the ship. Nanna straightway died of grief, and was laid with Balder on the pyre, which was now kindled. Thor hallowed it with his hammer, when before his feet ran the dwarf Litr, whom Thor kicked into the fire. Odin was there, with Frigg, the Valkyries, and his ravens; Frey drove in his chariot with his boar Gullinbursti or Slidrugtanni. Heimdall rode Golltop; Freyja drove her cats. Many of the Frost-giants and Hill-giants were also present. On the

pyre Odin laid the ring Draupnir, and Balder's horse was led to
the fire with all his trappings.

When Hermod told his tidings to the Æsir, they sent messengers all over the world to pray that Balder should be wept
out of Hel. People, living things, earth, stones, trees, metals,
wept — ' as thou must have seen that all these things weep
when they come out of the cold into the heat.' As the messengers went home, they found a giantess sitting in a cave, Thokk
by name. They begged her to weep for Balder: she refused,
and here Snorri quotes a verse of a lost Eddic poem.

> ' With waterless tears will Thokk weep
>   That Balder ascends the pyre;
>   Neither in life nor death loved I the karl's son,
>   Let Hel hold what she has.'

Thokk was Loki. Snorri then relates the vengeance taken by
the gods on him.[11] He also tells of Balder and Hod in the
renovated world.[12] His narrative is based on poems now lost,
the stanza about Thokk being one of these, on the Eddic poems,
and on the *Husdrapa*, already cited.

The *Eddas* do not tell how Vali took vengeance on Hod, but
this is assumed, and, in *Hyndluljod*, asserted. Thus Snorri
gives as one of the kennings for Hod, ' foe of Vali,' and for
Vali himself ' foe and slayer of Hod.' [13] As we have seen, the
poetic references to Balder's death do not mention Loki as the
agent who caused Hod's action. If Hod had merely been
the unwitting slayer, there would have been no reason for seeking an avenger to put him to death. In Snorri's narrative, where
he acts under Loki's advice, vengeance is not taken on him, but
on Loki. In the earlier form of the myth, before *c.* 1000 A.D.,
Hod alone was responsible for Balder's death.

The story of Balder and Hod is also told by Saxo Gramma-
ticus, Hod being called by him Hotherus, and he is a son of
Hodbrodd, king of Sweden, and fosterling of Gewar, king of
Norway. Hotherus was skilled in all accomplishments, and

these so pleased Nanna, daughter of Gewar, that she fell madly in love with him. Balder, Odin's son, saw Nanna bathing, and he desired to have her (as Frey did on seeing Gerd), resolving to slay Hotherus. Hotherus, led astray by a mist when hunting, came to a lodge where certain *virgines silvestres* or Wood-maidens greeted him by name. They told him that by their guidance and auspices the fortunes of war were mainly determined. They took part invisibly in battles, and secretly assisted their favourites to victory, for they could win victory or inflict defeat as they willed. They told him of Balder's love for Nanna, but counselled him not to attack him in war, for he was a demi-god (*semi-deus*), sprung secretly from celestial seed. Lodge and maidens now vanished, and Hotherus found himself in the open fields. Hotherus, much amazed, told Gewar of this, and asked him for Nanna. Gewar said that he would gladly favour him, but feared Balder's wrath, as he also had asked for her. Balder's body was proof against steel, but, said Gewar, there was a sword which would cause his death, as well as a bracelet which had the power of increasing its owner's wealth. These were in the possession of Miming, a satyr of the woods. The way to his abode was full of obstacles, over frozen ground. Hotherus must harness a car with reindeer and, having reached the place, pitch his tent so that its shadow would not fall on Miming's cave and, by the unusual darkness, prevent his coming out. Hotherus followed these instructions, and when Miming emerged from the cave, he aimed a spear at him and laid him low. Then he bound him and demanded the sword and brace-let, which Miming now gave to him. Incidents are told of war with Gelder, king of Saxony, who coveted these treasures, and of assistance given to Helgi, king of Halogaland, to gain Thora, daughter of the king of the Finns and Perms.

Meanwhile Balder had sued for Nanna and was bidden by Gewar to learn her own mind. She would not be moved, and said that a god could not wed a mortal. Gods were apt to break their pledges! Hotherus, with Helgi's aid, joined battle with

Balder at sea. Odin, Thor, and all the gods fought for Balder. Thor with his club (*clava*) was carrying all before him, when Hotherus, clad in an invulnerable coat, cut the club in two, thus rendering it useless. The gods with Balder took to flight. Even Saxo is staggered by this, but he says that antiquity vouches for it.

Soon after, fortune turned and Balder defeated Hotherus, but was so tormented by dreams in which phantoms took the form of Nanna that he fell into sickness, and had to be driven about in a four-wheeled carriage. Hotherus took possession of Denmark, joining it with Sweden. Balder came to Denmark, the people there accepting him. Hotherus was again defeated, retiring to Sweden in despair. In a wild forest he once more met the Wood-maidens, who had formerly given him an invulnerable coat, as we now learn. He told them of his defeats and upbraided them with breach of faith. They said that though he had been defeated, he had inflicted as much loss on the enemy as they had on his forces. Victory would soon be his, if he could obtain a food of great deliciousness devised to increase Balder's strength. Hotherus plucked up courage, and now Balder and the Danes opposed him in battle until night ended the fight. During the darkness Hotherus went to spy on the foe, and learned that three maidens had gone out, carrying Balder's secret feast. Running after them, for their footsteps could be traced in the dew (an elfin trait), he entered their dwelling, saying that he was a musician, one of the company of Hotherus. He played to them, entrancing them with his music (another elfin trait), and at the same time he saw that the venom of three serpents was dropping from their mouths on Balder's food, thus dowering it with magic strength. Out of kindness two of the maidens would have given him a share of the food, but the eldest forbade it, saying that Balder would be defrauded if the strength of his enemy were increased. But these nymphs (*nymphae*) gave him a belt and a girdle which ensured victory. On his return, he met Balder and plunged his sword into him,

leaving him half dead. On the night following, Proserpine
(Hel) stood by Balder, and promised that on the morrow he
would have her embraces. In three days he died, and was given
a royal funeral by the Danes, his corpse being laid in a barrow
made by them.[14]

Saxo then tells how, in his day, certain men, chief of whom
was one Harald, sought to open the barrow to find treasure, but
were stricken with panic. It split open; water poured from it
and flooded the land; the guardian gods of the place (*land-
vætter* or perhaps the *haugbui*) thus terrifying the seekers, but,
as Saxo believes, with a magic and phantasmal flood, not an
actual one. Saxo gives interesting information about places
connected with Balder. A haven, the name of which he does not
mention, recalls the story of Balder's defeat at sea, perhaps
Balderslee, the traditional name of a village in Schleswig,
though it may be Balsnes, formerly Baldersnes, on the island
of Hitteren in Norway. After conquering Hotherus, Balder
pierced the earth and opened a spring at which his men quenched
their thirst. The traces of this spring at Baldersbrönd, a village
near Roskilde, were thought to exist in Saxo's time. Later tradition said that it was formed by a stroke of the hoof of Balder's
horse.[15]

Saxo next tells how Odin began to enquire regarding vengeance for Balder's death, and gives the story of his affair with
Rinda, which has already been related.[16]

Saxo's narrative both resembles and differs from the Eddic
account of Balder. The protagonists Balder and Hod (Hotherus) are the same, though Hotherus is not one of the Æsir, but
son of a king. As in the earlier Eddic myth, Loki does not
appear, nor is Hotherus blind. Balder is slain by Hod by means
of the mistletoe which grows at Valhall and is sought there by
Loki (*Edda*); by means of a magic sword sought by Hotherus
in the far North (Saxo). Balder's safety is secured by oaths
taken of all things not to harm him (*Edda*); he is invulnerable,
because of magic food and save for being wounded by Miming's

sword (Saxo). In the *Eddas* he is troubled by dreams. So in
Saxo's account he is troubled by dreams of Nanna and has a
vision of Hel. The vengeance *motif* appears in both: Rind has
a son Vali or Bous to Odin, who overcame her by spells.

On the other hand, Hotherus seems to be Saxo's hero, and
Balder is not presented in a favourable light. Nanna becomes
wife of Hotherus: in the *Edda* she is wife of Balder. The cause
of the enmity between the two is not given in the *Edda:* in Saxo,
it is rivalry for Nanna and, later, strife for the possession of
Denmark. In Saxo, too, the gods fight against the hero Hotherus, and, years after, he is slain by Bous, who himself dies of
his wounds. The oath taken from all things to weep Balder out
of Hel and Hermod's visit to Hel are lacking in Saxo. Balder
is buried, not burned on a pyre — the pyre on a ship is transferred to Gelder, who was slain in the war, and set by Hotherus
on the corpses of his men, laid on a pyre of ships. The Wood-
maidens and the three *nymphae* who prepare Balder's magic
food are not in the Eddic story. Saxo's narrative is mainly
euhemeristic, save that Balder is a demi-god in the earlier part
at least, and the gods fight for him: the action takes place on
earth, and each protagonist has his army and fleet.

The problems here are: Is Saxo making use of a Norse or of a
native Danish source or sources? Has he changed a myth of
the gods into a saga about heroes? Was there a form of the
Balder story which had no reference to the gods? Why should
Balder be so well spoken of in the *Eddas,* but regarded un-
favourably by Saxo?

Definite solutions of these problems are hardly possible.
The native Balder saga is maintained by Kauffmann, who thinks
that this saga told of héroes, one of whom, Balder, was a demi-
god, but that, on reaching Iceland, it became a myth of the gods,
modified by Christian influences.[17] Others regard Saxo's source
as Icelandic, or partly Danish, partly Norse, and think that he
or his source had euhemerized a myth of the gods. Saxo's narrative seems to indicate two sources. In one of these, mainly

mythical, the quarrel between Balder and Hotherus is about
Nanna. The gods intervene, yet Balder is put to flight, this
narrative probably ending with his death and burning on a
pyre — this being transferred to king Gelder. In the other,
completely euhemerized, there are no gods: Balder and Hotherus are mortals, and the quarrel is about the possession of Denmark.[18] Not impossibly Saxo's narrative may be based on a
form of the Balder myth of earlier date than the Eddic.[19]

The references in *Voluspa* and in Snorri (or his source) to
the mistletoe by which Balder was slain, do not seem to have
been written by men familiar with this plant, which is described
as a tree, not a parasitic plant on a tree. In Saxo, Balder is slain
with a magic sword. No name is given to it, as was usual with
magic swords, but in other documents we hear of a sword called
Mistelteinn. Thus in the *Hromundar-saga Greipssonar* Hromund possesses the sword Mistelteinn which he took from a
berserker or his ghost out of a hill. Two magicians, Bildr and
Voli (Balder and Vali), oppose him. Bildr is slain. Voli hurls
Hromund's sword out of his hand, wounds him, but is himself
slain. Hromund loved Svanhit: Bildr and Voli would not per-
mit him to be her bride. The story thus bears some resemblance to Saxo's narrative of Hotherus, Balder, and Bous
(Vali).[20] In composite words *teinn* is ' sword,' as in Lævateinn,
the name of the sword by which alone Vithofnir could be killed,
as Balder could be slain only by Miming's sword.[21] The sword-
name might easily be mistaken for that of the plant, which
would then be supposed to be the instrument of Balder's
death.[22]

The meaning of the Balder myth has been sought in many
directions, and German and Scandinavian scholars have suggested numerous interpretations of it, evolving many new
myths in the process. The myth, like others existing in com-
parative isolation, must be more or less of a sealed book.
Bugge's hypothesis that an earlier Balder myth was reconstructed with stress laid on the fundamental moral elements of

life, as a result of the influence of English and Irish Christianity
on the heathen Norsemen in the West, is worked out in great
detail.[23] Balder is identified with Christ; all the stress is laid
on his death. While the hypothesis is ingenious, the elements
of the new myth taken over from Christian sources — biblical,
theological, legendary — are too numerous and too various for
the theory to be convincing. One would also have thought that
a Balder restored from Hel and death would have formed part
of a myth due to Christian ideas, as our Lord's Resurrection and
conquest of death and Hades had such a large place in Christian
thought. Miss Phillpotts, who sees in many of the Eddic poems
the words of folk-drama, and considers that a lost poem in
dialogue form about Balder's death constituted a folk-play
representing the slaying of a god, would like to believe that
Balder rose again, or that the representation of his funeral and
the general weeping would have effect in inducing him to return.[24] But if one thing is clearer than another in the Eddic
references to Balder, it is that he does not return and cannot return. Only after the Doom of the gods does he appear in the
renewed world.

The name of Balder, whether god or hero, is thought to
occur in the Merseburg charm which tells how

> ' Phol and Wodan rode to the wood,
> Balder's colt there wrenched its foot.'

If so, this would prove that Balder was known in Germany.
The question is whether ' Balder ' is here a personal name or
an appellative meaning ' lord ' and referring to Odin, whose
horse would then be in question. Grimm found place-names in
Germany constructed, as he thought, both from Phol and
Balder, and he connected the name Phol with that of the Celtic
Belenus, a god of light, Slavic Bèlbôgh, ' white god,' and
Lithuanian *baltas*, ' white.' He considered that Phol and
Balder were differing forms of one word.[25] The enigmatic
Phol has also been explained as Apollo, possibly an early *inter-*

pretatio Romana of a German Balder; or as S. Paul; or as a native German god; or as the name of Wodan's horse.

The name Balder appears in Anglo-Saxon genealogies as Bældæg, Baldag, and once as Balder, son of Woden. The AS *bealdor*, *baldor*, akin to these names, like ON *baldr*, meant ' prince ' or ' lord,' though Balder means ' the white or shining one,' and Bældæg means ' bright day.'

The only indication of a cult of Balder occurs in the fourteenth century *Fridthjofs-saga* which speaks of a temple in Baldershog in Norway, enclosed by a fence. It contained many images, and Balder was most reverenced. Neither men nor oxen must do mischief there, nor sexual relations occur. On festivals the images were anointed by women. This notice is generally regarded as fictitious.

Place-names in Sweden, Norway, and Denmark show traces of Balder; and he is still named in Danish folk-lore.[26] The name of the plant Baldrsbrá is widespread in Scandinavia, but is applied to different plants.

CHAPTER XI

LOKI

LOKI is the son of giants and is yet included among the
gods. Snorri gives a detailed account of him and relates
several myths in which he plays a part. He is mentioned in
*Voluspa, Thrymskvitha, Hymiskvitha, Svipdagsmal, Regins-
mal, Hyndluljod,* and *Baldrs Draumar,* and he is the subject
of *Lokasenna.* Some of the notices in these poems are included
in Snorri's references. Two of the myths in which Loki plays
a part are the subject of poems by Eilif Gudrunarson and Thjodolf of Hvin — those of Thor and Geirrod and of Idunn and
Thjazi. A third skald, Ulf Uggason, wrote a poem on Heimdall and Loki, cited by Snorri. Apart from these notices, Loki
is not mentioned, e.g., in the Sagas, though his name survived in
folk-tradition.

Snorri says of him: ' Included among the Æsir is he whom
some call the slanderer of the Æsir or the author of deceit and
the shame of gods and men. He is named Loki or Lopt; he is
son of the giant Farbauti and the giantess Laufey or Nal. His
brothers are Byleist and Helblindi. To outward appearance
Loki is beautiful and comely, but evil in disposition and most
fickle in nature. He excelled in sleight and had stratagems for
all occasions. He often brought the Æsir into great difficulties,
but then delivered them with his cunning. His spouse is called
Sigyn, and their son is Nari or Narfi.' [1]

Loki joined in adventures with Thor — the visit to Utgard-
Loki and to the giant Thrym. He was the cause of Thor's
combat with Geirrod and his daughters.[2] He was also joined
with Odin and Hœnir — in the work of creating the first pair,
in connexion with Andvari's treasure, and in the story of Idunn.[3]

Hence he is called ' the friend of Odin,' ' the staunch friend of Hœnir,' by Thjodolf of Hvin.[4] In *Lokasenna* he recalls to Odin that in earlier days they had mixed their blood in the rite of blood-brotherhood, and Odin had promised to pour no ale unless it were brought for both. In the same poem Frigg bids Odin and Loki preserve silence on the deeds they had done long ago. Idunn reminds Bragi that Loki had been chosen as ' wish-son ' or adopted son by Odin.[5] In a skaldic poem quoted in *Heimskringla* Odin is called ' Lopt's friend,'[6] and Snorri speaks of him as ' Evil companion and bench-mate of Odin and the Æsir.'[7] Some have thought that Saxo's Mit-othin may have been Loki in disguise.[8] In the *Sorla-thattr* (thirteenth century) Loki, son of a peasant Farbauti and his wife Laufey who was thin and meagre and hence called Nal or ' Needle,' is caustic, cunning, and tricky. He became Odin's serving-man. Odin always had a good word for him, though he often laid heavy tasks upon him, all of which he performed. Loki knew almost everything that happened and told it to Odin. This is introductory to the story of Loki's stealing the Brisinga-men from Freyja.[9]

Snorri's statement that Loki got the gods into trouble, but saved them by his cunning, is illustrated by different myths. The demand of the giant artificer who rebuilt Asgard that the gods should give him Freyja and the sun and moon, was believed by them to have been suggested to him by Loki, and they adjudged him worthy of death unless he found means of evading the demand. He then changed himself into a mare, which was pursued by the giant's helpful stallion Svadilfari. This caused the work to be suspended and it was not completed in the agreed time. Thor slew the giant and, some time after, Loki gave birth to Sleipnir, Odin's horse.[10]

Again, by means of Loki's agreement with the giant Thjazi he brought the goddess Idunn into his power. When the gods discovered this, Loki was threatened with torture or death. He escaped by borrowing Freyja's feather-dress, flying to

Jötunheim, and bringing back Idunn, whom he transformed
for the occasion into a nut. The Æsir slew Thjazi when he
pursued Loki to Asgard, but in *Lokasenna* Loki claims to have
been himself first and last in the fight with the giant.[11] When
Thjazi's daughter Skadi came to Asgard to avenge her father,
Loki caused her to laugh — one of the terms of reconciliation
demanded by her.[12]

When Loki flew to Geirrod's abode in Frigg's feather-dress
and was there captured and starved by him, he ransomed his
life by promising to bring Thor there without his hammer or
girdle of strength. Here, however, Thor required no strata-
gem on Loki's part in order to overcome Geirrod.[13]

Odin, Hœnir, and Loki were brought into the power of
Hreidmarr after Loki had slain his son in the form of an otter.
Odin sent Loki to Svartalfheim, and there he captured the
dwarf Andvari, who was in the form of a fish, and forced him to
give up his treasure. This treasure was to form the gods' ransom to Hreidmarr, and it was to cover the otter's skin completely. The dwarf begged to be permitted to keep one ring,
but Loki took it also, and he then declared that it would be the
ruin of everyone who came into possession of it. Returning
with the gold, Loki gave it to Odin who covered the skin with it,
but retained the ring. One of the hairs of the otter's nose remained uncovered, and Hreidmarr insisted on its being covered,
so Odin had to give up the ring. Loki now said that both ring
and treasure would be a curse to every possessor of them.[14]
Snorri tells this story, but it is also the subject of *Reginsmal*,
where the otter is called Otr, and Loki borrows Ran's net in
order to catch Andvari, who says that the gold, not the ring,
will be a curse.

When Loki cut off Sif's hair out of mischief, Thor would
have broken all his bones, had he not sworn to get the Black
Elves to make Sif hair of gold, which would grow like other
hair.[15]

In *Thrymskvitha* Loki, by crafty counsel, aids Thor to recover his hammer from Thrym. We are not told that Loki had caused the hammer to be stolen, but this may once have been the introduction to the story.[16]

Two forms of the story of Loki's theft of the Brisinga-men from Freyja are given. One is that related in the *Sorla-thattr*, already cited; the other is obscurely referred to in a poem, a fragment of which is cited by Snorri, and in Snorri's account of Heimdall. Here Loki has apparently stolen it from Freyja for his own purposes. Heimdall contends with him for it and both are in the form of seals.[17]

Loki does mischief for mischief's sake. He is a thief (of the Brisinga-men) or he causes theft (Idunn and her apples). He dislikes others to be praised, even a servant, as when he slew Fimafeng at Ægir's banquet.[18] He is foul-mouthed and slanderous, as *Lokasenna* shows. Some account must be given of the contents of this poem. The prose Introduction tells how Ægir invited many of the gods and elves to a feast. All went well until Loki, angry at the guests' praising Fimafeng for his ability, slew him. The gods shook their shields and howled at Loki, and drove him out to the forest. At this point the poem begins. Loki has returned and asks Eldir of what is going on in the hall. Eldir tells how the talk is of weapons and war, and that none has a friendly word for him. Loki says he will go in, bringing hatred to the gods and mixing venom with their ale. He enters and says that he has come from a far journey and asks for a drink. The gods are silent, till Bragi speaks and says that there is no place for him here. Loki appeals to Odin on the ground of their old brotherhood sworn in the morning of time, and Odin bids Vidar find a place for the ' wolf's father,' lest he should speak evil. Vidar obeys and Loki pledges all present:

> ' Hail to the Æsir! hail to the Asynjur!
>   And all the holy gods;
> Save only to that one of them,
>   Bragi, sitting there on the bench.'

The poem now takes the form of a ' flyting ' between Loki and
most of the guests present, in which much scurrility is spoken,
and many mythological incidents, some of them otherwise
unknown, are referred to. Bragi is accused of cowardice.
Idunn begs him to weigh Loki's kinship with Odin and speak
no taunt to him. Loki turns on her and accuses her of an
amour with her brother's slayer. She does not refute this
taunt, but merely tries to calm Bragi, who is overcome with ale.
Gefjun now intervenes and begs that no bandying of words
will continue, for Loki is known as a slanderer and hates everyone. Loki accuses her of misconduct with a youth who gave
her a necklace. Odin tells Loki that he is mad to raise Gefjun's
anger, for she knows men's destinies just as Odin himself does.
Loki turns on Odin and tells him that he does not justly assign
victory, and often gives it to him who deserves it least. Odin
says this may be, but Loki had been eight winters under the
earth milking cows in woman's form, and even giving birth to
children. Loki retorts that Odin had once wrought magic
spells in the guise of a witch in Samsey (Samsö, north of
Fünen).

These two taunts — a man bearing children as a woman, a
man taking woman's form — were not uncommon in the
Scandinavian North, but were regarded as most deadly insults.
Gods and goddesses in turn address Loki and strive to silence
him, but in vain. He accuses Frigg of misconduct with Odin's
brothers, Vili and Ve, and when she says that if Balder were
alive, he would fight with him, Loki boasts that it is he who
caused his death. Freyja, ' a witch strong in evil,' is accused
of sharing her favours with all the gods and Alfar, and with
being her brother's lover. Njord intervenes, wondering why
this womanish god, who has borne children, should come here.
Loki taunts Njord with being a hostage from the Vanir and
with having a son, Frey, by his sister. Tyr now says that Frey
is best of heroes. Loki bids him be silent, for he is no peace-
maker and had lost his hand by the Fenris-wolf, and his wife

had a son by Loki for which crime no fine was ever paid. Frey reminds Loki that the wolf is bound till the Doom of the gods and that soon he, too, will be fettered if his tongue is not quiet. Loki says that Frey bought Gerd with gold and his sword, and now weaponless must await Muspell's sons when they ride through Myrkwood.

At this point Byggvir, Frey's servant, intervenes, and says that if he were of such birth as Frey, he would crush Loki to marrow and break all his bones. Loki taunts him — little creature that he is — with cowardice. Now Heimdall speaks and tells Loki he is drunk. Skadi says that soon the gods will bind Loki with his son's bowels. Loki cries that he was first and last among those who slew her father, and reminds her of his amour with her.

Sif comes forward, pours ale for Loki, and says that she at least is blameless, but she also is reminded of misconduct with him. Beyla, wife of Byggvir, cries that the mountains are shaking and Thor, absent slaying trolls, is coming, and will silence the slanderer. She is also vilified, and now Thor enters and bids Loki, wretched wight, be silent or his hammer will close his mouth. Loki says he need not threaten so much: he will be less fierce when he fights the Fenris-wolf. Thrice again does Thor threaten him: Loki still taunts him — with hiding in a giant's glove (p. 92) and with his difficulty in opening Skrymir's wallet. Finally he says that he has spoken all he wished to say: now he will go, because Thor is such a great fighter, but he warns Ægir that no more feasts will he give, for the fire will soon consume all that is here.

A prose conclusion, which is out of place, as Loki's imprisonment followed on Balder's death, tells how he hid as a salmon in Franang's waterfall, where the gods caught him. He was bound with the bowels of his son Vali, and his son Narfi was changed into a wolf. Skadi fastened a venomous snake over his face, so that its poison dropped on it. Sigyn, his wife (who is included among the Asynjur by Snorri), held a shell under the poison, but when she drew it away full of venom, some drops fell on Loki's face. He then struggled so much that all the earth shook, and that is called an earthquake.

This poem belongs to the pagan period (tenth century) and was written by a pagan who knew the old myths, and who treats the deities with a kind of Aristophanic humour. These myths were discreditable, but like the Greek poets condemned by Plato, he does not hesitate to tell them. The prose Introduction is of later date, for the poem itself tells how Loki had come from a long journey late to the feast, and had thus not been expelled for slaying Fimafeng. The gods receive him coldly, knowing his enmity to them. In spite of his dexterity in scurrility, none of the gods dare silence him, not even Odin. Thor alone, when he enters, and not even he immediately, can do this. Was the poem written by a Thor worshipper?

Lokasenna shows Loki at enmity with all the gods, though he is plainly shown to be a blood brother of Odin. As clearly is he called the father of the Fenris-wolf. Loki's wife was Sigyn: their sons Vali and Narfi. But in *Hyndluljod* his amour with the giantess Angrboda resulted in the birth of the Fenris-wolf and the Midgard-serpent. To these Snorri adds a third, Hel. When the gods learned that these were being nourished in Jötunheim, and knew that they boded ill to them from their mother's blood, still more from their father's, Odin sent gods to bring them to him. The Midgard-serpent was now cast into the sea and lies about all the land. Hel was cast into Niflheim. The Fenris-wolf was bound.[19]

Hyndluljod also tells of Loki's eating the cooked heart of a woman which he found in the embers. Through this he became with child, and gave birth to a monster. Nothing further is known of this myth, nor of that of which Odin speaks in *Lokasenna* — Loki as a cow-maid under the earth for eight winters and there bearing children. This has been explained as a nature myth. Loki is the subterranean fire, regarded as female, producing vegetation through warmth. The eight winters should be regarded as eight winter months during which frost reigns and warmth retreats within the earth and works in secret. The cows which Loki milks are warm springs! [20]

Loki's transformations were numerous — into a mare, a seal, a fly on two occasions, a flea, a milkmaid, a woman, a giantess, a salmon. By means of the feather-dress he became a bird.

Loki's worst action, showing him as foe of the gods, is found in the myth of Balder. Here he plays an evil part, without any compensating good. Balder's death, brought about by him, as already told, brings near the Doom of the gods. This led to Loki's punishment. He ran off and hid in a mountain, making a house with four doors, so that he could see in all directions. He transformed himself into a salmon by day and hid in Franang falls. When he sat in the house he took twine and knitted meshes as a net is made. When he found that the Æsir were at hand, Odin having seen his hiding-place from Hlidskjalf, he cast the net into the fire, and leaped as a salmon into the stream. The Æsir went into the house and there Kvasir saw the ash made by the burning net and realized that it was a device for catching fish. The Æsir now made one of the same pattern and, by its means, tried to catch Loki, who evaded them, until Thor waded to mid-stream. When Loki tried to leap over the net, he caught him. Loki slipped through his hand, but Thor was able to grip him by the tail. Hence the salmon has a tapering tail. The Æsir now took Loki's sons, and changed Vali into a wolf. He tore his brother Narfi to pieces, and with his bowels the gods bound Loki to three flat stones set on edge in a cave. These bonds turned to iron. The rest of this myth is given by Snorri as it is told in the prose appendix to *Lokasenna*. Loki now lies in bonds till the Doom of the gods. The sibyl refers to this in *Voluspa*:

> ' Bound saw I in the hot spring's grove
> A monstrous form, the repulsive Loki;
> There sat Sigyn sunk in pain
> For the woe of her spouse.' [21]

At the Doom of the gods Loki breaks forth. To this the dead seeress, consulted by Odin about Balder's dreams, refers. No one shall now consult her until Loki frees himself, shakes off his fetters, and the destroyers come to the Doom of the gods.[22] How he breaks loose is not told, but *Voluspa* describes how he stands at the helm of a ship with the people of Hel. Snorri gives further details. Loki, Hrym, and the Frost-giants come forth. The champions of Hel follow Loki, who fights with Heimdall, each slaying the other.[23] Thus Loki acts as opponent of the gods.

The myth of Loki's bonds resembles one in Iranian mythology. The hero Thraêtana conquered the dragon Azhi Dahaka and bound him to the rock Damavand. There he lies till the Last Day, meanwhile causing earthquakes by his struggles. In the end he breaks loose and takes part with hosts of evil against the gods.[24]

We have seen that Thor and Loki visited Utgard, the giants' region, where its lord, Utgard-Loki, practised deception on them. While it is possible that Loki's name has been used in the name of the lord of Utgard, it can hardly be that he, Loki, and Logi ('Fire') which devours all, are one and the same being. Loki is as prominent in the story as the others.

Snorri gives several kennings for Loki, based on his relationships and his deeds. He is 'Foe of the gods,' 'the sly god,' 'Slanderer and cheat of the gods,' 'the bound god,' 'Thief of the giants, of Brisinga-men, of Idunn's apples.' Other by-names are 'Wolf's father,' 'the cunning Loki.'[25] He calls himself Lopt, and this name is also given to him by others.[26] Its meaning is 'the airy one,' or it is connected with *lopteldr*, 'lightning.' The name Lodur, which occurs only in *Voluspa*, as that of the associate of Odin and Hœnir, is generally supposed to be an earlier name of Loki, who was 'companion' and 'friend' of Hœnir according to Thjodolf of Hvin. This name is regarded as equivalent to Luhþurar, 'the Fire-bringer.'[27]

Loki's original nature has been sought in the meaning of his

name, which may be connected with Logi, German Lohi, ' fire.'
Hence he is a Fire-demon, fire having the same destructive
power as he delighted in. The name has also been derived
from Lucifer, a name of the devil, and his personality regarded
as a reflexion of the devil's.[28] Others connect it with *lúka*,
ljúka, ' to close,' ' to bring to an end,' *lók*, ' the end.' Hence
Loki would be ' the one who closes or brings to an end,' because
his deeds lead up to the end of all, the Doom of the gods.[29]
None of these meanings is quite satisfactory, though the suggestion that Loki was originally a Fire-demon has some evidence in its favour. His father is Farbauti, ' the dangerous
striker,' i.e., the storm; his mother is Laufey, ' the leafy isle,'
or Nal, ' needle,' the needle-tree or fir-tree. Loki is a creation
of the storm which, in lightning, brings down fire on the wooded
isle.[30] Or, again, referring to the primitive production of fire
by friction, by means of the fire-drill, Farbauti is the piece of
stick, the drill, which by rubbing on a soft piece of wood, Laufey,
produces fire.[31] Here, again, these meanings are problematical.

Loki's twofold nature is undoubted — he is tricky and destructive, yet he has the power to set things right. He is a friend
of the gods, yet he brings trouble upon them. In addition to
this, he appears in darker colours. He is father of monsters, a
base slanderer, the cause of Balder's death, a monster chained
under the earth, the leader of hosts of evil against the gods.
Thus, for some reason not known to us, Loki becomes monstrous and sinister, whereas he was merely mischievous at first.
If he was originally a Fire-demon, fire is both beneficent and
dangerous, and in this may be seen both the twofold aspect of
Loki's character, and also his later emphatically destructive
aspect. If he represents fire, then his giving vital heat to Ask
and Embla would be appropriate. Whether or not we are to
regard him as a spirit of fire, his twofold aspect, no less than
other traits, suggests the characteristics of elfin beings. These
other traits are shape-shifting, skill in theft, craft, and trickiness.
He is beautiful in form, but of evil nature. He travels swiftly

through the air either by means of bird's plumage or shoes by which he ran through air and over water.[32] He is chosen to go to the dwarfs' land in order to get them to forge Sif's hair. His conduct to these dwarfs is of an elfish kind. He is also associated with dwarfs in the making of Menglod's hall, and, like a dwarf, he forged the sword Lævateinn in the Underworld.[33]

We may thus conclude that Loki, whether originally an embodiment of fire or not, was a spirit of an elfin kind, raised to divinity and included among the Æsir, just as Æsir and elves are constantly named together. He was also an embodiment of the mischief-maker, so common in all states of society, whose mischief has often dire results for himself or others. He is like the Greek Thersites or the Conan of the Celtic Fionn saga.[34] Such persons were common in actual life: why should there not be one of them associated with the gods? If Loki was an elfin Fire-spirit, then he might have been regarded as personifying the volcanic fires known in Iceland. This has been already hinted at in the interesting interpretation of the milkmaid myth. Some later folk-lore is also thought to point to Loki's connexion with fire or heat. A Norse saying when the fire crackles is: ' Loki is beating his children,' and the skin of the milk is thrown into the fire as a dole. On hot days when the air shimmers, or in spring when the mists rise from the ground in the sunshine, a Danish saying is: ' Loki is driving out his goats.' The sun appearing through clouds and drawing up moisture seems to be referred to in the sayings: ' Loki drinks water,' or ' Loki is passing over the fields.' In Sweden when a little child's tooth falls out, it is thrown into the fire with the words: ' Lokke, Lokke, give me a bone tooth; here is a gold tooth.' In Iceland chips and refuse for firing are called ' Loki's chips,' and subterranean sulphur fumes ' Loki's vapour.' [35]

The elfish Loki rose in character and became the companion of gods. Olrik tried to trace different conceptions of Loki in myth and folk-lore. Thus he regarded him as in part a once beneficent being. As stealer of Brisinga-men he is the Prome-

thean stealer of fire for the benefit of mankind, this famous
jewel being supposed to represent fire (*brisingr*, ' fire '; * *brising*, ' bonfire '), though it is never stated that this necklace did
good to men.   Loki also invented the fishing-net — a myth
inserted in Snorri's account of his capture.[36]

The myth of Loki's binding and breaking loose before the
Doom of the gods has been by some traced to the account in
Revelation of Satan's binding and breaking out of the abyss.
But there may already have been in the North myths of a monstrous being bound under the earth, whose movements caused
earthquakes — a not uncommon myth.[37]   If such a being bore
a name resembling Loki's,[38] then the two would tend to be confused, and the elfish Loki would become more demoniacal and
monstrous, parent of monsters, foe of the gods, and cause of
Balder's death.   We have seen the close resemblance of the
Iranian myth of Azhi Dahaka, found also in Armenia,[39] to that
of Loki.   Olrik maintained that the Eddic myth of Loki chained
and breaking loose had its *provenance* in a series of myths of
giants or animals bound and causing earthquakes, found in the
Caucasus region and radiating forth in all directions.[40]   The
Iranian myth is one of the series, but such a myth may have
been native to Scandinavia.

If Loki owes some of his more monstrous traits to the early
medieval devil, he is, on the whole, an original figure of Norse
mythology, one of those beings who, possibly kindly in origin,
is dowered with a more complex character as time goes on, and
ends by being wholly sinister and monstrous.

Loki's wife Sigyn is counted among the goddesses: her function of guarding him from the venom of the snake may point to
her being a guardian-goddess against poison.   To the more
monstrous Loki the giantess Angrboda was joined and was the
mother of monsters.

CHAPTER XII

LESSER GODS

HŒNIR

NOTHING is known of a cult paid to this god, but what is said of him in the *Eddas* points to his being one of the older Æsir. Snorri gives no separate account of him, but mentions him mainly in connexion with other gods.[1] In *Voluspa* he is associated with Odin and Lodur in the creation of Ask and Embla, giving them soul or reason, and the three gods are called 'mighty and benevolent.' He is also joined with the same gods (if Lodur is Loki) in the stories of Idunn and of Andvari.[2] A ballad of the Faroe Islands introduces the same gods, calling them Ouvin, Honir, and Lokkji. A peasant had lost his son to a giant at a game of draughts, and prayed the three gods to help him. Ouvin made a field of barley spring up in a night, and hid the boy in an ear of the barley. When the giant cut this down, the ear fell from his hand and Ouvin brought back the boy to his father. Next Honir hid him in a feather on the neck of one of seven swans. The giant caught them, but the feather fell out and the boy escaped. Finally Lokkji changed him into an egg in a flounder's roe. This also escaped from the giant, who was slain by Lokkji. All this has been interpreted mythologically, but it is nothing more than the invention of a poet to whom the association of the three gods was known, making use also of a common folk-tale *motif*.[3]

This association of the gods is remembered by the skalds. Hœnir is 'bench-mate,' 'friend,' 'companion' of Odin, and Loki is Hœnir's 'companion' and 'staunch friend.' Snorri

calls Hœnir ' the swift god,' ' the long-footed god,' and ' king
of clay ' or ' moisture,' or, as some interpret the Norse words,
' king of eld ' (*aur-konúng*).[4]   What lies behind these titles
is unknown, and the myths which may have given rise to them
have not survived.   In a Saga fragment Hœnir is called ' the
most timorous ' of the Æsir.' [5] This may refer to the account
of his being sent as a hostage to the Vanir, when his apparent
goodliness proved illusory, as already narrated.[6]   In this story
he is a big, handsome being, but stupid, unlike the Hœnir who
gave reason to Ask and Embla.

   After the Doom of the gods, Hœnir survives and appears in
the renewed world.   There he chooses the *hlaut-viþr*, i.e., a
slip of wood with runes engraved on it.[7]   This perhaps signifies
his knowledge of the future.

HEIMDALL

   Heimdall (ON Heimdallr) is an enigmatic being, and he has
been regarded as a mere creation of the skalds, a poetic form of
the old Heaven-god.   But this is to over-emphasize the poverty
of Teutonic polytheism, as well as the argument from silence.
Though enigmatic, Heimdall stands out as an actual mythic
being.

   Heimdall, called also Vindler, is included among the Æsir
by Snorri and in *Grimnismal:* he is ' of the race of the gods,'
according to *Hyndluljod*, and a son of Odin.[8]   In the Eddic
poems he is ' whitest of the gods,' and, like the Vanir, he knows
the future.   His abode is in Himinbjorg, where in a pleasant
house, he, the watchman of the gods, drinks mead.   The name
Himinbjorg, ' Heaven mountain,' is still used in Norway for a
steep mountain sloping down into the sea.   Heimdall is ' the
man mighty in arms,' and, as watchman of the gods, he has a
horn, the Gjallar-horn, which meanwhile rests under the ash
Yggdrasil, if the *Voluspa* poet is not here making it take the
place of Odin's eye.   It is curious that the divine watchman's

horn should not be beside him. Before the Doom of the gods, this horn will be blown as a warning.[9]

The human race, high and low, are Heimdall's children, or, as in *Rigsthula*, where he is called Rig, he is ancestor of the jarls, yeomen, and thralls. He went along the shore and came to a dwelling, where he called himself Rig. There he begat a son Thrœll on his hostess Edda, and he was the first of the thralls. Then he went to another house, where Amma bore to him Karl, the first of the yeomen or karls. In a third dwelling he was received by Fathir and Mothir, and the latter became by him mother of Jarl, the first of the jarls. As Rig, Heimdall is called the brave, old, wise god, the bold, robust walker, and he knows well to speak wise words. Heimdall is ' the kinsman of men,' endowed with unusual strength, and is celebrated in weapons. He is son of nine giantesses, Gjolp, Greip, Eistla, Eyrgjafa, Ulfrun, Angeyja, Imd, Atla, and Jarnsaxa. This account of his parentage is given in *Hyndluljod*, and by the skald Ulf Uggason, as well as in a fragment of the lost *Heimdalar-galdr*, cited by Snorri: —

> ' I am the offspring of nine mothers,
>   Of nine sisters am I the son.' [10]

In *Lokasenna* Heimdall opposes Loki, and is told by him to be silent, for in the old time an evil fate was fixed for him. Now he must stand with stiff neck and keep guard as watcher of the gods.[11] We have already seen how he advised Thor to disguise himself as Freyja and thus go to the giant Thrym.

Snorri combines much of this and gives further details about Heimdall. He is ' the white god,' great and holy, born of nine sisters. He is also called Hallinskidi, ' ram ' (?), and Gullintani, ' Golden teeth.' His horse is Gulltopp, ' Gold top,' on which he rode at Balder's funeral. He dwells in Himin-bjorg, close by Bifrost, at the end of Heaven by the bridge head, where Bifrost joins Heaven. He is warder of the gods, and sits there to guard the bridge from the Hill-giants. Less sleep does he need than a bird; by night or day he sees equally well a hundred leagues; he hears grass growing on earth and wool on sheep, as well as everything that has a louder sound. He has the Gjallar-horn, the blast of which is heard through all worlds.[12]

The statements regarding Heimdall as watchman of the gods point to the reality of his personality. The dualistic form of Eddic mythology — gods opposed by giants — may early have suggested this need of watchfulness, therefore of a watchman ever guarding the frontier of the gods' realm from the approach of their enemies, just as a watchman was needed against enemies among men. For this reason it is said of him that he needs little sleep, though this, as well as his miraculous sight and hearing, belongs to universal folk-tale formulae. Such powers are distributed among various beings who help a hero in his adventures.[13] This ' white god ' or ' whitest of the gods ' may be a god of light, light being essential to such functions as his.

As son of nine giantesses, perhaps the nine daughters of Ægir and Ran, who are the waves, though their names differ, he was born at the edge of the world. If we regard these giantesses as personifications of the waves, or, possibly, of mountains, Heimdall might be regarded as a personification of the day dawning out of the sea or over the mountains that look down upon it. Another suggestion regarding his birth is that the myth alludes to nine reincarnations of the god.[14]

The skalds called a sword ' Heimdall's head,' ' for it is said that he was pierced by a man's head.' This was told in the lost *Heimdalar-galdr*, and since then a head was called ' Heimdall's fate,' and a sword ' man's fate.' Heimdall's sword was also called ' head.' [15] Does this mean that there was some myth of Heimdall's having been slain by a head, or is it merely an obscure way of referring to his death at the future Doom when he and Loki slay each other? If the former, then Heimdall must have been reborn, for he is still to die at the last battle, and this would lend support to the theory of his nine reincarnations.

In *Hyndluljod* it is said of his ninefold birth that he was nourished ' with the strength of earth, with the ice-cold sea, and with the blood of swine.' As Heimdall was born at the world's edge, i.e., where sea and land meet, this may account for the reference to earth and sea, while ' the blood of swine ' would mean sacrificial blood. The lines are believed by some editors to have been transferred to *Hyndluljod* from *Guthrunarkvitha* where earth, sea, and swine's blood are components of the magic drink given by Grimhild to Gudrun.[16]

Heimdall is called ' the foe of Loki,' ' the seeker of Freyja's necklace,' ' the frequenter of Vagasker and Singasteinn, where he fought with Loki for the necklace Brisinga-men.' According to Ulf Uggason's *Husdrapa*, Heimdall and Loki were then in the form of seals, and Snorri quotes some lines of the poem which refer to this without throwing much light upon it.[17] Loki must have stolen and hid the necklace, perhaps in some cliff by the sea, and he and Heimdall, transformed to seals, fought for it, and Heimdall apparently recovered it. Examples of such transformation combats occur in Celtic and other mythologies. The enmity between Loki and Heimdall culminates at the Doom of the gods when each slays the other.

As men are ' Heimdall's sons,' as he is ' kinsman of men and of all rulers,' and ' holds sway over men,' Heimdall is in some sense regarded as creator or progenitor as well as ruler of men and orderer of their classes.[18] In the prose Introduction to *Rigsthula*, probably later than the poem itself, Rig (from Old Irish *rig*, ' king ') is identified with Heimdall, and it is said that ' old stories ' tell the narrative which is the subject of the poem. Some critics think that Odin, not Heimdall, is Rig. While this is possible, the references in the other Eddic poems to Heimdall in relation to men, support the identification of the Introduction. In the third son, Jarl, Rig took peculiar interest, calling him by his name, Rig-Jarl, teaching him runes, and bidding him possess his wide heritage. The poem serves as a eulogy of kingship, and to trace the descent of a royal house to a god.

Grimm compared Heimdall at Heaven's bridge to the angel guarding Paradise with a sword, and his horn blown before the Doom to the trumpet blown by the angel at the Last Day. Heimdall's strife with Loki is a parallel to that of Michael and Satan. Such Christian conceptions might have influenced the myth of Heimdall, but granting a bridge from Heaven to earth and an expected attack on the gods' abode, nothing is more likely than that it should have a divine watchman with a horn.[19]

Of a cult of Heimdall nothing is known, though his name occurs in certain place-names.

ULL

Ull (ON Ullr) was son of Thor's wife Sif by an unknown father, and stepson of Thor, called ' Ull's glorious step-sire ' and his kinsman.[20] He is fair of face and has all the accomplishments of a warrior, therefore men do well to call on him in single combats. He is so excellent a bowman and snow-shoe runner that none may vie with him. Hence he is called ' Snow-shoe-god,' ' Bow-god,' ' Hunting-god,' and ' Shield-god.' This is Snorri's account of him.[21] His ring is mentioned in *Atlakvitha* as that on which oaths were taken, probably a ring attached to or laid on an altar-stone, and the custom of swearing on such a ring is mentioned in Sagas. Odin singles out Ull by name along with the gods when he is bound between two fires, as recounted in *Grimnismal:*

> ' Ull's favour and that of all gods
>   Has he, who first in the fire will reach;
>   The dwelling can be seen by the sons of the gods,
>   If one takes the kettle from its hook.' [22]

Odin here refers to the torments he is suffering between the fires. Let some one draw away the kettle from its hook and the gods will be able to look down through the roof-opening which served as a chimney, and see his perilous position.

Ull dwells in Ydalir, ' Yew-dales,' an appropriate place for a god of the bow, since bows were made of yew. One manuscript of Snorri's *Edda*, in the passage which tells of the steeds of the gods, says that Ull had many horses.[23]

Ull's name means ' the lordly,' ' the majestic,' and is the equivalent of Gothic *wulþus*, ' glory.' The few notices regarding him suggest his former importance, waning before that of other gods. Many place-names, especially in Sweden, contain his name, and show that his cult was widespread.[24] As Snow-shoe-god Ull's original sphere would be the more northerly parts of Scandinavia, unless he is to be regarded as ruling more particularly in winter. He has been regarded as a Finnish god, or a god worshipped in the region where Finns and Scandinavians mingled. Skadi, who may have been a Finnish goddess, is also characterized by her snow-shoes. Ull would thus be her male counterpart. The shield, according to the skalds, was ' the ship of Ull,' [25] that on which he travelled — a reference to a lost myth, though *skjold*, ' shield,' may be an error for *skid*, ' snow-shoe,' the snow-shoes on which he journeyed over the snow-fields. An interesting comment on this skaldic periphrasis, which may point to its origin in folk-custom, is found in what Plutarch says of the Cimbri, when opposing the Romans in the Alps. They climbed to the tops of the hills and, placing their broad shields under their bodies, let themselves slide down the slopes — a primitive kind of toboggan.[26] Ollerus in Saxo, the equivalent of Ull, used a bone marked with runes to travel overseas, and quickly passed over the waters. This seems to mingle the travelling on skates made of bone with the skaldic conception of the shield as a ship.[27]

Ull took Odin's place when he went into exile and bore his name, as Saxo relates. This points to his high place, as does also the phrase ' Ull and all the gods ' in *Grimnismal*, where he is singled out by name as if of great importance. That he, as the glorious god, was a form of Tiuz, ousted by Odin, is doubtful. More likely he was a native Scandinavian, possibly Finnish, god, whose place and cult were taken by Odin — a fact indicated in Saxo's story of Odin and Ollerus.

Recent research in Scandinavian place-names has caused some scholars to see in Ull and Frey a pair of alternating divine brothers, gods of fertility. They are believed to have been worshipped on two hills near Leira in Sjællend — the place where a nine-yearly sacrifice formerly took place. These hills are the Hyldehög and Frijszhög, and their popular names as recorded three centuries ago, point to the belief that Ull and Frey were buried there. These twin gods were associated in a fertility cult with goddesses, and the cult seems to have contained the representation of a ritual marriage. On a rock called Ullaber (? Ullarberg) near Ullensvang, within recent times a gathering was held on Midsummer Day and a girl was dressed up as a bride.[28] The close connexion in one stanza of *Grimnismal* between Ull's abode, Ydalir, and Frey's, Alfheim, whereas those of other deities have each one stanza allotted to them, has also led to the supposition of a connexion between Ull and Frey.[29]

VIDARR

Vidarr is 'the silent god,' a son of Odin, 'Sigfather's mighty son.' His mother is the giantess Grid, whom Thor visited on his way to Geirrod's land. Vidarr is nearly as strong as Thor, and the gods trust him in all struggles, for he is their avenger. Snorri says that he is 'the divine dweller in the homesteads of the fathers.'[30] But *Grimnismal* speaks of his abode thus:

> ' Underwood and luxuriant grass
>   Fills Vidi, Vidarr's land;
>   There springs the youth from the back of his horse
>   Ready to avenge his father.'[31]

The latter part of the stanza refers to Vidarr's deed at the Doom of the gods.

As one of the Æsir present at Ægir's banquet, Vidarr was bidden by Odin to rise up and let Loki sit down in order that he might not speak words of contempt. Vidarr obeyed and presented Loki with a cup of ale.[32] He is the one god present who escapes the acid of Loki's biting tongue.

At the Doom of the gods, after the Fenris-wolf swallows Odin, Vidarr speeds to meet him and thrusts his sword into the monster's heart, thus avenging Odin. Snorri quotes this notice from *Voluspa*, but himself gives a different account. He has told how Vidarr has a thick shoe, hence he is 'possessor of the iron shoe.' When Odin met his fate, Vidarr strode forth and set one foot — that on which he wears the shoe — on the lower jaw of the wolf. With one hand he seized the upper jaw, and tore the two apart, killing the monster. This agrees with *Vafthrudnismal:* 'He will tear the jaws of the wolf, so that he will die.' Hence Vidarr is called 'Foe and slayer of Fenris-wolf,' and 'Avenger of the gods.'[33] With Vali, he survives the conflict, unharmed by the sea and Surt's fire, and dwells in Ithavoll.[34]

Though Snorri speaks of Vidarr's shoe as of iron, he gives another description of it, taken from folk-belief. The materials for this shoe have been gathering through the ages, the scraps of leather cut by men from their shoes at heel or toe. He who desires to aid the gods should throw these scraps away. This tradition, which resembles that about the ship Naglfar, formed from dead mens' nails, must be based on some folk-custom.[35]

Out of these sparse data and from the supposed source of the god's name, whether from *vid*, 'forest,' or from Vidi, the plain on which he dwelt, elaborate conceptions of Vidarr have been formed. Kauffmann says: 'In the dark solitude of the forest the silent god watches over order and justice in the lives of the gods and men. He is the guardian of peace, and as such the appointed judge of those who disturb it.' He is the god who lives 'untouched by wrong; silent and aloof he dwells, far from all crime, the lord of righteousness. . . . His temple among the Norwegians, as among the German tribe of the Semnones in the time of Tacitus, was the forest with its darkness and awe. In him we recognize the *Deus Requalivahanus*, " the god dwelling in darkness." ' Kauffmann also identifies Vidarr with Heimdall and Hœnir, all forms of one and the same god.[36]

On the other hand Rœdiger regards Vidarr as the god of the heath-land, wide-spreading, silent, remote. He is a divine personification of the heath with its brooding silence and its undergrowth, its thick grassy and mossy surface, symbolized by the indestructible shoe.[37]

While the ingenuity of these views does credit to the mythopœic faculty of their authors, they are entirely hypothetical as far as Scandinavian mythology is concerned.

Although no proof of a cult of Vidarr exists, here again the god's name is found in place-names — Vidarshof, Vidarsgarth, and the like.[38]

BRAGI

Bragi, Odin's son and husband of Idunn, is famous for wisdom, and especially for fluency and skill in speech. He knows most of skaldic art (*skaldskap*), and hence, says Snorri, this art is called after him, *bragr*, and the man or woman who excels in it is called ' *bragr*-man ' or ' -woman.' The word, *bragr*, however, which means both ' skaldic art ' and ' the foremost,' is not derived from Bragi's name. Snorri gives the kennings for Bragi — ' Husband of Idunn,' ' First maker of poetry,' ' the Long-bearded god ' (hence a long-bearded man was called ' *skegg-* ' or ' beard-Bragi ').[39]

In the Eddic poems Bragi is mentioned thrice. He is ' best of skalds '; runes are said to be carved on his tongue; both he and Idunn were guests at Ægir's banquet. When Loki re-entered the hall, Bragi said that the gods would never give him a place at their board. Odin, on the ground of their pact of brotherhood, permitted Loki to have a place, and Loki bade all the gods ' Hail,' but excepted Bragi by name. Bragi said that

he would give him a horse and sword from his hoard, and a
ring, if he would refrain from making mischief among the gods.
Loki said that he had none of these things, and that of all present he was the most cowardly in fight and most afraid of darts.
Bragi retorted that were he outside the hall he would carry
away Loki's head in his hand as a punishment for lying. Loki
taunted him with being valiant on his bench, and ironically
called him ' the bench-gracing Bragi.' If he is angry, let him
fight: a bold man does not sit considering. Idunn now inter-
vened, and said that Bragi was drunk with ale.[40] Whether
Loki's accusation was based on a lost myth is unknown.

Critics maintain that Bragi was a creation of the skalds or
actually the poet Bragi Boddason (*c.* 800 A.D.) thus apotheo-
sized by them and regarded as Odin's son. This Bragi was
most noted of all skalds; though, on the other hand, he himself has been regarded as mythical! In *Eiriksmal* (*c.* 935)
Bragi, the god or the poet, is Odin's favourite poet. He won-
ders at the noise of a host approaching Valhall and thinks that
it must be Balder returning. In *Hakonarmal* Odin bids Bragi
and Hermod go forth to meet the dead Hakon and invite him to
enter Valhall. Bragi tells him how his brothers await him in
Odin's hall and invests him with its honours.[41]

On the whole, Bragi may be regarded as distinct from the
poet of that name. He would be worshipped by skalds as god
of poetry, like Ogma among the Irish Celts and his counterpart
Ogmios among the Gauls.[42] As god of poetry, he takes Odin's
place, for to him this function was attributed, and as ' the long-
bearded god ' (*sidskeggia ás*) he resembles him, for Odin himself was called Sidskegg and Langbard. In Odin's court this
divine skald, whose personality is at least so well marked as to
be assigned Idunn for a consort (after slaying her brother — a
myth referred to in *Lokasenna*,[43] but otherwise unknown),
has the same place as the skald at a king's court, and he greets
the heroic dead who enter it. His eloquence is emphasized by
Snorri, and he is the narrator in *Bragarædur* and *Skaldskapar-*

mal. In the first he discusses the poetic art and its origin; in the second he shows how poetry should be composed and tells a number of myths. The wood called Braga-lund in *Helgi Hundingsbana* is ' Bragi's wood.' [44]

The cup drunk by the heir at a feast after the death of a king or jarl and in his memory, was called *bragar-full,* ' cup of the foremost,' i.e., of kings or jarls. Drinking it, an oath was taken by the heir, and he was then conducted to his father's seat. The same name was given to the cup drunk at sacrificial feasts, after those drunk to Odin, Frey, and Njord. A vow was made to perform some great deed which might become the theme of song.[45] In *Helgakvitha Hjorvardssonar* Hedin refused an offer made to him by a troll-wife on Yule-eve, and she said: ' Thou shalt pay for this when thou emptiest the *bragar-full.*' That night he vowed at the drinking of the cup to possess Svava, the beloved of Helgi, but repented this so bitterly that he left home and wandered through wild regions.[46] The name of this cup is sometimes connected with that of Bragi, as if it had been drunk in his honour, but it is rather derived from *bragr* in the sense of ' the foremost ' or ' the best,' i.e., king, chief, or hero.

FORSETI

Forseti, ' the President,' ' he who has the first seat,' the right-speaking god, is son of Balder and Nanna. His hall is called Glitnir, ' the Glittering '; it rests on golden pillars and the roof is decked with silver. There he dwells and sits in judgment, reconciling those who are at strife, and who come before him with quarrels arising out of lawsuits. He was thus a god of justice, one to whom the disputes of men must in some way have been submitted. The place-name in Norway, Forsete-lund, ' Forseti's grove,' preserves his name, and points to a seat of his cult.[47]

The Frisians worshipped a god Fosite, who had a temple on the sacred island of Helgoland or Fositesland. Cattle grazing

near it or anything about it might not be touched, and water
from the sacred stream must be drawn in silence. Any one pro-
faning the temple was sacrificed to the god, according to the
Frisian folk-law. S. Boniface had striven to convert the
Frisians, but the heathen among them had put him to death.
His successors carried on his work, but found the Frisians jeal-
ous of their temples, sacred springs, and holy places in woods
fields, or moorlands. In the early years of the eighth century,
Willibrord, when in Helgoland, baptized some of the people in
Fosite's spring. His companions slew some of the sacred animals. The anger of the people was roused: one of the party
was offered in sacrifice, and the rest sent back into Frankish
territory.[48]

Fosite is assumed to be the same as Forseti, and his cult to
have passed from the Frisians to the Norsemen, who had relations with them. The Norse poets then made him son of
Balder.

A curious story is connected by some students with this god.
Charlemagne desired the twelve Asegen from the seven Frisian
Seelands to tell him what the Frisian law was. They declared
that they could not do this, and asked for two days respite, and
then for three more. At the end of this time, being still unable
to obey the command, they were doomed to punishment, but
received the choice of death, slavery, or being set in a ship without sails or rudder. They chose the last, and one of them proposed to call on God for help. As Christ had appeared to His
disciples through closed doors, so He would send one who
would teach them what the law was and bring them to land.
They prayed, and now a thirteenth person was seen among
them, with an axe on his shoulder. By its means he steered the
ship to land. He threw the axe on the shore and there a well
began to spring forth. Hence this place was called Axenthove.
Then the stranger taught them the law and vanished. They
now returned to Charlemagne and told him what the law was.[49]
This mysterious personage who thus revealed the Frisian law

is presumed to have been Fosite, giver of law and justice, though the axe would rather suggest Donar.

VALI

Vali or Ali, called 'brother of the Æsir,' is son of Odin and the giantess Rind, who is counted as one of the goddesses by Snorri. Vali is described as daring in fight and a clever marksman. Like Vidarr he is said to be 'a dweller in the homesteads of the fathers.'[50] He was born expressly to avenge Balder's death. In *Baldrs Draumar* the seeress says to Odin:

> 'Rind bears Vali in the western halls,
> When one night old will Odin's son fight.
> His head he will not comb nor his hand wash
> Till Balder's foe is laid on the pyre.'

Voluspa also says of him that 'Balder's brother is soon born,' and repeats in almost identical words the passage in *Baldrs Draumar*. The Lesser *Voluspa* in *Hyndluljod* speaks of Vali as swift to avenge Balder's death, when he slew his brother's slayer. Hence, as Snorri says, Vali is called 'Balder's avenger,' 'Foe and slayer of Hod.'[51]

The *Eddas* relate nothing further of Vali's origin nor of his act of blood-revenge. In Saxo Vali is called Bous, and the blood-vengeance is long delayed. Bous dies of a wound received in his fight with Hotherus.[52]

The passages cited from the *Edda* suggest that while Balder's corpse was still on the pyre, his slayer's body was laid beside it. On the other hand, the vengeance seems to be delayed — Vali accomplishes it when one night old, but does not cut his hair or wash his hand till it is completed. The latter points to a period of waiting, and is the heroic aspect of an oath of blood-revenge or of the intention to do a doughty deed. The infant hero who arrives quickly at maturity and vigour is a commonplace of folk-tale and hero-tale — as with the heroes Cúchulainn, Fionn, Magni, son of Thor, Apollo, etc.[53]

Detter and Neckel explain Vali's name as derived from Wanilo, ' the little Van,' as if he were one of the Vanir, while Neckel assumes that Vali was the avenger, not of Balder, but of his father Frey. Such attempts at explaining away the statements of the *Edda* are futile. Sievers' derivation of Vali from * *vanula,* 'shining,' does not agree with anything told of this god.[54]

Vali takes no part in the strife at the Doom of the gods, but in the renewed world he shares with Vidarr the seats of the gods. While Vidarr and Vali are sons of Odin by giantesses; avengers, one of Odin, the other of Balder; and sharers of the blissful future, they are not necessarily identical, as has been maintained. That both are later creations of poetic fancy, i.e., to fit into the Doom drama, is possible.

In *Svipdagsmal* the dead Groa recites protective charms to her son, among others one that Rind sang to Ran. Ran is here not the Sea-goddess, but, as the parallel demands, a hero and even a son of Rind. Hence Ran is assumed to be another name for Vali. The *Eddas* say little of Rind, but from the Swedish place-name Vrindravi, ' Rind's sanctuary,' it is believed that she must have been the object of a cult.[55]

HOD

Hod (ON Hǫþr), whose name nears ' war,' ' battle,' is son of Odin, and is of great strength. He is the blind god among the Æsir. Gods and men would desire him not to be named, for the work of his hands will be long remembered.[56] This work was Balder's death: hence he is ' Balder's opponent,' ' Balder's murderer.' [57] Snorri tells how Loki caused Hod to slay Balder. Of Vali's vengeance upon Hod, no myth has survived, and it is possible that in the earlier form of the Balder story, Loki was not the cause of Hod's slaying Balder. Loki does not appear in Saxo's version of the story, as we have seen.

The *Voluspa* poet and Snorri tell how Hod will sit down with Balder in peace in the renewed world.[58]

One of the periphrases for Balder is ' Hod's adversary,' [59] and this agrees with Saxo's story, in which Balder was adversary of Hotherus (Hod), who is here a hero and king of Sweden, not a god. The kennings for Hod were ' the blind god,' ' thrower of the mistletoe,' ' companion of Hel,' ' foe of Vali.' [60]

A curious theory of Detter's as explaining the Balder myth is that Hod was really Odin. Balder and Vali were brothers, connected with Frey, Vali being ' the little Van,' one of the Vanir. Odin, the one-eyed or blind god of war, sought to cause strife between the brothers. He placed his spear in the form of a mistletoe-twig in Vali's hand. Vali threw it at Balder, who was slain.[61]

CHAPTER XIII

MIMIR

AMONG Water-spirits Mimir is supreme and has a prominent position in the Eddic poems. If not a god, he is
brought into close contact with gods, especially Odin, whose
uncle he may have been.[1]

In the *Voluspa* Odin pledged his eye with Mimir, presumably to obtain secret knowledge from him. The eye is hidden
in Mimir's well, and Mimir daily drinks mead out of Odin's
pledge. But in another stanza a stream is said to issue from this
pledge and it waters the tree Mjotvid, which Snorri, in his
reference to this verse, takes to be Yggdrasil. Mimir's well is
thus under the tree, the well which in verse 19 is called ' Urd's
well.' The redactor of the poem which spoke of Odin's eye
given as a pledge and hidden in a well beneath the tree which
was watered by it, has added a new and contradictory verse.
The well is that of the Water-spirit Mimir, and he daily drinks
from this eye. As Boer says: the redactor ' replaces the clear
nature picture (of Odin giving a pledge in return for something
else; i.e., water, which falls on the tree) with a meaningless one,
that of Mimir drinking from the pledge.'[2] The pledge, Odin's
eye, is generally regarded as the sun, the eye of the Heaven-
god, seen reflected in the water or sinking into the sea — phenomena which may have given rise to the myth. Where the
redactor speaks of Mimir's drinking from this pledge, it is
thought of as a cup or shell — a quite different myth from that
of the eye.

From Snorri's account of this myth, Mimir's well is under
that root of the ash Yggdrasil which turns towards the Frost-

giants. In it wisdom and understanding are stored. Mimir keeps the well and is full of ancient lore, because he drinks of the well from the Gjallar-horn. Odin came and craved one draught of the well, but did not obtain it till he had given his eye in pledge. Then Snorri quotes the *Voluspa* stanza which tells how Mimir drinks from Odin's pledge.[3] This contradicts what has just been said about the Gjallar-horn. There must have been different versions of the myth of Odin's eye and of Mimir's relation to it.

In *Svipdagsmal* Mimameid, 'the tree of Mimir,' is given as a name of the world-tree.[4]

At the Doom of the gods Mimir's sons, i.e., the rivers and brooks, are in violent motion.[5]

Another aspect of Mimir is given in *Vafthrudnismal*. Mimir, called Hoddmimer, ' Hill-Mimir ' or ' Mimir of the treasure,' is owner of a wood ('Hoddmimer's holt '), and in it are hidden a human pair, Lif and Lifthrasir ('Life' and 'He who holds fast to life '). They survive the terrible Fimbul-winter at the end of the world. Meanwhile they feed on morning-dew, and from them come the folk who will people the renewed earth. According to Snorri, who quotes this verse, this human pair lie hidden in the holt during the fire of Surt.[6] Whether this holt or grove is identical with the world-tree is not clear. It may have been regarded as existing underground at its roots where Mimir's fountain was.

Another series of Mimir myths is connected with his head, cut off by the Vanir, as already told.[7] Odin smeared it with worts that it should not rot, and sang words of magic (*galdra*) over it, and gave it such might that it told him of hidden matters. In *Sigrdrifumal* the Valkyrie Sigrdrifa instructs Sigurd in the wisdom of runes, and she says that he must learn 'thought-runes' which Hropt (Odin) devised from the fluid which 'dropped from Heiddraupnir's head and from Hoddrof-nir's horn.' These are evidently names of Mimir. Then she continues:

'On the hill he stood with Brimir's edge, [a sword]
 His helmet was on his head;
Then spake for the first time wise Mimir's head;
 Giving utterance to true words.'

These were now carved on various objects. The occasion of this incident is unknown.[8] *Voluspa* tells how, at the approach of the Doom of the gods, Odin spoke with Mimir's head, obviously seeking its advice. The poet must thus have known the myth of the cutting off of the head, but forgot what he had already told of Mimir himself. Snorri, who quotes this stanza of *Voluspa*, gives a different turn to it in his prose narrative. Odin rides to Mimir's well and takes counsel of Mimir himself, not of his head.[9]

Mimir's head may at first have been nothing more than the source of the stream of which he was the guardian spirit or in which he dwelt, the source being the stream's 'head,' or 'Mimir's head,' and the name afterwards taken literally. An explanatory myth was then supplied, as well as stories of the wisdom-giving head which are not without parallels in Scandinavian custom and belief. In the *Eyrbyggja-saga* Freysten found a skull lying loose and uncovered on a scree called Geirvor. It sang a stave foretelling bloodshed at this spot and that men's skulls would lie there.[10] This was deemed a great portent.

Mimir's connexion with Odin is shown by the title given to the latter by the skald Egill Skallagrimsson — 'Mimir's friend.'[11]

Mimir's name in its different Eddic forms — Mimir, Mim, Mimi — is connected with words meaning 'mindful,' 'to brood over,' and it seems to have meant 'the thinking one.' Inspiration, knowledge, prophecy were often associated with springs and streams, or with the spirits inhabiting them, and of these Mimir is an example, raised to a high place in Scandinavian myth. The name occurs in place-names of rivers, etc., in Germany (Mimling) and Sweden (Mimeså near the Mimessjö), as well as in personal names, and bears witness to the widespread belief in a Water-spirit bearing this name.[12]

In the *Thidriks-saga* Mimir the smith is Siegfried's master in smith-craft, as he is of Velint (Volund) in the *Vilkina-saga*, and in both he has supernatural attributes and possesses a wonderful sword. The Miming of Saxo's Balder story, called *satyrus silvarum*, has also a magic sword and a magic bracelet which increases its owner's wealth, like the ring Draupnir. The German hero-saga *Biterolf* speaks of Mime the old, a clever master-smith, who made the best swords that the world has ever seen.[13]

Saxo's Miming, *satyrus silvarum*, might be a dwarf or a Wood-spirit, and the smiths who bear the name Mimir have elfin traits. Whether they are identical with the Eddic Mimir is uncertain. An elfin or dwarfish Wood-spirit, clever at smith-work, and full of wisdom, might also be connected with wells or springs, found often in forests. If they are all identical, we see how, all over the Teutonic area, one out of the host of spirits of the woods and waters rose to pre-eminence. Mimir as a Water-spirit was known in late Swedish folk-lore, haunting the Mimeså.[14]

In Snorri's list of giants, Mimir is given as a giant's name, though the notices of him do not suggest a giant personality. But if the son of Bolthorn, who gave Odin nine mighty songs, was Mimir, then he was at least a giant's son. Mimir would then be the brother of Bestla, Odin's mother.[15]

CHAPTER XIV

ÆGIR

ÆGIR is god of the sea (*ægir*, 'sea') or rather a Sea-giant. In primitive thought the sea was regarded as a mighty being, which was personified or regarded as more or less distinct from the sea. The kennings for Ægir show that, even in late times, there was not a clear distinction between sea (*ægir*) and Sea-god (Ægir). Snorri says that *sæ*, 'sea,' is called 'husband of Ran, 'visitor of the gods,' father of Ægir's daughters,' 'land of Ran.'[1] The skald Ref speaks of 'Ægir's wide jaws,' as if the sea itself was a vast being. Into these jaws Ran wiles the ships.[2] Ægir, the personal name, or *ægir*, 'sea,' is connected with Gothic *ahva*, Latin *aqua*, ON *á*, 'water,' 'river.' The ON name of the river Eider (Egidora), Ægisdyr, is literally 'door of the sea.'[3]

Ægir is also called Gymir in the Introduction to *Lokasenna* and in skaldic verse. Ran, his wife, is 'Gymir's Volva'; the breakers or the murmur of the sea are 'Gymir's song'; the sea is 'Gymir's dwelling.'[4] Ægir's father is Fornjot, a giant, who is also father of wind and fire.[5]

Though on the whole depicted as a friend of the gods in the *Eddas*, Ægir is of the giant folk. His name is given in Snorri's list of giants,[6] and *Hymiskvitha* calls him *bergbui* and *jötun*, and describes him sitting 'merry as a child' (*barnteitr*) like other giants. Why the sea should be a Mountain-giant (*bergbui*) is not clear. Kindly and good-humoured, Ægir represents the peaceful rather than the stormy sea.

The gods feasted in Ægir's halls. *Hymiskvitha* opens by describing a feast at which the gods found the ale scanty. They consulted the divining-twigs and the blood and found that there was abundance in Ægir's dwelling. Thor bade Ægir furnish a banquet for them, but Ægir, in order to cause trouble, said that Thor must procure a vessel large enough to brew ale for all the gods. This is introductory to the story of Thor's adventure with the giant Hymir to whom he goes to procure this vessel.

Lokasenna continues the story. Ægir prepared the banquet in his halls, and to it came many gods and elves. The ale served itself and the banquet was proceeding gaily, but the gods praised Ægir's servants, Fimafeng and Eldir, for their cleverness, and this annoyed Loki, who slew Fimafeng. The bulk of the poem is taken up with Loki and his slanders of the gods and goddesses. Ægir takes no part in this: only at the end, ere Loki goes away, does he address Ægir:

> ' Ale hast thou brewed, O Ægir,
> But nevermore wilt thou prepare a banquet.
> All thy possessions flames shall play over,
> Fire shall burn thy back,'

i.e., the fire which is to consume the world.

In explaining why gold is called ' Ægir's fire,' Snorri speaks of this banquet. Ægir had gone to Asgard to a feast and, on leaving, invited Odin and the Æsir to visit him three months hence. When the guests (all but Thor) had assembled, Loki bandied sharp words with the gods and slew Fimafeng.[7] Nothing further is told by Snorri of the banquet, and neither here nor in the story of Thor and Hymir does he speak of the mighty vessel.

Lokasenna tells how, in place of fire, bright gold served to give light in Ægir's hall. Snorri enlarges upon this. Ægir caused bright gold to be brought in and set on the floor. It illumined the hall and served as lights at the banquet. Hence gold is called ' fire,' ' light,' or ' brightness ' of Ægir, of Ran, or of Ægir's daughters. Gold is also ' fire of the sea.'[8] As Ægir seems to personify the calm sea, the brilliant gleam of the sun on its surface may have given rise to these kennings and to the myth of the light-giving gold in his hall.

As brewer of ale for his banquet to the gods, Ægir is called by Egill ' ale-brewer of all the gods,' and as one present at their banquets he is ' the visitor of the gods.' [9]

Ægir also bears the name Hler, and the island Hlesey (Hler's island, Læsö in the Kattegat) was his dwelling. Snorri begins his *Bragarædur* with this statement, making Ægir a man versed in magic. He visits the gods in Asgard and partakes of their banquet, and as he sits next to Bragi, he learns many things from him of the doings of the Æsir and the methods of skaldic art. Hler may have been a local name of the Sea-giant in Denmark and in the west of Norway. In different accounts Hler alternates with Ægir as Fornjot's son, who rules the sea.[10] Hler may also be the giant Læ who dwells in Læsö according to the *Annales Lundenses*, or, as in another account, Olaus' *Chronica regum Danorum*, a Hill-giant or troll, with many heads, dwelling within the rocks.[11]

CHAPTER XV

FRIGG

THE name of Frigg, Odin's consort, OHG Frija, Lombard Frea, AS Frig (cf. Sanskrit *préya*, 'wife'), means 'the beloved,' 'the wife.' Odin is 'the dweller in Frigg's bosom' and 'Frigg's beloved.'[1] Snorri makes her daughter of Fjorgyn, but in *Lokasenna* Fjorgyn is her husband, i.e., Odin. From them are descended the races of the Æsir.[2] She is called 'mother of Balder,' 'co-wife of Jord, Rind, Gunnlod, and Grid,' and she is 'lady of the Æsir and Asynjur.'[3] As foremost of the goddesses and always heading the lists of these, she has the hall Fensalir, 'Sea-hall,' which is most glorious, but she shares Hlidskjalf with Odin.[4] She speaks no prophecy, yet she knows the fates of men.[5] Like Freyja she has hawk's plumage, and is called 'mistress of the hawk's plumage.'[6]

Others of the goddesses are associated with Frigg — Fulla, Gna, Hlin, Lofn, either as her servants or hypostases of herself, creations of the skalds. From what is said of her and of these other goddesses, Frigg may be regarded as a genial, kindly divinity, promoter of marriage and fruitfulness, helper of mankind and dispenser of gifts. She stands beside Freyja as one to whom prayers were made.[7] She was invoked by the childless, e.g., king Rerir and his queen prayed for offspring to the gods, and Frigg heard them as well as Odin.[8]

In her hall Fensalir, Frigg wept bitterly for Valhall's need as a result of Balder's death — her first grief. She comes prominently into the Balder myth, and she is grieved because Odin must fall before the Fenris-wolf — her second grief.[9] R. M. Meyer finds in this reference to Fensalir an explanation of its meaning. As Sigyn weeps for Loki in the forest where he is punished, so Frigg weeps for Balder on the sea-shore by his pyre. Fensalir would thus be the shore, and Frigg's abode was really with Odin in Hlidskjalf.[10]

In *Vafthrudnismal* when Odin consulted Frigg regarding his journey to the giant Vafthrudnir, she desired him to stay at home rather than go to this strongest of giants. Like others who seek advice, Odin did not follow Frigg's guidance. She then bade him go, journey, and return in safety. ' May wisdom not fail thee, Aldafadir, when thou comest to speech with the giant! '

Yet Frigg could at times act cunningly to Odin. In *Grimnismal* we see both of them sitting on Hlidskjalf, Frigg thus sharing Odin's oversight of the world. He drew her attention to her fosterling Agnar, who begat children with a giantess in a cave, while his brother Geirrod, Odin's fosterling, is a king and rules his land. We have already seen how Frigg announced Odin's coming as a supposed magician to Geirrod's hall, and how he was tortured between two fires.[11] This act of Frigg's corresponds to her craft in winning Odin's help for her favourites in the Lombard story. Some myths told worse things of Frigg. When she begged Loki and Odin at Ægir's feast not to make known what things they did in old days, Loki accused her of misconduct with Odin's brothers, Vili and Ve.[12] This, as we have seen, is amplified in the *Ynglinga-saga*. Corresponding to it is Saxo's story of Mit-othin, the earlier part of which introduces Frigg. Speaking of Odin and his worship, Saxo says that the kings of the North, anxious to worship him more zealously, made a golden image of him and sent it to Byzantium (Asgard). Its arms were covered with bracelets, and Odin was delighted. But his queen Frigga, desiring to be more adorned, called smiths and had the gold stripped from the image. Odin hanged them and set the image on a pedestal, and by his art caused it to speak when a mortal touched it. In her desire of adornment Frigga yielded herself to one of her servants, who broke the image and gave her its treasures. In disgust Odin went into exile, and Mit-othin took his place. Odin returned only after Frigg was dead. Probably we are to assume that Mit-othin, like Vili and Ve, took Frigga as wife.[13] The possible meanings of these myths have already been given.[14] Frigg, who gives herself for the sake of personal adornments resembles Freyja, who does the same — another suggestion of their ultimate identity or that myths told of one were also told of the other.

The opening part of the prose Introduction to *Grimnismal* shows Frigg, with Odin, in a more pleasing light. They appear as an old peasant and his wife dwelling by the sea. King Hraudung had two sons, Agnar and Geirrod, who went fishing in a boat. They were driven out to sea and wrecked on the coast where Odin and Frigg dwelt. With them they spent the winter, not knowing who the peasant and his wife were. Odin nourished Geirrod and taught him out of the treasures of his wisdom. Frigg took Agnar in charge. In spring Odin gave them a ship, and as he and Frigg accompanied the lads to it, Odin took Geirrod apart and spoke privately to him. The youths had a fair wind and reached their father's place, but as Geirrod sprang ashore, he pushed out the boat with Agnar, saying: ' Go where evil spirits may have thee.' The vessel was driven out to sea, but Geirrod was well received by the people and made king, for his father was dead. This explains why Odin and Frigg are respectively foster-parents of Geirrod and Agnar. The goddess Hlin was defender of Frigg's favourites or fosterlings.

Nothing is known in detail of the cult of Frigg, nor can it be proved that she was originally an Earth-goddess, consort of a Heaven-god, but later assigned to Odin. Her name occurs in that of the sixth day of the week as the equivalent of *Dies Veneris*, OHG Frîadag, Frîjetag; AS Frigedaeg; Old Frisian Frigendei; ON Frjadagr. The occurrence of these names shows that Frigg was known both to Scandinavians and West Germans, and that she was equated with Venus.[15] The English

Ælfric speaks of her as 'that foul goddess Venus whom men call Frigg.' The Lombards knew her as Frea; the Thuringians, as Frija, whose sister was Volla, the Norse Fulla, according to the Merseburg charm. Geoffrey of Monmouth says that, after Woden, the Anglo-Saxons worshipped among others the most powerful goddess after whose name the sixth day was called Fredai.

Reminiscences of Frigg appear in tradition. In Sweden, at the religious observance of Thursday, when the house was prepared for the visit of deities, the expression was used 'Hallow the god Thor and Frigg.' On the same day no spindle or distaff could be used, for Frigg herself then span. In the evening an old man and woman might be seen sitting at the distaff, viz., Thor and Frigg. Why she was thus associated with Thor is unknown. In Sweden the stars forming the belt in the constellation Orion are called 'Frigg's spindle and distaff.' Thus she was associated with women's work. In Iceland an orchis from which love-philtres are made is called Friggjargras, and a certain fern is called Freyjuhar.[16]

CHAPTER XVI

LESSER GODDESSES

IDUNN

IN his formal list of the Asynjur, Snorri does not mention
Idunn, but elsewhere he includes her among them.[1] She
was wife of Bragi and dwelt at Brunnakr's brook. As goddess
of immortality she is described by Kauffmann as keeping 'the
venerable father of singers young even in old age — a beautiful
symbol of the undying freshness of poetry,' and by Gering as
indicating the immortality of song.[2] She guarded in her coffer
the apples which the gods tasted when they began to grow old.
Thus they grew young, and so it continued to the Doom of the
gods. Gangleri, to whom this was told, said that the gods
have entrusted much to Idunn's care. Then he was told how
once the gods' ruin was nearly wrought, and this is the subject
of the myth of Thjazi and Idunn. Idunn was called 'keeper of
the apples,' and they are 'the elixir of the Æsir.'[3] Hence also
her name, from the prefix *id*, 'again,' and the termination *unn*,
common in female names. This gives the meaning 'renewal,'
'restoration of youth.' Idunn is a common woman's name in
Iceland.[4]

In *Lokasenna* Idunn besought Bragi at Ægir's banquet not to
speak ill of Loki. Loki accused her of hunting after men and
of winding her white arms round the neck of her brother's murderer. She replied that she would not speak opprobrious words
of Loki, but would soothe Bragi, excited by beer, so that he and
Loki would not fight in anger.[5] Nothing else is known of the
subjects of Loki's accusation.

The myth of Thjazi is told by Snorri and by the poet Thjodolf of Hvin (tenth century) in the *Haustlong*. Odin, Loki,

and Hœnir had wandered over wastes and mountains, and found a herd of oxen, one of which they slew and roasted. Twice they scattered the fire and found that the meat was not cooked. Perplexed at this, they heard a voice from a tree saying that he who sat there had caused the fire to give no heat. A great eagle was the speaker, and he said that the ox would be cooked if they gave him a share. To this they agreed, but the eagle, the giant Thjazi in disguise, took a thigh and two forequarters of the ox. Loki snatched up a pole and struck him, but, as the eagle flew off with the pole sticking in his back, Loki, hanging on to the other end, was carried off and his feet dashed against rocks and trees, while his arms were nearly torn from their sockets. He cried out, but Thjazi would not free him until he promised to induce Idunn to come out of Asgard with her apples. He accepted these terms, and in due time lured Idunn from Asgard by telling her of apples more wonderful than her own, growing in a wood. When she went there, Thjazi as an eagle carried her off to his abode, Thrymheim. The Æsir soon began to grow old, and consulting together, recalled that Idunn had been seen leaving Asgard with Loki. He was now threatened with torture or death and promised to seek Idunn in Jötunheim. Borrowing Freyja's bird-plumage, he flew off there and found that Thjazi had gone to sea, leaving Idunn alone. Loki changed her to a nut, and flew off with her, grasped in his claws.

Thjazi returned and gave chase, but when the Æsir saw the pursuit they collected bundles of wood-chips and made a fire with them. Thjazi was flying too swiftly to stop; his wings caught fire and the gods slew him. Of this death of Thjazi, Thor boasts in *Harbardsljod*, as if he were the sole slayer. Loki also maintained that he was first and last at the deadly fight when Thjazi was slain.[6]

This myth has been explained in terms of nature phenomena. Idunn is the luxuriant green of vegetation which falls as booty to the giant, the demon of autumn storms, but is brought back

by Loki, the warm air, in spring.[7]   But if the gods were believed
to owe immortal youth to magical apples, then inevitably the
Jötuns, their enemies, would seek to gain possession of these.
As apples were unknown in Iceland and only known in Norway
at a later time when grown in monastic gardens, the Idunn myth
has been regarded as one formed by skalds out of biblical conceptions of the fruit of the Tree of Life, the myth of the Garden
of the Hesperides, and Irish stories of magic apples.[8]   None of
these sources, however, quite accounts for the myth, and it is
quite likely that there is here a primitive conception, possibly
worked upon by outside sources, of the immortal youth or
strength of gods being dependent on certain magic foods, like
Soma, nectar and ambrosia, or, in Irish myths, Manannan's
swine, Goibniu's ale, or the apples of the Land of Youth.[9]

GEFJUN

Snorri includes Gefjun among the Asynjur.   She is a virgin
and on her attend all who die maidens.[10]   At Ægir's banquet she
tried to stay the strife by saying that Loki is well known as a
slanderer and hater of all persons.   Loki bids her be silent: he
cannot forget him who allured her to lust — the fair youth to
whom she surrendered herself for the sake of a necklace.   Odin
then cried: ' Mad thou art and raving, Loki, in rousing Gefjun's
wrath, for she knows the destinies of all as well as I.'   Gefjun
was called upon in the taking of oaths.[11]

Certain statements in these notices of Gefjun may show that
she is like, if not identical with, Frigg and Freyja.   She is mistress of dead maidens, and maidens, e.g., Thorgerd, go to
Freyja after death.   Her surrender of herself for the sake of
a necklace recalls the Brisinga-men myth.   Her prophetic
knowledge, equal to Odin's, makes her like Frigg who knows
all fates of men.   While these common factors may not establish identity, they show that goddesses worshipped in different
localities tended to have the same traits or that similar myths
were apt to be told of them.   Gefjun's name also resembles one

of the names of Freyja, viz., Gefn (cf. AS *geofon*, ' sea,' but more probably the name means ' giver ').

The same, or, as some think, a different Gefjun, is the subject of a story told by Snorri in the *Edda* and in his *Heimskringla*. In the Eddic account Gylfi, king of Sweden, gave a wandering woman named Gefjun, of the kin of the Æsir, as much land as four oxen could plough in a day and a night. This was in return for the pleasure which her skill had given him. She took four oxen out of Jötunheim (her sons by a giant), and yoked them to the plough. The land was now cut so deep that it was torn out and drawn by the oxen out to sea, where it remained in a sound. Gefjun gave it the name Selund (Seeland). The place once occupied by it in Sweden became water, which was now named Log (Lake Malar). The bays in that lake correspond to headlands in Seeland. Snorri then quotes a verse from the poet Bragi's *Shield-lay* describing this act.[12]

In the *Heimskringla* this story is connected with the wandering of the Æsir over Denmark to South Sweden. Odin sent Gefjun over the sound to seek land, and there Gylfi gave her the gift. Now she went to Jötunheim, where she bore four sons to a giant, and turned them into oxen. Then follows the account of the formation of Seeland. Odin's son Skjold married Gefjun, and they dwelt at Hleidra (Leire). Here also the Bragi stanza is quoted.[13]

This story is cosmogonic: it tells how an island was formed. In the original myth Seeland could hardly have been regarded as torn out of a part of Sweden at such a distance from it. This geographical inconsistency arose from the fact that Gylfi was regarded as king of Sweden. This piece of euhemerism dates from the thirteenth century. Gylfi may originally have been a god. Olrik, comparing the myth with traditional plough-rites at New Year surviving in Scandinavia and England, in which the plough is paraded, drawn by men masked as oxen under the lead of a woman (or a man masquerading as a woman), suggests that it was derived from such ritual. The rite was a fertility charm, and Gefjun was a Danish goddess of fertility and agriculture.[14] That Gefjun was a Danish goddess is shown by her connexion with Skjold, the eponymous ancestor of the Skjoldings or Danish kings. Skjold is ' the god of the Ska- nians,' *Skánunga god,* and the Skanians were the people of Den- mark or of part of it, the island Skaane. Possibly Gefjun is Nerthus or a form of Nerthus. Her name, if connected with *gefa,* ' to give,' or with Gothic *gabei,* ' riches,' would be in keep- ing with her attributes both as a giver of fertility or as a giver of land to Denmark. The name would then be found again in the *Gabiæ* or *Alagabiæ* of Romano-German inscriptions, ' the Givers ' or ' All-givers.'[15] If the myth is derived from the ritual, it is also linked to stories regarding the origin of islands or of land obtained by various stratagems with a plough or the hide of an ox.[16]

The association of an eponymous king, Skjold, with a god- dess, has a parallel in *Hyndluljod* where Freyja is associated with Ottarr, connected with a royal house. Gefjun must once have been worshipped in Seeland.

SIF

Sif was Thor's wife, and he is often known merely as ' Sif's husband.'[17] She was famous for her golden hair, and was called ' the fair-haired goddess.'[18] The myth told about her hair will be given in Chapter XXVI. Sif poured mead for Loki at Ægir's feast, wishing him ' Hail!' and saying that he knew her to be blameless among the deities. To this Loki replied that he knew one who had possessed her, viz., himself.[19] In *Harbardsljod* Harbard taunts Thor by saying that Sif has a lover at home, and that he should put forth his strength on him rather than on Harbard.[20] Perhaps this lover was Loki. When Hrungnir came to Asgard in giant-fury, he threatened to carry off Sif and Freyja.[21] Sif was mother of Thrud by Thor, and of Ull by some other father.[22]

SAGA

Saga is named by Snorri as the second goddess after Frigg. She dwells at ' a great abode,' Sokkvabekk, ' Sinking stream,' a waterfall, and here where cool waves wash her abode, Odin and she drink joyfully each day out of golden vessels.[23] Some scholars regard Saga as a mere reflexion of Frigg. Her name has no connexion with the Icelandic Sagas, but means ' she who sees and knows all things,' as Odin does, and her dwelling — a water-world — resembles Frigg's Fensalir, also near the waters. As the liquor drunk is presumably a draught of wisdom, and as Saga dwells in or beside a waterfall, she may be a Water-spirit, a female counterpart of Mimir. With such elfins, no less than in wells and streams, secret knowledge was supposed to reside. Unfortunately the myth which told of Odin's connexion with her is not now extant.[24] In *Helgakvitha Hundingsbana* a cape called after her is mentioned, Sagunes.[25]

SOL AND BIL

Snorri says that Sol and Bil are reckoned among the Asynjur. Sol is the sun, regarded as female, and, in another passage, Snorri tells how she and her brother the moon are children of Mundilfari, both of them so fair and comely that he called them Sol and Mane. Sol was married to the man Glen. The gods were so angry at Mundilfari's insolence in giving them these names, that they set Sol and Mane in the sky, making Sol drive the horses that draw the chariot of the Sun, while Mane steers the course of the moon, and determines its waxing and waning.[26] Snorri thus distinguishes between the actual sun and moon and those worshipful beings who direct their courses. In *Vafthrudnismal* Mundilfari is spoken of, and his children Sol and Mane are said to journey daily round the Heaven to measure time for men.[27] Here they are rather the actual sun and moon.

In the Merseburg charm Sunna, the sun, is named as sister of
Sinthgunt. The sex of the sun agrees with popular German
folk-lore regarding it.[28]

Snorri also says that Mane raised the two children of Vidfinn,
'Wood-dweller,' from the earth as they came from the well
Byrgir. Their names were Bil and Hjuki. On their shoulders
they were carrying the basket Sægr on the pole Simul. These
two follow the moon, as one can see from the earth. As Swedish
folk-lore still speaks of the spots on the moon as two people
carrying a basket on a pole, this may be taken as the meaning of
the myth. There may be some reference to the 'Man in the
Moon' myth, and even the nursery rhyme of Jack and Jill has
been supposed to have a link with Bil and Hjuki.[29] Why Bil
is called a goddess is unknown, but in *Oddrunargratr* the phrase
linnvenges bil, in the sense of 'goddess of gold,' is used as a
kenning for 'woman.' [30]

FULLA

Fulla is said to be a maid who has loose tresses and a band of
gold about her head. She bears Frigg's coffer, and has charge
over her foot-gear, and is acquainted with her secret plans.
Hence Frigg is 'Mistress of Fulla'; a kenning for gold is 'the
snood of Fulla,' with reference to her golden fillet. After his
death, Balder's wife Nanna sent Fulla a golden ring from Hel.[31]

As has been seen, the Introduction to *Grimnismal* tells how
Frigg sent Fulla with a message to Geirrod about Odin. The
Merseburg charm tells how Vol, sister of Frija (Frigg) tried
to charm the horse's foot. Vol is Fulla, and she was thus known
in Germany and regarded as Frigg's sister. In the Balder story
she takes rank with Frigg, since they are the only goddesses to
whom Nanna sends gifts from Hel.

The name Fulla means 'fulness,' 'abundance,' and the Dame
Habonde or Abundia of medieval folk-belief may be a reminiscence of Fulla, who perhaps distributed Frigg's gifts out of her
coffer. If Frigg was an Earth-goddess, Fulla or 'fulness'

would be an appropriate companion for her. She is perhaps no more than a form of Frigg.

LOFN, SJOFN, HLIN, GNA

Other goddesses associated with Frigg are Lofn, Hlin, and Gna. Lofn is kind to those who call on her, willingly hears prayer, and is mild. She has the permission of Odin and Frigg to bring together in marriage those to whom it had been forbidden before or who had found difficulties in the way. From her name, such permission is called *lof*. Akin to her, though not mentioned in connexion with Frigg, is Sjofn, who is zealous in turning the thoughts of men and women to love. From her name love is called *sjofni*. Hlin is set to guard men whom Frigg wishes to preserve from danger. Gna is sent by Frigg into different lands on her affairs, and rides the horse which can run through air and sea, called Hofvarpnir, 'Hoof-tosser.' Snorri, from whom this account of these goddesses is taken, then cites lines from a lost Eddic poem which recounted a myth of Gna, riding forth on an errand for Frigg. Some of the Vanir once saw her riding through the air, and one of them said:

> 'Who flies there? Who travels there?
>   Who glides through the air? '

Gna replied:

> 'I do not fly, though I do travel,
>   Gliding through the air
> On Hoof-tosser's back, on the swift Gardrofa
>   Begotten by Hamskerpir.'

Things high in air are said ' to raise themselves ' (*gnæfa*), after Gna's name. Apart from this notice by Snorri, nothing is known of Gna, except that her name is used as a kenning for ' woman.' [32]

Some of these goddesses may be merely forms of Frigg herself. In *Voluspa* a new grief is said to come to Hlin when Odin goes to fight with the Fenris-wolf. Hlin is here a name of Frigg and means ' Protector.' [33]

EIR, VAR, SYN, SNOTRA

Other goddesses are named by Snorri. Eir is the best physician. One of the servants of Menglod in *Svipdagsmal* has the same name, and Menglod had some connexion with the healing art. She sat on the hill Lyfjaberg, ' Hill of healing,' and ' it will long be a joy to the sick and suffering. Each woman who climbs it, however long she has been sick, will grow well.' There is doubtless some reference here to folk-custom, and to local goddesses of healing. Eir is ' the one who cares for ' (ON *eira*, ' to care for,' ' to save '). Her name is used in the sense of ' goddess ' in kennings for ' woman.' [34]

Var listens to oaths and complaints made between men and women: hence such compacts are called *varar*. She takes vengeance on those who break them, and she is wise and desirous of knowledge, nothing can remain hidden from her. Var is mentioned in *Thrymskvitha*, when Thrym says at his marriage with the supposititious Freyja: ' In the name of Var consecrate our union.' Var has thus to do with the marriage-bond, and marriage was one of Frigg's concerns. [35]

Syn, ' Denial,' guards the doors in the hall and shuts them before those who should not enter. She is appointed as guardian in law-suits where men would deny something: hence the saying that Syn is present when one denies anything. [36]

Snotra, ' Prudent,' is wise and decorous of manner: hence after her name prudent persons are called *snotr*. [37]

THORGERD HÖLGABRUD AND IRPA

The giantess-goddess Skadi may have been of Finnish origin, but she was included among the Asynjur. On the borderland of Finns and Scandinavians, viz., in Halogaland, we find a cult of two sister-goddesses, Thorgerd Hölgabrud and Irpa, who are never included among the Asynjur. Snorri says that Thorgerd's father was Hölgi, king of Halogaland, which was named after him. Sacrifice was made to both father and daughter. A cairn was raised over Hölgi, consisting of a layer of gold and silver (sacrificial money) and a layer of earth and stones. Hölgi was the eponymous king of the region said to be named after him.[38]

According to Saxo, Helgo, king of Halogaland, was in love with Thora, daughter of Cuso, king of the Finns. Being a stammerer he induced Hotherus to plead his cause with her, and he was so successful that she became Helgi's wife.[39] Saxo's Thora is Thorgerd, who was really Hölga's (Helgi's) wife, not his daughter, hence Hölgabrud, ' Hölgi's bride.'

The jarls of Halogaland seem to have regarded Thorgerd and Irpa as their guardians. Nothing is known of Irpa's origin. Jarl Hakon of Lather, in the later part of the tenth century, was devoted to their cult. In some of the Sagas we hear of temples of these goddesses, their images standing on each side of Thor, wearing gold rings.[40]

Hakon took Sigmund Brestisson to a secluded temple in the forest, full of images, among these one of Thorgerd, before which he prostrated himself. He then told Sigmund that he would sacrifice to her, and the sign of her favour would be that her ring would be loose on her finger, and the ring would bring good fortune to Sigmund. At first the goddess seemed to with-hold the ring, but when Hakon again prostrated himself, she released it.[41]

The *Jomsvikings-saga* tells how Hakon sought Thorgerd's and Irpa's help during the naval battle with the Jomsvikings. At first Thorgerd was deaf to his prayers and offerings, but when he sacrificed his son to her, the goddess came to his aid. From the North there came thunder, lightning, and hail, and Thorgerd was seen with Hakon's people by the second-sighted. From each of her fingers seemed to fly an arrow, and each arrow killed a man. This was told to Sigwald, who said that they were not fighting men but evil trolls. As the storm diminished Hakon again appealed to the sisters, reminding them of his sacrifice, and now the hail grew worse, and Thorgerd and Irpa were seen with his ships. Sigwald fled, because he could do nothing against such demons.[42]

A late Saga, that of *Thorleifs Jarlaskald,* tells how Hakon removed a spear which had belonged to Hörgi (Hölgi) from the temple of the goddesses. He desired to be revenged on Thorleif and asked help from them. A human figure was carved, and by means of their magic and that of the jarl, the heart of a dead man was inserted in it. By magic also the figure was made to walk and speak. It was despatched to Iceland, armed with the spear, and Thorleif was slain.[43]

In the story of Olaf Tryggvason the temple was destroyed by him and Thorgerd's image stripped of its gold and silver adornments and vestments, and afterwards destroyed with that of Frey. In the *Njals-saga* there is another account of a destruction of the temple. Hrapp went into it and saw a life-size image of Thorgerd with a great gold ring on her arm and a wimple on her head. These he took from her, as well as a second ring from the image of Thor in his wagon, and a third from the image of Irpa. Then he dragged the images forth and set fire to the temple. When Hakon found the images stripped of their gear, he knew what had happened, but said that the gods did not always avenge everything on the spot. ' The man who has done this will no doubt be driven away out of Valhall, and never come in thither.' [44]

These goddesses were revered as guardians, and their cult was prominent towards the close of the pagan period. They were probably of the class of female supernatural beings called Disir, of whom more will be said later. Their aid was given through magic and through their power over the forces of nature. Whether they were actually Finnish goddesses accepted in parts of Scandinavia, or whether, because of their magic, they came to be so regarded, is differently answered by different students. In Christian times an evil reputation attached to Thorgerd and she was called Thorgerd Hölgatroll.[45]

There is some connexion between Thorgerd, the bride of Hölgi, Saxo's Helgi and Thora, and Helgi and the Valkyrie Svava in *Helgakvitha Hjorvardssonar*.   In this poem Helgi is silent and forgets names, just as Saxo's Helgi stammered and was ashamed to be heard speaking.   Svava guards Helgi and is betrothed to him.   The horses of Svava and her fellow Valkyries drop hail and dew on woods and dales: she and they have power over nature just as Thorgerd had.   In this poem, however, the wooing by another is transferred to Helgi's father Hjorvard, and Atli woos Sigrlin on his behalf.[46]   As we shall see Valkyries were included among the Disir.

CHAPTER XVII

RAN

THE skalds had many names for the sea in its different aspects. Its hurtful character was personified in the Sea-goddess Ran, 'Robbery,' though she was rather demoniac than divine. Of terrifying nature, she was yet wife of Ægir, the sea in its calmer mood. The sea was called ' Husband of Ran,' ' Land of Ran,' ' Ran's road,' and the wave ' with red stain runs out of white Ran's mouth.' [1] Ægir and Ran had nine daughters whose names show that they are personifications of the waves. Among the riddles which Gestumblindi asked of Heidrik was: ' Who are the maidens who go at their father's bidding, white-hooded, with shining locks? ' The answer was, the waves or Ægir's daughters (*Ægis meyjar*).[2] In *Helga-kvitha Hundingsbana* the noise of Kolga's sister (Kolga was one of Ægir's daughters) dashing on Helgi's ships is like that of breakers on the rocks, and ' Ægir's fearful daughter ' seeks to sink them. But the vessel was wrested from ' the claws of Ran.' In *Helgakvitha Hjorvardssonar* Atli says to the monstrous Hrimgerd that she had sought to consign the warriors to Ran.[3]

In the first of these passages Ran tries to drag down the ships with her hands. She also possesses a net with which to catch sea-farers, and the gods first became aware of this when they were present in Ægir's hall. The skald Ref speaks of Ran's wiling ships into Ægir's wide jaws. Hence to be drowned at sea was ' to go to Ran.' [4] The drowned were taken by Ran to her domain: she was goddess of the drowned and dangerous to sea-farers. Yet not all the drowned went to her halls. When Thorsteinn and his men perished at sea, they were seen by his shepherd within a hill near their dwellings.[5]

In the *Egils-saga* Bodvar, Egil's son, was drowned, and his father cried: ' Ran hath vexed me sore. The sea has cut the bonds of my race. . . . I shall take up my cause against the brewer of all the gods (Ægir) and wage war with the awful maids of the breakers (Ægir's daughters), and fight with Ægir's wife.' [6] Folk-belief held that it was good to have gold in one's possession when drowning. In the *Fridthjofs-saga* Fridthjof says in the storm that some of his people will fare to Ran and they should be well adorned and have some gold. He broke a ring and divided it among them, saying: ' Before Ægir slays us, gold must be seen on the guests in the midst of Ran's hall.' [7] The fate of the drowned was not altogether bad. A piece of folk-belief about the drowned is preserved in the *Eyrbyggja-saga,* and it describes how Thorod and his men, drowned at sea, came as ghosts dripping with water to drink the Yule-ale several nights in succession. They were welcomed by their relatives, and it was a token that the drowned who thus came to their own burial-ale would have good cheer of Ran. This old belief, as the Saga says, had not been set aside though men had been baptized and were Christian in name.[8] In Ran's halls the drowned feasted on lobsters and the like.[9]

In later folk-belief Ran was still to be seen reclining on the shore combing her hair, like a mermaid, or in winter drawing near to the fires kindled by fishermen on the shores of the Lofoden islands. Swedish folk-belief also knew Ran as Sjörå, ' lady of the sea.' [10]

Ran, the ' cruel and unfeeling,' may be regarded as originally a demoniac being of the waters, who tended to be viewed also as a guardian goddess of the drowned, whom, if she slew, she entertained in her water-world halls.

Personification of the waves is found in Celtic mythology, Irish and Welsh. They were the Sea-god Manannan's horses or the locks of his wife. They bewailed the loss of Dylan, ' son of the wave,' and sought to avenge him. Nine waves, or the ninth wave, had great importance in folk-belief.[11]

CHAPTER XVIII

NATURE

HOW far the Eddic deities are derived from animistic spirits of different departments of nature is a moot point. The origin of nature worship must be sought primarily in the fact that man viewed rivers, hills, trees, thunder, wind, and the like, as alive in the same sense as he himself was. As he was alive, moving and acting, so things around him, especially those which moved and acted, or in any way suggested life, were alive. They had varying capabilities and spheres of action. Some were in motion — rivers, clouds, sun and moon, trees swayed by the wind. Some were vast entities — a huge tree, a broad river, a high mountain. Some acted or did things — the clouds poured down rain, the trees swayed in the wind, or brought forth leaves and fruit, earth produced vegetation, thunder crashed and rolled, the sun gave light and heat. Some seemed beneficial to man; some were antagonistic. They did more or less the things which man did: they were alive: they possessed power. Hence the more alive they were and the more power they possessed, man saw stronger reasons for standing in awe of them and even propitiating them. When man discovered himself possessed of a soul or spirit, he naturally ascribed such a soul or spirit to these powers or parts of nature. And as man's soul could leave his body in sleep or at death or become separable from it, so could the spirit or soul of a mountain, a tree, a river. Thus in time the spirits of parts of nature might be and were conceived as altogether detached from them. Thus a way was open to ever-increasing hosts of nature spirits, no less than to the dowering of certain nature spirits — those of greater entities, e.g., the sky, a mountain, earth, sun, moon — with a

more elaborate personality. These were on their way to be regarded as divine, as gods or goddesses. So also groups of nature
spirits were conceived as having a chief, on the analogy of human
society, and these in time might become personal divinities of a
part of nature. Such deities tended to become more and more
separate from the objects which were their source, more and
more anthropomorphic, yet lofty divine beings, ruling sky, sun,
moon, earth, sea. Hence the number of such gods found in all
polytheistic religions, separate from, yet connected in some way
with, these natural objects. They tend to become ever wider in
their sphere of influence, yet betray by certain links the source
from which they sprang. All deities were not necessarily nature
spirits, but many of them were, though the connexion may be
difficult to trace.[1]

In Teutonic polytheism some of the deities can be traced to a
source in nature. Tiuz was perhaps at first the sky. Odin,
whatever he became in later times, may have originated in connexion with the wind on which the souls of the dead were
thought to be borne. Thor is in origin the personified thunder,
though this connexion was forgotten in Icelandic literature, because in Icelandic and Old Norse the word for ' thunder ' corresponding to the name of Thor had gone out of use. The connexion of other deities with nature has been noted in discussing
the separate divinities. Some of the giants originated in hostile
nature powers, embodiments of frost, ice, storm, the mountains.
Individual names of giants throw little light on their origin, but
Thrym, Thor's opponent, whose name means ' noise,' and is
connected with ON *thruma*, ' thunder-clap,' is a kind of counterpart of Thor as Thunder-god. Another giant being, the eagle
Hræsvelg who causes the winds, is a personification of the wind.
So, too, the Midgard-serpent is the personification, in gigantic
animal form, of ocean as it was supposed to encircle the earth.

In the following sections we shall see how different parts of
nature were regarded by the Teutonic peoples and especially by
the Scandinavians.

EARTH

Jörd, mother of Thor by Odin, is said to be both wife and daughter of Odin by Snorri, who counts her among the Asynjur. He and the skald Hallfred speak of her as daughter of Anar (Onar) and Night. The kennings for Jörd were, among others, ' Flesh of Ymir,' ' Daughter of Anar,' ' Odin's bride,' ' Co-wife of Frigg, Rind, and Gunnlod.' She is also called Hlodyn. ' The hard bones of the green Hlodyn ' are spoken of by the skald Völu-Steinn.² Inscriptions to *Dea Hludana* are found in Lower Germany and Friesland, on altars consecrated to her by fishermen. The meanings proposed for Hludana vary with the suggested derivations. These remain uncertain, as does the identity of Hlodyn and Hludana.³

Still another name for Thor's mother is Fjorgyn, which must be a title of Jörd's. But there was also a male Fjorgynn, Frigg's husband, i.e., Odin, though Snorri, mistaking the meaning of *mær*, ' beloved,' ' maiden,' ' wife,' calls Frigg ' daughter of Fjorgynn.' ⁴ In these two similar names or appellatives we may see those of a primitive Sky-god and Earth-goddess, their son being Thor. When Odin took the place of the Sky-god, Fjorgyn or Jörd was regarded as his wife and Thor as his son. The name is connected with Sanskrit Parjanya, Lithuanian Perkunas, Latin *quercus*, ' oak,' and Gothic *fairguni*, ' mountain,' OHG Fergunna, the name of a mountain covered with oaks. Hence the supposition that Heaven and Earth, as a divine pair, were venerated on a wooded mountain. The union of such a pair was regarded in many mythologies as the source of all things, Earth being a female. Often, too, they were parents of gods and men.⁵ If such a divine pair were venerated by the Teutons, what Tacitus says of Nerthus as Mother-Earth is significant. Jörd, Fjorgyn, perhaps also Freyja, were forms of the Earth-goddess.

Tacitus speaks of a temple of the goddess Tamfana, worshipped by the Marsi, which Germanicus levelled to the ground.

The tribes had held a festival of the goddess early in winter, and, when drunk, were surprised by Germanicus and put to the sword.   Various derivations have been proposed for Tamfana, e.g., a connexion with Icelandic *þamb*, 'fulness,' *þǫmb*, 'abundance'; with ON *tafn*, 'sacrificial animal'; and Latin *daps*. Tamfana was apparently a goddess of fertility, of harvest, hence a form of the Earth-Mother.[6]

Anglo-Saxon formulae of the tenth century for restoring fertility to fields which had suffered from hostile magic are interesting, as showing how memories of an older Earth cult survived into Christian times.   The ritual was partly sacrificial, with spoken spells.   One of these runs: '*erce, erce, erce, eorthan modor.*'   The mother of Earth, rather than Earth herself was invoked.   A similar Lettish phrase forms a parallel — Semmesmâte, 'mother of Earth.'   The meaning of *erce* is uncertain. Grimm connected it with the traditional German Frau Harke or Herke.   Some connexion with *ero*, 'earth,' is also possible. The other charm runs: 'Hale be thou, Earth (*folde*), mother of men; be faithful in God's embrace, filled with food for use of men.'   This was said before beginning to plough.[7]   *Folde*, 'Earth,' occurs also in ON as 'fold,' and a similar appeal is found in *Sigrdrifumal* where Brynhild cries: 'Hail to the gods, hail to the goddesses, hail to the generous Earth' (*fjolnýta fold*).[8]   The Earth, as a productive source of what is good for men, and as spouse of the Heaven-god, lies behind these formulae.   Ritual survivals of an old Earth cult are collected in Sir James Frazer's *Golden Bough.*

Obscure references to the magic or strengthening power of Earth occur in the Eddic poems, as in the formula from *Guthrunarkvitha* and *Hyndluljod* already mentioned.   In *Havamal* Earth is said to cure drink: hence before drinking ale one should exorcise it through the magic strength of Earth.   Because of the magic strength of Earth, a newly born child was laid upon it. The vitality or soul of the child issued from Mother-Earth. When the child had again been lifted up by the midwife and acknowledged by the father, it could only be exposed in exceptional cases. Scandinavian terms for 'midwife' are *jord-gumma, jordemoder,* 'earth-mother.'[9]

Children or their souls were believed to come from Mother-Earth, as this rite shows, and as is found in many folk-beliefs regarding their coming out of hollow trees, i.e., from the earth, out of ponds, lakes, wells, or caves.[10] Connected with this was the rite by which men swore brotherhood. They let their blood flow together into a footprint. Another rite was called 'going under the earth.' A long sod was cut so that its ends were fast to the earth. It was propped up with a spear, and the parties to the pact crept through it. All then let their blood from a cut vein flow on the earth under the sod, afterwards touching it, swearing to avenge each other, and calling the gods to witness. The mixing of blood with the earth signified that all had come from a common mother.[11]

SUN AND MOON

The myth of Sun and Moon as children of Mundilfari has already been referred to. Sun is 'Moon's bright sister,' and she drives the horses Arvak, 'Early-wake,' and Alsvid, 'All-strong,' harnessed to the chariot of the sun which the gods had fashioned for lighting the world out of the glowing matter from Muspellheim. Under the horses' shoulders the gods set wind-bags to cool them, though in some records this is called 'iron-coolness.' Moon steers the course of the moon.[12] The poems on which this account of Snorri's is based say that the horses wearily drag the weight of the sun, but the gods have set under their yokes a cool iron.[13]

In giving the kennings for 'sun,' Snorri cites verses of Skuli Thorsteinsson (*c.* 980 A.D.) which refer to the sun as 'goddess.' The Eddic poems also call the sun 'shining goddess,' and in front of her stands Svalin, 'Cooling,' as shield, otherwise mountains and sea would be set on fire. The sun is 'Glitnir's goddess,' Glitnir being the sky, the heavenly palace of Forseti.[14] Snorri also says that Sol, 'Sun,' is reckoned among the Asynjur.[15] When the giant artificer asked for sun and moon as well as Freyja for his reward, this shows that they may be regarded as deities.[16] Some of the names given to the sun in *Alvissmal* are interesting. Dwarfs call it 'deceiver of Dvalin '; elves name it ' fair wheel.' The sun deceives Dvalin, a dwarf, because dwarfs turn to stone if caught by its light. The name ' elf-beam ' for the sun refers to the danger which elves encounter from it.[17]

In *Voluspa* the poet says that the sun cast her hand over the rim of Heaven and had no knowledge of where her home should be. The moon knew not what might was his, nor the stars where their stations were, till the gods held council. Then they gave names to night and new moon, full moon, morning, evening, midday, and vesper. This account of the sun is best explained as a description of the Northern midsummer night, when the sun is at the edge of the horizon, but does not sink beneath it, and remains near the moon. This suggested to the poet a disordered state of things: hence he added a stanza telling how the gods set order among the heavenly bodies.[18]

The analogy of other religions would suggest that with all these myths a cult of sun and moon existed in Scandinavia. Cæsar, on insufficient evidence, says that the Germans worshipped no other deities than those which were objects of sight and benefited men by their power — the sun, the moon, and fire (Vulcan).[19] This points to some cult or magical rites, and is partly corroborated by what Tacitus says. Beyond the Suiones (Swedes) is a sluggish sea, supposed to engirdle the earth. The setting sun is so vivid there as to obscure the stars. People believe that the sun can be heard emerging from the sea, and horses and rays streaming from his head are seen. These horses correspond to the Eddic horses of the sun. Tacitus also tells how Boiocalus, king of the Ansivari, invoked the sun and stars. Cæsar's opinion about a cult of the moon is not corroborated from other sources, yet superstitious beliefs about new and full moon found in later times may have existed in his day and have given occasion to his assertion. The Suevic prophetesses, e.g., warned the tribesmen not to fight before new moon.[20] Sunna is mentioned in the Merseburg charm as one of the Idisi. Procopius says that in Thule, by which he means Scandinavia, the sun does not appear at the winter solstice for forty days. Watchers on the mountains look for its rising and inform the people that this will happen in five days. A great feast is then held.[21] In later centuries the Church forbade the cult of sun and moon or observances in connexion with them. They were not to be called lords, said S. Eligius. The Saxon *Indiculus Superstitionum* mentions the custom of the pagans who say: *Vince, luna*, at an eclipse. The Anglo-Saxons were told in the laws of Canute that heathenism honoured heathen gods, sun and moon. The worship of sun, moon, and stars, new moon, and the shouting and noise at an eclipse, by which the moon was supposed to be aided, are denounced in Burchard's collection of ecclesiastical decrees.[22]

In folk-custom there are many survivals of rites by which the power of the sun was supposed to be increased and fertility aided. Further reference need not be made to these, but the mention of the chariot of the sun in the *Eddas* is interesting because of certain archaeological finds.

In the Stone Age symbols of the sun were carved on stones in Scandinavia — circles with or without inner rays in the form of a cross, or with several rays from centre to circumference, or concentric circles, sometimes with an inner cross or with lines joining the two circles. These circles show that the sun was regarded as a disc or wheel rolling through the sky. This symbolism was continued in the Bronze Age,[23] but now more interesting finds show the reverence for the sun in that period. In 1902 a bronze disc decorated with spirals and overlaid with gold was found at Trundholm in Seeland. It stood on a bronze wagon with six wheels, set upright on the axle of the hindermost pair. Resting on the axles of the two foremost pairs of wheels is the figure of a bronze horse. The wagon on which is the disc of the sun does not appear to have been drawn by the horse; both horse and disc are on the wagon.[24] Other representations of the sun, whether ornamental or used in cult or magic, have been found. A bronze disc, with concentric ring ornamentation, and with triangular pendants attached to the upper part of the disc, was found at Eskelheim in Gotland. It was probably part of the ornamentation of a horse's trappings.[25] More elaborate is a decorated bronze disc, fifteen inches in diameter, mounted on a ring of metal, six inches deep, with ten wheels, each with four spokes from a central ring. This was found at Ystad in Schonen.[26] All these different kinds of discs represented the sun.

Snorri tells how Gangleri spoke of the sun's swift course, as if hasting to destruction. To this Har replied that he who seeks her comes close and she cannot but run away. Two wolves cause this trouble. Skoll pursues her, and Hati Hrodvitnisson leaps before her, and he is eager to seize the moon. They are progeny of a giantess in Ironwood who bears many giants for sons. Hrodvitnir, 'Mighty wolf,' is the Fenris-wolf, father of the brood.[27]

This account is based on verses of *Grimnismal* and *Voluspa*. The former says:

> ' The wolf is called Skoll, who in Ironwood
> Follows the glittering goddess;
> Hati the other, Hrodvitnir's son,
> Runs before the bright bride of Heaven.'

The latter tells how the giantess in Ironwood bore Fenrir's brood. Among these was one in troll's form, the robber of the sun. Nothing is said of the moon, as in Snorri's account.[28] In *Vafthrudnismal* Fenrir himself swallows the sun at the Doom of the gods, but the sun bears a daughter before that, and she will follow her mother's path.[29] This deed of Fenrir's belongs to the end of the world: the pursuit of the sun by his wolf-sons goes on always. Both incidents refer to the myths of an eclipse as caused by a monster devouring sun or moon, which was driven off by people making noises. Snorri gives another myth. One of Fenrir's brood, mightiest of all, is Managarm, ' Moonhound,' who will be filled with flesh of all who die and shall swallow the moon, sprinkling Heaven and the air with blood. This precedes the great storms and darkening of the sun at the Doom of the gods. Snorri is paraphrasing and quoting a passage in *Voluspa* which, however, speaks of the swallower of the sun (*tungl*, ' sun,' not ' moon ') and not of Managarm, whom he must have introduced from some other source.[30]

Vafthrudnismal says that Delling, ' Day-spring,' is father of Day. Nor is father of Night. The steed which draws the shining Day to benefit mankind is Skinfaxi, ' Shining mane,' the best of horses in the eyes of heroes; his mane burns brightly. The horse which brings Night for the noble gods is Hrimfaxi, ' Frosty mane.' Foam falls from his bit each morning, and thence come the dews in the dales — a statement made also of the Valkyries' steeds. Night as daughter of Nor is named also in *Alvissmal*.[31]

Snorri elaborates this. Night's father, Narfi, is a giant in Jötunheim. Night is swarthy and dark, as befits her race. She was given first to the man Naglfari (who bears the same name as the corpse-ship in *Voluspa*), and by him had a son Aud. Then she was married to Anar, and from them Jörd was born. Next Delling, of the race of the Æsir, had her, and their son was Day, radiant and fair like his father. All-father took Night and Day and gave them two horses and two chariots, and sent them up into the Heavens to ride round about the earth every two half-days. Night's horse, Hrimfaxi, bedews the earth with foam every morning. Day's steed, Skinfaxi, illumines earth and air with his mane.[32]

This elaborate genealogy may be due to knowledge of such theogonic genealogies as that given by Hesiod. The skalds worked this up, and Snorri has put it into prose. Thus it is not genuine Scandinavian mythology. The parallels are Night, Nox; Nor, Erebus; Day, Dies; Jörd, Terra; while Aud (Authr) perhaps is Æther, and Anar is Amor.[33] The origin of Day from Night is genuine mythology, as with the Celts and others, who held that night precedes or gives rise to day, darkness to light. The light of day comes gradually out of the darkness of night, whereas darkness falls over the light of day, extinguishing it. Man also, asleep and inert during darkness, rises to fresh activity with the light. A pre-existing state of darkness, out of which light and life have proceeded, is thus very widely presupposed. Tacitus says of the Teutons that they count the number of nights, not of days, for night seems to precede day.[34]

'Delling's door' is mentioned in *Havamal*. Before it the dwarf Thjodrörir 'sang might for the gods, glory for elves, and wisdom for Hroptatyr' (Odin). This door would be that through which day or the sun came forth. In the *Hervarar-saga* one of Gestumblindi's riddles is: 'What is the marvel outside Delling's door, which shines on men in every land, and yet wolves are always struggling for it?' The answer is, the sun, the wolves being Skoll and Hati.[35]

FIRE

Cæsar's reference to a cult of Vulcan means a cult of the visible fire. Superstitious reverence for fire, e.g., on the hearth, or fire as a sun-charm, as a medium of sacrifice, or the like, may lie behind his words. In Scandinavia a fire-ritual was used in establishing a claim to property in land. Fire was carried round it, or a fiery arrow shot over it.[36] Consecrated fires burned in temples, for such a fire in a temple in Iceland belonging to Thorgrim was never allowed to go out. There were also fires in the midst of temples over which kettles hung and across which toasts were carried.[37] The Anglo-Saxon laws of Canute speak of the honouring of fire as a heathen rite.[38]

Needfire, fire kindled by means of friction, was used in many rites, especially where new fire was required. This is mentioned in the *Indiculus Superstitionum* — *de igne fricato de ligno, id est nodfyr*, and also in one of Charlemagne's Capitularies — *illos sacrilegos ignes quos niedfyr vocant*.[39] It was used to kindle fire in time of cattle-plague, and through such a fire cattle were driven, all fires in houses having first been extinguished. Bonfires at midsummer festivals were also kindled from needfire.[40]

Fire plays its part in Eddic cosmogony — in the Muspellheim conception, and in the final conflagration. The giant Surt with the flaming sword is guardian of this final fire and he will burn up the world. It may be that Surt was a Volcano-god or a Volcano-demon, originating in Iceland.[41] A story in the *Landnama-bók* may be cited in this connexion. Thorir was an old man, his sight dim. One evening he saw a huge, ill-looking man rowing in an iron boat. He came to a house and dug beside it. During the night fire and lava burst from this place and did great destruction. The huge man was obviously a Fire-demon or Fire-giant.[42]

Fire was used in Scandinavia as elsewhere to cure diseases. Hence the sayings in *Havamal* that ' fire is the best gift for men ' and that ' fire cures diseases.'[43]

MOUNTAINS, HILLS, AND ROCKS

Many hills were called after Odin, either as places of his cult or as indicating that the dead, whom he ruled, were within them. Others were called after Thor. Folk-belief peopled certain hills with the dead, especially in Iceland, and these were held to be sacred.[44] Hill-giants are demoniac beings inhabiting hills, or personifications of the hills. A cult of mountains as such in Scandinavia is not easily proved. Agathias in the sixth century says that the Alemanni worshipped mountains.[45] The ecclesiastical prohibitions include sacrifices *super petras et saxa*, whether these are to be regarded as hills or great stones or out-crops of rock or megalithic monuments. Some stones seem to have been ruins of older temples and shrines — 'stones (*lapides*) which in ruinous places or woods are venerated,' is a phrase in one of the canons of the Synod of Nantes.[46] Examples of the cult of spirits dwelling in stones are found in Iceland, and the *Landnama-bók* tells how Eywind settled Flatey-dale up to the Gund stones, and these he hallowed or worshipped.[47]

TREES

Trees and groves were sacred among the Teutons, the grove being a temple, a centre of religious and political life, the scene of cult and sacrifice. Tacitus mentions several such groves in connexion with the cult of Germanic deities — the *silva Herculi sacra* near the Weser; the *lucus Baduhennae* in North-west Germany; the grove where the Semnones sacrificed to the *regnator omnium Deus*; the island *castum nemus* of Nerthus; the grove where the brothers called Alcis were worshipped.[48] Lives of Christian missionaries and other documents show the reverence for such groves at a later time among the Frisians, Lombards, Saxons, and others. On the branches of the trees sacrificial victims were hung. Adam of Bremen describes a grove near Upsala where animals were sacrificed, and other groves were sacred in Scandinavia. We read in the *Landnama-bók* of the Icelander Thore who hallowed and worshipped a grove and offered sacrifice to it.[49] Where Christianity prevailed, such groves were cut down and destroyed.

Single trees were also held sacred, such as those worshipped by the Alemanni, mentioned by Agathias, or others spoken of in contemporary documents over a period of several centuries.[50] They were sacred in themselves or dedicated to a god, e.g., the *robur Jovis* dedicated to Donar at Geismar or the huge tree with spreading branches ever green in winter at Upsala, with a spring beside it at which sacrifices were offered. A living man was sometimes thrown into this spring, and the whole place was tabu.[51]

Trees were associated with the souls of the dead, with elfins and spirits, as well as with the spirit indwelling in the tree. Many superstitions prove this, and trees, branches, and twigs figure prominently in fertility rites. As spirits of the dead dwelt in trees, so the Swedish Tomte or Brownie, successor to an ancestral ghost, dwells in the *Vårdträd* or ' ward-tree,' the lime or elm growing before the house. If it is cut down, the prosperity of the house ceases, or, again, the Tomte dies with the tree and then dwells in the house in the rafters made from it. The Tomte acts as a guardian spirit of the house and family. Such protective trees are also associated with a community.[52] Analogous to this is the North German belief in the Klabauter-mann, a helpful Brownie of a ship, dwelling in the mast made from a tree which, as a sapling, was split in order to pass a sickly child through it, and then joined together again. If the child died its soul passed into the tree. Such trees have a peculiar form after this treatment and are used in ship-building.[53]

As we shall see in a later Chapter, the mythic ash Yggdrasil and the tree Lærad are linked to such sacred trees as the *Vårdträd* and the sacred tree described by Adam of Bremen. There may be a hint at the sacredness of trees in the myth of the creation of Ask and Embla out of tree-stumps.

Earlier and later folk-belief knew many varieties of more or less elfin beings connected with the woods, in whom may be seen earlier forest spirits, sometimes in new shapes and names. The fairies and *fées* were fond of the woodlands, though those are seldom directly linked to Tree-spirits, except e.g., where trees are sacred to certain elves, or where mortals sleeping below trees are subject to fairy enchantment. Even peculiarly wood-land or tree elfins are more or less independent of their environ-ment. The spirit animating a tree, rock, or stream always tended to be separable from it, and as there are many trees, rocks, or parts of a river, there would be many spirits animating

these, but apt to appear apart from them and to assume a distinct
form. Teutonic folk-lore knows the distinctive forest elfins by
different names — OHG scrato, MHG holzmuoja, holzrûna,
waldminne (cf. AS wuduælf); in South Germany Fanggen,
Saligen or salige Fräulein ('blessed maids,' a euphemism),
wilde Leute; in Mid-Germany Moosweibel, Moosfräulein,
Holz- or Buschfrauen. In North Germany they are little
known or have assumed the qualities of dwarfs. Corresponding
to these are the Danish Skogsnufa, ' Forest-maidens,' Askefruer,
' Ash-women '; the Swedish Skogsrå, 'Wood-goblin,' Skogsfru,
' Wood-wife, and the Löfviska. Male Wood-spirits are less
common — Waldmännlein, Wildmannel, Schrat, and the
Swedish Skogsman. The Ivithja, a female forest being mentioned in Hyndluljod, and the Troll-wives called Iarn-
vithja, ' Ironwood women,' by Snorri, were more monstrous
than elfin, and nothing definite is known of them.[54]

The Teutonic Schrat (Scrato), Latin Pilosus, is a wild,
shaggy, male Wood-spirit, also a form of the nightmare spirit,
with eyebrows meeting, who appears singly. Another form is
Schretel, Schretzel, a small elfin in houses. The woodland
Schrat is akin to the Fauns of classic tradition and to the Tree-
spirits of Teutonic paganism to whom temples and trees were
dedicated.[55] The *wildiu wîp* of early Teutonic belief were beautiful, long-haired forest spirits, usually appearing singly. They
are the *agrestes feminae* mentioned by Burchard, who says that
when they will they show themselves to their lovers, and with
them these say they have pleasure, and when they will they
leave them and vanish.[56] In *Gudrun* Wate learned the healing
art from one of them. They were famed for spinning. In one
version of *Wolfdietrich* to the sleeping hero came a shaggy
Wood-wife, Rauhe Else, or Rauh Ells, on all fours like a bear,
asking his love. He called her a devil's child: she cast spells
over him and he became like Nebuchadnezzar. When she next
sought his love, he agreed, if she would be baptized. She
carried him to her own land, bathed in a Fountain of Youth, and

became the lovely Sigeminne.[57] Similar amours occur in later story, and such *wildiu wîp* and *agrestes feminae* resemble the *puellae, dominae, matronae*, seen in forests in medieval legend, native Teutonic *fées*, like Saxo's *virgines sylvestres* and the Eddic Swan-maidens who love the forest.

The Moos- and Holzweibel and Buschfrauen, akin to dwarfs though taller, live in companies, in the heath, in hollow trees, or underground, though they also appear singly. They may be golden-haired, but are mostly shaggy, clad in moss or with moss on their faces, which are old and wrinkled. Their backs are hollow, their breasts pendent. The shaggy, mossy woodland gave the type of these woodland folk, of Rauhe Else, and of the Fauns. The less common males of these groups are both kindly and tricky to the woodman. They have a queen, the Buschgrossmütter. They beg or take food. When bread is baked, a loaf is left for them at a certain spot, for which one of their own loaves is afterward placed in a furrow or on the plough, and they are angry if it is not accepted. For other services they give a reward of a twig or leaves which afterwards turn to gold. They both cause and cure diseases. As worms or insects they creep from trees into men's bodies, and these must then wish them back into the tree in order to be rid of them. But in time of plague a Holzfräulein will give herbs which are effective against it, and if a Wildmännlein was caught and intoxicated, he supplied secret knowledge, e.g., of cures. On the whole, these Teutonic Wood-folk are kindly; they help with harvesting, hire themselves to peasants, tend cattle, and bring good luck to the house, or one will act like a Kobold or Brownie in a house, requiring only bread and cheese as wages.[58]

Wood-folk care for and protect the creatures of the wild. The Skogsfru is Lady of those pursued by the hunter, and may put him on their track. Sometimes the Wood-folk themselves appear as animals — the Holzfrauen as owls, the salige Fräulein of Tyrol as vultures, guarding the chamois, the Fanggen as wild cats; the Danish and Swedish Wood-wife has a semi-animal form or wears beast-skins or a cow's tail. Wood-wives and Moss-wives are pursued by the Wild Huntsman or the devil, and seek human protection. Three crosses were marked on a fallen tree in order that the Wood-wife might sit within them, for the Wild Hunter fears the cross, and for such aid men were richly rewarded.[59] But a wood-cutter who re-fused this aid was seized and clasped by a Moss-wife, and after-wards became ill. A peasant who mimicked the Hunter as he pursued a Moss-wife found part of her body hanging at his door next morning. This pursuit of the Wood-wives resembles the North German belief in the Wind's Bride, driven before the Hunter.[60]

Some of the Wood-folk are earlier Tree-spirits. Whoever would fell a tree must kneel before it with uncovered head and folded hands. In Denmark, where the Elder-mother dwelt under an elder-tree, he who desired to take part of it had to ask her permission thrice. The life of the Fangge is bound up with that of a tree, like a Dryad's. If any one twists a young tree until the bark comes off, a Wood-wife dies, for she lives beneath the bark.[61] All this is in accord with animistic beliefs about Tree-spirits. The antiquity of the Wood-folk as com-pared with man and his modern ways, is seen in their prefer-ence for old methods. They say that there has never been a good time since people began to count the dumplings in the pot and the loaves in the oven, or to ' pip ' or mark loaves and put caraway seed in them, which they cannot endure — a distaste shared by certain dwarfs. Hence they cannot now enjoy the peasants' bread, and these in turn lose their prosperity.[62]

Where the Wood-folk are supposed to dwell together (as in Mid-Germany), they have many elfin and dwarf characteristics, e.g., abducting women and children. The solitary Wood-wife resembles a *fée*; the solitary male is rather a gigantic or monstrous being. As spirits of the dead often took up their abode in trees, according to older Teutonic belief, there is some connexion between them and the Wood-folk, as there is between a House-spirit, with its seat in the ' house-tree,' and the ancestral ghost. In South Tirol where the Wild-folk hang on a traveller's back until he faints, there is an example of Wood-spirits acting like the Mahr or nightmare. A Moss-wife also attacked a strong peasant and so weighed upon him that he sickened and became wretched.[63] The characteristics of really distinct supernatural beings are apt to be ascribed impartially to the different groups.

WATER

The universal belief in the sacredness of streams, springs, and wells is due to the fact that water, moving, glittering, making audible sounds, is thought to be living and also tenanted by spirits. These spirits were made more and more personal, though still linked to the waters to which they owed their origin. The waters are both beneficent and dangerous. They cleanse, heal, give drink to the thirsty, fertilize, but they seek and take human life on occasion — the rushing, swollen stream, the cataract, the tempestuous sea.

The sacred fountain was often near a sacred tree, as at Upsala. Such fountains gave oracles and healed the sick when the due ritual was observed. In Christian times resort to wells and springs in the old pagan manner was forbidden, though often the guardianship of these was transferred to a saint, who now performed miracles by its means.

In Scandinavia there are occasional references to the cult of water, e.g., the worship of a cataract by Thorsteinn in Iceland, who sacrificed and carried all leavings of food to it. He was a seer and predicted how many of his sheep would perish in winter. One autumn he said: ' Kill what ye will, for I am now fey, or the sheep are, or perhaps both.' That night he died, and all the sheep rushed into the cataract and perished.[64]

Sometimes human victims were sacrificed to the waters or to the spirits dwelling in them, as when the Franks in 539 A.D. threw the women and children of the Goths into the river Po

as an offering and in order to know the future.[65] Before beginning a long voyage Scandinavian sailors offered a human victim
to protect them against the rapacity of Ran.[66] The Normans
also offered victims to the Sea-god before setting out on their
raids.[67] The human sacrifices to the Frisian deity Fosite, after
violation of his sacred spring, were offered on the sea-shore, and
if Mogk is right, they had originally been offered to a Sea-
demon, in accordance with a long-continued Frisian belief that
the sea demanded the sacrifice of those guilty of robbery. Human victims were thrown into the sacred waters at Upsala.[68]
Less sinister offerings were also made to springs and wells, and
survivals of these in Christian times were denounced in canons
of Synods and in Penitentials.

The varied extents of the waters — the broad and deep ocean,
the lake, the mere, the river, now larger, now smaller, no less
than their varied appearance, terrible or attractive, helped to
give form and character to the beings associated with them.
Many of these were dangerous, some because of their specious
beauty. Death and danger lurked in the depths of lakes or
swollen rivers, but were not unknown to the limpid, sparkling
stream or the clear pool, in which dwelt beautiful Water-elfins.
These, like other spirits, were regarded by ecclesiastical writers
as demons, and stories told how their wailing or spiteful cries
were heard when they realized that a new faith was ousting their
supremacy.

The more monstrous Water-spirits were like the giant Hati's
wife who, whether a Sea-demon or not, tried to wreck the ships
of Helgi and Atli, as her monstrous daughter, Hrimgerd, confessed.[69] These are types of the Hafgygr and Margygr, ' Sea-
giantess,' of old Norse literature. The Anglo-Saxon poem,
Beowulf, gives vivid pictures of the terrible beings who haunted
inland waters or marshes. The mother of Grendel, seen on
moors, fens, and fastnesses, dwelt in a mere surrounded by
gloomy trees and rocks. She is called *merewîf*, *brimwylf*, and
grundwyrgen. The mere was of unknown depth; its waves

mounted murkily to the clouds; fire was seen on its surface by night. There, too, sea-snakes, dragons, and *niceras* were seen, ' those that, in early morning, often procure disastrous going on the sea-road.' These *niceras*, like the OHG *nichus*, feminine *nichessa*, seem to have betokened actual sea-monsters, but the words also included Water-spirits. The different forms of the word are AS *nicor*, plural *niceras*; Middle English *nykyr*, meaning also ' siren '—' nykeren that habbeth bodyes of wyfmen and tayl of nisse'; [70] ON *nykr*; Norse and Danish Näk; Swedish Näck; German Nix, English Nix, Nixie. The widespread use of the word is significant of a common belief.

Other words denoted the Water-spirit, e.g., the German Wasserman or a local form, Hakemann, who seized children with a hook; the older Wazzerholde, Wasserjungfrau, Wasserfräulein, Seejungfer, Seeweibel; the Danish Havfolk, Havmaend, Havfrue; the Swedish Strömkarl and Vatten-elfvor ('Water-elves'), the Hafsman and Hafsfru; the Norse Grim or Fossegrim. The Norse Näk is also known as Säetrold or Vigtrold. Medieval literature knows the Merminne, Merwîp, Merwîf, Merfrouwe, female supernatural beings of the sea and waters. The Marmennil, the present-day Marbendill, is mentioned in the Sagas. The *Landnama-bók* tells how Grim pulled up a Marmennil and demanded to know the future from him or he would never see his home again. He prophesied Grim's death, and other matters which came true. [71]

The male Water-spirit is usually old, like a dwarf, with green hat and teeth, or even green hair and eyes, though he may appear as a golden-haired boy, as a kind of centaur (in Iceland and Sweden), as a horse, or in full or half fish form. He is to be recognized by his slit ears and by his feet, which he keeps hidden. Although his dwarf aspect does not appear prominently in older tradition, the dwarf Andvari in *Reginsmal* took the form of a fish and dwelt in the water. [72]

All Water-elfins love music, and the Näk sits or dances on the water, playing enchanting music on his golden harp. The

Strömkarl's lay has eleven variations, the eleventh belonging peculiarly to him, and if a mortal plays it, every person and thing must dance. If a black lamb was sacrificed to him, the offerer's head being averted, he taught him this music; as did also the Fossegrim to the person who offered a white he-goat on a Thursday evening. If it was lean, the pupil got no further than tuning his fiddle: if fat, the Fossegrim guided his hand, grasping it till the blood came, and now he could play so that trees danced and waterfalls stood still.[73] The Näk assumed youthful form to entice girls. The Swedish Näck has a passion for women in childbed, and takes the husband's form, though his equine hoofs remain. If the woman does not perceive these and admits him into her bed, she becomes demented. The Icelandic Nykr, as a grey horse, tempts someone to mount him, and then dashes into the water — a trait of other Water-spirits.[74] The Nix and his kind were cruel, and even Water-maidens staying too long ashore at a dance, or other Water-spirits intruding on his domain, were slain by him. The drowned were his victims, one or more yearly, and here may be seen a relic of human sacrifice to the waters. The Nix also slew and ate children born to him by his captive human wife. Like other elfins, the Water-man knows where treasure is hid, and will communicate the secret to favoured mortals.[75]

Other elfin traits are seen in the communities of Nixen or of each Nix and his family in their gorgeous palaces under the water, or in an Icelandic story of Water-elves who entered a house every Christmas Eve to hold revel, some of their number watching for dawn. Each time, they killed the servant, left alone in the house; but one Christmas Eve the servant concealed himself, and, long before dawn, struck the planks of the house and cried: ' The dawn! the dawn! ' All fled to the water, leaving costly vessels behind, and some were killed in their haste to escape.[76] The Nix and his kind abduct women as wives, for whom, in turn, human midwives are required. The midwife is warned by the wife not to eat food or take more than her due when offered to her, and sometimes valueless articles given to her turn to gold.[77]   Young children were stolen by them, and a Wasserkopf — a Nix's child with a large head, or a Wechselbalg or changeling was left in place of the stolen child.[78]

The female Water-spirits have many different names in the older literature,[79] and the Norse Sea-goddess Ran corresponds to these in so far as they are hostile to man and are unpleasing of aspect.   But not all are of this kind, though there might be danger to mortals in too close an acquaintance with them.   These have more of an elfin character.   They are beautiful, and sit combing their long locks in the sun, but they may also have a homely appearance, as when they come ashore to market, when they may be recognized by the wet edge of skirt or apron.   According as they pay much or little for what they purchase, a dear or a cheap season will follow.   Sometimes they are naked, but hung round with moss or sedge.   The Nixe's exquisite song beguiles unwary youths, who, like Hylas, are drawn into the waters.   The drowned are also her victims, and children falling into wells come into her power.[80]   In earlier Teutonic belief the Nixen are hardly distinguishable from the Swan-maidens, and like most of these water beings possess prophetic gifts.   Hence they are also called *wisiu wîp*.   The *Nibelungenlied* tells how Hagen heard water splashing on the Danube, where certain *wisiu wîp* or *merewîf* were bathing.   They would have fled, but he seized their garments, and they floated before him like water-hens.   On his restoring their garments, they foretold what would befall the Nibelungs.[81]

These female water beings sometimes marry men, but their husbands must not see them naked or enquire into their origin — common forms of tabu in such supernatural marriages.   As the Swan-maiden was powerless without her wings, so the Nixe who comes ashore to dance is grieved if her partner retains her gloves, and in one story several of them returned sorrowfully to the water, which was seen to be reddened with blood, because

their father had slain them.[82]   Youths in love with Nixen have
followed them to their home, like one who descended with an
Elbjungfer into the water at Magdeburg, but was slain by her
relations.   In a variant, she herself was the victim, and her
lover, standing by the water, saw it reddened with her blood.[83]
The Nixen have flocks and herds which come ashore, and mingling with ordinary animals, render them prolific.

The attraction of the woods has been well expressed by Emer-
son and Meredith, and men still delight in their mystery, their
silence and their voices.   They were more dreadful when
peopled with supernatural beings, akin to the evil Forest-spirits
of savages, 'in their obscured haunts of inmost bowers.'   In
bygone ages vast forests stretched across large parts of Europe,
and wide morasses occupied land now under cultivation.   From
these strange sounds were heard, or by night the Will o' the
Wisp flitted eerily over them.   On wide moorlands moss-
covered boulders protruded from the heath, or grey stones, with
a suggestion of shadowy forms lurking among them, stood
singly or in circles, or grass-grown tumuli dotted its surface.
Such was the region encircling small reclaimed areas, and we
do not wonder that men peopled it with the objects of their
imagination or their fear — demons, spirits, divinities of wood,
stream, immemorial rocks, and fells, and with ghosts of those
who lay under the ' howes of the silent vanished races.'   Some
were monstrous, some beautiful, but all were more or less dangerous.   In the forest men worshipped the gods, for the earlier
temples were often groves, not to be approached lightly.   The
men of the township would go in procession to a sacred well, to
a hoary tree in which an image was set, to rocks or boulders in
which dwelt a spirit, or to the circle or tumulus to invoke the
dead.   They lit fires or placed candles by tree, stone, or well, or
by the cross-ways, and offered sacrifices there.   Even after the
Germanic peoples became Christian, these beliefs in the lesser
supernatural beings and these customs continued.   Through

long centuries the Church continued to condemn them, but they were too deeply rooted to be easily displaced.

Thus the Council of Tours, 567 A.D., denounced the pagan observances at sacred trees or springs or stones, called ' places of the pagans,' and some years later the Council of Auxerre speaks of vows offered at these instead of in churches. These and similar decrees concerned the Frankish population.[84] Eligius, bishop of Noyon (ob. 658 A.D.), who laboured among the Frisians, denounced the veneration of stones, wells, trees called sacred, bringing lights to these or offering vows at them or in sacred enclosures (*cancelli*) or at cross-roads.[85] The eighth century *Homilia de Sacrilegiis* shows that Frankish Christians were still resorting to the old altars, groves, trees, and rocks, to offer animal or other sacrifices and to celebrate feasts, or to pray at springs or rivulets. There was an observance of *Neptunalia in mare*, perhaps some feast of a Water-god or Water-spirit.[86] S. Boniface counted as capital sins among the Germans to whom he taught Christianity, offerings at stones or to springs and trees.[87] In Charlemagne's time, as his *Admonitio Generalis* shows, the cult at trees, fountains, and stones still continued, with the placing of lights at these, and other customs. Such practices were forbidden, and these sacred things were to be destroyed.[88] Among the Saxons, who were still pagan, the use of votive offerings at fountains, trees, and groves was punishable by fines varying according to a man's quality.[89] Sacrifices at fountains are mentioned in the *Indiculus Superstitionum*.[90] How difficult it was to root out these customs and beliefs is seen in the fact that the Penitential of the tenth century ' Corrector ' in Burchard's collection of decrees still enquires: ' Hast thou gone to any place other than the church to pray — to fountains, stones, trees, or cross-roads, and there burned a candle or torch in reverence to such a place, or offered or eaten there bread or any such oblation, or sought there the welfare of body or soul? '[91]

Such superstitions remained popular in spite of all prohibitions and continued long after the time here spoken of, not only among the common people but among those of higher rank. Few, indeed, of the superstitious customs and beliefs of the Middle Ages cannot be traced to the earlier centuries when pagans began to flock into the Church in large numbers without clearly understanding the new religion and without having abandoned either their pagan ways of looking at things or many of their customs. But the rites and beliefs to which they ad- hered were rooted in a far distant past, and had been dear to the folk for long generations. The springs and wells and rocks had been sacred from prehistoric times, and, in the thought of the different religions, were inhabited by divinities or spirits. Hence the old sacred wells were still visited, as well as sacred stones and trees, in the hope of gaining a boon — healing, fruit- fulness, prosperity — from them or from the spirits, mainly now of an elfin kind, supposed to dwell in them. A small offer- ing was made or a candle lit to propitiate the *genius loci*. The old sacred place, familiar for generations, and visited in a hope- ful mood, seemed friendly and easily propitiated. Men thought, wrongly no doubt, that it was nearer to their lives than the Church's sacred Persons, though the Virgin and the saints were beginning to assume a familiar form and to be invoked about the minor ills and blessings of life as well as about things which loomed more largely and terribly on the human horizon.

Those who persisted in such practices were excommunicated or subjected to penance, lighter or heavier, or to a fine. They had been deceived by the demons inhabiting these sacred spots, and the rites were execrable in the sight of God.

CHAPTER XIX

ANIMALS

CERTAIN monstrous or giant animals play a part in Eddic
mythology — the Fenris-wolf, the Midgard-serpent, the
eagle of the winds. Some animals seem to have received a cult,
according to statements in the Sagas, but this was rendered by
individuals, like Brand to Freyfaxi. The Saga of Olaf Tryggvason tells of Ogvald, who was a great sacrificer to a certain
cow. He took her with him wherever he went and thought that
his health benefited by her milk, and, when she died, she was
buried in a tumulus near his own.[1] The *Landnama-bók* recounts how the viking Floci set out to seek the Snowland. He
made ready a great sacrifice, and hallowed three ravens to tell
him the way.[2]

Animal forms entered into the art of the Norsemen, and, of
these, the dragon or snake is prominent. It appeared on the
bows of Norse galleys and was borne into battle as a standard by
different Germanic tribes. On swords the snake was engraved,
like that one of which the Valkyrie told Helgi — ' on the edge
lies a blood-stained serpent, on the back a serpent's tail is
twisted.' The snake was supposed to run from the hilt to the
point and back again. Snakes or dragons also ornamented helmets, adding strength to them as to the sword.[3] Whether this
implies a cult is uncertain, but the *Life* of S. Barbatus shows
that the Lombards worshipped the golden image of a viper.
Having come into possession of the saint, it was melted down
and made into a chalice and paten.[4]

The dragon or serpent occurs often in Norse stories, e.g., that
of Fafnir, whether as a guardian of treasure or in other aspects.
Serpents often appear in tales of the Other World and in the

Eddic description of Nastrand (p. 319). Nidhogg and many serpents dwell in Hvergelmir and gnaw the roots of Yggdrasil. Two of these, Ofnir and Svafnir, bear names by which Odin calls himself in *Grimnismal,* and we know that Odin took snake form occasionally.[5] A design on a helmet from a Swedish grave in which Odin figures, shows an upreared serpent before him.[6] The snakes of the Other World have been regarded as forms of the souls of the dead, and Odin as god of the dead might sometimes have been regarded as a serpent.[7] Some foundation for this may be seen in many stories, though these are not peculiar to the Teutons, of snakes in meadows and houses feeding out of the children's milk-bowl, coming beside them, watching over them, and revealing treasure to them. It is unlucky to kill such snakes. Folk-belief also tells of two snakes attached to a house, revealing themselves when the master and mistress die, and then themselves dying. Such snakes are soul-animals, forms taken by dead ancestors.[8] The soul as a snake is illustrated by a story recorded of king Gunthram of Burgundy by Paulus Diaconus. The king was sleeping in a forest after hunting, when a snake crept out of his mouth and crossed a rivulet by means of the sword of one of his nobles. It now passed into a mountain, soon afterwards returning and entering the king's mouth. When he woke, the king told how he dreamed that he had crossed a river and entered a mountain full of gold. This gold was now sought and found.[9] The soul takes the form of other animals as will be seen in considering the Fylgja.

The stories of Balder and Hotherus, of Fafnir's heart, eaten by Sigurd, and others, show that the serpent was regarded as an animal which gave health, strength, and wisdom.

The beliefs concerning serpents point to two aspects of these reptiles, beneficent and malignant, though this is far from being peculiar to the Teutons.[10]

Animals are also associated with the gods — ravens and wolves with Odin, the boar and the cat with Freyja, the horse and the boar with Frey, goats with Thor. Whether this denoted an earlier cult of these animals, as in other religions where an animal is connected with a deity, cannot be verified now. The boar may have been regarded as the embodiment of a Fertility-spirit, and so associated with Frey, a god of fertility.

It is possibly significant that, in the Eddic poems and tales, animals are frequently found (apart from the special animals of the gods), e.g., in the account of Balder's funeral, in *Skirnis-mal*, in *Hyndluljod*, in the Volsung poems (pike, otter, talking birds, a dragon). Equally significant is the prominence given to metamorphosis or animal disguise — Fafnir as a dragon, Andvari as a pike, Ottarr as a boar, Odin as a snake, Loki in different animal forms. These indicate primitive traits in the poems, and point to their origin among the folk themselves, rather than among the more cultured classes.

CHAPTER XX

THE ALFAR OR ELVES

ALONG with the Æsir and Vanir the *Eddas* speak of the Alfar or ' elves.' These are represented in later Teutonic folk-belief, and equivalents of the name are OHG and MHG *alp, alb*, AS *ælf*, Old Danish *elv*, Old Swedish *älf*. In Germany the older use of *alp* or *alb* (plural *elbe, elber*) in the sense of ' spirit,' ' genius,' ' fairy,' ' ghostly being,' shows that beings like the Norse Alfar were known there also, as does the word *elbisch* in the sense of mental unsoundness caused by such beings. The word *alp* does not occur by itself before the thirteenth century, but it is found in proper and compound names. The plural forms, probably denoting friendly spirits, are found in MHG poetry. Gradually, however, *alp* was used rather in the sense of ' nightmare,' and the words *tverc, zwerg*, ' dwarf,' *wiht, wicht*, ' wight,' and their synonyms took its place. The modern German *Elfe* was derived from English literary sources in the eighteenth century. Whether the word Alfar is connected etymologically with Sanskrit *ṛbhus* is uncertain. The enigmatic *ṛbhus*, whose name is variously explained as ' dexterous ' and ' shining,' were seasonal divinities and skilful artificers with magical power, three in number. They have been regarded as in origin ' no more than elves who gradually won higher rank.' [1]

The Eddic Alfar are the earliest known elves, akin to the Anglo-Saxon *ylfe* (singular *ælf*). The scanty notices of them show that they had a loftier nature than the elves of later beliefs. They are not said to be dangerous or mischievous, nor are they yet confused with evil trolls through Christian enmity to the old paganism. They are joined with the Æsir, as in the recurrent phrase ' Æsir ok Alfar,' used partly but not wholly for the sake of alliteration, and also with both Æsir and Vanir. In the prose Introduction to *Lokasenna* ' many Æsir and Alfar ' are said to have been present at Ægir's banquet, and Eldir said to Loki: ' None of the Æsir and Alfar here present has a good word for thee.' Loki says that Bragi is the most cowardly of all the Æsir and Alfar present, and he accuses Freyja of misconduct with everyone of these. In *Voluspa* and *Thrymskvitha* the question is asked: ' How is it with the Æsir, how is it with the Alfar? ' and the latter poem gives the reply: ' Ill is it with the Æsir, ill is it with the Alfar.' In *Havamal* Odin says: ' I know all the Æsir, I know all the Alfar,' and in the next verse we learn that Thjodrörir sang ' strength to the Æsir and prosperity to the Alfar.' The same poem speaks of Odin carving runes for the Æsir, and Daenn carving them for the Alfar. In *Skirnismal* Frey complains that none of the Æsir or Alfar is willing that he and Gerd should come together. Odin, in *Grimnismal*, speaks of the land lying near the Æsir and Alfar as holy. Æsir, Alfar, and Dvalinn's people (dwarfs) are conjoined in *Fafnismal* as progenitors of the Norns.[2]

In *Skirnismal* Gerd asks Skirnir: ' Art thou of the Alfar, or of the Æsir, or of the wise Vanir? ' The sacred mead with which the magic runes was sent forth is with the Æsir, the Alfar, the wise Vanir, and with men, says *Sigrdrifumal*.[3]

These phrases show that the Alfar are akin to divine beings. They dwell in Heaven, in Alfheim, which is ruled by Frey,[4] and they act with gods and share their feasts. A similar combination was known to the Anglo-Saxons, one of their spells coupling *êsa* and *ylfa*.[5] Though their creation is not mentioned, the Alfar are a distinct group, supernatural, and with special qualities. Unlike the dwarfs no individual Alf is spoken of, save Daenn in *Havamal*, the name also of a dwarf in other poems. Volund (Weyland the smith), however, is called ' prince ' and ' lord ' of Alfar.[6]

Only one kind of Alfar is spoken of in the poems, but Snorri

gives three groups — Ljösalfar, ' Light elves,' Dökkalfar,
' Dark elves,' and the inhabitants of Svartalfaheim, the Svartalfar, ' Black elves,' whom, however, the context shows to be
dwarfs. Snorri says that Alfheim is the place where the Light
elves live, but the Dark elves dwell down in the earth, unlike
the others in appearance but more so in nature. The Light elves
are fairer than the sun, but the Dark elves are blacker (*svartari*)
than pitch.[7] These Dark elves are not again mentioned, but
Snorri relates how Loki swore to get the Black elves to make
for Sif hair of gold, and then he went to those dwarfs called
Ivaldi's sons, who made it.[8] Odin sent Loki into Svartalfaheim
to the dwarf Andvari in order to get his treasure.[9] He also sent
Skirnir into Svartalfaheim to certain dwarfs who made the
fetter Gleipnir.[10] The Black elves were thus dwarfs, and as
Dark elves dwell in the earth, they are presumably identical
with these. In spite of Snorri's distinction, there was perhaps
but one class of Alfar, since no others are named in the Eddic
poems, in old writers, or in folk-tales, even if the elves of later
belief are ' a sort of middle being between Light and Dark
elves.'[11]

Snorri further states that at the southern end of Heaven there
are two other Heavens superimposed, and in the uppermost is
believed to be the hall Gimle, reserved for the righteous, but at
present inhabited by the Light elves.[12] There may be here a
reflexion of Christian ideas of successive Heavens, and possibly
an identification of Light elves with angels. Alfheim, the region of the Light elves, is a heavenly abode, and in *Alvissmal*
Heaven is called ' Fair roof ' by the Alfar, as if it stretched over
their aerial home, and the sun is its ' Fair wheel.'[13] Unfortunately the *Eddas* say nothing regarding the functions of the
Alfar. ' Light,' as applied to them, has no moral significance,
and merely refers to their appearance.

Certain elfin groups of later Scandinavian belief, associated
with the air and with trees, and not specifically an underground
race, may represent the older Light elves, though neither they

nor those of German tradition dwell in Heaven. Grimm connected with the Light elves the Teutonic White Women, appearing at noon, sitting in the sunshine or bathing, contrary to
the avoidance of sunlight by most fairy folk. This trait of the
White Women recalls the Eddic name for the sun, *alfrodull*,
'shining on the elves,' 'elf-ray,' 'elf-light,' perhaps because
they rejoiced in it.[14] But it might equally mean that it was a
danger to them, and in *Hamthesmal* dawn is called 'the grief
of Alfar.'[15]

In later folk-belief the elfin beings who most probably represent the earlier Alfar are generally a race dwelling on the earth
or under the earth; yet distinct from dwarfs, though these have
many elfin traits. Other groups of beings haunting the forests,
the waters, the mountains, are also akin to elves. These also
were objects of belief in earlier times and survivals of cult paid
to them were frequently condemned in the earlier Middle Ages
and even later. Whether the Anglo-Saxon glosses which speak
of *wudu-elfenne, munt-elfenne, dun-elfenne, feld-elfenne, sæ-
elfenne*, represent a mere translation of Dryads, Oreads, Naiads,
and the like, or actual groups of native elfins, cannot be definitely known.

The older German *elben* seem to have been merged in the
various kinds of dwarfs and underground folk known to later
tradition. Beautiful, fairy-like women, akin to the medieval
fées, are known to German tradition, the White Women
(Weisse Frauen) already mentioned. They are seen on hills
or in woods, or haunting old castles. Sometimes spellbound in
hills, they guard treasure; they carry flowers or a bunch of keys;
or are seen turning over pods of flax. If a mortal takes such
flowers or pods, they turn to gold. The White Woman tries to
induce a mortal to do something which will release her from
enchantment, but usually the purpose fails. Some of these
White Women are ancestral spirits; more usually they represent
older native goddesses or nature spirits, and the spell under
which they suffer may be a symbol of the ban laid by Christian-

ity on the divinities of the older faith.   Like Water-elfins they
are seen basking in the sun, combing their tresses, or washing in
a brook.[16]

In Iceland the Alfar (elves) preserve the conception of the
Eddic Alfar, and resemble fairies, though the word has now the
equivalence of the German Zwerge and Norse Unnerjordiske.
Like the Ljösalfar they do not fear the light, but appear in the
sunshine.   The name Huldu-folk, ' hidden folk,' is thought to
be preferred by them as a milder term than Alfar, and they are
also called Liuflingar, ' darlings,' an obvious euphemism such
as is often applied to supernatural beings.   Their dwellings are
in hills, stones, and rocks, or even in the sea, and they seem to
have ousted the Dvergar, now unknown to folk-belief.[17]   Another class of beings, the Trolls, are more monstrous than
elfin — giants, fiends, demons, as in the *Eddas* and Sagas, yet
they possess certain elfin characteristics.[18]

Though the elves as such are little known in Norway, there
are different classes of beings who have elfin traits.   The Trold-
folk or Tusser, trolls, gnomes, or sprites, may be as large as
men, and they possess houses, cattle, and churches.   Music is
heard from their abodes in the mountains whither they often
carry mortal maidens.[19]   Huldra (from *at hylja*, ' to hide,' ' to
cover '), a mountain fairy or wood nymph, already mentioned
in the thirteenth century, appears as a beautiful woman among
the hills, clad in blue or grey, but she possesses a tail or is hollow
behind.   Her melancholy song causes sadness, others describe
it as fascinating.   Fond of dancing, she appears at merry-
makings, and once when her partner, espying her tail, but not
wishing to betray her, said: ' Fair maid, you will lose your
garter,' she vanished, afterwards rewarding him with gifts and
cattle, of which she has a special brand.   When a man marries a
Huldra, the result is not always happiness.[20]   Huldra may be
regarded as queen of the green-clad Huldre-folk, or fairies, who
dwell in mounds, where their mournful music, the Huldreslaat,
is heard, and into which they invite men.   The Huldreman

seeks to obtain a human wife, and a youth who discovered one with his sweetheart fired a silver bullet at him, seized her, and rode off, pursued by the Huldre-folk. The subterranean folk, who are at enmity with the Huldre-folk, bade him ride on the rough and not on the smooth as they saw him approaching his house. He rode through a rye-field and escaped his pursuers, but they afterwards burned his house.[21]

The subterranean folk, or elves, described in some parts of Norway as diminutive naked boys, wearing hats, live in mounds and by lofty trees. They love music and dancing, and are described as mischievous. The dwarfs live under the earth, and are reputed to be long-armed and skilful.[22] The Vætter are tutelary spirits dwelling in Vætte-hougar or mounds, at which offerings are laid, or in waterfalls, but they are sometimes described as Trolds or Nisse — the House-spirits, like boys dressed in grey with black hats.[23]

Danish legend connects the elfin race with the rebel angels, who, when cast out of Heaven, fell into mounds or barrows — the Trold-folk, Bjerg-trolds, or Bjerg-folk — or into the moors — the Elver-folk or Elle-folk.[24] These Trold-folk differ from the Icelandic Trolls, and resemble the dwarfs. Their mounds, which contain treasure, may be seen raised on red pillars on S. John's Eve, but they also dwell under human habitations, coming up into these through a hole. They wear dark clothing, and are described as like boys in size, or, as in Jutland, four feet high, with clumsy heads, red hair, and a red cap. They love dancing, and are friendly to men, but old ballads tell of their stealing maidens, and of the seductive power of their females over men.[25]

The Elle-folk, whom legend describes as Adam's children by Lilith, and as called Elle because of the double ' l ' in her name, live in mounds on the moors, or in alder (*elle*) trees. The males, who resemble old men, are seen basking in the sunbeams, like the Ljösalfar, and entice maidens to join them. The females, who are beautiful but hollow as a dough-trough behind,

are seen dancing in the Elle-dance by moonlight. Their ravish-
ing music, often irresistible to susceptible youth, has fatal results. Their cattle feed on dew, and the cattle of men suffer
by mingling with them, or by feeding where the Elle-folk have
danced.[26] Much of the lore about the Elle-folk and the Trolds
is similar — their dances, the pillar-mounds, and their kindly
or hostile relations to men. The Danish Vetter have similar
traits, but are on the whole regarded as evil, since they suck the
breasts of children.[27]

In Sweden the same likeness in the traits of beings with different names exists. The Eddic Alfar survive in the Älvor or
Hög-folk who dwell in mounds or hills. They are more slender
and refined than mortals, and are ruled by a king and queen,
whose kingdom and laws resemble those of men. Many tales
and ballads describe the beauty and musical voices of the females, their dancing in woods, hillsides, and meadows where the
grass in the circle grows more luxuriantly than outside it. Into
the circle mortals are enticed. The dancers must disappear by
cockcrow, otherwise they remain stationary but invisible, and if
any one touches them unawares sickness and pain follow. Fever
is caused by meeting with these elves. Should a man place his
ear to an elf-mound, he hears their music, and if he promises
them redemption it becomes sweeter, but changes to lamentation
if he does not.[28] Offerings for the sick used to be laid in round
hollows cut out of rocks or stones (prehistoric rock-carvings).
The older Alfar are mentioned on a runic stone at Lagnö, which
depicts one seizing two serpents.[29]

The Rå is a harmless elfin, heard in workshops and houses,
but silent whenever any one seeks the cause of the noise. The
sound of his working is a good omen, but if he is heard lament-
ing, this betokens an accident. The Rå resembles, but is distinct from, the Vätter, guardians of houses beneath which they
live, playing with the children, or feasting when the household
sleeps. They are unknown in a house tenanted by a Nisse or
Brownie.[30]

The older literature mentions the Löfjerskor, perhaps the same as the Lund-folk, ' Grove-folk,' or Lundjungfrur, ' Grove-damsels,' invisible spirits of the heathen groves. Groves and trees, especially lime-trees, are still associated with the Alf and the Rå. Those who protect such trees or seek the help of these elfins benefit by this: but if any one breaks a branch he suffers for it.[31]

The origin of the elves and fairies of popular belief, including the older Alfar, has been sought in different directions. They were souls of the dead, nature spirits, lesser divinities, reminiscences of older races, products of dream or imagination. Probably all these mingle together in the elfin belief wherever found.[32] There is, however, some evidence that the Alfar or a certain class of them were, if not originating in, yet connected locally with the dead, perhaps because both dwelt in mounds or tumuli. Olaf Gudrudsson after his death and while dwelling in his burial-mound at Geirstad was known as Geirstadar-álf. His kinsmen sacrificed to him for a fruitful year.[33] This evidence, however, is too scanty for us to assume that all the dead were called Alfar.

The religious or mythic aspect of the older Alfar is seen in the *álfablót* and in survivals of sacrifices to elfin beings at trees or stones, and to the House-spirit or Brownie. But, on the whole, this aspect has vanished and given place to a merely superstitious regard for these beings, who are the subjects of innumerable folk-tales.

To the Alfar was offered a sacrifice called *álfablót*, resembling the *disablót* made to the Disir. A description of this is given in the *Kormaks-saga*. Thorward enquired of Thordis, a wise-woman, how his wounds could be cured. She told him that near by was a hillock in which lived Alfar. He must take a bullock and redden the hillock with its blood. Then he must make a feast to the Alfar with the meat, and he would get well.[34] Here the Alfar in their hillock resemble the dead in their barrows. In the time of Olaf the Holy the inland people of Norway were still heathen or inclined to the old heathen ways. The skald Sigvat was on a journey with his companions to the east. In Gautland they came to a homestead where, on asking admission, they were told that an *álfablót* was going on, and they must not come in.[35] The nature of this act of worship is not described.

On Helga-fell or Holy-fell, a hill regarded as very sacred by Thorolf, an early emigrant to Iceland, men were forbidden to commit that form of defilement known as *álf-reka*, 'elf-driving,' obnoxious to the Alfar.[36]

CHAPTER XXI

VÆTTIR

THE Eddic poems and the Sagas speak of a class of spirits called Vættir (singular Vætr). Parallels to the Norse word occur widely in the Germanic region: OHG *wiht,* applied to spirits and men, like the English ' wight,' which may mean a person as well as a spirit (cf. Chaucer's ' elves and wights '); MHG *wihtel, wihtelen,* glossed *elbe, lemures, lares cum corporibus morantes, vel nocturni dæmones.* Later dialect forms are Wichtlein, Wichtelmann, diminutive beings of a fairy or dwarf kind, of whom many stories are told. The AS *wiht* had the generic meaning of 'creature' or sometimes a demoniac being or devilkin.

The word Vættir may be regarded as covering any divine or semi-divine spirits, but it is applied to a class of spirits of a tutelary kind, guardians of the land or of parts of it, and related to the land much as the Fylgja was to a person. Such spirits were called Land-vættir, not easily distinguished from the Alfar, and they may have included, if they are not ultimately derived from, the spirits of the dead. In the Gulathing's law the king and bishop are ordered to enquire whether men believe in Land-vættir (*genii locorum*) who dwell in tumuli and cataracts.[1] There is no clear evidence of a cult of the Vættir.

We shall first pass in review the Eddic references to Vættir. In *Helgakvitha Hjorvardssonar* Helgi asks Hrimgerd whether one Vætr or many invaded the ships, and she replies that there were three bands of nine. These are Valkyries, and the name is thus applied to them. Of Agnar it is said in *Sigrdrifumal* that he found no Vætr to shield him. In *Oddrunargratr* the ' hollar

Vættir,' good or friendly Vættir, are appealed to for aid, and
along with them Frigg, Freyja, and favouring gods, as if they
were included among the Vættir.[2] The word is occasionally
used, with or without a qualifying adjective, in the sense of
a miserable being. Brynhild is called 'a miserable Vætr,'
and Gollrond is described by Gudrun as 'a Vætr,' in the sense
of 'a witch.' Thor addressed Loki as 'wretched Vætr.'[3]
These, however, are secondary uses of the word, which
has the more general sense of friendly spirits in the other
passages.

The Vættir occupied the land unseen, except by the second-
sighted, and they had to be treated properly, lest they should
leave a district, which would suffer in consequence. For this
reason men would avoid a district known to be haunted by
them, though a bold person would take such land where none
had dared to settle, like Olver who occupied land at Grims
River in Iceland.[4] This unwillingness to injure their suscepti-
bilities explains the curious heathen law of c. 930 A.D., known
as Ulfliot's law, which announces that men must not approach
land with a figure-head on their ship. It must be taken off, so
that the land would not be approached with gaping heads and
yawning jaws, which would frighten the Land-vættir. The
Norse ships had fearsome decorations for figure-heads, ' grim
gaping heads of ships,' as a poem by Hornklof in the *Heimskringla* describes them.[5]

King Harald Gormsson of Denmark bade a wizard Finn
take a ' skin-changing journey ' to Iceland in order to see what
tidings of it he might obtain, the king having hostile ends in
view. The Finn took the form of a whale, but when he approached Iceland he found its hills and fells full of Land-vættir,
both small and great. At four successive places he was hindered from landing: at Vapreafjord by a dragon, followed by
worms, frogs, and adders blowing venom at him; at Breida-
fjord by a great bull which waded out and bellowed at him,
accompanied by many Land-vættir; at a third place by a

Mountain-giant with many other giants; and at Eyjafjord by a great fowl with many others. These all appear to be guardian spirits of the four chief families of Iceland, dwelling in these four places. Hence there may not be a clear distinction between the Vætr and the Fylgja, or they are here acting in combination. As in other examples, they have the form of animals or giants.[6]

A woman with second-sight saw all the Land-vættir following Beorn in the south-west of Iceland to a moot, and his brother to fishing and fowling. Beorn dreamt that a Bergbui or giant asked him to be his partner. He agreed, and now his stock was increased, because a buck came to his she-goats.[7] Grettir met a huge man called Hallmund who was wounded, and said that he would help him for the aid which Hallmund had formerly given him. Hallmund took him to his cave, where his huge daughter cured the wounds of both. Friendship was sealed between them and Hallmund gave Grettir counsel. Hallmund was a Land-vætr, and, like many of these, interested in the welfare of men.[8]

By magical means the Land-vættir might be compelled to do a man's bidding. Egil Skallagrimsson was incensed against king Eirik and his queen Gunnhild. He was leaving Norway for Iceland, but first landed on an island near the coast, taking with him a hazel-pole. Setting on this a horse's head, he fixed it on a rock looking towards Norway. Then uttering a curse formula, he said: ' I erect this insulting-post (*nith-post*) and turn it against Eirik and Gunnhild.' Turning it towards the land, he added: ' I turn this insulting-pole against the Land-vættir of this land, that they go astray and not one of them light on his dwelling till they drive Eirik and Gunnhild out of the land.' On the pole runes embodying the curse were written. The horse's head on the post had the effect of the gaping heads of ships already referred to, and the curse illustrates the old runic magic.[9]

Though the Vættir were beneficent, this story shows how

they might become harmful. There were certain spirits of the Vættir kind regarded as harmful — Uvættir, like the German Unhold. They might hinder the land from being appropriated by settlers. They did harm to men by disease or sickness, but it was possible for these to be healed by those who had such a gift.[10] In *Odin's Raven Song* treacherous Vættir are said to have confounded the runes.[11]

With the coming of Christianity all spirits such as the Vættir were regarded as evil. Tradition held that they had now deserted the regions once guarded by them. Just before Christianity came to Iceland, the seer Thorhall was in bed looking through the window of his room, when his host, Sidu-Hall, who had accepted Christianity, observed him smiling. ' Why do you smile? ' he asked. Thorhall replied: ' I see many mounds opening and all spirits, small and great, are packing their gear and making ready to depart.' [12] This is an early example of a story, of which there are many variants in Germany, of the Wichtelmänner leaving the country in a body, for one reason or another.[13] In Christian custom, however, means were used to expel all such spirits, and one of these is found in the processions at Ascension-tide and at other times through the fields with the sprinkling of holy water and the saying of prayers directed against them.[14]

In spite of this the Vættir are remembered in one form or another. In Norway they are still looked upon as tutelary spirits, dwelling in Vætte-hougar, mounds at which offerings used to be laid, in trees too sacred to be touched, or in waterfalls, though they are also called Trolds or Nisser. In some districts they differ but little from the Huldre-folk.[15] The Danish Vetter have traits similar to those of Elle-folk and Trolds, but are on the whole regarded as evil.[16] The Swedish Vätter are elfin in character, guardians of houses, beneath which they live, playing with the children, the females even suckling a weakly child. When the household sleeps, they feast, but they are unknown in a house tenanted by a Nisse or Brownie. They ask help of women for their females in childbirth, rewarding them well.[17] The Faroe Islanders also believe in Vættrar which dwell in houses, where milk is placed for them. They are small and handsome, and give prosperity to a house, but leave it if a new-comer is unkind.[18]

CHAPTER XXII

THE FYLGJA

IN the Fylgja we meet with an interesting Norse conception, though one not peculiar to that region. The belief may be traced to the idea that the soul or one of the souls which, in primitive belief, a man is supposed to possess, could leave the body and become visible to its owner or another person, either as a double of the man or as an animal. It was seen in dreams and in waking life. Such a soul tended to become a separate entity, connected, however, with its owner and mainly appearing before his death. So it was with the Norse Fylgja or 'Follower.'

The Fylgja was a kind of guardian spirit most usually in the form of an animal. But in one of two examples of a Fylgja in the Poetic *Edda*, that of Helgi appeared to his brother Hethin as a Troll-wife riding a wolf bridled by snakes. He refused her advances, and she threatened vengeance upon him at the 'king's toast' that night during the Yule feast. At this toast Hethin vowed that he would have Svava, the beloved of Helgi. Then grief seized him and he fled until he found Helgi and told him of his vow. Helgi bade him not to grieve, for he was about to fight a duel and feared he would not return. Hethin now knew that he had seen Helgi's Fylgja or, as the poem puts it, his Fylgjur (plural), as if he had more than one.[1] The other reference is in *Atlamal*. An eagle was seen flying through the hall by Kostbera, who interpreted it as the *hamr* of Atli, betokening an evil fate, for with blood it sprinkled those present. *Hamr* is literally 'skin,' 'covering,' but here perhaps signifies Fylgja, Atli's soul in an animal covering.[2]

The animal Fylgja often had some corresponding aspect to that of the character of its owner — bulls and bears attended great chiefs, foxes people of crafty nature. In the *Njals-saga* Hauskuld saw in a dream a huge bear going out of the house with two cubs, and entering another house. He knew that its match was not to be found and so regarded it as the Fylgja of the peerless Gunnar.[3] Einar dreamed that he saw a huge ox going to the farm of his powerful brother Gudmund. At the high seat it fell dead. From this he was able to foretell his brother's death.[4] The boy Thorsten Ox-foot rushed into a room where an old man called Geite was sitting and fell on the floor. Geite laughed because, as he explained to the boy: ' I saw what thou couldst not see,' — a white bear-cub over which Thorsten had fallen, his Fylgja in that form.[5] A bear which fought by the side of Hrolf Kraki was regarded as the Fylgja of Bjarki, one of his heroes, who was meanwhile asleep. When Bjarki himself appeared on the battle-field, the bear vanished.[6] Eyjolf slew his enemy, but was himself lamed by a fall from his horse. He was told by a seer that the Fylgjur of his enemy's kinsfolk had caused this, whereupon he indignantly asked if they were stronger than those of himself and his friends.[7] An Icelander dreamed that a pack of wolves fell on him and his followers. Two of them were killed by him. A seer, who explained the dream, said that the wolves were Manna-hugir, ' men's spirits,' hostile to him. At the fight which followed close upon this dream, the Icelander slew two of his foes.[8] Manna-hugir is thus an alternative name for Fylgjur. Thord saw a goat wallowing in its gore and told Njal of this. Njal could not see the goat, and said that Thord must be fey, as he had seen his Fylgja. Next day he was slain.[9]

A man who was near death or who was fey was apt to see his own Fylgja. Dreaming of attacking animals also foreshadowed a fight with the men whose Fylgjur they were. A man's Fylgja protected him, but its death was followed by that of its owner, though whether this means that the Fylgja never survived its owner's death is doubtful.

The Fylgjukona, 'Following woman,' always had woman's form and was even more definitely a guardian spirit than the animal Fylgja. She might be guardian of an individual or of a family, and there might be more than one of them, three, nine, or a multitude. The name Hamingjur was also applied to them. Hamingja (singular) is from *hamr*, which meant 'a caul' as well as 'skin' or 'covering,' and as the caul was supposed to bring good luck to the child born with it, so the word Hamingja, as applied to fortune-bringing guardian spirits showing themselves in a certain form, came to be used in the abstract sense of 'happiness,' 'good luck.' [10]

These guardian spirits accompanied men, shielded, warned, consoled, and cheered them. They appeared to their *protégés* urging them to action. When one member of a family died, his Fylgjukona would pass from him to another kinsman. In *Viga-Glums-saga* Glum dreamed that a huge helmeted woman, whose shoulders touched the mountains, came up from the sea. He asked her to come into his house. On awaking he explained the dream as meaning that his mother's father, Vigfuss, must be dead. This woman was his Hamingja, for he had been held high in honour. She must be seeking to take up her abode with Glum. Soon after came news of the death of Vigfuss. This helmeted woman resembles a Valkyrie.[11] Other examples of family guardian spirits, called Œttar-fylgja or Kyn-fylgja, occur in the Sagas. As the skald Hallfred lay dying on board ship, he saw a huge woman wearing a birnie going over the waves, his guardian spirit, whom he now knew would pass from him. She asked his brother to accept her, but he refused, whereupon the skald's son Hallfred said that he would take her, and now she vanished.[12] The Troll-woman, Helgi's Fylgja, who desired Hethin's company, may have wished to be his guardian after Helgi's death.

With the coming of Christianity the belief in these female

guardian spirits was apparently altered. They were divided
into white and black groups, the former those of the new Faith,
the latter those of heathenism. This is illustrated in the *Saga of
Olaf Tryggvason.* Thidrandi, son of Hall, heard a knocking
at the door. Opening it, he saw no one; but going by the wood-
pile he heard the noise of people riding into the horse-garth
from the North. These were nine women in black with
drawn swords. Others were heard coming from the South, nine
women in white. Before he could return to the house, the
women in black wounded him. In this condition his friends
found him, and before his death he told what he had heard and
seen. The seer Thorhall said that the black women were the
Fylgjur of Hall and his kinsmen (more properly Hamingjur),
who followed the old faith, and they had attacked Thidrandi
because it was about to be overthrown. These Disir had fore-
seen this and they were angry because the usual respect would
not be paid to them. The brighter spirits, now about to connect
themselves with the family, must have wished to help him, but
had not been in time.[13] Here, as in other examples, these Kyn-
fylgjur resemble Valkyries, and the name Disir, ' goddesses,' is
applied to them as it was to Valkyries and Norns.

In the *Gisla-saga* Gisli was visited by two dream-women
(*draum-konur*), one of whom, described by him as a Valkyrie
and sent by Odin to speak his will, was evil and foretold evil.
She seems to represent the dying paganism. The other was
milder, and appeared almost as a Christian guardian angel.
Gisli was standing midway between the two faiths, pagan and
Christian. Once he saw a hall with his kinsfolk. In it were
seven fires, some burning brightly, others were low. The
milder dream-woman told him to leave the old beliefs and
witchcraft and to be good to the poor and weak. The fires were
symbols of his life: those burning brightly indicated the number
of years that he had to live. On one occasion she rode a grey
horse, and bade him follow her to her house, where he saw
benches with pillows of down. Here, she told him, he would

come when he died. The evil dream-woman often came to
Gisli, wishing to sprinkle blood over him and to bathe him in it,
and looking spitefully at him. She appeared more often as his
death drew near, saying that she would prevent what the other
had foretold from coming to pass. In this story the belief in
Fylgjukonur has been influenced by the Christian conception of
good and evil angels, associated with a man's soul, for which
they strive.[14] In *Njals-saga* Hall, a pagan, would only consent to become a Christian if S. Michael became his ' Fylgju-
engill ' or guardian angel.[15]

The resemblance of the Fylgjukona to other kinds of spirits,
e.g., Valkyries, is interesting. Valkyries also guarded chosen
heroes and came to their aid when called upon.[16] The Fylgjukonur are sometimes called Spa-disir, ' Prophetic women.'

Such beings as the Fylgja are still known in Iceland, Norway,
and Sweden. Their names are as follows: in Iceland, Fylgja;
in Norway, Fölgie (usually an animal) and Vardögr; in Sweden,
Vålnad or Vård. They are generally good, protective spirits,
and care is taken, e.g., when a man leaves the house, to allow his
protector to leave with him, lest danger meet him, especially
from his evil spirits. Sometimes they are warning spirits, telling
by knocking or rattling the latch that their owners are coming,
or that death or misfortune is at hand. Such a spirit will appear
as a double of its owner, even to the person himself, as his double
was seen by the hero of Stevenson's *Ticonderoga*, giving thus a
warning of his death.[17] This Highland superstition of the
double, used in *Ticonderoga* with such effect, or, as the Rev-
erend Robert Kirk, Episcopal minister of Aberfoyle in the
seventeenth century, called it in his *Secret Commonwealth of
the Elves*, the ' co-walker,' seen by persons with second-sight,
resembles that of the Vardögr. Kirk, however, thought that
the co-walker was a fairy.[18]

CHAPTER XXIII

THE NORNS

THE Teutonic peoples seem to have been much impressed by the idea of overruling fate or, at first, of powers controlling the destinies of men and even gods, and it enters largely into their literature. ' Fate none can escape,' is the terse saying of Gudrun in *Atlamal*.[1] Different words expressed this conception. The OHG *wurt*, Norse *urþr*, AS *wyrd* (English ' weird '), had the meaning of ' fate ' and are glossed *fatum*, *eventus*. *Wurt* may be connected with the Indo-Germanic *uert*, ' to turn,' with which are linked OHG *wirt*, *wirtel*, ' spindle.' Hence *wurt* would have the meaning of a fate spun, just as the Norns spun the threads of human fate.

In literary sources, e.g., the poem *Heliand*, *wurd* means the spirit of death or death in the abstract as the fate of man. ' Wurd took him away ' means ' Death took him away.' In *Beowulf* we find ' Wyrd ravished him away '; ' it shall befall us as Wyrd decideth.' Wyrd ordains, or weaves, or deceives, or harms. The weaving of fate, *wyrd gewæf*, occurs in an AS manuscript and also in *Beowulf*.[2] The word *metod*, ' measure ' or ' fate,' the power that metes out or dispenses, is used in *Heliand*, as in the phrase *metodo giscapu*, ' determined by fate ' (AS *meotod*, ON *mjotuþr*). The OHG *scephanten* is glossed as *parcæ*.

Besides the general use of *urþr* in the sense of ' fate ' (the word occurring in the plural *urþer*, ' fates '),[3] the Norse people believed in embodiments of fate in one or more supernatural beings, the Norns (ON Norn, plural Nornir), the chief of whom was herself called Urd (*Urþr*). The name, which still occurs in Faroese lore as Norna, is of uncertain derivation, but some students connect it with Swedish dialect forms, *norna, nyrna,* ' to tell secretly,' ' to warn,' and with Middle English *nyrnen,* ' to recite,' ' to utter.' It has also been connected with * *nornhi,* ' twisting,' ' combining.' [4]

There may first have been a number of spirits of fate, with a later more personalized Fate-goddess, the Norn Urd. But in Eddic literature there are three Norns, and ' many Norns ' are also spoken of.

Snorri says: ' There is a fair hall by the ash under Urd's well, and out of it come three maids — Urd, Verdandi, Skuld. They determine the course of men's lives and are called Norns. Yet there are many Norns — those who come to each child that is born and shape its fate, these are of the race of the gods; the second are of the Alfar; the third are of the dwarf kin.' For this statement Snorri cites *Fafnismal:*

> ' Of different origin are the Norns,
>   Not all of one race;
>   Some are of the people of the Æsir,
>   Some of the people of the Alfar,
>   And some are Dvalinn's daughters.'

At this point Gangleri interposes. ' If the Norns determine the fates of men, then they give unequal portions. Some have a pleasant, luxurious life, others have few possessions or little fame; some have long life, others short.' To this the reply is: ' Good Norns, of honourable race, appoint good life; those who suffer evil fortunes are ruled by evil Norns.' Snorri also says that the Norns who dwell by Urd's well take water of it every day and sprinkle it over the ash, so that its limbs may not rot or decay. [5]

We turn now to the Poetic *Edda.* The decision of the Norns, viz., death, is spoken of in *Fafnismal,* as if it were lying in wait at the beginning of life's voyage, in youth. The same poem describes the Norns as helpful in need, bringing the babe from the mother. It also says that the Norns have decided that Sigrdrifa

(Brynhild) shall not wake from her magic sleep. At the birth of Helgi, according to *Helgi Hundingsbana,* it was night in the house when Norns came and shaped his life. He would be most famous of warriors and best of princes. Mightily they wove the threads of fate, the golden threads, and made them fast in the moon's hall (the sky). The ends were hid in the East and West, between which his lands would be, and one of the Norns, here called ' Neri's kinswoman,' cast a chain to the North and bade it ever be firm. This betokened the widespread fame of the hero, especially in the North.[6] In *Sigrdrifumal* Mim's head bade runes to be written on the nails of the Norns, and the same poem describes birth-runes as those which give help in childbirth, when the Norns (here called Disir) are asked to aid.[7]

Yet the Norns were apt to be regarded as evil, or certain Norns were evilly disposed, as Snorri says. Thus the dwarf Andvari, transformed to a pike, told Loki that an evil Norn in old days doomed him to dwell in the waters.[8] Brynhild said that grim Norns had shaped for her the longing she had for Sigurd. Hostile fates (*urper*) had caused the complex situation arising from Sigurd's having Gudrun as wife, while she herself is Gunnar's.[9] Gudrun says that Norns awakened her with terrible dreams, which she then relates.[10] In another poem she speaks of the Norns whose wrath she seeks to escape in death, but in vain.[11] Helgi blames the Norns for his slaying Bragi and Hogni.[12] Hamther also speaks of the Norns (Disir) driving him to slay Erp, and, as he is dying, says that no one outlives the night when the Norns have spoken.[13] Angantyr found his brother dead on the field of battle, and said that he had brought him to death, for evil is the doom of the Norns. In the *Saga of Harald Fair-hair* when Einarr slew Halfdan, he sang: ' The Norns have ruled it rightly,' and in *Egils-saga* Kveldulf accused the Norns for snatching away his son Thorolf.[14] Odin, as Hnikar, warned Sigurd that Talar-disir, evil goddesses, presumably Norns, would be at both his sides, willing that he

should receive wounds.[15]   Thus death and disaster were due to
the decree of the Norns. 'The Norns have done both good and
evil,' says a runic inscription on the timber church at Borgrund,
and their evil aspect may be seen in the name for wolves —
'hounds of the Norns,'[16] and in the myth that the peace and
golden age of the gods were first broken when three giant-
maidens, of great might, came out of Jötunheim. This is told
in *Voluspa*, and these giant-maidens are generally regarded as
embodiments of fate, or Norns, mightier than the gods. The
same phrase, 'three maidens' (*þriar meyjar*), is applied to the
maidens in this passage and to the Norns themselves in a later
passage.[17]   Similarly three hosts of maidens, who come of the
giants' kin, according to *Vafthrudnismal*, are thought to be
Norns, though here kindly of nature.[18]

There is no escaping the fate fixed for men by the Norns, as
Gudrun found when she sought but could not obtain death as
a relief from her ills. So Svipdag says that no one can tear the
decrees of Urd, however undeservedly these are laid upon
him.[19]

The belief in three Norns, one of whom was apt to give an
evil destiny, where the others had promised what was good, is
illustrated by certain stories. In the *Nornagests-thattr* (written *c.* 1300 A.D.) the stranger Nornagest was persuaded to tell
before King Olaf how he came by his name. He said that
prophetic women (Volor, Spakonur) travelled through the
land, foretelling to men their fates. They were invited into
houses and gifts were given to them. They came to his father's
house when Nornagest was in his cradle, two candles burning
beside him. Two of them said that he would be greater than
any of his kindred or any sons of chiefs in the land. The third
and youngest Norn, because the crowd of people present had
pushed her off her seat, said that the child would live only as
long as the lighted candle beside him burned. The eldest now
blew it out and bade his mother keep it and not relight it.
Having heard this, Olaf persuaded Nornagest to be baptized.

He had long ago obtained the candle and now he lit it, saying that he was three hundred years old. After his baptism, the candle flickered out and he died. The Norns are regarded in this story more as actual women with prophetic powers than as supernatural. The story, which is the subject of a Faroese ballad, is, like others summarized in this volume, an interesting example of the literary use of the situation created by the coming of Christianity to Scandinavia and the passing of the old paganism. The same literary use of a like situation is found in Irish and Welsh literature.[20]

Some scholars have seen in the story of Nornagest an influence from the classical tale of Meleager and the three Parcae. That story, however, has quite a different ending; and possibly both are variants of an earlier folk-tale. The candle, with which is bound up the hero's life, is a Life-token, so well known in innumerable stories, and a similar incident occurs in medieval tales, as well as in later folk-tales, e.g., the German 'Dornröschen,' or Perrault's 'La Belle au bois dormant,' where three, seven or even thirteen *fées* or spae-wives appear at a child's birth, the last one wishing it evil, because of a fancied slight, while the others wish it good.[21]

Saxo Grammaticus, who calls the Norns Parcae and Nymphae, and makes them sisters, says that the ancients consulted their oracles about the destinies of their children. Fridleif sought to find the fate of his son Olaf, and, after offering vows, went to the temple of the gods where he saw three Nymphs sitting on three seats in the *sacellum*. The first was benignant and bestowed on Olaf beauty and favour in the sight of men. The second gave him the gift of great generosity. The third, mischievous and malignant, wished to mar these gifts and ordained to him niggardliness, which was afterwards always mingled with his generosity.[22] This story suggests a cult of the Norns, but whether we are to understand that their images sat in the *sacellum*, resembling those of the Celtic Matrae, or that the Norns actually appeared, is not clear. Saxo's Wood-nymphs, who aid Hotherus, have some traits of the Norns, but are on the whole more akin to Valkyries. So also have the three maidens who prepared Balder's magic food. The eldest maiden, who refused Hotherus a share of this food, is like the evilly disposed Norn.[23]

Three Norns, or three chief Norns, are spoken of by Snorri, copying *Voluspa*, which alone of the Eddic poems names the three. The ash Yggdrasil grows by Urd's well:

> 'Thence come the maidens, great in wisdom,
> Three from the hall beneath the tree,
> Urd one is called, the second Verdandi,
> (On a wooden tablet they scored), Skuld the third.
> Fast they set the lot of life
> To the sons of men, the fate of men.'

Urd is also named in *Havamal* where Loddfafnir says that he was by Urd's well and heard Har (Odin) speak of runes and giving counsel. In *Svipdagsmal* Groa chants a rune to Svipdag by which the bolts of Urd on every side shall guard him on the road that he goes.[24]

The names of Skuld and Verdandi do not occur again in the *Eddas*, save that Skuld is named as a Valkyrie in *Voluspa*.[25] These names appear to be due to a learned error in the twelfth century and interpolated into *Voluspa*. 'Urd' was taken for the preterite stem of *verþa*, ' to be,' and called the Norn of the past. From the same verb came 'Verdandi,' the Norn of the present; and from *skulu*, denoting the future tense, came ' Skuld,' the Norn of the future. Some influence from the conception of the Greek Moirae, denoted as Past, Present, and Future in Plato's *Republic*, or, more directly, from the seventh century encyclopædist, Isidore of Seville, who speaks of the Fates in the same manner, may be admitted here.[26] Yet there may have been an early belief in three Fates, even if these names are influenced from the sources mentioned. This is supported by the *Voluspa* passage about the three giant-maids, if these are Norns, and by the Helgi poem in which three Norns

are implied.   Three groups of Norns are known to the poet who
wrote *Fafnismal*.   This grouping into three may have reflected
the chief functions of the Norns — giving life, giving good or
evil destiny, and taking away life.

The Norns, like the Valkyries, are sometimes called Disir
(singular Dis).   The Disir are linked to the Idisi of the Merseburg charm.   Dis was used of a woman of higher rank and appears in such female names as Asdis, Vigdis, Freydis; but it
generally betokens female supernatural beings.   We do not
know for certain that these were originally spirits of dead
women.   The word Disir is used generically, and seems to
include Norns, Valkyries, and Kyn-fylgjur.   ' Dis ' was applied
to goddesses: Freyja was the Vanadis, ' Lady of the Vanir,' and
Skadi the Öndurdis, ' Snowshoe Lady.'   The word is used in
the Sagas to denote spirits, and ' Spadisir ' is used of armed
female guardian spirits and of prophetic women.[27]

Whatever the Disir were, sacrifice called Disablot was offered
to them, apparently at harvest or in winter.   The *Heimskringla*
tells how king Adils was at a Disablot in Upsala, and rode his
horse through the Disarsalr or ' hall of the Disir.'   The horse
tripped and fell, and the king was killed.   In connexion with
this Disablot there was a market and a Disathing or court, the
name surviving as that of a fair called Distingen.[28]   The Disablot is mentioned in other Sagas, e.g., the *Hervarar-saga*.   A
great Disablot was held at king Alf's at harvest-time.   Alfhild
performed the sacrifice, and in the night, as she was reddening
the high place, Starkad carried her away.[29]

A trace of a cult of the Norns is also seen in Saxo's story of
Fridleif.   Certain survivals point to the nature of the cult, and
show how the belief in these or similar goddesses of fate continued in later times.   The German Penitential of the ' Corrector ' has the following question, asked of women: ' Hast thou,
as certain women at certain times do, prepared a table in thy
house and placed food and drink with three knives, that if those
sisters called by the ancients Parcae come, they are there re-

freshed; and dost thou believe that they are able now or in the future to benefit thee? ' The Penitential of Baldwin of Exeter (twelfth century) also condemns this custom, performed in hope of good gifts being bestowed on children.[30] The 'Corrector' cites as an example of a gift conferred by the Parcae, the power of changing into a wolf at will.[31] In the Faroe Islands the *nornagreytur* or 'Norn groats' is the first food eaten by a mother after childbirth — a relic of an earlier offering to the Norns, who are supposed to show their goodwill to a child by setting marks on its nails, the *nornaspor*. Those who have white marks are believed to be lucky. Traces of this are found in Norse and German folk-lore. White nail-marks betoken that something new or pleasant is about to happen.[32]

The medieval belief in *fées* or in a group of three *fées* seems to have had its origin, especially as they were associated with the birth of children, the prosperity of a household, or the death of its members, in three sources — the Roman Parcae, the Celtic Deae Matres, and the Scandinavian Norns (possibly also the Valkyries). In Teutonic folk-story three beings like *fées*, though sometimes of the hag kind, are found, e.g., in 'The Three Spinners' and its variants. Such beings appeared suddenly, haunted wells, bestowed gifts on children, and span. Two of them might promise a good, and the third an evil, destiny.[33] The belief in Nornir and Valkyries must have been carried to France by the Northmen and there have influenced the *fée* superstition. The practice of placing food for the Parcae already noted is referred to in *Guillaume au court Nez*; and, in *La Jus de la Feuillié* of Adam le Bossu, three *fées* visit a house in Arras where a table has been set for them, but as no knife has been provided for one of them, she bestows ill fortune. The same custom was long observed in Brittany and Provence, where, at a birth or on the last day of the year, a table was spread for three *fées* in order to propitiate them and cause them to bring prosperity to the household or endow the child with happiness, just as, in Iceland, food was set out for the elves in order that they might be propitious to the household.[34]

The AS *wyrd* is represented in English and Scots by ‘ weird,’ e.g., ‘ he maun dree his weird ’ (suffer his destiny). Some link with Teutonic Fate-goddesses is therefore to be found in the ‘ three weird sisters ’ of our earlier literature. Holinshed relates that three women ‘ in straunge and ferly apparell, resembling creatures of an elder world,’ met Macbeth and Banquo and foretold their destinies. ‘ These women were either the weird sisters, that is the goddesses of destinie, or else some nimphs or feiries, endued with knowledge or prophecie by their Nicromanticall science.’ They are Shakespeare’s witches or weird sisters, the Fatae or Parcae of Boece’s *History*. A story of ‘ The weird Sisters ’ is mentioned in *The Complaynt of Scotland*, but it is now unknown, and the additions to Warner’s *Albion’s England* (1616 A.D.) speak of ‘ the weird elves,’ as Spenser has ‘ three fatal Impes ’ in his *Ruines of Time*, and Chaucer ‘ the fatal sustrin ’ (sisters), akin to ‘ the weird lady of the woods ’ in Percy’s ballad, who prophesied from a cave about Lord Albert’s child, then stole him away and nurtured him.[35]

Whatever the ultimate origin of the Norns and similar dispensers of destiny may have been, they had human counterparts in actual prophetesses or magic-wielders, like the old Scots ‘ spae-wife,’ who foretold an infant’s future, or the Norse Spakona or Volva. In some references to these it is not easy to say where the human aspect ends and the supernatural begins. As Grimm says: ‘ prophesying, inspiring and boon-bestowing women were always supposed to pass through the country, knocking at the houses of those whom they would bless,’ and ‘ tales of travelling gifting sorceresses were much in vogue all through the Middle Ages.’[36] In the story of Nornagest the Norns are called Volor and Spakonur, and are said to travel through the land. In *Viga-Glums-saga* a Volva or spae-wife called Oddibjorg goes about the land, prophesying and telling stories, her prophecies depending on the kind of entertainment which she receives.[87] Quite possibly the supernatural Norns were a reflection of such actual women who claimed and were believed to possess powers of prophecy and even of influence on human destiny.

CHAPTER XXIV

VALKYRIES

THE Valkyries attained their greatest development in Viking times, with the growth of war and of Odin as War-god and chief deity, and skaldic poetry doubtless aided in this. Yet their personality is of more remote origin.

The ON Valkyrjor (singular Valkyrja) means 'Choosers of the slain' (*valr*, 'the host of the slain,' i.e., in battle, and *kjósa*, 'to choose'—a word used for the acceptance of sacrifice by a god). They were also called Valmeyjar, 'Battle-maids'; Hjalmmeyjar, 'Helmet-maids'; Oskmeyjar, 'Wish-maids,' because they performed the wish of Odin (or, perhaps, 'Adopted-maids,' i.e., adopted by Odin, just as dead warriors in Valhall were his 'Adopted sons,' *oska-synir*); Herjan's (Odin's) Disir. The names Hjalmvitr, Folkvitr, and Sarvitr, meaning respectively 'Helmet'-, 'Battle'-, and 'Wound-wight,' also occur. To these names correspond the AS Sigewîf, ON Sigrmeyjar.[1]

Snorri describes them in their final form. They serve in Valhall, carry drink, and attend to the table-service and ale-flagons. Odin sends them to every battle. They choose or determine men's feyness and award victory. Guth, Rota, and Skuld, the youngest Norn, ride to choose (*kjósa*) the slain and decide fights.[2]

The Eddic poems have several references to purely supernatural Valkyries and also to Valkyries who are maidens of mortal descent with certain supernatural powers. The latter are found in the heroic poems. In *Grimnismal* Odin tells how certain Valkyries bring the horn at his will, and carry beer to the warriors in Valhall. These are Hrist or 'Shaker,' Mist or goddess who causes paralysing terror, thus making the enemy as if bound with fetters. In the field of battle which, as Tacitus says, was called Idistaviso by the Cheruscans, or according to the suggested reading which has won general acceptance, Idisiaviso, some have seen a place called after the Idisi — 'field of the Idisi,' as if they had aided in a victory there. Idisi means 'women' or, more definitely, 'supernatural women,' like the Greek νύμφη.[25]

The Anglo-Saxon word Wælcyrge (equivalent of Valkyrie) is glossed Bellona, Erinys, Tisiphone, Parca, *venefica*. Another gloss speaks of eyes as 'Wælcyrigean eágan' or 'gorgoneus,' as if their eyes were terrible as a Gorgon's.[26] The Wælcyrge was thus a sinister being, and other references rather suggest a supernatural witch than a Valkyrie. The older War-maidens may have degenerated into witch-like beings. An Anglo-Saxon charm against pain supposed to be inflicted by a little spear thrown by supernatural beings from the air calls it *êsa gescot, ylfa gescot, hægtessan gescot* ('shot of Æsir, of elves, of witches'). Though the charm refers more immediately to witches, these are described rather as Valkyries riding through the air. 'Loud were they, yea, loud as they rode over hills; haughty were they as they rode over lands.' Then it speaks of these 'mighty women' mustering their hosts and sending forth their whizzing spears.[27] Wulfstan, archbishop of York (1022–23 A.D.), refering to Danish invaders and Anglo-Saxon traitors, says of them that 'here in England there are witches and Wælcyrgean.'[28] Thus the name had become one of ill omen. The word Sigewîf, 'Victorious women,' mentioned in a charm, may point to the older functions of the Anglo-Saxon Wælcyrge, though here referring merely to bees, the charm forming a blessing of bees. Kemble renders it: 'Sit ye, victorious women, descend to earth; never fly ye wildly to the wood; be ye as mindful to me of good, as every man is of food and landed possessions.' Bees were supposed to have prophetic powers.[29]

Saxo's *virgines silvestres* in the Hotherus story resemble Valkyries in their functions — taking part invisibly in battle, giving victory to their favourites, governing the fortunes of war; but they have traits of the Waldfrauen of German lore and also of *fées* and elfins. Very often a hero, misled by a mist as Hotherus was, meets supernatural beings in a wonderful dwelling, which afterwards vanishes with them.[30] This glamour incident runs through all folk-belief and occurs in Snorri's *Edda*. The woodland traits of Saxo's Valkyries recall the Valkyrie-Swan-maidens of *Volundarkvitha,* as we shall see in the next Chapter.

Thus supernatural women resembling Valkyries were known elsewhere than in Norway.

In their power over the fate of men in battle and their prophetic gifts as displayed, e.g., by Brynhild [31] and by the *virgines silvestres* in Saxo's story, who, by *auspiciis ductibus,* decide the fortunes of war, the Valkyries have affinity with the Norns, the youngest of whom, Skuld, is said to be a Valkyrie. The Valkyries in *Volundarkvitha* are spinners, like the Norns, and one is called Alvitr, ' All-wise.' An episode in the *Njals-saga* is also significant. Before the battle of Clontarf in 1014 A.D. between Irishmen and Norsemen, Daurrud in Caithness had a vision in which he saw twelve women riding through the air to a bower, while blood dropped from the sky. Looking in, he saw them engaged in a horrible kind of weaving. The reels and shuttles were arrows and a sword, the spindles spears, the weights men's heads, the web was of human entrails. They sang a song — the *Daurrudar-ljod* — given in the Saga, as they wove the web for the coming battle and prophesied the course of the future. This weaving-song shows that the women were Valkyries, about to ride to the fight, guiding its destinies, and, as ' corpse-choosing spirits,' taking charge of the slain. Their gruesome weaving forebodes the course of the fight, and the woof is ' war-winning.' The weaving ended, they tore the web in two: six rode to the North with one piece; six to the South with the other. Their

prophecy will now come to pass. A similar conception of weaving fates of warriors occurs in *Beowulf* in the phrase *wigspéda
gewiofu*, 'the weavings of victory,' as if a battle's fate were
woven by higher powers.[32]

The Norns wove the fate of men in general: Valkyries could
be represented as weaving the fate of battle and the fateful death
of warriors. Norns and Valkyries are both included among the
Disir, the Valkyries being 'Herjan's Dis' and Sigrun 'the
southern Dis.' Snorri speaks of the kennings for 'women' as
'the names of goddesses, Valkyries, Norns, and Disir.' In the
Asmundar-saga Asmund saw in a dream women with weapons
standing over him, telling him he was singled out for supremacy,
and that they, his Spadisir, would aid him against his enemies.[33]
These women are like Valkyries, but also resemble the weapon-
bearing guardian spirits or Hamingjur. The Valkyries have
also, like the Norns, a prophetic aspect. Their appearance foretells battle, as already indicated, usually through a dream of
women pouring blood out of a trough, as examples in the Sagas
show.[34]

Besides having affinity with the Norns the Valkyries have
some traits of Swan-maidens, as we shall see in the next
Chapter.

To what earlier conception may the later aspect of the
Valkyries be traced? They resemble the War-goddesses or
War-spirits of Irish mythology, whose symbols or incarnations
were scald-crows, just as ravens were connected with Valkyries
— 'choughs of the Valkyries.'[35] Such Germanic War-spirits
would not at first be strictly personalized: rather would they be
a group, like the Idisi. Some then became more definitely
personal, like the German War-goddesses of inscriptions —
Vihansa, Hariasa, Harimella, or the goddess Baduhenna mentioned by Tacitus. The derivations of these names show that
the goddesses were connected with war and the host, and the
name Baduhenna is cognate to that of the Irish War-goddess
Badb.[36] With the growing dominance of Odin and the warrior

Valhall conception, the Valkyries took more definite shape as Odin's servants. The passage already cited from *Helgakvitha Hjorvardssonar* seems to connect them with the fruitfulness of the earth, but unless they and their steeds are poetically regarded as clouds dropping dew and moisture, they do not seem to have been regarded as nature spirits.

As War-spirits the Valkyries may be reflexions of actual female warriors such as were known in Germanic custom and referred to by Flavius Vopiscus, Dio Cassius, and Paulus Diaconus.[37] These are the 'shield-maids,' *skjald-meyjar,* of the Huns, spoken of in *Atlakvitha,* and apparently known also in Scandinavia. They took part in the famous Bravalla battle, according to the *Sogubrot* and Saxo, who says that they had women's bodies, but souls of men. Saxo also speaks of Alfhild, daughter of Siward, king of the Goths, who was a sea-rover with other like-minded maidens, and of Danish women who dressed as men and devoted themselves to war. 'They offered war rather than kisses, and preferred fighting to love'! [38] Such shield-maids may have given a hint for the existence of War-spirits, and it is possible that the ghosts of such women may have been regarded as spirits carrying on warfare in the unseen, as the spirits of warriors did, and so becoming spirits of battle, Idisi and Valkyries.[39] A curious belief, perhaps based on memories of shield-maids and their ghosts, is found in the Penitential of the German 'Corrector,' in a question asked of an alleged witch: 'Dost thou believe, as certain women are accustomed to believe, that in the silence of the night, when the doors are closed, thou, with other members of the devil, are raised in the air even to the clouds, and there dost fight with others, giving and receiving wounds?' [40]

The derivation of the Valkyries from nightmare demons, favoured by some scholars, rests mainly on the idea of the *herfjǫturr* as indicating 'panic terror,' a paralysis of the limbs equivalent to the effects supposed to be caused by the nightmare demon. But as only one Valkyrie bears a name, Herfjotur, resembling *herfjǫturr*, such a derivation is hardly likely. The German Walriderske, 'Rider of the dead,' is thought to be a folk-survival of the Valkyries in this earlier aspect.[41] There is no reason, however, to go beyond their origin in actual War-spirits.

CHAPTER XXV

SWAN–MAIDENS

THE world-wide myth of the Swan-maidens has its place in Scandinavian mythology. The main features of the myth are that the hero of the tale sees birds — swans, geese, or ducks — flying to a lake, where, doffing their feather dresses or wings, they become beautiful maidens, usually of a supernatural kind. Stealing up to their dresses, he takes one of them, and its owner is now in his power and becomes his wife. But long after, because she regains her dress or because her husband breaks a tabu concerning her, she flies away.

The story is sometimes told of a dog, seal, or wolf, or the captured woman has scarce a trace of the animal. There are also stories in which merely part of a woman's clothing is captured and there is no shape-shifting, and in these there seems to lie the key to the whole group — the idea that for one person to gain possession of an article of clothing, ornament, hair or nail clippings, or even to learn the secret name of another person, brings that person within his power. Any such thing contains the power of its owner, or is so much a part of him that whatever is done to it is done to him. To gain possession of it is to have its owner at one's mercy. With the weakening of such beliefs, the story would be told of supernatural women only, and it was now influenced by stories of the totemistic Beast Marriage group, in which a wife is both animal and human, and can take human form at will. When the incidents of this last group of tales were attracted into the group which told of a woman captured because a man gained possession of her garment or the like, the totemistic origin of the Beast Marriage stories had been long forgotten. But the animal skin now took the place of the garment. Two story groups thus coalesced as neatly as do the animal and human natures in the Swan-maiden.[1]

The widespread occurrence of the swan in these stories may be due to its grace and beauty, but its popularity in Scandinavian story may also be traced to the fact that the wild swan is so well known there.

The deities of the *Eddas* could assume bird form through donning a feather-dress, *fjaþr-hamr*, cognates of which word are found in other Teutonic languages.

The Swan-maiden story forms part of *Volundarkvitha*, the tale of Volund (Weyland the Smith), which reached Scandinavia from Saxon regions. It is told first in a prose Introduction, and then in the poem itself. Volund, Slagfid, and Egil were sons of a king of the Finns. They hunted wild beasts and went on snow-shoes. At Ulfdalir, where was a lake Ulfsjar, they built themselves a house. One morning they found on the shore of the lake three women spinning flax. Near them were their swan-dresses, *aptar-hamir*, for they were Valkyries. Two of them were daughters of king Hlodver — Hladgud the Swan-white and Hervor the All-wise: the third was Olrun, Kjar's daughter from Valland. The brothers took them to their dwelling: Egil had Olrun, Slagfid took Swan-white, and Volund took All-wise. For seven winters they dwelt there, and then the women flew off to find battles, and came back no more. Two of the brothers set out to seek them, but Volund remained behind. Nothing is said of the heroes' gaining possession of the maidens through their swan-dresses, but this must have been part of the original story. Nor do we hear that the maidens recaptured them, but as they flew away, they must have done so.

The poem which now goes on to tell this part of the story is fragmentary and confused. The three sisters are said to fly from the south through Myrkwood, following their fate. They rest by the shore, these southern maids, and spin flax. Then follow their names, and it is said of Swan-white that she wore swan-feathers, *svan-fjaþrar*. The account of their capture is lost, but the next lines tell how they threw their arms round the necks of the heroes. In the eighth winter they yearned for Myrkwood. The heroes returned from hunting to find them gone and sought them everywhere.

A German version of this story, whether derived from the original Saxon tale is unknown, occurs in a fourteenth century poem. Wieland (Volund) was searching for Angelburga when he saw three maidens bathing in a fountain, their doves' feather-dresses lying near. They had flown thither and, on touching the ground, had become maidens. By means of a magic root which made him invisible Wieland was able to gain the dresses. The maidens wept, but he insisted that one should marry him ere he gave them back. This was agreed to and Wieland chose that one of the three who proved to be Angelburga, long loved by him, but never seen till then.[2]

The theft of swan-dresses forms an incident in *Helreid Bryn-hildar*. Brynhild, who moves on her seat ' like a swan on the wave,' and her seven companions had hid their swan-dresses beneath an oak. There the king (Agnar?) found them and they were forced to do him service.[3]

Brynhild and her companions and the Swan-maidens of the Volund story are Valkyries. So also is Kara who appears in the form of a swan. The Swan-maidens of *Volundarkvitha* long to return to the wood — Myrkwood. Their names Hladgud and Hervor are explained philologically as indicating connexion with armies and war. They fly away to find battles. They thus resemble the Valkyrie Wood-maidens in Saxo's story, and have obvious Valkyrie traits. The Valkyrie Kara hovered as a swan over her beloved hero Helgi in battle. By magic charms she blunted the weapons of his opponents. In his fight with Hromund, Helgi swung his sword so high in air that it cut off one of her feet. She fell to the ground and was no longer able to protect him, so he was slain by Hromund.[4]

This curious mingling of Valkyries and Swan-maidens may have arisen from traits which they possessed in common —

flying through the air (though by different methods), knowledge of the future, links with an earthly hero; but in other respects they are quite distinct. While imagination dowered Valkyries with properties of Swan-maidens, the true Swanmaiden was never a Valkyrie.

The Swan-maidens of universal folk-story are usually of supernatural character, and perhaps they represent most closely Water-spirits, who would take the form of birds floating on the water. Such seems to be the nature of the three 'wise Waterwomen,' *weisen Meerweiber*, of the *Nibelungenlied*, whose garments Hagene took, thus getting them into his power and compelling them to prophesy. One said he would have great honour, thus inducing him to return their garments. Another then said that the first had deceived him. The poem does not say that their dresses were of feathers, but they are described as 'wonderful,' and the women are said to swim 'as birds upon the flood.'[5] In this episode there is no love *motif* nor does it occur in a story told by Saxo. Fridleif, king of Denmark, heard an unusual sound in the air and saw three swans flying and calling above him. They told how Hythin was rowing on the sea, while his serf drank out of gold. Better than Hythin's was the state of the serf. They then dropped a belt on which was writing by which their song was interpreted. Hythin, or rather his son (the text is confused), had been captured by a giant — the serf, and forced to row his boat. Fridleif must rescue him, and now he sets out to do this. These birds are Swan-maidens, urging Fridleif to an heroic deed.[6]

In German medieval romance and in tales current from Iceland to South Germany, the Swan-maiden appears. A medieval tale with many variants tells of a knight who saw a maiden bathing in a forest lake. He took a gold chain which she had laid aside and now she could not fly away. Because of the chain or necklace such women were called Wünschelwybere. She became his wife and bore him seven sons, each with a necklace by which they could become swans.[7] An old Swedish tale relates that a knight captured the swan-garment of a maiden and married her. Many years after she regained it and flew away, though she had borne him several children.[8] A more recent Swedish story has a hunter for hero. He saw three swans flying to a lake where, doffing their swan-dresses, they became beautiful girls. Their robes appeared like linen. Advised by his foster-mother, he took the dress of the youngest and most beautiful and so gained her as wife. Seven years later he showed her the dress and told her the story. She took it, and that instant became a swan and flew away.[9] The seven years recall the same period in the Volund story: it occurs often in fairy-tales, especially in those where a mortal is in the power of elfins and escapes at the end of that time.

The swan is often a prophetic bird in Germanic and other folk-belief, just as the Swan-maidens also sometimes foretell the future. In Eddic cosmogony two swans are fed in Urd's well, the well of the Norns, and from them comes the race of swans.[10] Whether this has any connexion with the Swan-maiden myth or with Norns as Swan-maidens is unknown.

The story of the Knight of the Swan had many variants, mainly Germanic. Vincent of Beauvais gives an early version in which a skiff drawn by a swan attached to it by a silver chain was seen on the Rhine at Cologne. From it a knight leaped ashore, and then swan and skiff disappeared. Long after, when the knight had married and had many children, the swan returned with the boat. The knight leaped into it and was seen no more. His descendants were living in Vincent's day.[11]

In other versions the knight is ancestor of Godfrey of Bouillon or of other noble persons, and is also identified with Lohengrin, son of Percival, the tale being thus linked to Arthurian romance.[12] The Swan-knight who comes and goes so mysteriously is a denizen of the Other World, and his disappearance was the result of his wife's asking his name or whence he had come. Grimm tried to connect this romance, of which still earlier forms must have existed, with the Danish hero-ancestor

Sceaf or his father Scyld, who, as a child, was conveyed in a boat to the land which he was to aid and rule, sleeping on a sheaf of corn (hence the name Sceaf), with weapons and treasure. At his death, his body was put in the boat which then disappeared as it had come.[13] There is, however, no swan in the legend of this culture-hero.

The origin of the Knight of the Swan is explained in later forms of the romance by connecting him with the story of the swan-children. Seven children were born at a birth to the wife of a king, each with a silver chain round its neck. Through the enmity of the king's mother they were exposed, but a hermit saved them. She then sent men to slay them, but they contented themselves with taking the chains, and now the children became swans. One of them, Helyas, was absent, and became protector of the swans, eventually regaining their chains, when they reassumed human form. One of them, however, had to remain a swan, for his chain had been melted to form a goblet. This swan later drew the skiff of Helyas, the Knight of the Swan.

This story existed separately before it was joined to the Swan-knight tale in the twelfth century, and in some versions of it the sister, not one of the brothers, is guardian of the others. One of the earliest versions is told by the monk Johannes in his *Dolopathos, c.* 1190 A.D. Here the mother of the swan-children is called a *nympha,* and was probably a Water-elfin.[14]

CHAPTER XXVI

DWARFS

THE Teutonic forms of the English word ' dwarf ' are: ON *dvergr*, OS *dvärgher*, AS *dweorg*, OHG *twerg*, OF *dweorh*. These can be traced back for at least twelve centuries, showing that the belief in dwarfs must have been held by the undivided Teutons. The word may be connected etymologically with the idea of hurting or oppressing, as by the nightmare spirit, or with that of deceiving or hurting through deception — a root-meaning akin to that of the various forms of the word ' elf.'

Eddic cosmogony tells of the origin of the dwarfs. A later addition to *Voluspa* shows the gods in council. Who would shape the dwarf race from Brimir's blood and the bones of Blaenn? Motsognir, mightiest of dwarfs, was created, then Durin. At Durin's command the dwarfs made many figures of human form in (or out of) the earth. Then follows a catalogue of dwarfs' names.[1] Brimir and Blaenn may be names of Ymir, from whose flesh and blood earth and sea were made. The phrase ' figures of human form ' does not make quite clear whether these were men created by dwarfs, or, more likely, dwarfs created in human form by the chief dwarfs.

Snorri quotes these stanzas, but gives his own prose version. The gods sitting in council recalled that the dwarfs had quickened in the mould and underneath the earth, as maggots in flesh. They had received shape and life in Ymir's flesh, but now, by the gods' decree, they had human understanding and form. They dwell in the earth and in stones.[2] Snorri had already told how the gods placed under each corner of the overarching Heaven a dwarf — Austre, ' East '; Vestre, ' West '; Nordre,

'North'; and Sudre, 'South,' names which appear in the
Voluspa catalogue. Heaven is therefore called 'Task or Burden of the dwarfs' or 'Helmet of Austre,' etc.[3]

With this Eddic account of the origin of the dwarfs may be
compared that in the German *Heldenbuch*. God made dwarfs
for the cultivation of waste lands and mountains, and made them
artful and wise to know good and evil and the uses of all things.
They erected splendid hollow hills. Giants were created to kill
wild beasts and dragons and so to give security to the dwarfs.
Heroes were also created for their aid.[4] This must be based on
some older pagan myth.

Of some of the dwarfs *Voluspa* says that they went from stone
dwellings through moist fields to sand fields — a poetic account
of a dwarf migration or of their power over various parts of
nature, rocks, earth, and moisture. Snorri quotes the passage,
and then divides dwarfs into those dwelling in mould and in
stones, and those who proceed from Svarin's mound to Aurvangr
on Jöruplain.[5] There is no doubt that the dwelling of dwarfs is
underground, within hills and rocks.

Some of the Norns are said to be daughters of the dwarf
Dvalin. Dvalin is a representative dwarf, since other dwarfs are
'Dvalin's host'; the sun is called by dwarfs 'Dvalin's deceiver'; and Dvalin gave magic runes to the dwarfs.[6] The
dwarf Thjodrörir, otherwise unknown, sang before Delling's
doors a magic song which gave strength to gods, ability to elves,
and wisdom to Odin.[7] Other dwarfs are named as doing certain
deeds or are otherwise singled out for notice. There are the
nine who, with Loki, built Menglod's palace. Daenn and
Nabbe made the boar Hildesvini for Freyja. Lit was kicked by
Thor into Balder's pyre. Fjalar and Galarr slew Kvasir and
thus obtained the mead of poetry. Alviss, 'All-knowing,' is
prominent in *Alvissmal*. The dwarf Sindri's race possess a
hall of gold in Nidafell, according to *Voluspa*. This is apparently in Hel, and near it is the giant Brimir's beer-hall. The
verse is a later interpolation. Snorri calls the hall itself Sindri,

and makes it a future abode of righteous men.⁸   Other dwarfs are named in myths cited in this Chapter.

As we have seen the Eddic dwarfs are hardly to be distinguished from the Dökkalfar and Svartalfar, although *Odin's Raven-song* mentions dwarfs and Dökkalfar separately.⁹   Certain dwarfs' names show a connexion with the elves — Alf, Gandalf, Vindalf, while Dainn is a name shared by both a dwarf and an elf.   Alberich (*alb* = ' elf ') was a king of dwarfs, and Volund, skilled in that smith-work for which dwarfs were famous, and himself taught it by a dwarf, was yet a ' prince ' and ' lord ' of elves.   Grimm, who identifies dwarfs and Svartalfar, points to Pomeranian folk-lore which divided dwarfs into white, brown, and black, according to their dress.¹⁰

Dwarfs were skilled in smith-work and their work was often of a magical kind.   Loki, having cut off Sif's hair, and threatened with vengeance by Thor, swore to get the Svartalfar to make hair of gold for Sif.   He therefore went to the dwarfs called Ivaldi's sons, and they made the hair, as well as the ship Skidbladnir and Odin's spear Gungnir.   Loki wagered his head with the dwarf Brokk that his brother Sindri would not make three equally precious things.   Sindri bade Brokk blow the bellows and not cease till the work was done.   Loki, transformed into a fly, stung Brokk three times in hope of making him stop blowing, but he could not hinder the precious things from being forged.   These were a bear with golden bristles, the ring Draupnir, and a hammer.   Sindri sent Brokk to Asgard to claim the wager.   Loki presented the spear to Odin, the gold hair to Thor, and the ship to Frey.   Brokk also presented his gifts — the ring to Odin, the boar to Frey, and the hammer to Thor, telling the magical virtues of each.   The gods sat in judgment on the gifts, and the decision of Odin, Thor, and Frey was to be final.   They decided that the hammer was best of all, their sure defence against the Frost-giants, and that the dwarf had won the wager.   Loki offered to redeem his head, but Brokk would not hear of this.   ' Take me,' cried Loki, but Brokk could not, for Loki wore the shoes with which he went through air and over water. Brokk asked Thor to catch him, and he did so. Loki told Brokk that he might have the head but not the neck. The dwarf took a thong and a knife and would have bored a hole in Loki's lips and stitched up his mouth, but the knife would not cut. Then Brokk wished for his brother's awl, and at once it was in his hand and pierced the lips. He stitched the lips together, but Loki ripped out the thong, called Vartari.[11] So the story ends, and apparently we are to understand that Loki outdid Brokk by his cunning. The dwarfs, as skilful artificers, were thus necessary to the gods for some of their most cherished possessions.

Regin, fosterer of Sigurd, was a dwarf in stature, wise, fierce, and clever at magic. He became king Hjalprek's smith and taught Sigurd, making for him the sword Gram. It was so sharp that when he thrust it into the Rhine and let a strand of wool float against it, the strand was cut in two. With this sword Sigurd cleft Regin's anvil, and afterwards slew Fafnir the dragon and Regin himself.[12]

Hogni's sword, Dainslef, was made by dwarfs, and it caused a man's death every time it was drawn. If one was only scratched by it, the wound would not heal.[13] A dwarf forged a sword for Egil, who had lost his hand, and this sword, fastened to his elbow, was wielded by him as well as if his hand had grasped it.[14] Volund fashioned seven hundred rings of gold adorned with gems, a wonderful sword, and also golden ornaments for king Nidud. When he afterwards slew the king's sons, he set their skulls in silver, and made gems of their eyes and a brooch of their teeth.[15] The *Thidriks-saga* tells how Velint (Volund) was placed for instruction by his father Vadi with the smith Mimir and then with two skilful dwarfs who dwelt in a hill. None could forge such swords, weapons, and armour as they. Velint slew them because they desired to kill him for being cleverer than themselves — a common folk-tale incident.[16] Dwarfs also made the famous Brisinga-men.[17]

When forced to exercise their skill, dwarfs would sometimes curse the weapon made by them so that it would bring disaster for generations after. Svafrlami, grandson of Odin, was hunting and saw two dwarfs standing by a stone. He forced them to make him a sword which would cut iron like cloth and always bring victory to its wielder. When he returned to get the sword the dwarfs told him that it would be the death of a man every time it was drawn, that it would be the instrument of three acts of villainy, and that it would cause Svafrlami's death. Svafrlami struck at the dwarfs as they fled within the rock, into which the blade sank deeply. He called the sword Tyrfing. It shone like a sunbeam, and it could be sheathed only when human blood was still warm upon it.[18]

In parallel stories the sword or treasure of dwarfs or supernatural beings is forced from them as a ransom for their lives, and again these bring disaster to their new owners or their successors, like the treasure which Loki took from Andvari.[19] This treasure is prominent in the Saga and the Eddic poems of the Volsungs, and the fulfilling of the curse is seen in these. In the German version the treasure belongs to the Nibelungs or Niflungar, who, though depicted as Burgundian kings and their people in some accounts (because these were the last possessors of the treasure), are in other versions, following an older tradition, subterranean beings, dwarfs or black elves. The Nibelungs are the 'children of Nebel' or 'darkness' (cf. Niflheim). Siegfried (Sigurd) acquired their hoard, a Tarnkappe or cloak of invisibility, and the sword Balmung.[20]

Besides skill in smith-work and possession of treasure, dwarfs are dowered with cunning, hidden knowledge, and supernatural power. Andvari was forced by Loki to tell what retribution will befall deceivers in the Other World, viz., wading through the stream Vadgelmir. Alviss can name earth, sun, moon, etc., according to the names given them by different orders of beings, and Thor says: ' In one breast I have never found so much ancient lore.' The dwarfs Fjalar and Gallar collected the blood of Kvasir, mixed honey with it, and so made the mead of poetry, or 'the dwarfs' drink.' [21]

The Eddic dwarfs and those of later folk-lore dwell in rocks or within hills, where they pursue their craft of metal-workers. Alviss is described by Thor as pale, as if he had lain with corpses, and he says that he dwells deep under the earth, his house is under a stone.[22] Svegdir, a grandson of Frey, sought the home of the gods and of Odin. After much travelling he came to a stead called Stone in the east of Sweden, where was a huge rock. There he saw a dwarf sitting, and was told that, to find Odin, he must enter the rock. Svegdir ran into it; the rock-door closed, and he was never seen again, like many others who, in popular tales, enter concealed doors in hills into dwellings of supernatural beings.[23] That mountains were an abode of dwarfs is shown by the Norse word for 'echo,' dverga-mal, literally 'speech of dwarfs,' the dwarfs being supposed to throw back the words spoken. Mountain-tops in Sweden are sometimes called Dvergemål-kletten, 'Dwarf-speech summit.'[24]

In their subterranean region, as later Sagas and stories show, the dwarfs have a beautiful kingdom and are ruled by kings. They come forth at night, for sunlight is fatal to them, turning them to stone, as Thor says to Alviss: 'Daylight is upon thee, O dwarf; now shines the sun in the hall.' The implication is that the dwarf was turned to stone, like dwarfs in other stories or the monstrous Hrimgerd.[25] Hence, from dwelling underground, dwarfs are pale of countenance.

Nothing is said in the Eddas of the dwarfs' hat or cloak of invisibility, the Tarnkappe, Tarnhut, Nebelkappe, or Helkappe of German dwarf traditions, though it must have been known in Scandinavia as the OS Helidhelm and ON Hulidshjalm show. This garment also gave its owner great strength, and if it fell into a mortal's possession, he could compel a dwarf to do his will or relinquish his treasure.

The more evil aspects of dwarfs in their relations with men as shown in later belief is suggested by some of their names in

the *Edda* — Althjolf, ' Mighty thief,' Hlethjolf, ' Hill thief,'
while in *Thidriks-saga* Alfrek (Alberich) is called ' the great
thief.' [26] Their love for beautiful girls or women is illustrated
by the desire of Alviss for Thor's daughter and the amour of the
four dwarfs with Freyja, just as in later German heroic poems
dwarfs carry off maidens into their hills. [27]

In all Teutonic lands, especially in their mountainous districts, dwarfs have been a subject of popular superstition, and
their traits as seen in the *Eddas* reappear along with many
others. They are called Bjergfolk, Unterjordiske, Unterirdische, Erdleute, Bergsmiedlein, Erdmännlein, Stillevolk,
Kleinevolk, and by other names. They seem now to be unknown in Iceland, though their name survives in place-names —
Dvergastein, Dverghól, etc. Dverge are still known in Norway
and the Danish Bjergfolk or Troldfolk closely resemble dwarfs,
and dwell in mounds containing rich treasure. The Swedish
Dvärg lives in the mountains with wife and daughters of rare
beauty. Dwarfs are also known in the Faroe Islands; and in
Orkney and Shetland the Trolls or Drows are akin both to
dwarfs and fairies, but the older belief in Dvergar is shown by
such a name as ' the Dwarfie stone,' a huge boulder on Hoy. [28]

The dwarfs of Germany have, on the whole, a wider field of
operation than the Norse dwarfs of the *Eddas*, perhaps because
the older *elben* are blended with them. They have skill in
smith-work and teach it to men, yet the hammering and ma-
chinery of men drove them away. They spin; they help men in
harvesting and hay-making. They give freely to those whom
they favour, but not to those who seek them out or annoy them.
Tales of dwarfs abound in the mining regions: on the plains the
Unterirdische are a kind of elfin equivalent of the mountain
dwarfs. The dwarfs have great treasures in their underground
dwellings, and music sounds from these places, whence they
come forth at night to avoid the sun. In them they have control
over metals and work at their smithies. An older description of
the dwarfs' hollow hills is found in the *Heldenbuch*, where the

dwarf king Laurin leads Dietrich and his friends into hills brighter than the sun because of their encrusted gems. They echo with the song of birds, and are full of dwarfs, singing, playing, and feasting.[29]

The dwarfs are like little men, sometimes no bigger than a thumb, deformed, with large heads, long beards, feet occasionally like those of a goose or goat. They are clad in grey, but their kings are more splendidly attired. These kings have large territories, and they and their subjects are often described in German medieval poetry and romance, which reflect on them the feudalism of the time.[30] Old tradition depicts them as leading simple lives, and a dwarf in *Ruodlieb* complains of human faithlessness which, with unwholesome food, is the cause of men's brief life. Dwarfs themselves are often of great age. Something of the old heathenism clings to them. They are even called ' heathen,' and dislike the building of churches and bell-ringing, no less than they do agriculture and the clearing of forests.[31]

The smith or other work of dwarfs was made available to men who laid metal to be forged or wool to be spun, with a piece of money, before their holes. Next morning the work was found done. This custom, referred to in several tales, is connected with Weyland (Volund) the Smith in England. At an ancient sepulchral monument at Ashbury in Berkshire, supposed to be the dwelling of Weyland, a horse requiring a shoe was left with a piece of money. When its owner returned, the horse was shod and the money was gone. This monument was already styled ' Welandes Smiththan ' in a charter dating from before the Norman Conquest, the tradition thus belonging to Saxon times. A similar legend was told in Greece of Hephaistos, and we may regard the story as based on early custom and enshrining the mystery and fear attaching from long past ages to metal-workers. It is also connected with the wide-spread custom of ' the silent trade.' [32]

The dwarfs sought human help when they required it, e.g.,

in dividing a treasure, as in an incident in the *Nibelungenlied*. The dwarf king Nibelung left his hoard to his sons who asked Siegfried to divide it, giving him the sword Balmung as reward. But as he was long at his task, they attacked him and he slew them. The folk-tale incident of a hero called in to divide magical things among disputants often describes these as dwarfs. The hero is able to make himself possessor of the things in question.[33] Or again dwarfs seek human aid in their fighting, like the dwarf king who gave William of Scherfenberg a girdle with the strength of twenty men, on condition of his aiding him and keeping silence about their pact.[34] Other services done to German dwarfs were sometimes rewarded with gifts which brought prosperity to a family as long as its representatives lived.[35] The most usual service was that sought for from human midwives, who were well rewarded for their trouble.

They also gave help to mortals, e.g., by means of their magic power, as in the well-known story of ' Rumpelstiltschen,' though here an equivalent was sought in return. As wise counsellors they advise men or warn them of danger, and those coveted magic articles which produce unfailing abundance are sometimes given by them to men. Frequently dwarfs or little red men come out of a magic snuff-box, or appear at the blowing of a flute, or when the ground is knocked on, and perform otherwise impossible tasks for him who summons them.[36]

Yet they were often hostile to men, and many stories relate how dwarfs, like other elfins, carry off women or girls to be their wives. They also, like fairies, substitute for mortal children stolen by them their own deformed offspring. The changeling is called Umskiptungar (Iceland), Skiftingar (Denmark, Norway, from *skipta*, 'to exchange'), OHG wihselinga, German Wechselbalg, Kielkröpf. Dwarfs also steal from men — corn and pease from the field, loaves from a baker, and the like.[37]

Less animistic than elves, the dwarfs seem to be more akin to men. Does this mean that they are a folk-memory of an actual race of small people? This theory has been seriously held or has been regarded as a possibility by different scholars. Dwarfs were an aboriginal, small race, driven to the hills by new-comers, but regarded by them with awe as being in league with the gods of the land and possessed of powerful magic. They and their deeds became more and more unreal as time passed on, until tradition made of them a supernatural folk, with greater powers and knowledge than men. We must remember, however, that dwarfs and pygmies belong to universal folk-lore, not only to that of the Teutonic or even of the Indo-European people. Even if an actual pygmy people, as in Africa, may be regarded by their neighbours as more or less supernatural,[38] the theory does not account for all the facts, and it is equally possible that a race of spirit-beings might have been invested with traits of an actual race.

The existence of pygmy races at the present time, Negrillos and Negritos, as well as their probably wide-spread existence in Neolithic times, has given support to this theory, especially when it is proved that certain characteristics of dwarfs are also those of these races. If traditional dwarfs are a folk-memory of actual people, then the tradition must be an early one, coming down through the generations from prehistoric times. But while some traits of dwarfs and of elfins generally may be traced to those of actual races of men, others are purely animistic in origin. Even where, as in Polynesia, Melanesia, or Africa, certain groups of fairy-like beings seem to be an actual race thus transmuted, many things ascribed to them are non-human — their tiny size, the supernatural powers of glamour and invisibility, their spirit nature. With every allowance for the facts, the existence of an early pygmy race cannot be the sole cause of the belief in dwarfs and elfins. The belief in the soul as a manikin, no less than general animism, has had great influence in its formation. What is said of dwarfs and fairies is also said of groups of beings with no human ancestry — Greek Nereids, Slavic Vily, foxes in Japan, vampires, ghosts, etc., and many fairy-like beings —

Nixies, mermaids, swan-maidens — have no link with an older human race.[39]

Primitive animistic or pre-animistic ideas are the basis of dwarf and fairy beliefs, attached now to groups of purely imaginary beings, now to all kinds of supernaturals, now linked with traditions of actual people. Much also must be assigned to the free-working fancy of imaginative men in the past, its results quickly assimilated by their fellows. And there is much in the saying that ' the wish is father to the thought.' Men wished to be invisible, to transform themselves, to fly, to possess magic weapons and other articles, abundant treasures, knowledge of the future. What more easy than to believe that certain beings had such powers and gifts, and that favoured mortals could obtain them on certain terms, and had actually done so from time to time!

CHAPTER XXVII

GIANTS

THERE are different names applied to giants in the *Eddas* and Sagas, as well as in German tradition. ON *jötun*, AS *eoten*, OD *jaetten*, from *eta*, ' to eat,' perhaps express their gluttony, and these names are continued in the ' Etin ' of Scots folklore. ON *thurs*, AS *thyrs*, OS *duris*, OHG *thuris*, perhaps mean ' powerful ' (cf. Sanskrit *turás*, ' strong '), though the corresponding Danish *tosse* means ' simpleton.' The OHG *risi* (sanskrit *uřsan*), ' strong,' appears in ON in Berg-risi, ' Mountain-giant.' The MHG *hiune*, German *Hüne*, signified in its root-meaning strength and daring, or perhaps great size, but was confused with the name of the dreaded Huns. The word ' troll,' formerly a more or less demoniac being, is now used in Scandinavian speech for ' giant ' or ' ogre.' Female giants were called *thursa-meyjar*, ' giant-maids,' *gygr*, and occasionally *gifr* or *grithr*.

Giants appear in the Eddic cosmogony. The first giant, Ymir or Aurgelmir, existed before earth and sea were formed, and he was made from venom dropping from Elivagar, ' Stormy Waves,' into Ginnunga-gap. According to Snorri, this venom congealed into ice, and the ice melted in contact with warm air from Muspellheim. Life quickened in it and Ymir was the result. He and all his descendants, the Frost-giants, were evil.[1] To Odin's question: ' How did Ymir beget children without a giantess? ' Vafthrudnir replied that beneath his arms a male and female grew, and foot with foot formed a six-headed son. This son was probably Thrudgelmir, mentioned in an earlier stanza of *Vafthrudnismal*. His son was Bergelmir, and Vafthrudnir remembered how he was born in a boat long ago.[2]

Snorri gives the same account and says that Ymir was nourished with the milk of the cow Audhumla.[3] When Ymir was slain so much blood flowed from him that all the Frost-giants were drowned save Bergelmir who, with his wife, escaped in a boat (or mill-stone).[4] Saxo also makes the giants an ancient people, the first of three races in far off time.[5]

The giants dwelt in Jötunheim, or in Utgard outside the limits of earth and sea, assigned to them by the gods. It is on the edge of Heaven, beyond Elivagar. The river Ifing, which never freezes, separates the realms of giants and gods. This region lies in the North or North-east, or East, according to various accounts in the poems and in Snorri.[6] It has fields with cattle, regions where hunting and fishing are carried on, and halls where the giants dwell. Saxo's giants have also herds or goats.[7] On its frontier, on a hill, sits Eggther, warder of the giants, and the cock Fjalar, whose crowing wakes them at the Doom of the gods.[8] At the end of Heaven, hence probably near Jötunheim, the giant Hræsvelg, 'Corpse-eater,' sits in eagle's form and makes the winds with his wings. His hill overlooks Hel.[9] Jötunheim was a mountainous region, and this, coupled with the fact that in later tradition mountains are the home of giants, explains the names Bergbui, Bergrisi, 'Mountain-giant.' But any distant region was apt to be called the home of giants and monsters. Saxo says that a wild region north of Norway and separated from it by the sea, was peopled with monsters, and perhaps Greenland is intended. Snorri speaks of giants, dwarfs, and 'blue men,' dragons and wild beasts, as existing in Sweden. Saxo also thought that Denmark had once been cultivated by giants, and found proof of it in megalithic remains and boulders on hill-tops. The statement in *Grimnismal* that the Frost-giants dwell under one of the roots of Yggdrasil, and beside Mimir's well, according to Snorri, is due to the systematizing of Norse mythology.[10]

The giants had separate dwellings in Jötunheim, e.g., Gymir, before whose house fierce dogs were bound. Thrym is called 'lord of the giants,' and has many giants under him, and Utgard-Loki is lord of Utgard. *Svipdagsmal* also speaks of 'the seat of the giant race.' Hence giants lived in some kind of community.[11]

Giants are of great size and are sometimes monstrous. This is shown by Skirnir's vast glove and by other indications. They have many heads, varying from three to the nine hundred possessed by Tyr's grandmother. According to Saxo, they are shaggy, monstrous beings, who can alter their shape or size.[12] The hero Starkad, sprung from giants, had many hands. Thor tore four of these off and now his giant's body was contracted and made human. Saxo records this, but discredits it. In another account, Starkad had eight arms, but perhaps the hero is confused with a giant of the same name overcome by Thor.[13] Giant women were sometimes beautiful, and beloved by gods or heroes. The giants were of great might. Vidblindi drew whales out of the sea like little fish. Others tossed huge rocks as if they were small stones. The giantess Hyrokkin could alone move Balder's funeral ship.[14] To giants as to dwarfs the sun was fatal, turning them to stone. The monstrous Hrimgerd was thus transformed, and 'men will mock at her as a harbour-mark.' In one of many stories of S. Olaf's encounters with giants, he cursed a giantess so that she became stone.[15]

Adjectives applied to giants indicate aspects of their character — 'haughty,' 'insolent,' 'dangerous,' 'joyous,' 'morose,' 'fierce,' 'hard,' 'energetic,' 'warlike.' In later tradition they are stupid, but in the Eddic poems they have a wisdom of their own, due to their great antiquity and early origin. Hence they are 'wise,' 'sagacious,' 'full of wisdom,' as Vafthrudnir was. Suttung owned the poetic mead, and runes were given to giants by the giant Alsvith, 'All-wise.'[16]

Giants were often violent, especially when thwarted, and their rage was called *jötunmodr*, 'giant frenzy.' Saxo tells how a giant fell into such a frenzy, biting his shield, gulping down

fiery coals, and rushing through fires.[17] They were nevertheless
often good-natured, ' merry as a child,' like Hymir in *Hymiskvitha*. Mostly they were hostile to gods and men, and Thor
was their great opponent, his hammer the great defence of the
gods against the Frost-giants. The gods feared that the Hill-
giants might cross Bifrost bridge (the rainbow) into their abode.
Hence what was red in it was burning fire, and Heimdall was
its guardian. Yet a giant rebuilt their citadel for the gods that
it might be strong against the giants. The breaking of the gods'
pledges to this giant, however, leads to their attack upon them
at the Doom of the gods, when the Frost-giants come out with
Loki and Hrym against the Æsir.[18] The giants sometimes out-
witted the gods, as in the story of Skrymnir, but more usually
gods, especially Odin, were cleverer than giants and cheated
them, just as Thor overcame them by force.[19]

Yet Odin's descent was traced from giants, and at Balder's
funeral Frost- and Hill-giants were present. Gods also married
giantesses or had amours with them — Frey, Njord, Odin, and
Thor (with Grid and Jarnsaxa).[20] Giants also sought to unite
with goddesses, Thjazi with Idunn, Thrym with Freyja. Gefjun had four sons by a giant.[21] Saxo tells several stories of
giants who carried off princesses; and the giantess Hardgrep,
who had nurtured Hadding, sought and obtained his love when
he was grown up. The Eddic giants also stole mortal women,
as Hrimgerd says her father Hati did. Hrimgerd herself desired Atli as a lover.[22]

Besides the giants who figure in the myths of Thor and Odin,
others are named and described. Brimir had his beer-hall in
Okolnir (' the not-cold,' presumably a volcano in the frost regions). From his blood came the dwarfs, and Odin has his
sword, unless Brimir is here the name of the sword itself.[23]
Hrimnir, a Frost-giant, has children called Heith, ' Witch,' and
Hross-thjof, ' Horse-thief.' Skirnir told Gerd that Hrimnir
would stand and stare at her fate if she refused Frey.[24] Hrimgrimnir, ' the Frost-shrouded,' dwells by the door of Hel, and

Gerd was threatened with him as her possessor.[25] Helgi told
the monstrous Hrimgerd that she would be mistress of the giant
Lothen, who dwelt in Tholley, ' Pine Island.' This very wise
giant was yet worst of all dwellers in the wild.[26] Alvaldi was
father of Thjazi, Idi, and Gangr. He was rich in gold, and at
his death his sons agreed to take the gold each in the same number of mouthfuls so that all should share equally.[27]

However monstrous the giants may be, they are anthropomorphic. A few other beings called giants are theriomorphic,
e.g., the brood of Loki, himself called a giant and the son of a
giant. The giantess Angrboda bore to him the Fenris-wolf and
the Midgard-serpent, giant animals of a supernatural kind.[28]
The wolves Hati and Skoll, who pursue the sun and moon, are
giants, offspring of the Fenris-wolf and a giantess.[29] The giant
Hræsvelg, who causes the winds, is in eagle form and is called
' the tawny eagle ' who gnaws corpses at the Doom of the gods.[30]
Giants also took animal form occasionally, and some of them had
animal names — Hyndla, ' She-dog,' Kött, ' Cat.' [31]

The Hill-giants were connected with hills and rocks. Suttung and Gunnlod dwelt in rocks, and the rocks were called ' the
giants' paths.' Thrymheim, ' Home of clamour,' where Thjazi
dwelt, was in the mountains. The giantess who accosted Brynhild had her home in the rocks.[32] The titles Bergbui, Bergrisi,
Berg-daner point to hills as the giants' dwelling, and some hills
were regarded as petrified giants, while some names of giants
suggest a connexion with stone. Hrungnir had a stone head and
heart, and a shield made of stone.

Frost-giants or Hrimthursar, are personifications of frost,
snow, and ice, or of the mountains covered with snow and ice.
As Ymir himself originated out of ice, so his descendants are the
Frost-giants, who appear at the Doom of the gods in a body, led
by Hrym.[33]

Fire-giants are suggested by the dwellers in the Fire-world
who, led by Surt, come forth to fight the gods. Surt's fire will
destroy the world; meanwhile he sits at the frontier of Muspell,

the region of heat, to defend it, brandishing a flaming sword. Icelandic folk-lore knows that in the Surtarhellir, a great lava-cave, there once dwelt the giant Svart or Surt.[34] The giantess Hyrokkin has a name which means ' Fire-whirlwind.' Logi in Utgard is fire which consumes everything. Ægir's servant was Eldir, ' Fire-man,' and other giants have names pointing to the same element. Eruptions were thought to be caused by giants.

Some giants were connected with the wild forest regions. Vitholf, ' Wolf of the wood,' named in *Hyndluljod,* may be the Vitolfus of Saxo, skilful in leechcraft, and living in the wilds. Those who sought him with flattering words to cure them he made worse, for he preferred threats to flattery. When the soldiers of Eirik menaced his visitor Halfdan, Vitolfus led them astray by a delusive mist. His name is from ON *viþr* (OHG *witu*), ' a wood,' and he resembles the Wild Man of the Tirol who aids by leechcraft only when he is threatened. He is akin to the giant Vidolf in *Thidriks-saga* and to the Bavarian giant Widolt, ' the Wood-lord.' [35] The Ivithjar, ' Wood-giantesses,' of whom Hyndla was one, and the giant Welderich, ' Lord of the woods,' belong to the same category. The *Eddas* speak of an old forest called Iarnvith, ' Iron-wood,' in which lived the giantess who bore Fenrir's monstrous brood. In that wood dwelt troll-women called Iarnvithjur, ' Iron-wood women.' [36] These giants of the woods resemble the shaggy Wood-spirits or Schrats of German folk-lore. Such giants resented the cutting down of timber in their domain, threatening the wood-cutter with death if he persisted.[37]

There were also giants of the waters, like Grendel in *Beowulf,* called *eoten* and *thyrs,* and his monstrous mother. Grendel might be a personification of the storm-flood which devastates the low-lying coasts of the North Sea. As Beowulf slew the mother of Grendel in the mere, so Grettir, as is told in the *Grettis-saga,* dived into a waterfall and entered a cave where he slew a giant who dwelt there. Both incidents are variants of a common theme.[38] Other giants associated with the waters are

Ægir and Ran. Akin to Ran is Hrimgerd who, with her mother, lay in wait for ships, and is called ' corpse-hungry giantess.' [39]

Possibly other elements of nature were typified in certain giants.

A curious genealogy of giants shows how the forces of nature were conceived of as giants, though the genealogy itself is of comparatively late date. Fornjöt, ' the old giant,' was progenitor of the giants, the first dwellers in Norway. He was father of Kari, the wind; of Hler, Ægir, or Hymir, the sea; and of Logi, the fire. Kari had a son Iökul, ' Icicle,' whose son was Snær, ' Snow.' Snær had four children — Snow-heap, Snow-drift, Black Frost, and Fine Snow. Some of these are euhemer-ized as kings in the *Heimskringla* and in Saxo, but the geneal-ogy suggests an old myth of the cold north wind producing ice and snow in their different forms. [40]

Different theories have been advanced regarding the origin of the giants. They have been regarded as an earlier and wilder race of men, with stone weapons, opposed to the more cultured race which uses the plough, as in stories where a giant's daughter carries home a ploughman and his plough and learns that he and his kind will yet do the giants harm. [41] The wilder traits of giants suggest a savage race, but the theory does not explain the universal belief in giants nor the great stature ascribed to them.

They are also regarded as an older group of gods dispossessed by newer deities and therefore hostile to them. This theory might apply to some giants, e.g., Thrym and Hrungnir, who are almost counterparts of Thor himself, but it cannot apply to all. No trace of a cult of giants is found in tradition, in spite of at-tempts to discover this. [42]

Another theory is that of Schoning, who, taking the word *jötun* in its sense of ' devourer,' considers that this group of giants at least, the Jötuns, were originally corpse-devouring demons of the Under-world, viz., Jötunheim, originally a realm of the dead. [43]

The giants may be looked upon as mainly personifications of the wilder elements and phenomena of nature, as these might be supposed to be arrayed against men and gods whose rule and attributes were those of order and growth. Probably no one theory accounts for the archaic belief in giants, but, if this one does not fit all the facts, it has the merit of fitting many of them. To this personification must be added the power of imagination, creating those strange and monstrous forms, and giving them such intense life and movement.

In folk-tradition giants were favourite subjects of story. Boulders, rocks, even islands were said to have been dropped by them as they were carrying them from one place to another. To this corresponds Saxo's theory of boulders on hill-tops and the Eddic myth of the rocks formed from Hrungnir's stone club.[44] Other stories tell of the huge print of a giant's hand or fingers on rocks which he had thrown.[45] Tradition also tells of rocks or even stone circles which were once giants turned to stone, sometimes because they opposed the preaching of Christian saints, e.g., S. Olaf.[46] As in other parts of the world, so in Scandinavia and Germany, the remains of archaic ages, old and (to the folk) mysterious buildings or ruins, were ascribed to giants, the *wrisilīc giwerc* of the *Heliand* and the *enta geweorc* of *Beowulf* and other Anglo-Saxon poetry, both phrases meaning ' giants' work.' Hence a giant is spoken of as a *smiþr*, ' artificer ' in the wide sense, like him who rebuilt Asgard, not merely ' a smith.'[47] Even old weapons were sometimes said to have been made by giants, as the phrase in *Beowulf* shows — *eold sweard eotenisc*.[48] Older tradition made giants fight with stone clubs and shields or with boulders flung at their enemies.

Apart from Eddic myths of giantesses, Snorri gives a prose account and cites an old poem, the *Grottasong*, about two giant-maidens, Fenja and Menja. Their story is mingled with versions of two wide-spread folk-tales, ' The Magic or Wishing Mill ' and ' How the Sea became Salt,' and it is also linked to the myth of Frodi and the golden age of peace. Frodi bought the two maids, huge and strong, and set them to grind the mill called Grotti, the stones of which were so large that no one could turn them, though whatsoever one asked for would be ground by this mill. Frodi bade the giantesses grind out gold, and this they did along with peace and happiness. Frodi allowed them no rest for longer than the time that the cuckoo was silent or a song might be sung. So they sang the magic *Grotta-song* and ground out a host against Frodi. The sea-king Mysing (Hrolf Kraki) came and slew Frodi, ending the celebrated 'Peace of Frodi.' He took the mill and the giantesses, and bade them grind out salt. They ground so much that the ship on which they sailed sank, and from that day there has been a whirlpool in that place in the sea where the water falls through the hole in the mill-stone. So the sea became salt.

In the song Fenja and Menja tell their story. They, mighty maidens who know the future, are in thrall to Frodi and must grind. So they will sing of what they are doing, and, since Frodi is so hard, they tell how unwise he was in buying them for their strength, without enquiring about their kindred — Hrungnir, Thjazi, Idi and Aurnir. These were brothers of Hill-giants, and of them were the maidens born. The mill-stone would not have come from the mountain, nor would Menja have been grinding, had her origin been enquired about. For nine winters the sisters had been playmates beneath the earth, moving huge rocks from their places. They had rolled the stone over the giants' garth: the ground shook beneath them: they slung the mighty stone till men took it. Then in Sweden they, as Valkyries, went to fight, caused wars, casting down and setting up kings. For years this continued and many wars did they cause. Now they are thralls, but they prophesy how they see fire and hear war-tidings, and how a host is coming against Frodi. Their song becomes a magic charm by which evils are ground out for the king. So they ground in giant frenzy, until the stone was broken, and Menja told Frodi that now they would cease from grinding.[49]

This poem is of the tenth century, and references to the story occur in skaldic poetry. The whirlpool is in the Pentland Firth, and traditions of the giant-maids still linger in the Orkneys. The mill-stone (which is not broken in the prose version) came to men through them, a stone which they had thrown, and possibly, as Boer suggests, they were identified with the mill-stones which they turned, as giants often are with the nature elements which they personify.[50] The appearance of giantesses as Valkyries is curious. In this myth, as in the story of Volund, supernatural beings held in bondage are content to work for a time, until their wild nature breaks out and causes disaster.

CHAPTER XXVIII

TROLLS

SNORRI often speaks of Thor's having gone to the East to slay trolls.[1] The word occurs once in the Poetic *Edda*, one of Fenrir's brood is said to be in the form of a troll.[2] The word included giants, but also meant beings with magic power, unearthly beings, and all kinds of monsters. The giant aspect of the troll perhaps came first, then the more demoniac. The word occurs in the Sagas in these different senses. Etnar saw a troll-karl (a giant) sitting on the cliffs and dangling his feet in the surf.[3] The *Grettis-saga* makes Grettir say that a rock-troll attacked Skaggi, when he himself killed him; and Thorkel's men exclaim: 'Surely trolls did not take him in daylight.'[4] A troll-wife came to a house by night and ate all the food stupidly left out. Then she tore and slit men asunder and threw them into the fire.[5] Another troll-wife was overcome by Grettir and killed, but men said that day dawned as they wrestled, so that she burst when Grettir cut off her arm. Now she is a rock in the likeness of a woman.[6] This agrees with popular traditions of giants or trolls of the mountains turned to stone when surprised by the sun or at the word of a saint. To many supernatural creatures the sun is believed in many parts of the world to be fatal. A giant slain by Grettir in a cave, as well as this troll-wife, haunted a district troubled by trolls, and was himself a troll.[7]

Men could be possessed by trolls, like Thorlaf, who, however, became a Christian.[8] One person would devote another to the trolls with the words: 'Trolls take thee and thy company!' This was a common Viking curse, and resembles Harbard's final words to Thor: 'Get hence where every fiendish being will have you! ' Egil said to Hermund in the *Bandaman-na-saga:* ' Though it was prophesied that I should die of old age, the better would I be content if the trolls took thee first! ' [9] With the coming of Christianity trolls became more demoniac, representing the supernatural powers of paganism. When Olaf was introducing the Faith to Norway, trolls and other evil beings tempted his men and himself. But by his prayers they were expelled from their haunts in the mountains. On the whole Olaf Tryggvason and the later S. Olaf took the place of Thor as enemy of trolls and giants. Sometimes, however, Olaf would agree with a troll to build a church, as the gods agreed with the giant to rebuild Asgard. [10]

' Half-trolls ' are spoken of in the Sagas. Grettir told how one of these ruled a certain valley, the giant Thorir, who made him his *protégé*. Halmund's song in the *Grettis-saga* speaks of his fighting giants, rock-folk, and half-trolls. [11]

Troll-women are mentioned in the *Eddas,* and these are sometimes giantesses, but occasionally a troll-woman is a witch, and one of these hailed Bragi by night in a forest. The word is also used as the name of a Fylgja, like that one who met Hedin. [12] This troll-woman rode a wolf bridled with snakes, but giantesses (Hyndla, Hyrokkin) also rode such steeds, and the skaldic term for a wolf was ' the grey horse of the giantesses.' [13]

In later folk-tradition the word ' troll ' was applied to less evil beings, though in Iceland it still retains its older meaning, and trolls there are more monstrous than elfin, though not lacking elfin traits. [14] In Norway Troldfolk or Tusser may be as large as men, and music is heard from their mountain-abodes, to which they carry off mortal maidens. [15] Danish legend connects its Troldfolk, who are akin to dwarfs, with the rebel angels, who, when cast out of Heaven, fell into mounds and barrows, or into the moors (these latter the Elverfolk). The mounds contain treasure and may be seen raised on red pillars on S. John's Eve. These trolls are small, with big heads, and are generally friendly to men, though old ballads tell of their stealing maidens and of the seductive power of their women over men. They can become invisible or transform themselves. They prophesy, and confer prosperity, strength, and other gifts on men. The stories told of them resemble those told elsewhere of fairies and elfins.[16] They dislike the ringing of church bells and any kind of noise, and this trait has suggested a reminiscence of the trolls' dislike of the noisy Thor and his hammer.[17]

The Swedish Dvärg (dwarf) is akin to the trolls or mountain-dwellers, though these are sometimes of giant form. Little trolls ride out with witches, or dance and feast under stones raised on pillars on Christmas-night, and the troll-women entice men into these when watching their dancing.[18]

The trows of Orkney and Shetland recall the old Norse trolls, the traditions about them being derived from Scandinavian settlers, but much influenced by Scottish fairy beliefs. They dwell in mounds, of great splendour within. They are small, clad in green, and fond of dancing by night, but, if surprised by sunrise, must remain above ground all day. On the whole, they are malicious, and are given to abducting women and children.[19]

CHAPTER XXIX

THE NIGHTMARE SPIRIT

SAVAGES regard nightmare as the oppression of a demon or ghost, and the *incubus* or demon lover was at first the nightmare, but personified like the Greek Ephialtes and the nightmare demons of most European lands. In ancient times and in the Middle Ages some medical enquirers regarded nightmare merely as a dream produced by congestion of blood-vessels, hindrance to breathing, or some other physical cause.[1] The popular view was quite different, and the various names for nightmare show this. Of these the German Mahr with its cognates in Scandinavian speech, ON Mara, Danish Mare, our own 'nightmare,' and the French *cauchemar*, are examples. In Upper Germany Mahr has been displaced by Alp, and the words Trut, Trude, Schrettele, and others are also in use. The Schrettele or Schrat is the medieval *pilosus*, a shaggy spirit.[2]

All of these were supposed to ride or press the sleeper, even to cause death. But the sleeper's feelings varied from great pain or oppression to mild or even voluptuous sensations. He might imagine himself attacked by an animal or a more or less monstrous or shaggy being (e.g., Fauns, Satyrs), or by a male or female person. All depended on his physical state, the position of his body, the nature of his bed, the materials of his bed-clothes, no less than upon his preconceived ideas aided by his dream fancies. The Mahr might even be imagined as changing into a straw, a piece of down, or vapour, if, on awaking, the sleeper found himself grasping these or his room filled with smoke.[3]

The form of the Mahr varies — now a giant, now a dwarf; now deformed, now handsome or lovely. A beautiful elfin was sometimes supposed to enter a room by the key-hole or a knot-hole, and, resuming larger proportions, to attack the sleeper. If, knowing the Mahr to have entered or having taken precautions to prevent its attack, he closed such means of egress, the Mahr was found next morning as a beautiful nude woman. She could be forced to promise never to return, or might beg to be set free.[4] Often, however, the Mahr was in the form of an animal. It was usually the soul of a person which had left its body in order to torment a sleeper. A witch might cause her soul to act as a Mahr, or it might be the soul of a woman secretly in love with the victim.[5] Stories show that the sleeper, finding the Mahr desirable, offered her love or married her. When a Norse husband asked his nightmare wife how she had entered, and she replied that she did not know, he showed her a knot-hole through which, now becoming small, she vanished. This corresponds to the broken conditions by which a man loses his fairy or Swan-maiden wife, of whom the nightmare is the equivalent. Or she might beg the husband to remove the plug from the hole. This done, she vanished, but might return to tend her children, like the fairy wife or dead mother in other tales. A Swedish story tells how a girl, as a nightmare, tormented a man who refused her love. When he placed a scythe by his bed as a means of riddance, she cried that she would die, and next morning she was found dead in bed.[6] The Mahr might be a spectre from the region of the dead, and when questioned regarding herself or whence she came, she vanished. When such a spectre was drawn back to earth by a former promise of marriage, there is a resemblance to the dead lover in the *Lenore* ballad and its parallels; and where the Mahr is a living woman or her spirit sent forth by her, she resembles the witch or fairy who uses a man as a steed and makes him hag-ridden.

Night is the usual time for the Mahr's attack, but it might occur to sleepers at noon, and then the Mahr is a form of the Midday demon.[7]

From old Icelandic literature the best example of an oppres-

sive nightmare spirit is recorded in the *Heimskringla*. Vanland, Svegdir's son, was king of Sweden, and abode one winter
with Snær (Snow) the old, and married his daughter Drift.   He
left her, but promised to return.   She sent for Huld the witch
in order that she might draw Vanland by spells or slay him.
Vanland was sleeping, and cried that a Mara was treading him.
His men tried to help him.   She went to his head and legs in
turn, breaking his legs and smothering him, so that he died.[8]

That the belief in the Mara was seriously regarded is shown
by the ecclesiastical law which ordained that a woman, proved
guilty of acting as one and riding a man or his servants, must pay
a money fine.   If she could not pay, she was outlawed.[9]

CHAPTER XXX

WERWOLVES

WHILE transformation of themselves or others was a property common to gods, spirits, giants, and human magic-wielders, there was one form of it which, found all over the world, developed into a belief which for centuries caused terror and is not now extinct among savages and in backward regions of Europe. This is the belief in lycanthropy, the power which certain persons have of becoming wolves or, in some regions, the fiercest animal there existing — bear, tiger, leopard, hyena, etc. The basis of this superstition is the belief in transformation, but its special form is due to mental aberration, persons of diseased mind imagining that they were wolves and the like, acting as such, and preying upon other human beings. Without the belief in transformation this form of mental aberration could not have arisen. The belief in lycanthropy was exploited by interested persons — magicians and sorcerers. It is one of the most deeply rooted of all superstitions and the most wide-spread. We are concerned with it only as far as it existed among the Norsemen and other members of the Teutonic race.[1]

People who could change their form by the soul's entering another body or by putting on, e.g., a feather-dress and so becoming a bird, were said in Norway to be *eigi einhamir*, ' not of one form '; they were *hamramr* or *hamhleypa*, ' changing form.'

The word for Werwolf (literally ' Man-wolf ') in Norse was Vargulf, a wolf worse than any other kind of wolf (*varg*, ' wolf '; *ulfr*, ' wolf '). Save for one reference, the *Eddas* do not speak of the Werwolf, but there are examples of it in the *Volsunga-saga*.

A she-wolf came night after night and ate one of Volsung's sons, set in the stocks by their brother-in-law Siggeir. Their sister Signy saved the last of the brothers, Sigmund. This wolf was held to be Siggeir's mother, who had thus changed her form.[2]

Signy's son, Sinfjotli, and his uncle Sigmund, came to a house in the forest where two men were asleep, spell-bound skin-changers. Wolf-skins hung above them, and every tenth day they came out of those skins. Sigmund and Sinfjotli put on the skins, each now howling as wolves, but thinking as men. Each went his way, agreeing that they should risk the attack of seven men, but no more. If more attacked one of them, he must howl for the other's aid. On one occasion Sinfjotli slew eleven men without seeking help. For this Sigmund bit him in the throat, and then carried him home and healed his wound. They now cast away the wolf-skins, devoting them to the trolls, and later burned them.[3]

The belief was mingled with and perhaps influenced by the custom of wild warriors and outlaws, e.g., the berserks, wearing wolf-skins or bear-skins over their armour or clothing themselves in these, while they were often victims of frenzy and acted as if they were animals. As the person who had the power of changing his form became preternaturally strong, so the berserks in their fury were very powerful, and, as was said of two brothers in the train of Earl Hakon of Norway, they ' were not of the fashion of men when wroth, but mad like dogs and feared neither fire nor steel.' [4]

The story from the *Volsunga-saga* is referred to in the *Edda* when Godmund says to Sinfjotli: ' Thou hast eaten wolves' meat . . . and often sucked wounds with cold mouth, and, loathsome to all men, slunk into the dens of wild beasts.' [5]

Other examples are found in the Sagas. The *Story of Howard the Halt* says of the dead Thormod that in life he was thought to have more shapes than one, and men held him ill to deal with.[6] The *Egils-saga* tells of Ulf, grandfather of Egil, that at times he would be subject to attacks at night, during which he changed his form. Hence he was called Kveldulf, ' Evening Wolf.'[7] In the *Eyrbyggja-saga* Thrand was *hamramr* in his heathen days, but this fell off him at his baptism.[8] Other persons are said to have had this power of changing their form, and a Norse gloss to the *Bisclaverit* of Marie de France says that in earlier times many men took wolf-form and dwelt in the forests.[9]

The word *hamramr* does not always refer to wolf-form. Thus Dubhthach and Storwolf were mighty skin-changers. They quarrelled and were seen by a second-sighted man fighting, one as a bull, the other as a bear. The bear was the stronger of the two. Next day the valley where they had fought looked as if an earthquake had occurred in it. Both men were worn out and lay in bed.[10] In a wild tale from *Hrolfs-saga kraka* Bjorn was transformed into a bear by his step-mother, who shook a wolf-skin glove at him. He lived as a bear and killed many of his father's sheep, but by night he was a man.[11]

Among the Anglo-Saxons the existence of the belief is proved by the use of the word ' Were-wulf ' in the laws of Cnut, e.g., at the council of Winchester, 1018 A.D., where preachers were told to guard their flocks from the fierce devouring Were-wulf, i.e., Satan. Gervase of Tilbury speaks of the English name ' Were-wolf ' and explains its meaning. He also says that at changes of the moon in England men became wolves.[12]

In Germany the belief is witnessed to by the OHG *wolfhetan*, the equivalent of ON *ulfhedinn*, and meaning one who puts on a wolf-girdle or skin (*ulfhamr*) in order to become a wolf.[13] The oldest literary testimony to the superstition is found in a sermon of S. Boniface (eighth century), who speaks of the belief of the Saxons in *fictos lupos*, obviously Werwolves.[14] Later evidence is supplied in the Penitential of the ' Corrector ' which speaks of the gift conferred by the Parcae of power to change into wolf-form or any other shape at will. ' Vulgar folly calls this creature *werewulff* ' — the German name. The connexion of this power with the German Parcae, equivalents of the Norns, is curious, but points to popular tradition or to the belief that the power was innate in certain men.[15]

Modern collections of Scandinavian and German folk-tales contain many Werwolf stories. In later medieval times the superstition was closely connected with witchcraft, and theologians turned their attention to lycanthropy as a branch of sorcery. The power of changing the form, or of deluding the eyes of others so as to make them believe that such a change had taken place, was ascribed to diabolic agency.

In Scandinavian and German belief the change was effected by donning a wolf-skin or a girdle of human skin, or by throwing these over another person. The girdle had sometimes magic signs upon it, and was held in place by a buckle with seven catches. When the buckle was broken off, the transformation ceased. The man was a wolf or bear by night, or he assumed the animal form for nine days, or even for three, seven, or nine years, the eyes alone retaining a human appearance. He howled and devoured like the actual animal.

CHAPTER XXXI

MAGIC

THE practices of divination, prophecy, and magic were common in the pagan North, but a distinction was drawn between lawful and unlawful magic. The deities wrought magic, but this was reflected upon them from human practice.

Magic songs, spells, incantations — *spjall, galdr, ljodh* — were used to effect the magic act. These were also called runes (*rún*, OHG *rûna*, AS *rún*), though this word betokened magic signs engraved on something and producing magic power. After being engraved, they were coloured. Hence the verse in *Havamal*:

> ' Runes thou shalt find, and fateful signs,
>   Most powerful signs, most mighty signs,
>   By the mighty poet (Odin) coloured, by the high gods made,
>   By the chief of the gods carved.' [1]

The colouring was made with blood, and this increased the power of the runes.

The Norse word *rún* was used in two senses. The primary meaning was ' a mystery ' or ' mysterious knowledge.' It also signified a letter of the alphabet, such as was used before the Roman letters came into use. The unlearned, who were the majority, would regard letters as a mystery; hence the word *rún* was applied to them. These runes had a magical significance besides an alphabetic value, and apparently some magical runes were not letters in the ordinary sense. In using them, besides engraving them on some object, there was a necessary ritual which gave power to them. This seems to be referred to in *Havamal*, where, besides cutting, interpreting, and colouring them, there are mentioned invocation, offerings, and the right method of slaughtering the victim.[2] The runes could not be used unless one knew their meaning, and there was danger in an ignorant use of them.[3]

Runes were ascribed to the gods, and *Havamal* also tells how Odin came into possession of them. He wrote them for the gods, as Dainn for elves, Dvalin for dwarfs, and Alsvith for giants. Another verse of *Havamal* shows that not only was advice given to Loddfafnir in the hall of Odin, but that there runes had been spoken and their meaning declared.[4]

Each rune had a name which represented a particular object, and, through this, good or evil magic was wrought. Hence to produce the magical result, the magic power of each rune must be known. Examples of imparting this knowledge are given in the *Edda*. Thus Sigrdrifa taught runes to Sigurd — victory, ale, birth, wave, branch, speech, and thought runes. Victory-runes are to be written on the sword-hilt and other parts of the sword, the name of Tyr (the name of the rune for the letter T) being uttered twice. Ale-runes, by which the wife of another will not betray a man's trust, are to be written on the drinking-horn and the back of the hand, the sign Naudr (the runic N) being written on the nail. Birth-runes, to relieve a woman in child-birth, are to be written on the palm of the hand and on the joints, while the Disir are called on to help. Similar explanations are given regarding the other runes. The poem then tells how Odin stood on a hill with Brimir's sword, his helmet on his head: then Mimir's head first spoke words of truth and wisdom. There follows a curious list of mythical and actual things on which runes were commanded to be written — the shield of the sun, the ear of Arvak, the hoof of Alsvith (steeds of the sun), the wheel of the car of Hrungnir's slayer, Sleipnir's teeth, the straps of a sledge, the paw of a bear, Bragi's tongue, a wolf's claws, an eagle's beak, bloody wings, the end of a bridge, the reliever's hand and the healer's foot, glass, gold, amulets, in wine and beer, on favourite seats, on Gungnir's point, or Grani's breast, on the nails of the Norns, and on the beak of the night-owl.[5]

Some of the actual objects on which runes in this list were to be written resemble the miscellaneous things found in Scandinavian graves — bones of a weasel, teeth of a horse, claws, vertebrae of a snake, etc.[6]

The poem continues by saying that runes thus engraved were scraped off and steeped in mead and cast far and wide. Some are with the gods, some with the elves, some with the wise Vanir, and some with men. There are beech-, birth-, and ale-runes, and the excellent magic runes for him who knows them rightly and reads them truly: they will benefit until the gods perish.[7]

Whether all the verses describing these runes are in a true series or drawn together from various sources is not clear. The account of the objects, mythical and actual, on which they are written seems to belong to an old myth of the value of runes, telling how they had been used. The scraping of the runes into mead and casting them abroad, so that they are now with gods, etc., is mythical, but it may be based on actual practice — drinking mead into which runes had been scraped from wood or bone. *Havamal* also speaks of runes being with gods, elves, dwarfs, etc.[8]

The enumeration of runes is preceded by a verse telling how Sigrdrifa gave Sigurd a magic drink:

> ' I bring you beer, O tree of battle,
> Mixed with strength and powerful fame;
> In it are magic songs and healing strength,
> Beneficent charms and love-runes.' [9]

As Sigrdrifa taught runes to Sigurd, so in *Rigsthula* Rig taught them to the first jarl, and his son in turn learned to use them — life-runes, everlasting runes; now he could shield warriors, dull the sword-blade, and calm the seas.[10]

Odin carved and coloured runes before speaking with a dead

man on the gallows, and he touched Gerd with a piece of bark on which spells (runes) were written, inducing frenzy in her. Grimshild carved runes on the cup from which Gudrun drank and by which he forgot Brynhild.[11] Runes were carved on a cup to destroy a poisoned drink within it, as Egil cut them on the cup which queen Gunnhild gave him. At once it broke. They were also carved on the insulting-pole which he set up.[12] Saxo tells how the giantess Hardgrep cut magic runes (*carmina*) on wood and placed them under a dead man's tongue, making him speak.[13]

The list of magic songs (*ljod*) in *Havamal* already cited in Chapter IV shows the different purposes for which they were used.[14] In *Svipdagsmal* the dead Groa chants charms at her son's request, while she stands at the opening of her barrow on a stone. These charms will help him in his dangerous quest of Menglod. The first is that which Ran taught to Rind. The second will guard him by means of the bolts of Urd. The third will make dangerous rivers fall away before him. The fourth will deliver his foes into his hands. The fifth will burst all fetters. The sixth will prevent wind and wave from harming his boat. The seventh will protect him against deadly frost and cold. The eighth will protect him from the curse of a dead Christian woman — perhaps a pagan view of the potency of a Christian's curse. The ninth will give him words and wit in a word contest with a giant.[15]

These different lists in *Sigrdrifumal*, *Havamal*, and *Svipdagsmal* show several points of contact. All three have charms which give power of speech and wit, such as Odin gave to his favourites.[16] All three have charms to still tempests and to give victory. Two have charms to break fetters and charms for healing. It is interesting to compare the fetter-breaking charm with the similar magic of the Idisi in the Merseburg charm. The power-giving spells of Odin in *Havamal* correspond to the magic ascribed to him in the *Ynglinga-saga*, and the passage in the Saga may be a paraphrase of the stanzas in the poem.[17]

Cursing spells were used, and an example of these is found in *Atlamal* where Vingi pronounces a conditional one on himself. He devotes himself to giants or to the gallows if he breaks his oath.[18]

Various names were used for magic. One of these, *seidr*, which, according to the *Ynglinga-saga*, owed its origin to Freyja, usually refers to harmful magic, though sometimes also protective magic. Gullveig practised it and so also did Odin according to Loki.[19] In using *seidr* a special seat was necessary, and the magician held a staff. Magic songs were sung to effect the result. The male magician was called *seidhmadhr*, the female *seidhkona*. Deadly results were ascribed to *seidr* — killing others, causing tempests, creating delusions. The *seidhkona*, while sitting on the seat, could send her soul out of her body in another form, while her body remained on the seat. If the soul was wounded or killed, the body of the witch showed similar wounds or fell dead.[20] This, as well as other kinds of magic, is regarded in the Sagas as a natural accomplishment of the Finns or Lapps, and often a magician was one of these. But it is improbable that all Norse magic came from Finland.

The Volva and Spakona, prophetess and spaewife, were mainly soothsayers (like the German prophetesses mentioned by Tacitus and Dio Cassius), practised in the art of divination, though some of them used the most hurtful *seidr*. The Volva travelled through the land with a retinue, especially during the winter nights when spirits were abroad. She visited one house after another, where she was well received, and a meal put out for her.[21] In *Orvar-Odds-saga* Heidr travelled with fifteen youths and fifteen maidens. The retinue sang the magic songs by which the Volva fell into a trance and learned the future. The power of the Volva was gained by sitting out for several nights. By this sitting out, *uti-seta*, spirits of the dead or other supernatural powers were conjured up and gave revelations to the Volva.[22] Even when dead the Volva could still supply hidden knowledge, when conjured up by the

proper spells.   Odin called up a dead Volva to enquire of her
about Balder's dreams, and possibly the utterance of the Volva
in *Voluspa* was made to Odin by a dead seeress.

The ærial flight of witches and sorcerers to a nocturnal gathering is found in widely separated regions.   Only in the later
Middle Ages and under theological influence was it attributed to
direct diabolic agency.   In pagan Scandinavia this flight was
practised by the Tunnrida, who sat on roofs or hedge-enclosures
of a homestead to destroy it, or rode and sported in the air,
usually after shape-shifting (*tun*, ' a hedged place ' or ' farm ').
One of the charms described by Odin in *Havamal* was used to
discomfit these ' House-riders ':

> ' A tenth I know when House-riders
> In flight sweep through the air;
> I can so work that they wander
> Bereft of their own form,
> Unable to find their way home.'

The witch's soul has left her body, assuming another form, and
in that, as a result of the charm, she must wander about.[23]

Other Eddic names are Myrkrida and Kveldrida, ' Dark-
rider,' ' Night-rider,' both names referring to the riding about
at night.   Odin used much seductive craft with Night-riders,
and in the *Eyrbyggja-saga* the following lines occur:

> ' There are many Dark-riders about,
> And often a witch lurks under a fair skin.'

Geirrid said this to Gundlaug in order to keep him from going
home at night   But he set out, and was found senseless, bruised,
and the flesh torn in lumps from his bones.   Men thought that
Geirrid herself had ridden him.   She was summoned to the
Moot as a Dark-rider and for causing Gundlaug's trouble.   But
on her oath that she was not responsible for this, the case was
quashed.[24]

In *Helgakvitha Hjorvardssonar* Atli says to the monster
Hrimgerd:

'Atli am I, ill shall I be to thee,
  Giant-women to me are hateful;
  Often have I been in the dripping bows,
  And slain the Night-riders.'[25]

A poem by Eilif calls Thor destroyer of *konor kveldrunnar* or
night-faring beings.[26]   The MHG *zeunriten* corresponds to the
Tunnrida: other MHG names are *nahtfara, nahtfrouwa,* 'night-
travelling women.'[27]

The witch-ride was performed on a *gandr* or 'staff' — the
gandreid. Witches, troll-women, and demoniac beings also rode
a wolf bridled with snakes, and the wolf was called 'the troll-
women's steed,' 'the dusky stallion on which the Night-rider
fareth.'[28]   The distinction between spirits or demons of a dangerous kind and the night-faring witches is not clearly sustained.

Examples of the witch-ride and of nocturnal gatherings occur
in the later Sagas.   Thus in the *Thorsteins-saga* (fourteenth
century), Thorstein overheard a youth call to his mother in her
burial-mound: 'Mother, give me staff and gloves, for I am
going to *gandreid*.'   These were thrown out of the mound.
The youth put on the gloves, rode on the staff, and went off.
Thorstein now repeated the same formula, received gloves and
staff, and rode after the youth to a mountain where many people
sat drinking round a king and queen.   Thorstein, whose staff
made him invisible, took a ring and a cloth, but at the same time
dropped the staff, and, becoming visible, had to ride off from the
throng on the youth's staff.[29]

In the *Ketils-saga* we learn how Ketil was awakened by a
great noise in a wood, and saw a troll-woman with hair waving
behind her.   At his question she told him that she was going to
the troll-thing.   To it the troll-king, Ofoti, Thorgerd Hölgatroll, and other mighty spirits were coming.[30]   An earlier
glimpse of the witch-gathering is seen in the Salic Law of the
Franks (*c.* 600 A.D.), which condemns in a fine anyone who calls
another *herburgium* or 'cauldron-bearer' for the Striae or
witches.[31]

Cattle which were troubled by a disease of the spine, causing palsy, were supposed to be troll-ridden.[32] Witches also caused disease in cattle and death. This was supposed to be done by an invisible arrow, the *hægtessan gescot* of an Anglo-Saxon charm already cited.[33] They did harm to crops and caused tempests. In the *Gisla-saga* Audbjorga went round a house widdershins, sniffed to all the points of the compass, and drew in the air. The weather changed and there came driving sleet, floods and snow, which caused the death of twelve people.[34] To the witch was also ascribed the power of blunting weapons and taking away a warrior's courage.[35]

Icelandic and Norwegian laws condemn these different practices, including the use of runes and spells, and one of these laws speaks of the troll-woman who, if proved guilty of riding a man or his servants, was fined three marks.[36]

CHAPTER XXXII

THE OTHER WORLD

IN this Chapter we consider the different views of Other World existence entertained in the pagan North.

HEL

The Norse word Hel with its cognates — Gothic *halja*, OS *hellia*, AS *helle*, OHG *hella* — denotes the general Underworld of the dead, a primitive conception of the Teutonic peoples. In Scandinavia alone is Hel also personified as ruler of this Underworld, but it is not always easy to differentiate person and place. Grimm thought that an early goddess of the dead gave her name to the region of the dead, but the reverse is more probably correct.

The abode of Hel is under one of the roots of Yggdrasil. Of Fafnir, Sigurd said that now Hel would have him, and Hogni said of the five sons of Butli that Hel has now the half. To come to Hel's seat is to die.[1] Hel has a dog, Garm, which barked at Odin when he went to consult the dead Volva. His breast is besprinkled with blood, and he howls loud before the Doom of the gods. Hel has also a rust-red cock which crows and awakens her dwellers.[2] Snorri tells how Hermod rode down to Hel to seek Balder's release from her. Her condition could not be fulfilled because of Loki, who said: ' Let Hel hold what she has! ' Hence Balder is called ' companion of Hel.' [3] Hel was said to be one of Loki's monstrous offspring, whom Odin cast into Niflhel or Niflheim, giving her power over nine worlds, to apportion their dwellings to all who were sent to her, those who die of sickness or old age. She has a great abode.

Her hall is Sleet-cold; her servant Hunger; her maidservant Tardy; her threshold Sinking to destruction; her bed Disease; her bed-cover Unhappiness. She is half black and half flesh-colour, and with down-hanging head she looks grim and fierce.[4] The personified Hel is somewhat monstrous, but Snorri, in this account, may have borrowed traits from Christian visions of Hell. Popular sayings, however, spoke of things 'black as Hel,' and *heljarskinn* meant a complexion of a deathly hue.[5]

The personified Hel in Saxo is called Persephone, who appears to Balder before his death, saying that soon she will embrace him. So king Frodi, when dying, heard voices calling him 'home to Hel.' A saying about the dead was: 'Hel will fold thee in her arms.' The curious *Solarljod* or 'Song of the Sun,' with its mixture of paganism and Christianity, speaks of the maidens of Hel calling to them a man about to die.[6] The poem of *Beowulf* may preserve a memory of the personified Hel. In describing the death of Grendel, the poem says: 'There Hel received him.'[7]

Hel as a place is deep down in the earth, enclosed, with one or more gates. Within is the hall of Hel, 'a high house.'[8] Near the entrance is Gnipahellir, 'Cliff-cave,' where Garm, best of hounds, is set to guard.[9] Hel is sometimes called Niflhel, which suggests a misty region (*nifl*, 'mist,' 'darkness'). But the description of it in *Baldrs Draumar* and in Snorri's account of Hermod hardly bears this out. Balder sat on a high seat. The hall had benches bright with rings and platforms decked with gold. There the dead ate and drank mead.[10]

The way to Hel is the Helveg, a troublesome road, though the plural is also used, as if there were more than one. When Hermod went to rescue Balder, he rode for nine nights through deep and dark vales to the river Gjoll, crossed by the Gjoll-bridge, thatched with gold. The maiden Modgud who guarded it asked his name, and said that on the previous day five companies of dead men rode over it, yet the bridge thundered no less under him alone. Why was he, who had not the hue of dead

men, riding on the Hel-way? Then, learning that he sought
Balder, she permitted him to ride on the Hel-way to the North.[11]
When Brynhild, burned on a pyre, went in a wagon along Hel-
way, she passed the house of a giantess who would have stopped
her.[12] Those who descended to Hel for tidings of the dead were
said to perform the Hel-ride. The dead might traverse Hel-
way on horseback: hence the custom of burying or burning the
horse with its owner. Saxo tells how when Harald's horse and
chariot were burned on his pyre by Ring, he prayed that Harald
might ride on this steed and reach Tartarus before those who
fell with him, and that Pluto, lord of Orcus, might grant a calm
abode to friend and foe.[13] Possibly Odin and Valhall, not Hel,
are here intended.

The Gjoll-bridge is perhaps ' the brig o' dread, na brader
than a thread,' which, in Yorkshire belief, the dead had to
cross.[14] The toilsome journey to Hel was aided by the equip-
ment buried with the dead, e.g., the Hel-skor (German Todten-
schuh), ' Hel-shoe.' The custom of providing shoes for the
dead existed in prehistoric Europe and continued as a general
custom. When Vestein was dressed for his barrow, Thorgrim
said to Gisli: ' It is the custom to bind on Hel-skua for folk to
walk to Valhall, and I shall do this for Vestein.' After putting
them on, he said: ' I know nothing about binding on Hel-shoes
if these loosen.' [15] The shoes are here for the journey to Valhall, but the old name is retained. In Yorkshire, where we may
see survivals of Teutonic custom, a pair of shoes given to a poor
man in life would cause the giver after death to meet an old man
who would present him with the same shoes at the edge of
Whinnymoor, a region full of thorns and furze, which otherwise the spirit would have to traverse ' wi' shoonless feet.'
This belief is illustrated by the Lyke-wake dirge, versions of
which are still known in the north of England.[16]

Snorri limits Hel to the old and those who died a ' straw
death,' i.e., in bed. This is in keeping with the views which sent
warriors to Valhall, women to Freyja, maidens to Gefjun, and

the drowned to Ran. Behind these views is the more primitive one that all, even warriors, go to the Underworld. The Eddic and skaldic conception of Valhall was mainly a product of the Viking age, and slain warriors were even yet said to go to Hel, e.g., Balder, Hjalmgunnar, warriors mentioned in *Atlamal*, Sigurd, and others. Thor threatened to smite Harbard and Loki and send them to Hel. Egil, after slaying three men, speaks of their faring to the high hall of Hel. Regin and Fafnir went to Hel, and Sigurd told Fafnir that a time comes when everyone must fare to Hel, *fara til Heljar*. Though this phrase may be used here and elsewhere in the conventional sense of 'to die,' still it points to what was once regarded as following death.[17] The same conception is seen as late as the time of the Saxon Widukind of Corvei, who says that gleemen declaimed after a victory: 'Where is there an *infernum* so large as to hold such a multitude of the fallen?' *Infernum* stands here for the Saxon *hellia*.[18] So also in Saxo's story of Hadding's visit to the Underworld, which has much in common with Norse conceptions, warriors are found there.[19]

Conversely even some of those who did not die in battle went to Odin in Valhall, e.g., king Vanland, killed by a Mara, and king Halfdan, who died in bed. These are said to have gone to Odin, though Halfdan was bidden to go to him by Loki's daughter, i.e., Hel.[20]

THE DEAD IN THEIR BARROWS

With the early conception of Hel as the general home of the dead, stands the equally early, if not earlier, conception of the dead living on in their barrows or burial-mounds, as well as that of their being within hills. The barrow or group of barrows was in itself a small Underworld. In primitive thought this passed over to the conception of a hollow region under the earth or in the hill where the barrows were set, while yet the grave or barrow was thought to be the dead man's abode. Hel, the hollow place, was thus an extension of the barrow where the dead feasted, occupied themselves with the welfare of their kindred, and where their presence in these barrows was a blessing to the neighbourhood.[21]

The dead were said ' to die into the hill,' and this belief with its corollary that they still lived in grave, barrow, or hill is decidedly primitive. Dead Norsemen were vigorously alive in their barrows. The *Eyrbyggja-saga* tells how Thorstein's shepherd saw the hill on the north side of Helga-fell open. Fires blazed in it: the clatter of ale-horns was heard. Words of welcome were spoken to Thorstein and his companions, who had just been drowned at sea, and those already in the hill said that he would sit in the high seat with his father.[22] A good example of the dead alive in their barrow is found in *Helgi Hundingsbana*, though it is combined with the Valhall conception. A hill was raised for Helgi and he went to Valhall. But at night one of Sigrun's maidens saw him ride with many men to the hill. She told this to Sigrun who went to see him and rejoiced at the reunion. Sigrun kissed him. His hair was covered with frost, his body damp with the dew of death. Helgi told her that her tears caused this dew, each tear falling like blood on his breast. Sorrow will now be forgotten. ' Now in the mound our brides we hold, the heroes' wives by their dead husbands ' — as if his followers were also visited by their living wives. Sigrun made ready a bed and said: ' I will make thee rest in my arms as once I did when you lived.' So they rested until Helgi had to ride back to Valhall ere the cock woke the warrior throng there.[23] Two beliefs are illustrated in this episode, besides that of the dead living in their barrow, viz., that excessive tears of mourners harm the dead, and that the dead can rejoin the living for a time — both wide-spread conceptions.

Stories in the Sagas show that the forgotten dead in ancient barrows would reveal themselves to the living; that the dead resented any desecration of their barrows, and that they would make known to the living any annoyance caused them, e.g., by a

thrall buried beside them.[24]   The *Hervarar-saga* tells how
Angantyr was buried with the famous sword Tyrfing, his eleven
brothers being buried in as many mounds beside his own.   His
daughter Hervor, who had taken to Viking ways, visited the barrows in order to obtain the sword.   She rode through the fire
which burned around them, and by incantations forced her
father to speak.   In spite of his trying to send her away and
telling her that the sword, lying beneath him surrounded by
fire, would bring destruction with it, she still persisted, and now
it came forth from the barrow of itself.[25]   Another story describes a visit paid by Thorstan to a barrow at the invitation of
a dead man.   In it were this man, Bryniar, and eleven men, besides other eleven, companions of Ord.   Bryniar and his men
had to give treasure to Ord, but their store was running short.
Thorstan, when asked by Ord for a gift, held out his axe, and
when Ord would have taken it, he cut off his arm.   A general
fight between the two groups of the dead now began.   Ord and
his men were slain, and Bryniar gave Thorstan Ord's ring
which, laid beneath a dumb person's tongue, would make him
speak.   He also told Thorstan that he would change his faith,
which they, the barrow-folk, could not do, for they were earth-
dwellers or ghosts.[26]   The *Njals-saga* tells how Gunnar's barrow was seen open with lights burning in it, and how he recited
lines in an audible voice.   His face was joyous.   Yet immediately after, his son Hogni, who had witnessed this, speaks of
Gunnar's going to Valhall.[27]

The barrow-dweller, the *haug-bui* or ' barrow-wight,' was
sometimes troublesome to the living, as many stories in the
Sagas show.   Grettir saw a fire in the barrow of Karr who
haunted the region near.   He broke open the barrow and was
removing its treasure, when Karr attacked him.   After a
struggle Grettir cut off Karr's head and placed it at his thigh —
a recognized way of laying such substantial ghosts.[28]   Another
story in the *Grettis-saga* relates to the godless Glam who was
slain by a spirit, and now began to haunt the farm on which he

had been a shepherd, riding on the roofs and nearly breaking them in. The hauntings continued for two winters. People who saw Glam went mad; others were killed; cattle were destroyed; farms were burned. After a terrific fight Grettir slew Glam, cutting off his head and placing it at his thigh. The body was then burned and the ashes buried deep.[29]

In other stories such substantial ghosts do immense harm, and even after their bodies have been burned, their vitality continues through the ashes. Thus a cow licked a stone on which the ashes of the vicious ghost of Thorolf had lain, and its calf continued the harm done by the ghost. Sometimes holy water and the saying of Mass, as well as a doom pronounced against the tormenting dead, were necessary before their hauntings ceased. While the ' ghost ' haunted, its body was undecayed. These animated corpses, for they can hardly be called ghosts, resemble vampires, for the quelling of which similar rites of riddance were observed — cutting off the head, impaling, burning, and scattering the ashes.[30] Many stories describe fights with the barrow-wight by a hero bold enough to invade the barrow and try to remove the treasure contained in it. Saxo gives such a story. Asmund and Asvitus had promised to die with each other. Asvitus died first and Asmund was buried alive with him. Soon after, the barrow was broken open, and Asmund came forth, ghastly and bleeding, for Asvitus had eaten his horse and dog and then attacked his friend, who, however, had been able to cut off his head and impale his body with a stake.[31]

All the dead did not act in these ways. They were helpful and interested in their descendants, and would appear to give information on different matters. Hence some cult was paid to the dead at their barrows or at the natural hillocks into which they were supposed to have died. The greater or more beloved they were, so much the more reverence was shown them. Jordanes says of the Goths that they regarded dead chiefs as *ansis* or *semi-deos*. Adam of Bremen speaks of the cult of dead men who had performed mighty deeds, and cites the *Vita S. Anskarii* which shows how the Swedes had neglected the gods through the coming of Christianity. Through a certain man they complained of this and said that if the Swedes desired more gods, they might worship their former king Eirik, who would now become one of the gods. A temple was therefore erected in his honour, and sacrifices offered to him. The *Indiculus Superstitionum* shows that the dead were regarded as holy and worshipful.[32] The Sagas give several examples of the worship of popular or great persons when dead, and of the sacrifices paid to them.[33] The euhemerized accounts of the gods also show how they, as supposed mortals, were deified and worshipped after their deaths.

In Iceland, hillocks or hills were believed to be abodes of the dead, especially one near the family dwelling, on which we may suppose the barrows to have been made.[34] The family barrow or barrows were usually beside the dwelling. The living believed that they would ' die into the hill.' One of the early settlers in Iceland, Thorolf, in reverence for the hill on the ness to which his high-seat pillars had floated, and which was near his homestead, called it Helga-fell, ' Holy fell.' He would allow no one to pray to it unwashed; it must not be defiled; and no living thing could be destroyed on it or brought from it to die. Things and Dooms were held on it, and Thorolf believed that he would die into it. On one occasion, as we have seen, it was found open and the dead were present in it. Another example is that of the place where the lady Aud was buried, one of several hillocks on which she had raised crosses. Her kinsmen, falling into heathenism, made it a place of worship and sacrifice, and believed that they died into these hills. Ari, the earliest chronicler, says that Selthorir and his kinsmen died into Thori's hill.[35]

The ' memory-toast ' was one drunk to kinsmen in their barrows.[36] The *erfi* or *erfiöl* was a feast in honour of the dead, e.g., the head of a house, at which many guests were present and much ale drunk in memory and honour of the departed. The

heir then occupied the high-seat for the first time.[37]   These
funeral feasts for the dead are also described by Saxo.[38]   The
sacrifices at Aud's hill were for her benefit, and the dead were
said to be present even visibly at their own funeral feasts.[39]

Evidence of this cult of the dead is seen in the denunciations
of the Church through canons of Synods and Councils in the
Teutonic area, as elsewhere.[40]

The dead were also enquired of at their mounds regarding
the future, as Odin did regarding Balder, and Svipdag of his
mother Groa.[41]   In *Harbardsljod* Harbard says that he had
learned the words spoken to Thor from the old men who dwell
in ' the grave-hills of home,' i.e., ancestral grave-hills.   Thor
replies that he is giving a fine name to cairns when he describes
them thus.   Cairns, as distinct from barrows, were piled over
criminals.   What Harbard had learned had been communicated
by wicked spirits.[42]   A shepherd slept on a mound in hope of
composing a dirge in honour of its occupant Thorleif, but could
get no further than ' Here lies a skald.'   One night the mound
opened, and a stately man emerged, who told the shepherd that
if he could remember a poem of eight lines which he would
recite to him, he would become a poet.   On awaking, he recalled
the lines and became a famous skald.[43]   Saxo tells how the
giantess Hardgrep, desiring to know the future, made Hadding
place a wooden slip engraved with runes beneath a dead man's
tongue.   He then uttered a prophecy.[44]   Odin knew a spell
which would make a hanged man talk, perhaps the *valgaldr* by
which he awakened the dead seeress in *Baldrs Draumar*.[45]

There is no example in the *Eddas* of the dead appearing in
dreams to the living to warn them or to foretell the future.   In
Atlamal dead women were seen in a dream by Glaumvor seeking
and calling her husband Gunnar to come quickly to their
benches.   They were apparently his kinsfolk, desiring his presence in the Other World.[46]   The belief that the dead communicated with the living through dreams was a common one, and
Saxo gives an example of it.   Hadding's dead wife appeared to

him foretelling his death by his daughter's instigation, and, now forewarned, he was able to prevent this.[47]

The dead ancestor was sometimes thought to dwell in a particular stone. In the *Cristne-saga* Codran and his kin are said to have worshipped at a stone in which their ancestor dwelt. He told Codran the future and of what he should beware. A bishop sprinkled the stone with holy water, and the ancestor complained to Codran that he and his children were being driven from their home by hot water. After a second sprinkling he appeared, dark and evil of face, beseeching Codran to drive away the bishop. After a third sprinkling, his appearance was lamentable. Codran told him that he had worshipped him as a strong god, but, as he had proved false and weak, he would now become a Christian.[48] A stone at which Thorstan worshipped and from which a voice was heard foretelling his death, was probably also a spirit stone.[49]

In spite of the power of the barrow-wight, men still sought in burial-mounds for treasure, and curses against such persons are known on grave-stones. With the coming of Christianity the barrow-wight became more or less demoniac, and later stories of encounters of living and dead are of a darker kind.

All this belief of the dead living in their graves, barrows, or hills, or in stones, may seem to conflict with the belief in Hel, still more with that in the heavenly Valhall. But all religions and mythologies show how apparently contradictory beliefs can be held concurrently.

VALHALL

The belief in Hel is as prominent as the Valhall belief in the Poetic *Edda*. Snorri and the skalds give it more emphasis, and it was a profound future hope to warriors in the Viking age, giving them courage in conflict and confidence that, if slain, Odin would receive them.

Valhall, ' Hall of the slain,' ' Hropt's (Odin's) battle-hall,' stands gold-bright and wide in Gladsheim, ' Abode of joy,' a heavenly place.   It is Odin's favourite abode.   Spears are its rafters, shields its roof, its benches are strewn with corslets.   A wolf hangs by its western door, over it hovers an eagle (perhaps carved figures above the door).   The cook Andhrimnir cooks the boar Sæhrimnir in the cauldron Eldhrimnir, as food for dead warriors, though few know on what they feast.   Odin's wolves sit beside him.   The river Thund surrounds Valhall and in it joyously swims ' Thjodvitnir's fish,' the sun.   The fallen find it hard to wade through this stream.   Valgrind is the outer gate of Valhall, and behind it are five hundred and forty doors in the wall.   Through each door eight hundred warriors will go to fight the Fenris-wolf at the Doom of the gods.   There is unfailing mead for the heroes, to whom the Valkyries bring it. Each day the warriors or Einherjar go forth to fight, felling each other, but they are magically healed by nightfall, when they feast.   They are waked each morning by the cock Gollin-kambi, ' Gold-comb.' [50]

Some of these details from *Grimnismal* and *Vafthrudnismal* require explanation.   The river Thund may be the sky in which the sun, the fish to be swallowed by the mighty wolf (Thjod-vitnir), runs its course, or perhaps it is the ocean surrounding Midgard, in which is the Midgard-serpent.   The three names, Andhrimnir, ' Sooty-face,' Eldhrimnir, ' Sooty-with-fire,' and Sæhrimnir, ' the Blackened,' are believed by R. M. Meyer to be formulæ of a riddle: — ' Sooty-face seethes the Blackened in Sooty-with-fire; ' the answer being ' the cook in Valhall seethes the boar in a cauldron.' [51]

Snorri repeats this description of Valhall, with additions.   The host of Einherjar in Valhall will not be too great in the day of the gods' need.   The boar's flesh suffices for all, and though killed and eaten, he is alive again each evening.   Something better than water is given to the warriors who have bought their place in Valhall so dearly.   From the udders of the goat Heid-

run flows mead enough to fill a tun daily, and all the Einherjar
could become drunk from it. When Gylfi (Gangleri) arrived
in Asgard, he saw a hall with many people, gaming, drinking,
or fighting. This was evidently Valhall. Snorri also says that
in Valhall swords were used instead of fire, just as gold gave
light in Ægir's hall.[52] Odin appoints dead warriors to Valhall
and Vingolf (not mentioned in the poems). Elsewhere in
Snorri Vingolf is the abode of goddesses, close by Gladsheim.
Warriors may have shared in this abode of goddesses, for
Freyja is said to decree who shall have seats in her hall Sessrumnir in Folkvang. She chooses half of the dead, Odin the other.
Sessrumnir may be the equivalent of Vingolf, the meaning
of which is variously given as ' Friend-hall,' ' Wine-hall,'
and ' Hall of the beloved,' where Valkyries serve the warriors.[53] In the *Lexicon Mythologicum* the dying Hadding's
words are given. He speaks of the Valkyries coming to him
and says that he will go to Vingolf and drink beer with the
Einherjar.[54]

The Einherjar were outstanding warriors, fallen in fight, and
chosen for Valhall by the Valkyries. They were Odin's *osk-
synir*, ' wish-sons ' or ' adopted sons,' and Odin himself was Val-
father, ' Father of the slain.' They are assembled in Valhall
partly to aid the gods in their day of need, when they will ride
forth with them to battle, though it is not known when the grey
Wolf (the Fenris-wolf) will come, and many as they are, their
number will seem small enough in that time.[55] While it is true
that all warriors did not go to Valhall and some went there who
were not warriors, the view of the skalds was that it was exclu-
sively for brave and noble fighters, men of high birth, heroes,
freemen. This is reflected in one of the Bjarka songs in Saxo.
The poet says: ' No humble and obscure race, no low-born ones,
no base souls are Pluto's prey, but he weaves the fate of the
mighty and fills Phlegethon with noble shapes.' Pluto stands
for Odin, Phlegethon for Valhall. So in *Harbardsljod* the
noble who fall in battle are said to go to Odin, while Thor has

the thralls. Yet Thor himself is called 'Einhere' in *Loka-senna*.[56]

In the *Eiriksmal* and *Hakonarmal* (tenth century), already cited, we have seen how the Valkyries were sent forth to bring the heroes to Valhall. In the former Sigmund and Sinfjotli are bidden by Odin to go out and welcome Eirik and those who follow him; in the latter Hermod and Bragi are sent to greet Hakon. Sigmund asked why Odin looked so much for Eirik's coming, and was told that he was such a mighty warrior. He died in fight because the gods need such as he against the day of the Wolf's coming. Hakon said that he mistrusted Odin because he had been slain; but Bragi told him that now the Einherjar will toast him and he will drink ale with the gods.[57]

The Valhall belief had entered deeply into the Viking mind, as is seen in the phrase used of a hero fallen in combat with another — 'to show him the way to Valhall.' Such heroes would wish each other a journey to Valhall before fighting. When a warrior was buried he was dedicated to Valhall in the funeral oration.[58]

How did the conception of the heavenly Valhall arise in Scandinavia? As Odin was father of the slain, lord of the Einherjar, and lord of ghosts (*drauga drǫttinn*),[59] so he had once been god of the dead in general. When he came to be regarded as dwelling in the sky, the abode of the dead or, at least, of those more directly associated with him, was also transferred there. Valhall in Heaven was thus an extension of the Underworld or of an abode of warriors within a hill. Valhall with its surrounding stream, wall, gate and doors, and its hall, is a replica of Hel. We have seen that the dead were supposed to go into hills regarded as sacred. Now certain hills in Scandinavia are called 'hills of the dead' (Dødeberg, Dødemandsbjœrge), and some Icelandic and Swedish hills bear the name Valhall.[60] Odin was connected with hills which bear his name in Germany and Scandinavia, like 'Sigtyr's mountain' in *Atla-*

kvitha. He was 'the Man of the mountain,' and 'the god of the fells ' (Fjallgautr).[61] Were these hollow hills into which the dead entered? With some such hills the Wild Hunt was linked, emerging from them and returning to them, and the dead took part in the Hunt.[62] The numerous legends of kings or heroes sleeping in hills with their followers are also in point here. The king or hero is an earlier deity, Wodan or some other.[63] Charlemagne's army fought a battle at the foot of the Odenberg in Hesse. At night the hill opened, king and soldiers entered, and then it closed upon them. Every seven or every hundred years they come forth in battle-array and after a time re-enter the hill. Other legends of armed men coming out of hills, fighting, and re-entering them, are known from medieval times.[64] The continual fighting of dead warriors, not in Valhall, is an early belief enshrined in folk-tradition. It is exemplified in the story of the Hjadnings' strife in its various forms. Snorri gives one version of this and connects it with Hoy in Orkney. The kings Hogni and Hedin fought because Hedin had carried off Hild, Hogni's daughter. They and their men fought all day, and at night Hild resuscitated the dead. They renewed the fight next day, and all who fell turned to stone. But they rose up armed in the morning and fought again. ' In songs it is said that the Hjadnings will fight thus till the Doom of the gods.' This continual fight is also mentioned in Bragi's poem, *Ragnarsdrapa* (ninth century). The story is also attached to the Brisinga-men myth, Freyja receiving back the necklace on condition that she should cause two kings and their armies to fight until a Christian ended the strife. The resuscitation theme occurs here also, and the fight continues for one hundred and forty-three years until one of Olaf Tryggvason's men agrees to kill all the warriors and so release them from their doom. Another version of the story is given briefly by Saxo. Hilda is said to have longed so ardently for Hedin, that after he and Hogni had slain each other, she resuscitated them by her spells in order to renew the fight.[65] Other legends deal with a similar theme, and Saxo in one of his stories of a visit to the Underworld shows us dead warriors fighting there.[66]

Valhall might thus be regarded as an Underworld abode of warriors transferred to Heaven as a result of Odin's growing importance in the Viking age. The warriors there awaited the final assault of demoniac powers. Meanwhile they fought, feasted, and caroused, as the dead feasted in Helga-fell. It is also significant that *valhall* is the name applied to the hall where Atli and his warriors drank wine.[67] Apparently fighting as an occupation after death was not a primitive belief, for the earliest tombs do not contain armour and weapons.[68]

Whatever the origin of the Valhall belief may be, it was not the only conception of Other World life entertained by the Northmen. It is quite possible that in earlier times the state of the dead was not definitely formulated in Teutonic belief. In later times different beliefs arose and some of these were held simultaneously. The dead active in their barrows are also linked with Valhall, as the Helgi poem and the reference to Gunnar in the *Njals-saga* show. So also, according to Thjodolf the skald, Halfdan, who died in his bed, was bidden to the Thing of Odin (Valhall) by 'Hvedrung's maiden,' i.e., Hel, for Hvedrung is Loki.[69] In the Helgi poem, as Niedner puts it, the Valhall belief has been superimposed on an older tradition of Hel or of the dead living in their barrows.[70]

RETRIBUTION AFTER DEATH

The belief in the punishment of certain crimes after death is found among savage and barbaric peoples,[71] and may quite well have been held by the Teutons. It is indeed spoken of in the *Eddas,* but the question of Christian influence has to be considered.

Snorri speaks of the future lot as dependent on the nature of the death — a common and primitive conception. Warriors went to Valhall, those dying of sickness or old age to Hel, the drowned to Ran, etc.[72] But he also says that All-father gave man a spirit which is immortal. All men shall live; the righteous with him in Gimle, evil men in Hel and thence to Niflhel, in the ninth world.[73] This contradicts the other passage, and suggests that Hel is an evil place. In a third passage, already cited, Snorri makes Hel a place of cold, famine, and disease.[74]

Christian ideas seem to have obtruded themselves — that of man's immortal soul, of the righteous in Gimle or Heaven, of the wicked in Hel and Niflhel. Snorri seems to have been in error in making Hel and Niflhel different places: elsewhere Niflhel is equivalent to Hel,[75] and the earlier sources (e.g., the Eddic poems) do not suggest that Hel is an evil place of misery.

These passages tell of man's fate after death. But Snorri also describes the places allotted to men at the renewal of the world. There will be many good and many evil abodes. Best will it be to exist in Gimle, where will be abundance of drink for those who like it in the hall called Brimir, which is in Okolnir. A good hall is that which stands in Nidafells, made of red gold, and called Sindri. In these the good and pure in heart shall dwell. Gimle is further described as fairest of all halls, brighter than the sun, at the south end of Heaven. When Heaven and earth have departed, it shall continue, and the good shall dwell in it. It is believed to be in the third Heaven, Vidblainn, and so invulnerable against the fires of Surt. On Nastrand, 'Corpsestrand,' is a great and evil hall, its doors facing north. All the snake-heads turn into it and spurt venom, so that it runs in two rivers along the hall. Perjurers and murderers wade these rivers. In Hvergelmir it is worse, for there the cursed snake tears dead men's corpses.[76]

In this account there seems to be a mingling of pagan and Christian beliefs, and some misunderstanding of his sources by Snorri. In *Voluspa* Gimle is a hill on which the hall stands:

> 'A hall I saw, fairer than the sun,
> Decked with gold, on Gimle's heights,
> There shall dwell true hosts
> And enjoy happiness never to end.'[77]

Even this stanza is suspect of Christian influence.   In *Voluspa*
also Brimir's hall has no connexion with the lot of the righteous
dead; while Sindri is the name of a dwarf, not of a hall:

> ' In the north stood on Nidafells
> A hall of gold for Sindri's people;
> On Okolnir another hall stood,
> The beer-hall of the giant Brimir.' [78]

Sindri's people are dwarfs.   The next stanzas describe a place of
punishment, which Snorri connects with life after the Doom of
the gods.   But, unless their position in *Voluspa* is misplaced, this
must be a present place of punishment, not one in the renewed
world:

> ' A hall I saw stand far from the sun,
> On Nastrand, its doors facing the North;
> Venom streams down from the smoke-hole,
> For serpents are winding round the walls.
>
> There I saw wading through rivers wild
> Oath-breakers and murderers
> [And such as entice other men's wives];
> There sucked Nidhogg the dead
> And the wolf tore men.' [79]

The composition of this second verse is doubtful.   Line three
may be interpolated; lines four and five may belong to a stanza
with no reference to punishments for sin after death.   According to *Grimnismal* the dragon Nidhogg gnaws the root of
Yggdrasil.   Snorri says that the dragon gnaws that root which
is over Niflheim and below which is Hvergelmir, a well in Hel.
In the concluding stanza of *Voluspa*, possibly also interpolated
or out of its proper place, the dragon Nidhogg comes flying from
Nidafells bearing the bodies of men on his wings. [80]
   That perjurers, murderers, and adulterers were punished
after death would be in keeping with Teutonic ideas of the
enormity of these crimes, and the punishments meted out in
life for committing them.   In *Sigrdrifumal* an evil fate is said
to await the perjurer; and in *Reginsmal* Andvari says that perjurers will suffer long, wading through Vadgelmir's waters.

This river, not mentioned elsewhere, may be one of those which *Voluspa* assigns to oath-breakers as a punishment, and which are in Hel or on its confines.[81]

Snorri's reference to All-father, who is existing after the Doom of the gods, conflicts with the belief in Odin as All-father, slain at this final catastrophe. He has been influenced by his belief in the Christian God. Gimle, ' Gem-lee ' or ' Gem-roof,' is possibly a reminiscence of the Heavenly Jerusalem, the city of gold and gems, as described in the Book of Revelation.

VISITS TO THE OTHER WORLD

Stories of visits to the Other World, preserved by Saxo and in some of the Sagas, contain reminiscences of pagan beliefs. In their present form they belong to the twelfth and fourteenth centuries. They tell how men went to seek Odainsakr, ' the Acre of the Not-dead,' and Jörd lifanda Manna, ' the Land of living Men,' in the East or North, and apparently underground.

One winter day Hadding, a mythic king of Denmark, saw a woman rise out of the floor with hemlocks in her hand. He desired to know where such plants grew in winter, and, wrapping him in her mantle, she drew him underground through a dark cloud, along a worn path, to a place where were richly clad nobles, and then to sunny regions where the plants grew. A river, full of whirling missiles and crossed by a bridge, was passed, and on the other side two armies were fighting. The warriors thus showed the manner of their past life and of their death. A great wall barred further advance, but the woman wrung off the head of a cock and flung it over the wall, when the bird came to life again. Hadding now returned home, apparently by sea.[82]

This story must have been known in the tenth century, for ' Hadding's land,' the Other World, is spoken of in the second Gudrun poem. The region beyond the wall is probably the Odainsakr of other stories. The fighting warriors resemble the

Einherjar in Valhall, but they may be a reminiscence of its more primitive aspect, underground or within a hill. The river with missiles resembles the river Slid in *Voluspa,* full of swords and daggers, one of several rivers which run in Hel, according to *Grimnismal.* Its bridge recalls the Gjoll-bridge. The influence of Irish stories of Elysium, to which visitants with a magic branch or apple invite mortals, may be seen in this story.[83]

Saxo also tells of the visit of Gorm, king of Denmark, to Geirrod's abode, over ocean, down to Chaos, to a region of darkness. Thorkill acted as guide to the party, and when land was reached, he bade them kill no more cattle than sufficed for their needs, lest the guardian gods of the place (Land-vættir?) should not let them depart. This counsel was disregarded and three men had to be surrendered to the giants who beset them. They now sailed to a region of eternal cold, with trackless forests. Gudmund warned all on no account to speak. A giant-like man, Gudmund, brother of Geirrod, met them and conducted them past a river, on the other side of which were monsters, to his abode. Here Thorkill and the others refrained from food and from the love of the beautiful women of the place, for the one would cause oblivion and they would have to dwell with monsters, while the other would cause madness. Four men succumbed to the women's charms, and met this fate. Gudmund tried to entice Gorm with the delicious fruits of his garden, but, warned by Thorkill, he refused them. Gudmund now took the visitors over the river to a gloomy town, guarded by dogs and peopled by phantoms. Here was Geirrod's dwelling, filthy, swarming with snakes, its iron seats full of phantasmal monsters. Geirrod and his daughters were seen just as they had been overcome by Thor. In another place three of the party took some of its treasure and were horribly punished. In another room Thorkill's self-restraint was forgotten at sight of a beautiful mantle. The inhabitants attacked the voyagers, and all but twenty perished. These were ferried over the river by Gudmund and returned home.[84]

This story combines Polar travel with incidents of imaginary journeys. Gudmund appears in other tales. In the *Hervarar-saga* he is a king in Jötunheim, and dwells in Glasisvellir, 'glittering Plains.' He is wise and mighty, and he and his men live for generations. The heathen believed that Odainsakr was in his realm and that whoever went there cast off sickness and age and became immortal. After his death he was worshipped as a god.[85] In other sagas Gudmund rules Glasisvellir and is skilled in magic, but in one of these his land is tributary to Jötunheim, ruled by Geirrod, who meets his death by the magic power of Thorstein.[86] The *Story of Olaf Tryggvason* tells how Helgi Thoreson met twelve maidens in the far north, one of whom was Gudmund's daughter, Ingibjorg, with whom he stayed three days. In the sequel when, by Olaf's prayers, she could not keep him, she put out his eyes lest the daughters of Norway should love him.[87]

In *Eirik Vidforlas-saga*, Eirik reached Odainsakr by being swallowed by a dragon. It was a place of great beauty, with a tower suspended in the air and reached by a ladder. There Eirik and his companions found delicious food and wine and slept in splendid beds. A beautiful youth told Eirik in his sleep that this was Odainsakr, and Jörd lifanda Manna, and that it was near Paradise.[88]

Gudmund's is an Elysian region, but has dangers incurred through eating its fruits or loving its women. These are perhaps made darker by Christian redactors or authors of the stories. By analogy with Irish Elysian tales, the danger was that, by eating the fruit of the land or through love of its women, the visitor became bound to the region or, when he left it, found that time had lapsed as in a dream. This food-tabu — the danger of eating the food of gods, fairies, the dead, etc., is of widespread occurrence.[89]

Glasisvellir, Odainsakr, and Jörd lifanda Manna are Elysian wonder-lands, such as most races have imagined. But there may have been influence from Irish Elysium stories, notably *The*

Voyage of Bran, in which some of the voyagers come to grief by doing what they were advised not to do.[90] The tales, however, contain several points of contact with native beliefs regarding the region of the dead, e.g., rivers crossed by a bridge, dead men fighting, the mysterious region beyond the river, perhaps the equivalent of Hel. Geirrod's realm is more repulsive in Saxo's tale than in the Eddic myth of Thor and Geirrod, and here we may see the influence of Christian visions of Hell, though it preserves some features of the Eddic Nastrand with its snakes and venom, and even of Valhall, for its roof is made of spear-heads. Rydberg identified Gudmund with Mimir; and Odainsakr, the walled place in the Hadding story, and the tower in the Eirik story, with Mimir's grove where Lif and Lifthrasir, progenitors of the new race of men, are preserved.[91] To them the title ' living men ' might be appropriate. But more likely the names of this mysterious land were suggested to the Northmen by contact with the Celtic people of Britain and Ireland, in whose myths Elysium bore such names as ' Land of the Living,' Mag Mell or ' The Pleasant Plain,' and Tir na n-Og, ' The Land of Youth.'

CHAPTER XXXIII

COSMOGONY AND THE DOOM OF THE GODS

THE Eddic picture of the origin of the universe goes back to a time when neither gods nor men, Heaven nor earth, existed. There was a great abyss, Ginnunga-gap, 'Yawning chasm,' a conception probably due to popular belief in an abyss outside the ocean surrounding the earth. North of it had been made (by whom?) Niflheim, a frost and mist region, within which was the well Hvergelmir, 'Cauldron-rushing,' from which flowed several rivers. To the south was Muspell, light and glowing, ruled over by Surt. The streams or Elivagar from Niflheim, as they flowed, became ice, which spread into Ginnunga-gap. There the ice met warm airs from Muspell or Muspellheim and began to melt. Life was quickened in this by the power of that which sent the heat (whose was this power? there is perhaps a Christian influence here), and took form as a giant Ymir. From him came the Frost-giants.

From the dripping rime there sprang the cow Audhumla (explained as 'the rich, polled cow,' *audr*, 'riches,' i.e., its milk, and *humla*, 'polled'). Streams of milk from its udders nourished Ymir, and the cow was nourished by licking the salty ice-blocks. As she licked there came forth from the ice Buri, who was father of Borr. Borr married Bestla, a daughter of the giant race. They had three sons, Odin, Vili, and Ve.

Thus the giant race preceded the gods, as Saxo also indicates, and gods and giants were opposed to each other.

The sons of Borr slew Ymir, and his blood drowned all the Frost-giants save Bergelmir with his wife and household. The three brothers bore Ymir's body into Ginnunga-gap and made of it the earth.   Sea and waters came from his blood; gravel and stones from his teeth and such bones as were broken; rocks from his bones.   The sea was placed as a ring round the earth.   His skull became the sky, set up over the earth and upheld by four dwarfs.   The earth is ring-shaped, and on its coasts the gods gave lands to the giants.   Within the earth they erected a wall against the giants, made of Ymir's eyebrows.   This they called Midgard.   Of Ymir's brain, thrown into the air, they made the clouds.   The glowing embers and sparks from Muspellheim were set in the Heaven, above and beneath, to illumine Heaven and earth.   The gods assigned places to all, even to such as were wandering free.[1]

This is Snorri's account, based partly on sources now lost, partly on stanzas of *Voluspa, Grimnismal,* and *Vafthrudnismal.* *Voluspa* says:

> ' In time's morning lived Ymir,
> Then was no sand, sea, nor cool waves;
> No earth was there, nor Heaven above,
> Only a yawning chasm, nor grass anywhere.
>
> Then Borr's sons upheaved the earth
> And shaped the beautiful Midgard;
> From the south the sun shone on earth's stones,
> And from the ground sprang green leeks.' [2]

The first verse seems to contain the myth of Ymir formed in Ginnunga-gap.   The second gives a myth of earth raised out of an existing ocean, not made from Ymir's flesh.   The sun shone on it and growth began.   Whether both verses come from one hand or, as Boer holds, the second alone belongs to an earlier form of the poem, is immaterial.   The myth of earth raised out of ocean is found in other mythologies.[3]   The next verses tell how sun, moon, and stars were allotted their places, and how the gods gave names to night, new and full moon, etc.

In *Vafthrudnismal* the giant in response to Odin's question, tells how earth and sky arose, but does not speak of them as a work of the gods.

'Out of Ymir's flesh was shaped the earth,
The mountains out of his bones,
The Heaven from the ice-cold giant's skull,
Out of his blood the boisterous sea.'

This is succeeded by an account of the giants, the first of whom is said to have been made out of the venom from Elivagar. No mention is made of fire and heat, only of frost and ice.[4]

Grimnismal speaks of the origin of earth from Ymir's flesh, ocean from his blood, Heaven from his skull, the hills from his bones, and it adds that trees were formed from his hair, Midgard from his eyebrows, made by the gods for men, and out of his brain the clouds.[5]

In *Voluspa* three gods lift earth out of ocean, but the other poems merely mention gods, without specifying the number or saying how they came into existence. Snorri says that from Odin and Frigg came the kindred known as the Æsir, a divine race.[6] In an earlier passage he speaks of All-father or Odin living through all ages and fashioning Heaven, earth, and all things in them.[7] The latter is probably a reflexion from Christian views of Creation.

The conception underlying Snorri's main account is that giants, gods, and all things may be traced back to the union of water (ice and mist) and fire. The ice contains salt, and this plays an important part in the myth of Audhumla. An interesting comparison is found in Tacitus, who, speaking of the sacred salt springs near the Saale, says that the waters were made to evaporate on red-hot coals, and salt was thus obtained from two opposite elements, fire and water. This may point to an old Germanic cosmogonic myth with fire, water, and salt as elements.[8] Skaldic kennings illustrate the Eddic myth of Ymir. Heaven is ' skull of Ymir ' or ' burden of the dwarfs '; earth is ' flesh of Ymir '; the sea is ' blood of Ymir '; the hills are ' Ymir's bones.'[9]

Grimm cites passages from medieval ecclesiastical documents dating from the tenth century onwards, in which man is said to

have been created out of different materials. One of these says
that Adam's bones were made from stone, his flesh from earth,
his blood from water, his heart from wind, his thought from
clouds, his sweat from dew, his hair from grass, his eyes from
the sun. The four documents differ in details, but there is a
curious inverse parallel with the Eddic account, which ' uses the
microcosm as material for the macrocosm, and the other in-
versely makes the universe contribute to the formation of man.' [10]

Voluspa goes on to tell that the gods met at Ithavoll in the
midst of Asgard and built temples and altars, made forges to
work gold, wrought tongs and fashioned tools. This was during
their golden age. Then the creation of dwarfs is described.[11]
Snorri amplifies this. All-father gave counsel about the town in
the midst of Ithavall. A temple was made with twelve seats
and a thirteenth for All-father. It is all of gold and is called
Gladsheim. A second house was built for the goddesses, called
Vingolf. Houses were made for workshops; and tools, anvils,
hammers, and tongs were fashioned. The Æsir worked in
metals, stone, and wood, and fashioned their household wares
of gold. Hence that time is called the Age of Gold. Then follows the creation of the dwarfs.[12]

Voluspa next gives the myth of human origins. Odin,
Hœnir, and Lodur came forth to the land and found Ask and
Embla (Ash and Elm) unprovided with fate and without
strength, soul, breath, movement, heat, or colour. Odin gave
them soul, Hœnir sense, Lodur heat and goodly colour.[13]
Snorri says that Odin, Vili, and Ve, walking on the shore, found
two trees, which they shaped into human beings. Odin gave
them soul, Vili life, Ve hearing and sight. They named the
male Ask and the female Embla, and of them mankind was
begotten.[14] In an earlier passage, where biblical influence may
be seen, Snorri says that All-father made man, giving him spirit
which shall never die, though the flesh-frame rot or burn to
ashes.[15] The shaping of human beings out of trees may have
been suggested by wooden images, such as those which the

speaker in *Havamal* says that he found and on which he put clothes. Now they regarded themselves as champions. Such images, called *tremadr*, are mentioned in other documents.[16] In *Rigsthula* the different classes of men were begotten by Rig. The account given by Tacitus of the founders of the Germanic race is interesting by way of comparison. The Germans celebrate in ancient hymns a god Tuisto, issued from the earth, and his son Mannus, as the originators of their race. Mannus had three sons, progenitors of the Ingvæones, Herminones, and Istævones. Some, however, think that the god had other sons, progenitors of other tribes.[17] Mannus is thus the first man, born of a god who comes out of the earth, perhaps regarded as spouse of a Heaven-god. His sons were eponymous ancestors of three chief German groups. If Tuisto was thought to be produced by earth alone, and himself alone produced sons, he would resemble Ymir, who begat giants without a female (p. 275).

Separate cosmogonic myths occur here and there. A river, Van, is formed from the slaver out of the mouth of the Fenriswolf. Stars were made of the eyes of Thjazi or Aurvandill's toe; a well from the footprint of Balder's horse, etc.[18]

For the Eddic conception of the universe we begin with the earth, the middle of things, a general Teutonic conception — Gothic *midjungards*, OS *middelgard*, AS *middangeard*, OHG *mittigart*, ON *midgard*, literally 'boundary-wall,' i.e., the mountains by which the giants were shut out from the habitable earth, then the earth as the dwelling-place of man, or, as Snorri conceived it, a citadel. Thor is ' Midgard's warder ' (*veorr*) against the giants.[19] Earth is a vast disc, surrounded by the ocean or floating upon it, and in this ocean is the Midgard-serpent, lying about the land and surrounding it, his tail in his mouth, ' the girdle of all lands.' Around the shores of earth are mountains, rocks, wastes, and caves, and these are the dwelling of giants, Jötunheim or Utgard, though Utgard was also regarded as being beyond the ocean.[20]

According to one passage of Snorri, Asgard, the abode of the gods, is a city which men call Troy, in the midst of Midgard. It is the new Asgard, in place of the elder Asgard in Asia.[21] This conception of Asgard is due to Snorri's euhemerism and the desire to connect the Scandinavian people and deities with ancient Greece. The earlier pagan view of Asgard made it a heavenly abode, or possibly it was on the top of a lofty central mountain, which would give a link with Snorri's view of Asgard on earth.

Above all was Heaven, overarching and resting on earth. Between Heaven and earth was the bridge Bifrost or Bilrost, which the gods had made, the Ásbru or 'bridge of the Æsir.' It is the rainbow, of three colours. It is very strong and made with greater craft than any other structure. The red colour is fire, which keeps the Hill-giants off. Over this best of bridges the gods ride daily to their tribunal at Urd's well. Another name of the bridge is Vindhjalmsbru, 'Wind-helmet's (the sky) bridge.' At the Doom of the gods the sons of Muspell will cross it and break it down. Meanwhile Heimdall is its guardian.[22]

Valhall is Odin's hall in Asgard, where are also Gladsheim and Vingolf, but *Grimnismal* places Vainall in Gladsheim, 'the Place of joy.'

Separate dwellings of gods and others are enumerated in *Grimnismal* and by Snorri, and these appear mainly to be in Heaven. The chief of them are Alfheim, abode of the Alfar and Frey; Breidablik, Balder's abode; Valaskjalf, 'Seat of the fallen,' possessed by Odin and thatched with silver, in it is Hlidskjalf, 'Gate-seat,' whence Odin surveys all worlds. Valaskjalf may be Valhall. Thrudvangir, with its hall Bilskirnir, is Thor's abode.

Much speculation has been indulged in regarding the 'nine worlds,' spoken of in *Voluspa* and *Vafthrudnismal*, as well as in an interpolated stanza in *Alvissmal* where the dwarf says: 'Oft have I fared in the nine worlds all, and wide is my wisdom in each.' In *Voluspa* the Volva says that she knows ' nine worlds, nine rooms of the mighty World-tree.' The giant in *Vafthrud-nismal* says that he has been in every world, the nine worlds, even to Niflheim.[23] In all three passages the idea is that of comprehensive knowledge on the part of the speaker — dwarf, seeress, giant. This knowledge is possessed by different kinds of beings dwelling in different regions. Alviss knows the names given to various things by several orders of beings dwelling in earth, Heaven, Alfheim, etc. ' Nine worlds ' would thus be more a figurative phrase than one expressing local geography or cosmology. In *Voluspa* these worlds are connected with the World-tree, itself a comprehensive symbol.

Regarded as different regions, the nine worlds may be — 1. Asgard, 2. Vanaheim, 3. Alfheim (though this is one of the dwellings in Heaven), 4. Midgard, 5. Jötunheim, 6. Mus-pellheim, 7. Svartalfheim, 8. Hel or Niflhel. The ninth is un-certain. It may be obtained by dividing Hel from Niflhel or, preferably, by including a Water-world.[24] Undoubtedly the numbering of nine worlds is connected with the sacredness and importance of the number nine in religion, myth, folk-belief, and poetry.[25]

Below Midgard is Svartalfheim, the region of the dwarfs. Hel or Niflhel is also a subterranean abode. While Snorri speaks of Niflhel in this sense, he also speaks in error of Niflheim, apparently another form of the name, as a region in the North, the cold region of mist, whence streams flowed into Ginnunga-gap. In Niflheim Snorri places the well Hvergelmir, whence spring certain rivers, among them Gjoll, which is near Hel-gates. It is under the root of Yggdrasil which stands over Niflheim. In *Grimnismal*, the site of Hvergelmir is not given, but it is said that from the horns of the hart which eats the branches of Lærad, a stream drips into Hvergelmir and thence all the rivers run.[26]

THE ASH YGGDRASIL

To the seeress of *Voluspa* the World-tree with its nine divisions or worlds, is 'the mighty Fate-tree (or 'well-planned tree,' *mjǫtvithr*), deep in the earth.' The nine worlds are contained in the tree or symbolized by its divisions. In later passages the Volva speaks of an ash called Yggdrasil, reaching high aloft, wet with white water, thence come the dews that fall in the dales. It stands by Urd's well, and the three Norns dwell in a hall under it.[27] This reference to the three Norns may be interpolated, enlarging on Urd's connexion with the tree. Heimdall's horn is hidden under the tree, and a mighty stream pours from Odin's pledge (which is in Mimir's well) on the tree. At the Doom of the gods the tree shakes and its leaves rustle.[28]

The picture of the tree in *Svipdagsmal* is similar. Mimameith ('Mimir's tree'?) stretches its branches over all lands. No one knows what roots are beneath it. Few can guess what shall fell it, not fire and not iron. Then follows a piece of folk-lore. The fruit of the tree placed in fire is good for women in childbirth. What was within then comes out, such might has the tree for men. Gering points out that in Icelandic belief a hard legumen borne to Iceland by the Gulf Stream is used for the same purpose. On the highest bough stands the cock Vithofnir, glittering like gold, shining like lightning, ever-watchful, the terror of Surt and Sinmora.[29] If this bird is the same as Gollinkambi, who wakes the heroes in Valhall, the top of the tree must be in Asgard. The bird's watchfulness is a terror to the enemies of the gods.

These two passages give a picture of a wonderful world-tree, its roots on or under the earth, beside it Mimir's well — probably the older conception — or Urd's well. As we shall see, Snorri puts these two wells beside two separate roots of the tree.

A more elaborate picture is given in *Grimnismal*. The ash Yggdrasil is 'best of trees.' Beneath one of its three roots is

Hel; the Frost-giants beneath the second; mankind are beneath the third. A lost stanza may have spoken of the wise eagle that sits on the top of the tree, for the next stanza speaks of the squirrel Ratatosk which carries the eagle's words to the dragon Nidhogg below. Four harts nibble the uppermost twigs, perhaps a later amplification of the single hart of a succeeding stanza. Numerous serpents lie beneath the tree and gnaw its branches. Thus the tree suffers, for the hart bites its top; its trunk is rotting; and Nidhogg gnaws its roots. Meanwhile the gods ride daily to give judgments at the tree. Thor walks there.[30]

Snorri combines this information, but gives varying details. Of the three roots, one is among the Æsir, one among the Frost-giants, and one over Niflheim. Beneath each is a well or stream. As the Æsir are in Heaven, a root cannot be there, unless we assume that Snorri still regards Asgard as on earth. But later he says that the root is in Heaven, and underneath it is Urd's well. Mimir's well is underneath the root among the Frost-giants. The third root, over Niflheim, is gnawed by Nidhogg. The eagle in the tree knows many things. Between his eyes sits the hawk Vedrfolnir. Ratatosk bears envious words between the eagle and Nidhogg.[31]

Snorri thus upsets the whole conception of Yggdrasil by placing one of its roots in Heaven, with Urd's well there, and by setting Mimir's well among the Frost-giants.

Most of the details in *Grimnismal* may be no more than decorative *motifs*, perhaps derived from the presence of birds or other animals in sacred trees or groves, or, as R. M. Meyer supposes, from sculptured representations of trees with conventional animals.[32] Bugge thought that the poet had seen monuments in the north of England with ornamentation like that on the Bewcastle cross in Cumberland, if not that cross itself. On such crosses was carved a tree, in the foliage of which sat an eagle or hawk, squirrels and serpents, and ate of its fruits.[33] If the tree or the animals had any mythic significance, the key to it is lost, in spite of the ingenious conjectures of modern mythologizers.

The ash Yggdrasil has many prototypes. It recalls sacred trees beside sacred wells from which oracles were obtained. It is linked to the Vårträd or ' Ward-tree ' growing beside Swedish houses, which, if cut down, brings the prosperity of the house to an end — a significant fact when we remember that the gradual destruction of Yggdrasil denotes the approach of the Doom of the gods. It may thus have once been a mythic heavenly Vårträd, growing beside the hall of the gods. Such a tree is spoken of in a stanza quoted by Snorri — Glasir growing by the doors of Valhall, its leafage of red gold, the fairest tree known among gods and men.[34] *Grimnismal* also speaks of a tree, Lærad, growing beside Odin's hall. From the horns of the hart which bites its branches a stream falls into Hvergelmir, whence all the rivers flow. This also resembles a Vårträd, and both trees may be forms of Yggdrasil.[35] When *Grimnismal* speaks of the gods riding to judgment beneath Yggdrasil, this may be reminiscent of actual processions to judgment beneath a Vårträd or a temple tree.[36]

Yggdrasil also resembles the sacred tree growing beside a temple, like that one described by the scholiast to Adam of Bremen. Beside the temple at Upsala was a great tree with spreading branches, always green, even in winter. Its origin was known to none. Near it was a spring used for sacrifices.[37] The branches of Yggdrasil were also far-spreading; it was always green; beside it was a spring; no one knew its fate or its roots. The Old Prussian holy oak at the sanctuary called Romove also offers an analogy to Yggdrasil. It had three divisions, each sacred to a god, and an image of each stood in each section. Before the god Perkuna of one division burned perpetual fire; before Potrimpo was the snake fed by the priests and priestesses; before Patollo the heads of a man, horse, and cow. This tree was also evergreen.[38]

The full name of the Eddic tree was Askr Yggdrasils, ' the

Ash which is Ygg's (Odin's) Steed,' or ' the Ash of Odin's
Horse.' Yggdrasil was a kenning for Odin's horse Sleipnir.
The name may be due to the fact that victims sacrificed to Odin
were hung on sacred trees, riding the tree, gallows, or horse
sacred to him. Other explanations are given. It is the tree in
which is Odin's steed, the wind. Or Odin tethered his horse to
the tree, or, less likely, it is the tree on which Odin hung, hence
his gallows or steed.[39] In the same way the gallows was called
' the ice-cold steed of Signy's husband ' in a skaldic poem.[40]
But, as Chadwick points out, there is ' not a single reference to
the World-tree having served as Odin's gallows,' while ' the
name Yggdrasil may have been applied to the earthly Vårträd,
and transferred together with the conception of the tree to its
heavenly copy.' [41]

The mythic Yggdrasil was almost certainly a tree growing on
earth before it was transferred to the Other World and the region of myth.

This tree is also connected with wide-spread myths of a
World-tree growing on a mountain or in the centre of the earth,
and reaching to Heaven. Such a tree also resembles the mythic
World-pillars supporting Heaven. Both trees and pillars are
many-storied. The roots of the tree go down into the Underworld, its topmost branches pierce the sky, and it stands by a
spring, lake, or sea, or in the sea itself. As in a Yakut tale, a
goddess dwells at the root of the tree and foretells the future,
like Urd or Mimir. Tree or pillar is often the tethering-post
of deities, especially of the Over-god, as in the Yakut tale, and
this throws light on Yggdrasil as connected with Odin. Such
mythical pillars and trees are known all over Northern Asia, and
can be traced in India, Iran, Mesopotamia, and Egypt. The
eagle Garuda or Garide is believed to dwell in the tree. At its
roots is a dragon or snake at which the eagle pecks.[42] In some
of these myths a spring flows from the tree or from its sap, and,
as in Iranian belief, all the rivers of earth have their source in
it.[43] So out of Yggdrasil flows dew, called by men honey-dew,

on which bees are nourished, and the source of rivers is connected with the tree Lærad.[44]

Such mythic trees would be suggested by lofty forest-trees on which the sky seemed to rest, and, as in some Polynesian myths, which separated earth and Heaven. Then, as the sky seemed to recede into a remoter distance, arose the fable of one lofty tree reaching from earth to Heaven.[45] Myths of a Heaven-supporting tree are numerous, and they survive in tales of ' Jack and the Beanstalk.'[46] The resemblances of the Scandinavian tree to such mythic trees are numerous, and its origin need not therefore be sought in medieval Christian legends of the Cross as a World-tree, which, in fact, carry on the tradition of these mythical trees.

The myth of the sky as a tent-roof supported on a pillar or post occurs among the Lapps, Finns, and North Asiatic tribes, Japanese, and ancient Egyptians.[47] The Asiatic pillar is seven-storied, representing the seven Heavens, and it is the tethering-post of the stars or of the horses of the gods.[48] Posts with seven branches, on which sacrificial victims are hung, symbolize the mythical post. The Lapps also had such sacrificial pillars, representing the heavenly pillar supporting the world, with an iron nail at the top, a symbol of the World-nail which fixed the sky in place. The nail of the sky is the Pole Star, round which the Heavens are thought to revolve. This belief of the Lapps may have been borrowed from the Scandinavians.[49] Similar beliefs were entertained by the Celts and in ancient India.[50] The symbolism of the seven Heavens in tree or pillar, like the three divisions of the Romove tree, recalls the nine worlds or divisions of the Eddic tree.

This helps us to understand the Irminsul of the Saxons, a word denoting ' sanctuary,' ' image,' or ' pillar,' such as was destroyed by Charlemagne,[51] but its general significance was that of a pillar or tree-stump. Rudolf of Fulda says that the Saxons venerate leafy trees and springs, and worship a huge tree-trunk called Irminsul, which means *universalis columna,* as if it sustained all things.[52] The Irminsul must have been a symbol of a mythic World-pillar, and connected with the cult of a god Irmin. The nail of the sky may also have been known in Scandinavia, as its name, *veraldarnagli*, occurs in Icelandic folk-poetry.[53] The mythic World-mountain may be seen in the Himinbjorg, or 'Heaven-mountain,' situated at the end of Bifrost.

These various conceptions show that, whatever details may be due to Christian influences, the Eddic World-tree was a native conception. The theory that it was copied from the medieval legend of the Cross was advanced by Bugge, E. H. Meyer, and Golther, though Bugge admitted the existence in Scandinavian belief of a wonderful holy tree, which, under Christian influence, was transformed into a World-tree. In the medieval legend the Cross was a tree linked to the Tree of Life in Paradise. Its end, set in the earth, reached down to the Underworld, the top reached to Heaven, the two arms spread over the world. The Cross was our Lord's steed, according to medieval poetic usage, and 'steed' was a metaphor for 'gallows,' the victim being the Rider. The *point d' appui* here is the explanation of Yggdrasil as Odin's gallows, because he hung on it. As we have seen there is no evidence that the tree on which he hung was Yggdrasil. The dragon Nidhogg is the serpent of Eden, associated with the Tree from which the Cross was derived.[54] Be this as it may, the Yggdrasil conception is not entirely, if at all, due to such legends as these.

THE DOOM OF THE GODS

A phrase used in the Poetic *Edda* is *ragna rok*, 'fate or doom of the gods' (*ragna* being genitive plural of *regen*, 'powers,' 'gods'). It resembles the phrase *aldar rok*, 'destruction of the world,' used in *Vafthrudnismal*. Another phrase, with which it is often confused, is *ragna rokr*, 'the darkness of the gods,' which occurs in *Lokasenna* and is used by Snorri.[55] Used mistakenly as a proper noun, Ragnarok, the phrase is often rendered ' Twilight of the gods.'

This Doom of the gods, the central incident of a wider myth of the destruction of the world, is the subject of a great part of *Voluspa*, and shows that, as the gods are not eternal *a parte ante*, so their life at last comes to an end. In view of that Doom, Valhall must be filled with heroes, and even now Thor fights with the enemies of the gods.

The *Voluspa* poet connects the Doom with the coming of the three giant-maids, the Norns, which brought the Golden Age of the gods to an end. Now the gods are brought under the power of fate. The Doom is also linked to the first war, when gods fought the Vanir, and, more immediately, with the death of Balder.[56]

The verses describing these events do not all belong to the original poem, and may have been interpolated by a moralizing poet. The dualism which results in the conquest of gods by demoniac beings, who are themselves annihilated, is the foundation of the myth. This is bound up with fate, stronger than the gods, but the verse regarding this (the coming of the Norns) is isolated and is followed by interpolated verses about the dwarfs, which may have ousted stanzas continuing the subject.

Then follows an outrage perpetrated by the gods — a wild kind of justice, described in two interpolated stanzas. This is ' the first war in the world,' and concerns the slaying of Gullveig by the gods. She must have had some evil design in coming to the gods' world: hence they slew her, yet she ever lives. This may be connected with the war between Æsir and Vanir, if Gullveig was Freyja, a Vanir goddess. This war is also called the first war. During the contest with the Vanir, the wall of the gods' citadel was broken down. A moralized sign of the end is now introduced — a reference (intelligible only from Snorri's account of the myth) to the breaking of oaths made by the gods to the giant artificer, whom Thor slew. The gods have perjured themselves. Balder's death is the next step to the Doom.

The working of demoniac might through Loki against the gods has begun. Loki is put in bonds, but greater woes are coming, and ' Frigg weeps sore for Valhall's need.' The coming Doom was almost certainly the subject whispered by Odin into the dead Balder's ear.[57] As a consequence of the gods' violence and treachery, evils abound among men — oath-breaking and revenge, and these are punished in the Underworld.[58]

That the final destruction and Doom of the gods is a genuine Teutonic myth, we take for granted. There seem, however, to be different myths of the manner in which this would happen, and these are more or less combined in *Voluspa*.

1. A destruction of the world by its sinking into the sea, from which it had emerged, according to one cosmogonic myth.

' The sun becomes black, earth sinks into the sea,
From Heaven fall the bright stars.'

This is also described in *Hyndluljod:*

' The sea ascends in storm to Heaven,
It swallows the earth, the air becomes sterile.'

To this may be linked the swallowing of the sun by a monster — an eclipse myth used to heighten the effect of the myth of the world's destruction.[59] This myth of the sinking of the earth into the sea is perhaps connected with the daily apparent sinking of the sun into the sea, as seen by dwellers on the coast.

2. The world ends with a mighty winter, *fimbul-vetr*. In *Vafthrudnismal* Odin asks what of mankind shall survive the mighty winter. Vafthrudnir answers that Lif and Lifthrasir, hid in Hoddmimir's wood, will survive it. In Snorri's account they survive the destructive fires of Surt. *Hyndluljod* speaks of snows and furious winds which follow the sinking of earth in the sea, and in *Voluspa* mighty storms come in summer. Snorri says that this winter will precede the Doom. Snow will drive from all quarters, with sharp frost and wind; the sun will be without power. Three such winters will follow in succession

with no summer between. Over the earth are mighty battles. Brothers will slay each other for greed's sake: none spares father or mother in murder and incest. He then cites a stanza of *Voluspa* which refers to these evils:

> ' Brothers shall fight and slay each other,
> Sisters' sons break kinship's bonds;
> Hard is it on earth, with much unchasteness,
> Axe-age, sword-age,
> Shields are cloven,
> Wind-age, wolf-age, ere sinks the world;
> No man will ever another spare.' [60]

3. A third myth is that of the destruction of the world by fire. *Voluspa* tells how Surt comes from the South with ' the scourge of branches,' i.e., fire. In the stanza which describes earth sinking into the sea, it is said that steam rages and the preserver of life (fire); fire shoots high to Heaven itself. The fires of Surt are also mentioned in *Vafthrudnismal* as occurring at the end of the world. The possible destruction of the world by fire, viz., by the sun, is spoken of in *Grimnismal*. If it were not for the shield in front of the sun, mountains and seas would be set in flames. Snorri often refers to this final fire, and says that Surt will cast fire and burn the world. The sons of Muspell ride forth, Surt at their head, before him and after him burning fire. His sword is very good, from it shines a light brighter than the sun. As they ride over Bifrost, the bridge breaks down. In an earlier notice, Surt is said to sit at the world's end by Muspellheim. At the last he will go forth and harry, overcome the gods, and burn the world with fire.[61] Fire and heat were sources of life: now they are its destruction.

These separate myths, or at least the first and second, are combined in *Voluspa*, together with the myth of the freedom gained by chained monsters, the Fenris-wolf, Loki, and Garm, and all three appear in Snorri's account of the Doom, in which he quotes freely from the poem.

The doom begins with moral evils on earth.[62] The sons of

Mim (the waters or spirits of the waters) are in motion.[63]   The
Gjallar-horn sounds the note of Doom as Heimdall blows it.
All the Hel-ways are in fear.   Yggdrasil shakes; its leaves
rustle, for the giant, the Fenris-wolf, is free.   Odin consults the
head of Mim, but the wolf will slay him soon.   Then comes an
impressive stanza:

> ' How fare the gods?   How fare the Alfar?
> All Jötunheim roars; the gods take counsel.
> The dwarfs stand groaning before their rock-doors,
> The lords of the rock-walls.   Would ye know yet more? '

From the East comes Hrym, leader of the giants.   The
Midgard-serpent writhes in giant-fury.   The eagle Hræsvelg
screams aloud, gnawing corpses.   The ship Naglfar is loose,
steered, as Snorri says, by the giant Hrym and carrying the
giants.[64]   Another ship sails from the North with the people of
Hel, steered by Loki.   Wild hosts [65] follow the Wolf.   With
them is Byleipt's brother (Loki).   From the South comes Surt
with fire.   The hills are shattered; the giantesses fall; the dead
crowd Hel-way; Heaven is cloven.

To Frigg comes yet another grief: she sees Odin die by the
Wolf.   Frey seeks out Surt, Vidarr pierces the Wolf with his
sword, avenging Odin.   Thor advances against the Midgard-
serpent, and strikes a death-blow, but himself falls dead, suf-
focated by the venom.   Now the sun turns black; earth sinks
into the sea, stream and flame grow in fierceness, and fire leaps
up to Heaven itself.   It is the end.

Snorri's account of the advance of the gods and the fighting
is vivid.   The Wolf rushes forward, mouth gaping, the upper
jaw touching Heaven, the lower the earth, fire blazing from
eyes and nostrils.   The Midgard-serpent by its side blows
venom.   Heaven is cloven, and Muspell's sons, led by Surt,
ride forth, fire preceding and following them.   They ride to a
field Vigrid, and there come also the Fenris-wolf, the Midgard-
serpent, Loki, Hrym, and the Frost-giants.   The people of

Hel follow Loki. Heimdall blows his horn. Odin rides to Mimir's well to take counsel with him. Yggdrasil trembles: all in Heaven and earth are in fear. The Æsir arm themselves and ride to the field, with all the Einherjar from Valhall. Odin is in front, with golden helmet, birnie, and spear. Thor is beside him, but cannot aid him against the Fenris-wolf, as he must encounter the Midgard-serpent. The watch-dog of Hel, Garm, is loose, doing battle with Tyr, each slaying the other. Thor slays the Serpent, strides away nine paces, and falls dead, overcome by its venom. Frey fights with Surt and falls, for he lacks his sword, having given it to Skirnir. The Wolf swallows Odin, but Vidarr sets one foot on its lower jaw, and with his hand seizes the upper jaw, and tears them in two. Loki fights with Heimdall, and each slays the other. Surt then throws fire over the earth and burns it up.[66]

Snorri gives details not in *Voluspa*, e.g., Tyr's fight with Garm, and Heimdall's with Loki. He incorporates some incidents from *Vafthrudnismal* which also contains some notices of the Doom, viz., the field Vigrid, Njord's return to the Vanir before the end, the mighty winter which Lif and Lifthrasir survive, the swallowing of the sun, the fires of Surt, Odin's death by the Wolf, its slaying by Vidarr, and Thor's end.[67]

In spite of the large muster of forces, only a few are described as actual combatants — on one side Odin, Thor, Tyr, Heimdall, Frey, and Vidarr; on the other the Wolf, the Serpent, Garm, Loki, and Surt. No account of the participation of other gods or of the Einherjar is given. Some of these pairs of opponents are found in hostility to each other in non-eschatological myths — Thor and the Serpent, Heimdall and Loki.

The Doom is known to the poets who wrote *Baldrs Draumar* and *Grimnismal*. In the former the sibyl tells Odin that none shall seek her till Loki is free from his bonds and the destroyers come to the Doom of the gods. In the latter Thor is to dwell in Thrudheim ' till the gods are destroyed ' — a phrase used also in *Vafthrudnismal*.[68] Some of the skaldic poems also refer to it. In *Eiriksmal* Odin speaks of the time not being known when the grey Wolf shall come upon the seat of the gods. In *Hakon-armal* are the words: 'the Fenris-wolf shall be let loose on mankind ere such a good king as Hakon shall arise.' Verses by Kormak (*c.* 935 A.D.) say: 'the earth shall sink, the mountains drop into the sea' before such a fair woman as Steingud shall be born. Arnor Iarlaskald (*c.* 1065 A.D.) wrote: 'the bright sun shall turn black, the earth sink into the dark sea, the dwarfs' burden (Heaven) shall be rent, the sea rush up over the hills, ere such a one as Thorfinn shall be born.' These references are in conformity with the Eddic account. In the story of the Hjadnings' battle, it is said that the fight will continue till the Doom of the gods; and when the maiden saw the dead Helgi and his men riding to their barrow, she cried: 'Is this the Doom of the gods, that dead men ride?' [69]

How far Christian influences have coloured or moulded the ideas and incidents of the world catastrophe is problematical. Different critics assume more or less of such influence. While here and there echoes of Scriptural language and incidents may be found, the conception as a whole seems original, or at least based on native folk-lore and eschatological myths. Parallels from other mythologies exist, but it does not follow that there was borrowing from these. The swallowing of the sun by a monster is a wide-spread myth. Iranian mythology has a parallel to the mighty winter in its eschatology — the devastation caused by the rain of Malkōsh, when most of mankind die of excessive cold, snow, and famine. Rydberg and others regard the Iranian and Eddic myths as examples of an old Indo-Germanic belief.[70] The belief in the world's destruction by water and fire existed among the Celts, apart from Christian influence. There are classical references to this belief among the Celts, and it exists in native Irish documents. The prophecy of the War-goddess Badb about evils to come and the end of the world, and that of Fercertne in *The Colloquy of the Two Sages* have a certain likeness to the prophecy of Doom in *Voluspa*.[71]

One point requires further elucidation. Snorri says that the sons of Muspell ride with Surt at their head over Bifrost bridge. At the end of the conflict the fires of Surt consume the world. He has already spoken of the southern region of fire, Muspell or Muspellheim, at whose frontiers sits Surt waiting to go forth against the gods and destroy the world with fire. Muspell has the largest ship, Naglfar. From the sparks flowing out of Muspell, the gods made the chariot of the sun and the lights of Heaven.[72]

Two passages only of the Poetic *Edda* mention Muspell. Loki told Frey that when the sons of Muspell ride through Myrkwood he will be weaponless. In *Voluspa* the manuscripts have the reading ' the people of Muspell,' which is corrected by critics to ' the people of Hel.' [73] Bifrost is spoken of twice. In *Fafnismal* the gods assemble at Oskopnir ('the not yet created,' perhaps another name for Vigrid) to meet Surt, and Bifrost breaks down as they cross it. Elsewhere it is the hosts of Surt who break it down. A stanza in *Grimnismal* speaks of Thor wading through rivers, for Bifrost burns in flame. This may either refer to the time of Doom or express a myth of the sun's reappearance after thunder when the rainbow-bridge seems to be on fire.[74]

Is Muspell a word originating from pagan or from Christian conceptions? Grimm says that in it ' we find another striking proof of the prevalence of Old Norse conceptions all over Teutondom.' [75] The word occurs in the Saxon *Heliand*: ' the power of *mûdspelli* fares over men,' and ' *mûdspelli* comes in dark night as a thief.' The reference is to the Day of Judgment; and a Bavarian poem says of the fire which burns up the world: ' no friend can help another for the *mûspilli*.' [76] Thus the word refers to a world conflagration as in the *Eddas*. Did it first betoken the fire as a Christian conception, or was it originally applied to a similar pagan conception? Opinions are sharply divided here, as also on the root-meaning of the word. Grimm takes it to mean ' fire,' its component parts being *mud*, *mu,* ' earth,' ' wood,' ' tree,' and *spilli,* cognate with ON *spilla,* ' destroy ': hence the word is an epithet of fire.   Others connect *spilli* with OHG and AS *spell,* ' prophecy,' and regard *mud* as a Latin loan-word from *mundus* — hence ' a prophecy of the world,' viz., of its end.   In this sense the word, originating from Christian preaching about the end of the world by fire, took root in Teutonic thought and passed to Scandinavia.[77]   Other derivations have been suggested and there is a copious literature on the subject.[78]

There is every likelihood that the destruction of the world by fire was a native conception, as in other mythologies, though Christian influences may have worked upon it.   The Poetic *Edda* personifies the agents of destruction as ' Muspell's sons,' i.e., spirits of fire or Fire-giants.   Fire may have been personified as a giant called ' Muspellr.' [79]   Snorri then gives the conception of a southern region of fire, Muspell or Muspellheim, whether this originated with him or not.   The destruction of the world by fire was a Celtic conception, as has been seen, and this may have passed from Celts to Teutons or have been a belief common to both.

Why a myth of the destruction of the gods should have originated in Scandinavia is uncertain.   It does not appear to signify the defeat of Norse gods by the Christian religion, for there is no trace of such a conception in the sources.   We cannot even say that it arose out of a weakening of the old religion among the people.   They were still firmly attached to it when Christianity appeared in the North.   The best parallel to it is found in Scandinavian mythology itself (as in Greek) — the destruction of the older race of giants by the gods.

THE RENEWAL OF THE WORLD

The gods are gone, men destroyed, the earth sunk in the sea or burned, but now appears a new world.   This is the theme of the final stanzas of *Voluspa:*

'Now I see for a second time
Earth in fresh green rise from the sea;
The cataracts fall, the eagle flies,
He catches fish from the rocks.

The Æsir assemble on Ithavoll,
They speak of the mighty earth-engirdler,
They recall the mighty events of the past,
And the ancient-runes of Fimbul-tyr.

Then once more will the wonderful
Golden tables be found in the grass,
Which once in old time the gods possessed.

On fields unsown will fruits spring forth,
All evils vanish; Balder comes back.
Hod and Balder dwell in Hropt's battle-hall,
The hall of the mighty Battle-gods.

Then can Hœnir choose the prophetic wand.
The sons of the brothers of Tveggi abide
In spacious Vindheim.   Would ye know yet more?

A hall I see, brighter than the sun,
O'erlaid with gold, on Gimle stand;
There dwell for ever the righteous hosts,
Enjoying delights eternally.

From on high comes a Mighty One
To the great judgment, ruling all.
From below the dark dragon flies,
The glistening snake from Nithafjoll;
On his wings bears Nidhogg, flying o'er the plain,
The corpses of men.   Now must I sink.' [80]

There is thus a new earth without ills, where fruits unsown
ripen — a typical Elysian or Golden Age world.   Some of the
gods return — those who were not destroyed, Balder, Hod,
Hœnir, the sons of Tveggi's ('the Twofold,' Odin) brothers,
of whom nothing is known.   They speak of the things of the
past, of the Midgard-serpent, of Odin's runes (Fimbul-tyr,
'the mighty god ').   They find the golden tables on which the

gods had once played a kind of draughts in the Golden Age
(cf. v. 8: ' In their home at peace they played at tables '). The
mysterious ' Mighty One ' is almost certainly a borrowing from
Christianity, just as the hall on Gimle is a reflexion of the Christian Heaven. The final stanza about Nidhogg is apparently
not in its right place. Its last words, however, belong to the
end of the poem, and refer to the Volva, who, having delivered
her prophecy, sinks back whence she came. Some have taken
the verse as meaning that the dragon tries to rise, but is defeated and sinks for ever. This is unlikely, and ' she must sink '
= ' I must sink ') refers to the seeress.

Hyndluljod also speaks of the High God to come:

> ' There comes another, a Mightier,
> Yet dare I never his name forthtell;
> Few are they who can further see
> Than when Odin shall meet the Wolf.' [81]

The new world, as well as other details, is known to the poet of
Vafthrudnismal. During the mighty winter Lif and Lifthrasir
survive. The sun (Alfrodull) will bear a daughter ere the
Wolf swallows her, and this daughter will follow her mother's
ways when the Powers fall. Odin then enquires about the
maidens who shall fare over the sea. Vafthrudnir's reply shows
that three throngs of maidens descend over Mogthrasir's
dwelling-place. They will be guardian spirits to men, though
they come of giant stock. These are perhaps kindly Norns.
The giant then tells Odin that, after Surt's fires have sunk,
Vidarr and Vali shall dwell in the realm of the gods, and Modi
and Magni, sons of Thor, shall have his hammer Mjollnir. [82] In
this forecast of the new world, there is a further conception. Lif
and Lifthrasir (' Life ' and ' Vitality '), progenitors of a new
race of men, are hidden in Mimir's grove, possibly Yggdrasil if
Mimameid, ' Mimir's tree,' mentioned in *Svipdagsmal*, is the
World-tree. This corresponds to the Iranian myth of the *vara*
or ' enclosure ' of Yima, the first mortal, whose reign is a Golden
Age. He was commanded to make this *vara* and fill it with

happy mortals, who will repeople the earth after the devastating winter has passed.[83]   There will be a new sun, and certain gods will reappear, their names differing from those in *Voluspa*. The giant maidens who act as guardian spirits, presumably to the dwellers on the new earth, descend over Mogthrasir's ' thorp ' or dwelling-place; and, as Boer suggests, Mogthrasir, ' he who desires sons,' may be the same as Lif, progenitor of the new race.[84]

Snorri combines the *Voluspa* and *Vafthrudnismal* passages in his account of the new world.   But he adds a description of places of bliss and punishment, and here, as we have seen, he seems to have misunderstood his sources.[85]

Apart from the reference to Gimle, which appears to be for the righteous dead, the poems say nothing about the lot of the dead in the renewed world.

NOTES

NOTES

Introduction

1. Bugge [a] and [b].
2. Phillpotts [a], *passim.*
3. Cf. Boer.
4. Some scholars interpret Harbard as Loki or a giant. Harbard is one of the names of Odin in *Grim.*, 49.
5. On the Sagas see the Prolegomena to Vigfusson's edition of the *Sturlunga-saga,* Oxford, 1878, and Craigie [c].

Chapter I

1. *Gylf.*, c. 20.
2. ib., c. 35.
3. Saxo, i. 30 [25], iii. 94 [78], vi. 225 [183], etc.
4. Adam of Bremen, iv. 26, 27.
5. Procopius, ii. 15.
6. For these charms see Grimm [a], i. 224, 401; de la Saussaye, pp. 126 ff.; Golther [a], pp. 383 ff., 437, 487; *CPB*, i. 482.
7. See p. 38.
8. *MGH Leg.*, Sect. ii, i. 222.
9. Alcuin, *Vita S. Willibrordi,* c. 10; Adam of Bremen, iv. 3. See p. 162.
10. Grimm [a], i. 165.
11. See my *Celtic Mythology* in this Series.
12. Mogk, 'God' (Teutonic), *ERE* vi. 303.
13. Mogk, 'Æsir,' in Hoops, i. 130; *Grim.* 44.
14. Jordanes, c. 13, § 78.
15. *Vol.*, 6, 9, etc.; *Hav.*, 78, 142; *Alviss.*, 20, 30; *Hym.* 4; *Alviss.*, 10.
16. For *tivar* see *Grim.*, 5; *Hym.*, 4; *Thrym.*, 13; *B Dr.*, 1; *Vaf.*, 38, 42; *Hav.*, 149. For *sig-tivar, val-tivar,* see *Vol.*, 44, 49, 58; *Grim.*, 45; *Lok.*, 1 and 2; *Faf.*, 24; *Akv.*, 31; *Hym.*, 1; *Vol.*, 52, 62.
17. *Land.-bók,* iii. 10; *Volsunga-saga,* c. 26.
18. See p. 52.
19. *Grim.*, 6, 37, 41; *Lok.*, 32; *Vol.*, 8; *Grim.*, 13.   See p. 80 for Thor's anger. It is called *asmodi,* 'god-like anger,' as the giant's rage is *jötunmodi,* see *Skaldsk.*, c. 17.

20. *Gylf.*, c. 23 f.
21. *Vol.*, 18; *Gylf.*, c. 6 f.
22. See Mogk, ' Dreiheit,' in Hoops, i. 487; Tacitus, *Germ.*, c. 2; *Gylf.*, c. 6; *HHj.*, 28.

CHAPTER II

1. *Thrym.*, 14; *Vaf.*, 39; *Sigrd.*, 18; *Skir.*, 17, 18.
2. *Vaf.*, 39; *Vol.*, 24; Ulf Uggason in *Skaldsk.*, c. 7.
3. *Gylf.*, c. 35; *Skaldsk.*, cc. 6, 7, 20, 37.
4. *Brag.*, c. 1. See p. 53.
5. *Gylf.*, c. 23; *Vaf.*, 39; cf. *Lok.*, 34, 35.
6. *Ynglinga-saga*, c. 4.
7. *Skaldsk.*, cc. 32, 37.
8. De la Saussaye, pp. 248–9; Gering, p. 6.
9. Golther [a], pp. 223, 305; Chadwick [b], p. 61. For Svia-god and blot-god, see *Ftb.*, iii. 246 and *Olafs-saga Trygg.*, c. 173.
10. *Ynglinga-saga*, c. 5; Golther [a], p. 222.
11. *Vol.*, 24; *Ynglinga-saga*, c. 5.
12. See MacCulloch [b], pp. 23, 35. On the subject of this chapter cf. Weinhold [b], pp. 611 ff.; K. Krohn, pp. 93 ff.

CHAPTER III

1. *Brag.*, *ad fin.*
2. *Ynglinga-saga*, c. 1 ff.; see p. 106.
3. Saxo, i. 24 [20].
4. ib., i. 30 [25], iii. 90 [75], 94 [78], 98 [81].
5. ib., vi. 225 [184].
6. ib., iii. 94 [78].

CHAPTER IV

1. Grimm [a], i. 123 ff.; William of Malmesbury, *Gesta Pontificum Anglorum*, i. § 5; Roger of Wendover, *Flores Hist.*, i. 346.
2. Grimm [a], i. 130.
3. Tacitus, *Germ.*, c. 9, cf. *Annales*, xiii. 52, *Hist.*, iv. 64.
4. Paulus Diaconus, *de Gestis Langobard.*, i. 9.
5. Bede, *Hist. Eccl.*, i. 15. 36; Grimm [a], i. 165.
6. *MGH Leg.*, Sect. ii., i. 222; cf. p. 18.
7. Paul. Diac., i. 8; Grimm [a], i. 134. According to Saxo, who refers to Paulus, the people were prompted by Frea to take the name Langobardi, i. 343 [285].
8. See p. 18.
9. Adam of Bremen, iv. 26, 27.
10. *Heimskr.*, 6; *Ftb.*, iii. 246.

11. Cæsar, vi. 17.
12. Grimm [a], iii. 919 ff.
13. Mogk, p. 334; Grimm [a], iii. 919.
14. *ZfDM* i. 315 f.
15. E. Meyer, *Sagen aus Schwaben*, i. 1 f.; Panzer, *Bayrische Sagen*, i. 67; Vernaleken, *Mythen und Bräuche in Österreich.*, p. 23 f.
16. Grimm [a], iii. 919.
17. E. H. Meyer, p. 382 f.; Grimm [a], iii. 918 f.
18. *Yngl.-saga*, c. 2; Saxo, iii. 96 (80); *Vaf.*, 44, ff.
19. *Hav.*, 155; *Hynd.*, 3; *Reg.*, 18.
20. *Grim.*, 48; *Brag.*, c. 1.
21. Saxo, i. 29 [24].
22. *Gylf.*, cc. 15, 42; *Grim.*, 44.
23. *Gylf.*, cc. 15, 49.
24. ib., c. 51.
25. *Vaf.*, 5; *Grim.*, 53 f.; *Hym.*, 2; *Faf.*, 43; *Gylf.*, c. 20; *Skaldsk.*, c. 54.
26. *Grim.*, 29 f.
27. *Hakonar-saga Sverrisonar*, c. 20.
28. Grimm [a], i. 152 f.
29. *Reg.*, 18; *Akv.*, 32.
30. Saxo, iii. 95 [78], vii. 296 [247], *Land.-bók*, v. 12. 4.
31. For these names see *Yngl.-saga*, c. 7; *Gylf.*, c. 20; *Brag.*, c. 1; *Skaldsk.*, c. 2; *Islendinga Sögur*, i. 307.
32. See *Vol.*, 1, 29; *Grim.*, 48; *Gylf.*, cc. 15, 20.
33. *Grim.*, 8; *Gylf.*, c. 20; *Hynd.*, 6.
34. *Gylf.*, c. 36.
35. *Odr.*, 15.
36. *Fra d. Sinf.*
37. *BDr.*, 3, 13.
38. *Lok.*, 24.
39. Saxo, iii. 94 f. [78 f.]; *Skaldsk.*, 55.
40. *Harb.*, 20, 43.
41. *Hav.*, 145 ff.
42. *Yngl.-saga*, cc. 7, 14; *Vol.*, 47; *Sigrd.*, 14.
43. See MacCulloch [a], pp. 34, 102, 242, [b], pp. 101, 104.
44. *Sigrd.*, 13; *Hav.*, 111 f.
45. *Grim.*, 47.
46. *Yngl.-saga*, cc. 5, 7.
47. *Gylf.*, c. 30; *Skaldsk.*, cc. 2, 55.
48. Saxo, iii. 96 [79].
49. *Harb.*, 18, 20, 30; *Skaldsk.*, c. 19.
50. *Hav.*, 96 ff.
51. *Hav.*, 13, 103 ff.

52. *Reg.*, Introd.
53. *Vol.*, i, 28; *BDr.*, *Hav.*, 104, 161; *Vaf.*; *Harb.*, 44.
54. *Skaldsk.*, c. 2; *Vol.*, 27 ff.; Gering, pp. 6 ff.; Boer, *Vol. in loc.*
55. *Vol.*, 27, 29; *Gylf.*, cc. 15, 51.
56. *Grim.*, 7; *Gylf.*, c. 35; Gering, *Edda*, p. 71.
57. *Hav.*, 79, 138 ff., 143.
58. Boer, i. 46.
59. Bugge [a], i. 317; *Yngl.-saga*, c. 10.
60. *Gautreks-saga*, c. 7; cf. Saxo, vi. 227 [184]. Karl Blind recorded a song which he heard sung by a Shetland woman, and which is supposed by some to be an echo of the myth of Odin on the tree:

> ' Nine days he hang pa de rütless tree,
> For ill wis da folk in' güd wis he,
> A bluidy maet wis in his side,
> Made wi' a lance, 'at wid na hide.
> Nine lang nichts i' da nippin' rime,
> Hang he dare wi' his necked limb.
> Some dey leuch, bitt ithers gret.'

61. *Brag.*, c. 1. See also passages from the skalds giving various names of poetry, *Skaldsk.*, c. 3, and cf. *CPB* i. 277, 280, Odin is ' lord of the ancient mead.' For the saliva rite see E. S. Hartland, *Legend of Perseus*, London, 1894–96, ii. 260; ' Saliva ' in *ERE* xi. 100, 101.
62. Cf. the Sampo myth in the *Kalevala*, *ERE* vii. 642.
63. *Hynd.*, 3; Craigie [a], p. 20; *Skaldsk.*, c. 3.
64. *Yngl.-saga*, i. 17, 18.
65. *Hav.*, 78, 144.
66. *Vol.*, 23; *Harb.*, 24; *HH* ii. 33.
67. Saxo, vii. 307 [255].
68. *Harb.*, 40; *Lok.*, 23; *HBr.*, 8; *Faf.*, 43; *Sigrdr.*, 4.
69. *Hynd.*, 2; *Sigrdr.*, prose to 4.
70. *HH* ii. 27 prose; *Hynd.*, 2.
71. *HH* ii. 37 prose.
72. Saxo, i. 38 [32], vii. 298 [248].
73. Saxo, viii. 317 [263].
74. Saxo, i. 38 [32], vi. 226 [184].
75. *Eiriksmal* in *CPB* i. 261 ff.
76. *HH* i. 16.
77. Mogk, ' Human Sacrifice (Teutonic),' *ERE* vi. 866; Saxo, iii. 95 [78], viii. 296 [247].
78. *Heimskringla*, i. 12, 17; Saxo, ii. 80 [66].
79. Montelius, 139 f. See Plate VII.
80. *Skaldsk.* c. 48; Adam of Bremen, iv. 26 f.
81. *CPB* i. 279; *Grim.*, 54; Metcalfe, p. 386.

82. Mogk in Hoops, iv. 559; *Fl.-Bók*, iii. 246.

83. *Harb.*, 24.

84. *Gylf.*, cc. 3, 9; *Vol.*, 60; *Grim.*, 44.

85. *Gylf.*, cc. 17, 50; *Grim.*, 6.

86. *Gylf.*, cc. 3, 7, 20.

87. *Harvarar-saga*, c. 12; *CPB* i. 87 ff.; Kershaw, pp. 113 ff., 216.

88. *Gylf.*, c. 6; *Vol.*, 4; *Hynd.*, 31; *Hav.*, 140.

89. *Lok.*, 26; *Heimskringla*, i. 13.

90. Saxo, i. 31 [26].

91. Saxo, iii. 98 [81].

92. *Tacitus*, *Germ.*, 43; cf. Schuck, *Studier i Ynglingatal, passim*.

93. Balder — *Vol.*, 32; *Grim.*, 21, 22; BDr., 8, 9; *Hynd.*, 31. Thor — *Skaldsk.*, c. 4; *Lok.*, 59; *Grim.*, 24; *Hym.*, 2, 22, 36; *Thrym.*, 21, 32; *Alviss.* 6.   Vali — *Gylf.*, c. 30; *B Dr.* 11; *Vol.*, 33. Hod, etc., *Gylf.*, cc. 8, 10, 11, 13; *Vol.*, 54; *Grim.*, 17.

94. Prologue to *Gylf*.

95. *Gylf.*, c. 38; *Skaldsk.*, 60; *Grim.*, 20.

96. *Story of Olaf Trygg.*, c. 27, in *Saga Library*, iii. 258, and iv. 271.

97. *Gylf.*, c. 38; *Grim.*, 19; *HH* i. 13.

98. *Gylf.*, cc. 15, 42, 49; *Skaldsk.*, c. 17; BDr., 2; *Grim.*, 44.

99. *Skaldsk.*, c. 35; *Sigrd.*, 21, 22.

100. *Gylf.*, c. 49; *Skaldsk.*, cc. 5, 35.

101. *Story of Olaf Trygg.*, cc. 197, 198, in *Saga Library*, iii. 314.

CHAPTER V

1. Willibrord, *Vita Bonif.*, c. 8.

2. Migne, *PL*, lxxxix. 853 and 577.

3. Grimm [a], iv. 1739 f.

4. Cæsarius of Arles, *PL* xxxix. 224; Eligius, in Grimm [a], iv. 1737 f.

5. Burchard, § 92, in *PL* cxl.

6. Saxo, vi. 225 [183].

7. Tacitus, *Germ.*, cc. 3, 9, *Ann.*, ii. 12.

8. Golther [a], p. 247.

9. Grimm [a], i. 170.

10. For these see Kemble, i. 347.

11. Saxo, ii. 53 [44], 225 [183].

12. Adam of Bremen, iv. 26; Saxo, vii. 265 [220].

13. *Ftb.*, i. 320.

14. *Eyrb.-saga*, c. 5; *Laxd.-saga*, c. 192; *Viga-Glums-saga*, c. 9; *Fth.*, i. 488; *Olafs-saga Trygg.*, c. 69; *Ork.-saga*, ii. 737.

356 EDDIC MYTHOLOGY

15. Grimm [a], i. 186; Golther, p. 251.
16. *Egils-saga; Ftb.*, i. 389; *Land.-bók*, iv. 13.
17. *Skaldsk.*, c. 4.
18. *Gautreks-saga*, c. 7. See p. 52 *supra*.
19. Thor, son of Odin and Jörd — *Skaldsk.*, c. 4; *Lok.*, 58; *Vol.*, 55; *Harb.*, 9; *Hym.*, 2, 22, 36; *Thrym.*, 21, 32; *Alviss.*, 6. Sif — *Hym.*, 3, 15, 35; *Lok.*, prose Intro. and 54; *Harb.*, 48; *Thrym.*, 24; *Skaldsk.*, cc. 4, 21. Thrudh — *Skaldsk.*, cc. 4, 21, 48.
20. *Skaldsk.*, cc. 4, 17; *Hym.*, 34; *Harb.*, 9, 53; *Vaf.*, 51.
21. *Harb.*, 9, 39; *Gylf.*, c. 44; *Skaldsk.*, cc. 17, 22, 23; *Hym.*, 39.
22. *Lok.*, 58; *Thrym.*, 1.
23. Adam of Bremen, iv. 27; *Eiriks-saga*, c. 13.
24. *Ftb.*, i. 388.
25. Dudo, *de Mor. et Actis Normannorum*, in *Memoires de la Soc. des ant. de la Normandie*, 1869, xxii. 129 f.
26. *Land.-bók*, iii. 14. 1.
27. ib., iii. 8. 2.
28. ib., v. 36.
29. *Eyrb.-saga*, c. 3.
30. *Land.-bók*, i. 3. 7, i. 7. 6, iv. 11. 1.
31. See Introd. to *Eyrb.-saga*, in *Saga Library*, ii. p. xxxi.
32. *Njals-saga*, c. 98, ii. 72.
33. *Land.-bók*, iv. 2.
34. *Olafs-saga Helga*, c. 72.
35. *Ftb.*, i. 283; *Saga of Hakon the Good*, c. 18 (*Saga Lib.*, iii. 169).
36. *Gylf.*, c. 21; *Grim.*, 4, 24.
37. *Gylf.*, c. 21; *Skaldsk.*, c. 54; *Sigrd.*, 15.
38. Metcalfe, p. 485; Grimm [a], i. 166 f.; Mogk, p. 357; *Alviss.*, 3; *Haustlong*, in *CPB* ii. 16.
39. *Skaldsk.*, c. 4; *Hym.*, 21.
40. *Gylf.*, c. 44; *CPB* ii. 16; *Thrym.*, 21; cf. *Lok.*, 55.
41. *Grim.*, 29; *Gylf.*, c. 15.
42. *Gylf.*, c. 21; *Skaldsk.*, cc. 17, 35; *Lok.*, 57; *Hym.*, 37.
43. *Hym.*, 36; *Harb.*, 15; *Skaldsk.*, c. 17; *Lok.*, 57 ff.
44. Grimm [a], i. 179.
45. *Thrym.*, 30.
46. Dasent, *Story of Burnt Njal*, Intro., p. xxv.
47. Saxo, xiii, quoted in *Introd.* to Elton's trans., p. lxiii.
48. *Gylf.*, c. 53.
49. *Gylf.*, c. 21.
50. *Fms.*, i. 503; *Thrym.*, 1, 27; *Gylf.*, c. 44; Grimm [a], i. 177.
51. *Harb.*, 3, 39; *Gylf.*, c. 45.
52. *Gylf.*, c. 51; *Vol.*, 55 f.; but see *Lok.*, 58.
53. *Skaldsk.*, c. 4.

54. *ARW* iv. 282.
55. *Skaldsk.*, c. 17.
56. ib., c. 17; *CPB* ii. 16.
57. *Lok.*, 61, 63; *Sigrd.*, 15; *Hym.*, 16; *Skaldsk.*, cc. 4, 48. For a similar story of a ball sticking in the head see MacCulloch [b], p. 157.
58. *Harb.*, 14 f.
59. F. R. Schröder in *PBB* li. 33 f., quoting J. Scheffer, *Argentoratensis Lapponia*, Frankfort, 1673, p. 104, and Olrik, *Maal og Minne*, 1910, pp. 1 ff.
60. Grimm [a], i. 374; Saxo, iii. 106 ff. [87 ff.].
61. *Skaldsk.*, c. 18.
62. *CPB* ii. 19 f.; *Skaldsk.*, c. 18; see references to the myth in poems quoted by Snorri, *Skaldsk.*, c. 4.
63. Saxo, viii. 344 ff. [286]. For an explanation of Geirrod's daughters and the flood, see *PBB* li. 35.
64. *Gylf.*, c. 48.
65. *Skaldsk.*, c. 4.
66. See MacCulloch [c], pp. 143, 174.
67. *CPB* ii. 8, 24.
68. Faye, *Norske Folksagen*, pp. 3 f.
69. *Gylf.*, c. 42.
70. *Vol.*, 24; Grimm [a], ii. 547 f., iv. 1446.
71. *Skaldsk.*, c. 4.
72. *Harb.*, 19; *Skaldsk.*, c. 23; *Lok.*, 50.
73. *Skaldsk.*, c. 4.
74. *Harb.*, 23, 29, 32; *Hynd.*, 4; *Hym.*, 11.
75. *Gylf.*, c. 44.
76. *Lok.*, 60, 62; *Harb.*, 26.
77. See MacCulloch [a], pp. 366, 377, [b], pp. 118 ff.
78. Saxo, viii. 352 ff. [292 ff.].
79. ib.
80. On the tabu language see A. Olrik, *Nordisk Tidskrift*, 1897, p. 341; Phillpotts [a], p. 46.
81. Phillpotts [a], pp. 132 ff., 178.

CHAPTER VI

1. *AS* glossaries give Mars as the equivalent of Tyr, Kemble, i. 351.
2. Tacitus, *Hist.*, iv. 64, *Germ.*, c. 39, cf. *Ann.*, xiii. 57 for the Hermunduri and Mars.
3. Jordanis, *de Origine Actibusque Getarum*, c. 5.
4. Procopius, *de Bello Goth.*, ii. 15.
5. Mogk, p. 314.
6. Müllenhoff and Scherer, ii. 1 f.

7. On the altar found in 1920 the Alaisiagae are Baudihillie and Friagabi.

8. *Gylf.*, c. 25.

9. *Sigrd.*, 6.

10. *Skaldsk.*, c. 9.

11. *Gylf.*, c. 34.

12. See MacCulloch [a], pp. 84 ff., [b], pp. 25, 28.

13. *Lok.*, 37 f.

14. *Gylf.*, c. 44; Boer, ii. 94 f. See p. 92.

15. *Gylf.*, c. 51.

CHAPTER VII

1. *Gylf.*, c. 23.

2. *Vaf.*, 38; *Lok.*, 34.

3. *Skaldsk.*, c. 6.

4. *Grim.*, 16.

5. *Lok.*, 36. Cf. *Grim.*, 43; *Skir.*, Introd. and 39, 40.

6. *Gylf.*, c. 23; *Skaldsk.*, c. 6; *Vaf.*, 38.

7. Cf. *CPB* ii. 465.

8. Golther [a], p. 219.

9. Tacitus, *Germ.*, c. 40.

10. Mannhardt [b], pp. 567 ff.; Kock, in Mogk, p. 321.

11. Bing, ' Ull ' in *Maal og Minne*, 1916; Schuck, *Studier i Ynglingatal*, ii. 163 f.

12. *Land.-bók*, iv. 13; *Egils-saga*, 204; cf. *Skaldsk.*, c. 7.

13. *Gylf.*, c. 23.

14. Saxo, i. 37 [30].

15. F. v. d. Leyen, *Götter und Göttersagen der Germanen*, Munich, 1920, p. 55; Mannhardt [a], i. 415; F. R. Schröder, ' Njörds Nackte Fusse,' *PBB* li. 31. Cf. Grimm, *KHM*, no. 65, ' *Allerleirauh.*'

16. *Gylf.*, c. 23; *Grim.*, 11.

17. *Skaldsk.*, c. 6.

18. Saxo, i. 40 [37]; Grimm [a], i. 348.

19. *Lok.*, 49 f.; *Skir.*, Introd.; *Gylf.*, c. 50.

20. Gering, p. 39; Golther, pp. 239 f.

21. *Yngl.-saga*, c. 9; *CPB* i. 252. The *Volsunga-saga*, c. 1, makes Sigi a son of Odin. He slays Budi, thrall of a great and mighty man, Skadi, because he kills more deer at the hunt than he. Skadi has been regarded as a form of the goddess, changed by misunderstanding of the name to a male. If so, Sigi would be her son by Odin. Müllenhoff, *ZfDA* xxiii. 117.

22. Schuck, *op. cit.*

23. R. M. Meyer, p. 210 and *ZfDPh* xxxviii. 171.

24. *Yngl.-saga*, c. 22.

25. Vigfusson and Powell, *Origines Islandicae,* i. 309.
26. Craigie [a], p. 29.

CHAPTER VIII

1. *Skir.,* 38; *Lok.,* Introd.; *Brag.,* c. 1; *Skaldsk.,* c. 33; *Grim.,* 43; *Skir.,* 39; *Skaldsk.,* c. 7.
2. *Gylf.,* c. 24; *Lok.,* 35, 37; *Skir.,* 3.
3. ib., c. 24; *Lok.,* 37.
4. *Grim.,* 5 and Gering's note, p. 70.
5. *Grim.,* 43 f.; *Gylf.,* c. 43; *Skaldsk.,* cc. 7, 35.   See references to Sagas in Gering, p. 333.
6. *Skir.,* 8, 9; *Gylf.,* c. 37.
7. Thorgrim in *Skaldsk.,* c. 58; *Skir.,* 8.
8. *Skir.,* 21, 22.
9. *Gylf.,* c. 49; *Skaldsk.,* cc. 7, 35; *Hynd.,* 7.
10. *Hervarar-saga,* c. 10; *HHj.,* Prose to 31; *Gisla-saga,* cc. 5, 27; *Ftb.,* i. 337; cf. Craigie [a], p. 28.
11. Grimm [a], i. 51, 213 f.; R. Chambers, *Book of Days,* Edinburgh, 1864, ii. 754.
12. Tacitus, *Germ.,* c. 45.
13. Grimm [a], i. 214 f.; Kemble, i. 357; *Beowulf,* 604 f., 2895 f., 4299 f.
14. *Skir.,* 9; *Lok.,* 42; *Vol.,* 53; *Gylf.,* c. 51.
15. *Vol.,* 53; *Gylf.,* c. 37; *Skaldsk.,* cc. 7, 58; *Skir.,* 16.
16. *Lok.,* 32.
17. *Skir.; Gylf.,* c. 37; *Hynd.,* 31.
18. *Gylf.,* c. 51; *Lok.,* 42.
19. Saxo, viii. 313 [260]; *Lok.,* 43.
20. *Beowulf,* 2638; Grimm [a], i. 345.
21. Saxo, i. 36 [30], 90 [75], 313 [260].
22. Vigfusson and Powell, *Orig. Island.,* i. 309.
23. *Yngl.-saga,* cc. 12, 13.
24. *Skaldks.,* c. 43.
25. Adam of Bremen, iv. 27, 28.
26. Saxo, ix. 363 [301], vi. 228 [185].
27. *Ftb.,* i. 400; Vigfusson and Powell, *Orig. Island.,* ii. 484.
28. Phillpotts [a], pp. 119, 176.
29. *Land.-bók,* iv. 15. 3.
30. *Ftb.,* i. 307; *Hallfredars-saga,* c. 5; *Egils-saga,* c. 58; *Land.-bók,* iv. 7.
31. Vigfusson and Powell, *Orig. Island.,* ii. 473.
32. ib., ii. 478.
33. *Land.-bók,* iii. 5. 1.

34. *Olafs-saga Trygg.*, c. 49; *Hrafnkels-saga* in *Orig. Island.*, ii. 493.

35. *Vatnsdœla-saga*, c. 34.

36. *Olafs-saga*, c. 49; *Ftb.*, i. 337 f.

37. Craigie [a], p. 25.

38. *Orig. Island.*, ii. 473; *Viga-Glums-saga*, ed. Head, p. 75.

39. *Yngl.-saga*, cc. 23, 33; *Land.-bók*, v. 17. 2.

40. *Gisla-saga*, ed. Dasent, pp. 56 ff.

41. *Heimskringla*, i. 12; *Skir.*, 3.

CHAPTER IX

1. *Gylf.*, c. 35; *Skaldsk.*, cc. 20, 37.

2. *Gylf.*, cc. 24, 35; *Lok.*, Introd.

3. *Grim.*, 14; *Gylf.*, c. 24; *Skaldsk.*, c. 20.

4. *Gylf.*, cc. 24, 49.

5. ib., c. 35; *Skaldsk.*, c. 20; *Thrym.*, 12, 14, 18.   See p. 123.

6. *Brag.*, c. 1; *Thrym.*, 36.

7. See *Hynd.*

8. *Gylf.*, c. 35; *Skaldsk.*, cc. 20, 37.

9. ib., c. 24; *Skaldsk.*, c. 20.

10. *Yngl.-saga*, c. 4.

11. *Gylf.*, c. 24; cf. Grimm [a], i. 300.

12. *Odr.*, 8; *Hynd.*, 10.

13. *Olafs-saga Helga*, c. 101 (*FAS*, iii. 223).

14. *Egils-saga*, c. 78.

15. *Skaldsk.*, cc. 18, 19.

16. *Skidarimur*, in *Golther* [a], pp. 437–8; *Njals-saga*, cc. 98, 100.

17. *Gylf.*, cc. 14, 20.

18. ib., c. 24; *Skaldsk.*, c. 17.

19. Giant artificer, *Gylf.*, c. 42; *Vol.*, 25; Hrungnir, *Skaldsk.*, c. 17; Thrym, see *Thrymskvitha.*

20. *Sorla-tháttr*, in *FAS* i. 391; *Ftb.*, i. 275.   The story is introductory to the unending conflict of the kings, see p. 316.

21. *Beowulf*, 1200.

22. Mogk, in Hoops, i. 314.

23. *Lok.*, 30 f.

24. Thrym., 26, 28.

25. *Skaldsk.*, c. 18.

26. Mogk, p. 373.

27. Gylf., c. 35; *Skaldsk.*, cc. 20, 37.

28. Golther [a], p. 445.

29. Mogk [a], p. 373.

30. Gering, p. 19.

31. Cf. Chadwick [a], c. 12; Phillpotts [a], p. 164.

NOTES

361

Chapter X

1. *Vol.*, 32; *BDr.*, 8, 9; *Hynd.*, 31; *Lok.*, 27; cf. *Gylf.*, c. 22.
2. *Grim.*, 12.
3. Bugge explains this as a reference to the daughters of Ran. In their grief they will toss the ships up on the waves till their sails reach the sky.
4. *Vol.*, 32 ff.
5. *Hynd.*, 30.
6. *Skir.*, 21, 22; *Vaf.*, 54, 55; *Lok.*, 7; *Vol.*, 62.
7. *Vol.*, 62.
8. *CPB* ii. 23 f.; cf. *Skaldsk.*, c. 5.
9. *Gylf.*, c. 22; *Skaldsk.*, c. 5.
10. Thor actually killed Hyrrokin, according to skald Thorbjorn Disarskald cited in *Skaldsk.*, c. 4.
11. *Gylf.*, cc. 49 f.
12. ib., c. 53.
13. *Skaldsk.*, cc. 12, 13.
14. Saxo, iii. 83 ff. [69 ff.], 94 [78].
15. ib., iii. 89 [74], 94 [78]; Herrmann [a], p. 215.
16. See p. 47.
17. Kauffmann, p. 72.
18. Mogk, in Hoops, i. 159; Herrmann, [a], pp. 211 ff.; Olrik [c].
19. Cf. Golther [a], p. 378.
20. *FAS* ii. 372 f.; *Hervarar-saga*, ed. Bugge, p. 206.
21. *Svip.*, 42.
22. Cf. Golther [a], p. 379; F. Detter, *PBB* 1894, xix. 498, thinks *mistelteinn* the plant came first and was then regarded as a sword. G. Neckel, 'Mistel,' in Hoops, iii. 230, supports the plant theory.
23. Bugge [b], pp. xxxviii. ff.
24. Phillpotts [a], pp. 76, 128 ff. Miss Phillpotts thinks the account in Snorri is 'rather like a game which Snorri had either seen himself or had had described to him.' The comic elements mingle with the tragic, as in a folk-play — Thor kicks the dwarf into the fire; four berserks have to hold down the giantess's steed, etc. If the dwarf incident represents an older human sacrifice, still that would not be 'an unnecessary precaution if the god be thought to be irretrievably dead.' Human sacrifice was all too common at the funerals of those who *were* 'irretrievably dead.'
25. *ZfDA* lii. 169 f., liv. 195 f.; Kogel, i. 92; *PBB* xv. 207; Bugge [a], i. 301 (Paul); *ZfDPh* (Apollo) xxi. 145; Grimm [a], i. 224 ff.
26. Thiele, ii. 341.

CHAPTER XI

1. *Gylf.*, c. 33, cf. c. 44 'that As called Loki,' and *Skaldsk.*, c. 33, where he is included among the Æsir. For Lopt, see *Lok.*, 6; *Hynd.*, 43; *Fjol.*, 26. For Lodur, *Vol.*, 18. For Laufey, *Lok.*, 52; *Thrym.*, 17, 20; *Gylf.*, c. 49; *Skaldsk.*, cc. 16, 35. For Byleist, *Vol.*, 51; *Hynd.*, 42.

2. *Gylf.*, c. 44 f.; *Thrym.*; *Skaldsk.*, c. 18. See p. 83.

3. *Vol.*, 17; *Reg.* and *Skaldsk.*, c. 39; *Brag.*, c. 1.

4. *Skaldsk.*, c. 22.

5. *Lok.*, 9, 16, 25.

6. *Saga Library*, iii. 217 (*Story of Harald Greycloak*, c. 15).

7. *Skaldsk.*, c. 16.

8. See p. 63; Elton's ed. of Saxo. Introd., p. lxi; Mogk, p. 349.

9. See p. 123.

10. *Gylf.*, c. 42, cf. *Vol.*, 25, *Hynd.*, 42.

11. *Brag.*, c. 1; *Lok.*, 50 f.

12. ib., c. 1.

13. *Skaldsk.*, c. 18.

14. ib., c. 39.

15. ib., c. 35.

16. See p. 88.

17. *Fms.*, i. 391 ff.; *Skaldsk.*, cc. 8, 16.

18. *Skaldsk.*, c. 33; *Lok.*, Introd.

19. *Hynd.*, 42; *Gylf.*, c. 34.

20. ib., 43; *Lok.*, 23; and Gering's note, p. 34.

21. *Gylf.*, c. 50; *Vol.*, 35.

22. *BDr.*, 14.

23. *Gylf.*, c. 51.

24. Grönbech [b], ii. 213.

25. *Skaldsk.*, c. 16; *Lok.*, 10, 54; *Hym.*, 38.

26. *Lok.*, 6; *Hynd.*, 43; *Skaldsk.*, cc. 18, 22 and *CPB* ii. 19 f., 14 f.

27. *Vol.*, 18; *Skaldsk.*, c. 23 and *CPB* ii. 13 f.; Mogk, in Hoops, iii. 164.

28. Cf. Bugge [a], i. 73 f.

29. Uhland, vi. 14; Gering, *Edda*, p. 9.

30. Gering, *Edda*, p. 21.

31. Mogk, in Hoops, iii. 163.

32. *Skaldsk.*, c. 35.

33. ib.; *Svip.*, 42, 50.

34. See MacCulloch [b], p. 163.

35. Mogk, in Hoops, iii. 163; Golther [a], p. 409; Munch, pp. 297, 306; Grimm [a], i. 242.

36. Olrik, *Festskrift til Feilberg* (= *Maal og Minne*, 1911), p. 548 f. Cf. *Danske Studier*, 1909, pp. 69, 77 f., 83.

37. MacCulloch, ' Earth, Earth-gods,' *ERE* v. 128.

38. Cf. *CPB* i, Introd. p. cvi, for a theory of an old Titanic being, Wloki, chained beneath a mountain, and causing earthquakes, and combined with the mocking, spiteful Loki.

39. *Mythology of All Races*, vi. 265 f., vii. 76 f.

40. Olrik, *op. cit.*, in note 36, and ' Ragnarok-forestill ingernes udspring,' *Danske Studier*, 1913.

CHAPTER XII

1. *Brag.*, c. 1.

2. *Vol.*, 18; *Brag.*, cc. 1, 39; *Reg.*, Introd.

3. V. Hammershaimb, *Färöiske Kvädar*, Copenhagen, 1851, i. 140 f.; Grimm [a], iii, Introd., p. xl. For the interpretation of the story, Upland, vi. 193 f., vii. 367 ff.

4. *Skaldsk.*, cc. 15, 22; *CPB* ii. 14 f. Vigfusson regards Hœnir as connected with an old myth of a bird that laid the egg of the world. He is long-legged and ' lord of the ooze' (*aur-Konung*), and his name may be connected with Sanskrit Ṣakunas = Greek *cucuos*, the white bird, swan or stork. The picture is that of a creator walking in chaos and finally hatching the egg of the world (*CPB* i. Introd., p. cii).

5. *Fms.*, i. 373.

6. *Gylf.*, c. 23; *Yngl.-saga*, c. 4.

7. *Vol.*, 63.

8. *Gylf.*, c. 27; *Brag.*, c. 1; *Skaldsk.*, c. 8; *Grim.*, 13; *Hynd.*, 37.

9. *Thrym.*, 14; *Grim.*, 13; *Skir.*, 28; *Vol.*, 27, 46; cf. Boer on *Vol.*, 27.

10. *Vol.*, 1; *Rig.*; *Hynd.*, 38, 40; *Gylf.*, c. 27.

11. *Lok.*, 47 f.

12. *Gylf.*, c. 27, cf. cc. 15, 17, 49.

13. Cf. e.g., *Celtic Myth.*, in this Series, pp. 189, 190.

14. Phillpotts, p. 130.

15. *Gylf.*, cc. 27, 51; *Skaldsk.*, c. 8.

16. *Hynd.*, 39; *Gud.*, ii. 22.

17. *Skaldsk.*, cc. 8, 16.

18. *Vol.*, 1; *Hynd.*, 40; *Grim.*, 13.

19. Grimm [a], iv. 1360; Golther [a], p. 366; E. H. Meyer [a], p. 409.

20. *Gylf.*, c. 31; *Brag.*, c. 1; *Skaldsk.*, cc. 4, 14, 18, 21.

21. ib., c. 31; *Skaldsk.*, c. 14.

22. *Akv.*, 32; *Grim.*, 42.

EDDIC MYTHOLOGY

23. *Grim.*, 5 in Sijmons and Gering, i. 222.
24. Golther, p. 392; Munch, p. 296; Schück, *Studier,* ii. 184 ff.;
Mogk, in Hoops, iv. 372.
25. *Skaldsk.*, c. 48.
26. Plutarch, *Caius Marius,* c. 23.
27. See p. 64.
28. M. Olsen, *Hedenske Kultminder i norske Stedsnavne,* Kristiania,
1915, vol. i; J. Bing, in *Maal og Minne,* 1916, pp. 107 ff.
29. Munch, p. 325.
30. *Gylf.*, c. 29; *Brag.,* c. 1; *Skaldsk.,* cc. 11, 18, 33; *Lok.,* Introd.
31. *Grim.*, 17.
32. *Lok.*, 10.
33. *Vol.*, 54; *Gylf.*, c. 51; *Skaldsk.,* c. 11; *Vaf.*, 53.
34. *Gylf.*, c. 53; *Vaf.*, 51.
35. ib., c. 51.
36. Kauffmann, p. 80, *PBB,* xviii. 157 f., cf. Anderson, pp. 338,
339.
37. M. Rœdiger, *ZfDPh* xxvii. 1 ff.
38. Kauffmann, *PBB* xviii. 157.
39. *Gylf.*, c. 26; *Brag.,* c. 1; *Skaldsk.,* cc. 22, 33. Cf. *Lok., Introd.*
40. *Grim,* 44; *Sigrd.,* 16; *Lok.,* 8 ff.
41. *CPB* i. 260 ff.
42. See MacCulloch [a], pp. 25, 74 f.
43. *Lok.*, 17.
44. *HH* ii. 8.
45. *Yngl.-saga,* c. 40; *Story of Hakon the Good,* c. 16 in *Saga
Library,* iii. 165.
46. *HHj,* Prose to 31.
47. *Gylf.*, c. 32; *Brag.,* c. 1; *Grim.,* 15; Munch, p. 18; Bugge,
Stud., p. 290.
48. Alcuin, *Vita Willibrordi,* c. 10; *Lex Fris.,* tit. v. 1, in *MHG
Leg.,* iii. 663.
49. C. v. Richthofen, *Friesische Rechtsquellen,* pp. 439 ff.; Golther,
p. 389.
50. *Gylf.*, cc. 30, 36; *Skalds.,* c. 12; *BDr.,* 11.
51. *BDr.*, 11; *Vol.,* 33; *Hynd.,* 30; *Skaldsk.,* c. 12.
52. See p. 135.
53. See MacCulloch [b], pp. 141, 165; Grimm [a], i. 321.
54. Detter, *PBB* xix. 509; G. Neckel, *Studien zu den germ. Dichtungen vom Weltuntergang,* 1918, pp. 21 ff.
55. *Svip.*, 6; E. Brate, *ANF* xxix. 109 f.
56. *Gylf.*, c. 28.
57. *Vol.*, 34; *BDr.,* 10, 11.
58. *Vol.*, 62; *Gylf.*, c. 53.

59. *Skaldsk.*, c. 5.
60. ib., c. 13.
61. Detter, *PBB* 1894, xix. 455 f.

Chapter XIII

1. See p. 52.
2. *Vol.*, 19, 27, 29; *Gylf.*, c. 15; Boer, *in loc.*
3. *Gylf.*, c. 15.
4. *Svip.*, 30.
5. *Vol.*, 46.
6. *Vaf.*, 45; *Gylf.*, c. 53.
7. *Yngl.-saga*, c. 4. See p. 26.
8. *Sigrd.*, 13 ff.
9. *Vol.*, 46; *Gylf.*, c. 51.
10. *Eyrb.-saga*, c. 43. For Celtic head myths see MacCulloch [b], p. 101.
11. *Skaldsk.*, c. 2.
12. Golther [a], p. 179; Mogk [a], p. 305; E. W. Förstemann, *Altdeutsches Namenbuch*, Nordhausen, 1856–59, i. 931 f.; Grimm [a], i. 380.
13. Grimm [b], pp. 146 ff.
14. E. H. Meyer [a], pp. 280, 380.
15. Snorri, p. 209 (Rask's Norse text); *Hav.*, 141; *Gylf.*, c. 6; see p. 52.

Chapter XIV

1. *Skaldsk.*, cc. 25, 61.
2. ib., c. 61.
3. Munch, p. 305.
4. *Lok.*, Introd.; *Skaldsk*, cc. 25, 61; *Brag.*, c. 1; *Yngl.-saga*, c. 36.
5. *Skaldsk.*, c. 27.
6. Snorri, p. 210 (Norse text).
7. *Skaldsk.*, c. 33.
8. ib., c. 33.
9. *CPB* i. 278; *Skaldsk.*, c. 25.
10. ib., ii. 54; *Skaldsk.*, c. 27.
11. Herrmann [a], pp. 579, 600.

Chapter XV

1. *Skaldsk.*, (Thjodolf of Hvin), c. 2; *Vol.*, 53.
2. *Lok.*, 26; *Gylf.*, c. 9.

3. *Skaldsk.*, c. 19.
4. *Vol.*, 34; *Gylf.*, c. 35; *Brag.*, c. 1; *Skaldsk.*, cc. 19, 33; *Grim.*, Introd.
5. *Lok.*, 29 (Freyja's words); in *Gylf.*, c. 20, Snorri makes Odin say this.
6. *Skaldsk.*, cc. 18, 19.
7. *Odr.*, 8.
8. Golther [a], p. 432; cf. Grimm [a], l. 304.
9. *Vol.*, 34, 53; *Gylf.*, c. 49.
10. R. M. Meyer, p. 274.
11. See p. 61.
12. *Lok.*, 25 f.
13. Saxo, i. 31 [26].
14. See p. 64.
15. Grimm [a], i. 123 ff.
16. Mogk [a], p. 371; Grimm [a], i. 302; Golther [a], p. 433, citing G. O. Hyltén-Cavallius, *Wärend och Wirdarne*, pp. 236 ff.; Preyer and Zvikel, *Reise nach Island*, p. 356.

CHAPTER XVI

1. *Brag.*, c. 1; *Skaldsk.*, c. 33; *Lok.*, Introd.
2. Kauffmann [a], p. 44; Gering, *Edda*, p. 31.
3. *Gylf.*, c. 26; *Haustlong* in *Skaldsk.*, c. 22.
4. Golther [a], p. 449; *ANF* v. 24.
5. *Lok.*, 16 ff.
6. *Brag.*, c. 1; *Skaldsk.*, c. 22; *Harb.*, 19; *Lok.*, 50. The *Haustlong* is also in *CPB* ii. 14.
7. Gering, *Edda*, p. 33.
8. Bugge, *ANF* v. 1 f.
9. See MacCulloch [a], pp. 159, 377.
10. *Gylf.*, c. 35; *Brag.*, c. 1; *Skaldsk.*, c. 33.
11. Grimm [a], i. 311; *Lok.*, 19 ff.
12. *Gylf.*, c. 1. Cf. *CPB* ii. 8 for Bragi.
13. *Yngl.-saga*, c. 5.
14. Olrik, *Danske Studier*, 1910, pp. 1 ff. For the rites see R. Chambers, *Book of Days*, i. 94; Chadwick [a], pp. 234 ff.; F. Kauffmann, *ARW* xv. 617. Müllenhoff [a], ii. 361, however, thinks that the story is Swedish, not Danish, and identifies Gefjun with Freyja.
15. E. H. Meyer [a], pp. 213, 417; F. N. Robinson, 'Deae Matres,' *ERE* iv. 409 f.
16. Cf. E. H. Meyer [a], p. 416. The story is first told of Dido.
17. *Hym.*, 3, 15, 35, etc.; *Skaldsk.*, c. 4.
18. *Skaldsk.*, c. 21.

19. *Lok.*, 53 f.
20. *Harb.*, 48.
21. *Skaldsk.*, c. 17.
22. ib., cc. 4, 14, 21; *Gylf.*, c. 31.
23. *Gylf.*, c. 35, *Grim.*, 7.
24. Golther, pp. 345, 435.
25. *HH* i. 40.
26. *Gylf.*, cc. 11, 35.
27. *Vaf.*, 23.
28. Grimm [a], ii. 704.
29. *Gylf.*, cc. 11, 35; Grimm [a], ii. 717; Baring-Gould, p. 201.
30. *Odr.*, 31.
31. *Gylf.*, cc. 35, 49; *Brag.*, c. 1; *Skaldsk.*, cc. 19, 32, 36.
32. ib., c. 35.
33. *Vol.*, 33.
34. *Gylf.*, c. 35; *Svip.*, 52, 54.
35. ib., *Thrym.*, 30.
36. ib.
37. ib.
38. *Skaldsk.* c. 44.
39. Saxo, iii. 87 [72].
40. *Njals-saga*, c. 89; *Thorleif Jarlaskald, Ftb.*, i. 213; *Hardar-saga*, c. 19.
41. *Fœreyinga-saga*, c. 23.
42. *Jomsvikings-saga*, c. 44, cf. *CPB* ii. 30; *Fms.*, ii. 134.
43. *Tháttr Thorleifs Jarlaskald, Ftb.*, i. 213.
44. *Njals-saga*, c. 87.
45. See Gustav Storm in *ANF* ii. 124 f.; K. Liestøl [a], p. 49 f.
46. *HHj.*, prose to 6 and ff. Cf. Herrmann, p. 214.

Chapter XVII

1. *Skaldsk.*, cc. 25, 33, 61.
2. ib.; *Hervarar-saga*, c. 15.
3. *HH* i. 29 f.; *HHj.*, 18.
4. Ref. in *Skaldsk.*, c. 25; c. 33; Grimm [a], i. 311.
5. *Eyrb.-saga*, c. 11, cf. p. 307.
6. *Egils-saga*, c. 80; *CPB* i. 278.
7. *Fridthjofs-saga*, c. 6.
8. *Eyrb.-saga*, c. 53.
9. *Fms.*, vi. 375 f.
10. Metcalfe, p. 287; Mogk, in Hoops, iv. 438.
11. See MacCulloch [a], pp. 87, 179 f., [b], p. 99.

CHAPTER XVIII

1. See MacCulloch, ' Nature,' *ERE* ix. 201 ff.
2. *Gylf.*, cc. 9, 10, 36; *Skaldsk.*, cc. 4, 17, 18, 19, 23, 24, 57; *Lok.*, 58; *Thrym.*, 1.
3. W. Brambach, *Corpus Inscr. Rhen.*, Elberfeld, 1867, 150; W. Pleyte, *Verslagen der kon.-Akad. Letter-kunde*, 3, 6, 58; Grimm [a], i. 256 f.
4. *Vol.*, 56; *Harb.*, 56; *Lok.*, 26.
5. MacCulloch, ' Earth, Earth-gods,' *ERE* iv. 127 f.
6. Tacitus, *Ann.*, i. 51; Kögel, i. 1. 19; Müllenhoff, *ZfDA* ix. 258, xxiii. 23 f.; Golther [a], p. 458.
7. Grein i. 312 f.; Mogk, in Hoops, i. 625; Grimm [a], i. 253 f., 1237 f.; Golther [a], p. 455; Chadwick [a], c. 10.
8. *Sigrd.*, 4.
9. *Hav.*, 137; see p. 155; Mogk, in Hoops, i. 626, and in *ERE* ii. 662.
10. Mogk, in Hoops, i. 626, 663.
11. F. J. Hamilton-Grierson, *ERE* ii. 858; *CPB* i. 308; *Gisli-saga*, ed. Dasent, p. 23.
12. See p. 183; *Gylf.*, c. 11; Golther, p. 524.
13. *Vaf.*, 23; *Grim.*, 37.
14. *Skaldsk.*, c. 26; *Grim.*, 38; *Sigrd.*, 15; *Yngl.-saga*, c. 20; cf. *Grim.*, 15.
15. *Gylf.*, c. 35.
16. *Gylf.*, c. 42.
17. *Alviss.*, 16.
18. *Vol.*, 5 f., 73 f.; Gering, *in loc.*, citing Hoffory.
19. Cæsar, vi. 21.
20. Tacitus, *Germ.*, c. 45, *Ann.*, xiii. 55.
21. Procopius, *de Bello Goth.*, ii. 15.
22. Eligius, *PL* lxxxvii. 528 f.; *Ancient Laws and Institutes of England*, ed. B. Thorpe, London, 1840, p. 162; *Indic. Sup.*, in Grimm, iv. 1740.
23. S. Müller, *Solbilledet fra Trundholm*, p. 313.
24. ib., p. 174.
25. Helm, p. 185.
26. ib., p. 184.
27. *Gylf.*, c. 12.
28. *Grim.*, 39; *Vol.*, 40.
29. *Vaf.*, 46, 47.
30. *Vol.*, 40 f.; *Gylf.*, c. 12.
31. *Vaf.*, 12, 14, 25; *HHj.*, 28; cf. *Alviss.*, 29 f.
32. *Gylf.*, c. 10.

33. Golther [a], p. 523; Bugge [b], p. 100.
34. MacCulloch, ' Light and Darkness,' *ERE* viii. 48.
35. *Fms.*, i. 468; Kershaw, p. 120.
36. *Land.-bók*, v. 3, viii. 8; *Eyrb.-saga*, 1, 7.
37. *Islendinga-sögur*, 1; *Haconar-saga*, i. 309.
38. *Ancient Laws*, ed. Thorpe, p. 162.
39. Grimm [a], ii. 603.
40. ib.
41. *Gylf.*, cc. 4, 5; *Vol.*, 52; Phillpotts *ANF* 1905, xvii. 14 f.
42. *Land.-bók*, ii. 5.
43. *Hav.*, 68, 137.
44. See p. 310.
45. Agathias, *Hist.*, i. 7, in *PG* lxxxviii.
46. J. Hardouin, *Conciliorum Collectio*, Paris, 1715, vi. 1. 462; *Homilia de sacrilegiis*, edited by C. P. Caspari, *ZfDA* xxv. 313 ff.
47. *Land.-bók*, iii. 17 in *CPB* i. 421.
48. Tacitus, *Ann.*, ii. 12, iv. 73, *Germ.*, cc. 39, 40.
49. Adam of Bremen, ii. 46, iv. 27; *Land.-bók*, iii. 16, 17.
50. Agathias, *Hist.*, xxviii. 4.
51. Willibrord, *Vita S. Bonif.*, c. 8; Adam of Bremen, iv. 26.
52. Mogk, in *ERE* vi. 486, and in Hoops, i. 183.
53. Golther [a], p. 144; Mogk [a], p. 192, and *ERE* iv. 633; E. Hahn, *ZVV* 1911, xxi. 178 f.
54. *Hynd.*, 49; *Gylf.*, c. 12.
55. Grimm [a], ii. 480.
56. ib., ii. 432.
57. *Gudrun*, p. 429; *Das deutsche Heldenbuch*, ed. A. v. Keller, Stuttgart, 1867, pp. 228 f. Cf. Symons, in Paul's *Grundriss*,[2] iii. 476, and Bugge [b], p. 246.
58. Meiche, pp. 342, 344; Golther [a], p. 154 f.; E. H. Meyer [a], p. 129.
59. Grimm [a], ii. 483; Simrock, p. 440; Meiche, pp. 342 f.; Golther [a], pp. 152 f.; Thorpe, i. 252; Mogk [a], pp. 294 f., and in *ERE* iv. 634.
60. Grimm [b], i. 30, from Prätorius, cf. [a], iii. 929.
61. Mogk [a], p. 294; Keightley, p. 93.
62. Grimm [a], ii. 484; Simrock, p. 440; Thorpe, i. 252; Meiche, p. 33.
63. Golther [a], p. 156.
64. *Land.-bók*, v. 7. 10.
65. Procopius, *de Bello Goth.*, ii. 25.
66. Mogk, in *ERE* vi. 866.
67. See p. 75.
68. Alcuin, *Vita Willibrordi*, c. 10; Adam of Bremen, iv. 3; Mogk,

in *ERE* vi. 866. For other examples see C. von Richthofen, *Zur Lex Saxonum*, Berlin, 1868, p. 204, and for foretelling the future by water, Plutarch, *Cæsar*, c. 19.

69. *HHj.*, 19.
70. *Promptorium Parvulorum*, Early English Text Society, 1908, s. v. *nykyr*.
71. Grimm [a], ii. 491; Mogk, p. 146; Meiche, p. 357; Thorpe, ii. 21 f.; Craigie [b], pp. 238 ff.
72. *Reginsmal*, Introd.
73. Grimm [a], i. 52, ii. 492; Golther [a], p. 147; Thorpe, ii. 23.
74. Grimm [a], ii. 493; Craigie [b], p. 239; Thorpe, ii. 22.
75. Thorpe i. 249, 288; Simrock, p. 447.
76. Arnason, i. 95; Craigie [b], p. 228.
77. Grimm [b], i. 32, 43 ff., 202; Meiche, p. 364.
78. Meiche, p. 360; Thorpe, i. 248.
79. Grimm [a], i. 433 ff.; Mogk, in Hoops, iii. 205.
80. Thorpe, i. 246; Grimm [a], ii. 491, [b], i. 36 ff., [c], no. 79; Meiche, pp. 363, 372–3.
81. *Nibelungenlied*, stanza 1583 f.
82. Grimm [b], i. 37; Meiche, p. 366.
83. Grimm [b], i. 39; Thorpe, i. 247 f.
84. G. D. Mansi, *Sacrorum Conciliorum Collectio*, ix. 133; Hardouin, iii. 444.
85. Eligius, in *PL* lxxxvii. 528 f.
86. *Hom. de Sacrilegiis*, ed. Caspari, pp. 71 ff.
87. Boniface, in *PL* lxxxix. 853, *Sermo* vi.
88. *MGH Leg.*, sect. ii, Hanover, 1883, *Capit. Regum Francorum*, p. 55.
89. ib., p. 69.
90. Grimm, iv. 1739.
91. Burchard, in *PL* cxl. 961.

CHAPTER XIX

1. *Heimskringla (Saga Library)*, iii. 315.
2. *Land.-bók*, i. 2. 3.
3. *HHj.*, 9; Grimm [a], ii. 689.
4. Grimm [a], ii. 684.
5. *Gylf.*, cc. 15, 17; *Grim.*, 34, 35, 54.
6. Montelius, p. 140. See Plate VII.
7. Cf. Mogk, ' Schlangenverehrung,' in Hoops, iv. 132; E. Welsford, *ERE* xi. 420.
8. Grimm [a], ii. 686 f., [c], no. 105; Bolte and Polivka, ii. 459 f.
9. Paulus Diaconus, iii. 34; R. Chambers, *Book of Days*, i. 276.
10. See MacCulloch, ' Serpent-worship,' *ERE* xi. 399 ff.

CHAPTER XX

1. A. Berridale Keith, *Indian Mythology* (in this Series), pp. 57 f.
2. *Lok.*, 2, 13, 30; *Vol.*, 48; *Thrym.*, 6; *Hav.*, 143, 159, 160; *Skir.*, 7; *Grim.*, 4; *Faf.*, 13.
3. *Skir.*, 17 f.; *Sigrd.*, 18.
4. *Grim.*, 5; *Gylf.*, c. 17.
5. Grimm [a], i. 25, iii. 1244; T. O. Cockayne, *Leechdoms* . . . *of Early England*, London, 1864–66, iii. 53.
6. *Hav.*, 143 (Daenn, an elf); *Vol.*, 11 and *Hynd.*, 7 (Daenn, a dwarf); *Vkv.*, 12, 14, 34.
7. *Gylf.*, c. 17.
8. *Skaldsk.*, c. 35.
9. ib., c. 39.
10. *Gylf.*, c. 34.
11. Cleasby and Vigfusson, p. 42; Thorpe, i. 25.
12. *Gylf.*, c. 17.
13. *Alviss.*, 12, 16.
14. Grimm [d], p. 65; *Vaf.*, 47; *Gylf.*, c. 53; *Skir.*, 4.
15. *Ham.*, 1.
16. Grimm [a], iii. 962 f.
17. Craigie [b], p. 430, cf. also pp. 142 ff.
18. Cleasby and Vigfusson, p. 641; Thorpe, i. 218; Arnason, i. 114 f.
19. Thorpe, ii. 1, 11.
20. ib., ii. 2 f.; Faye, p. 39.
21. Thorpe, ii. 3, 6; Grimm [a], i. 271 f.; Faye, pp. 25, 39 f.
22. Thorpe, i. 25, ii. Introd., p. xi; Faye, p. 48.
23. Thorpe, i. 116.
24. Thorpe, ii. 115; Craigie [b], p. 93.
25. Craigie [b], pp. 94 ff., 422, 430.
26. Thorpe, ii. 116; Craigie [b], pp. 175, 430; Thiele, *passim*.
27. Craigie [b], p. 434.
28. Thorpe, ii. 63 f.; Mogk [a], p. 288.
29. ib., ii. 62; Munch, p. 288.
30. Craigie [b], pp. 170, 215, 422, 436; Wigstrom, pp. 108, 110, 154 f.
31. Thorpe, ii. 73.
32. See MacCulloch, ' Fairy,' *ERE* v. 679 ff.
33. *Ftb.*, ii. 7.
34. *Kormaks-saga*, c. 22; cf. *CPB* i. 414.
35. *Story of Olaf the Holy*, c. 92, in *Saga Library*, iv. 73.
36. *Eyrb.-saga*, c. 3.

Chapter XXI

1. Magnusen, p. 833; Thorpe, ii. 117.
2. *HHj.*, 27; *Sigrd.*, prose to 4; *Odr.*, 8.
3. *Gud.*, i. 21, 22; *Lok.*, 57, 59, 61, 63. In one manuscript the passage in *Hynd.*, 35, relating to the origin of seers (*vitkar*) from Vilmeith, reads *vættir* for *vitkar.*
4. *Land.-bók,* iv. 18. 6.
5. ib., iv. 13. 2; *Saga of Harald Fairhair*, c. 19, in *Saga Library,* iii. 112.
6. *Saga of Olaf Trygg.*, c. 37, in *Saga Library,* i. 268.
7. *Land.-bók,* iv. 17. 3.
8. *Grettis-saga,* pp. 169, 276.
9. *Egils-saga,* c. 60.
10. *Land.-bók,* iii. 14. 17, iv. 18. 6.
11. Thorpe's *Edda,* i. 29.
12. *FAS* ii. 197.
13. Grimm [a], ii. 459.
14. Munch, p. 42.
15. Thorpe, i. 116; Munch, pp. 44, 310.
16. Craigie [b], p. 434.
17. ib., pp. 170, 215, 422, 436; Wigstrom, pp. 108, 110, 154 ff.; Grimm [a], ii. 457.
18. *Faer. Anth.*, i. 326 f.; Craigie [b], pp. 138, 161, 216.

Chapter XXII

1. *HHj.*, prose to 30 and ff.
2. *Am.*, 18.
3. *Njals-saga,* c. 23.
4. *Ljosvetninga-saga,* c. 21.
5. *Fms.*, iii. 113; *Orig. Island.*, ii. 584.
6. *FAS,* i. 102 f.
7. *Ljosvetninga-saga,* c. 30.
8. *Thordar-saga,* c. 6.
9. *Njals-saga,* c. 41 and Introd., p. xix.
10. The word Hamingjur is used in *Vafthrudnismal,* 48, 49, in the sense of supernatural protective beings, possibly friendly Norns. See p. 241.
11. *Viga-Glums-saga,* ii. 8, ed. Head, p. 34.
12. *Hallfreds-saga,* c. 11.
13. *Olafs-saga Trygg.*, c. 215, in *Orig. Island.*, i. 419. In *Njals-saga,* c. 95, occurs the phrase: 'Thidrandi, whom the Disir slew.'

14. *Gisla-saga,* pp. 69, 73, 93, 100, and cf. Introd., p. xxviii (ed. Dasent).

15. *Njals-saga,* c. 96.

16. Grimm [a], i. 400, 419, iii. 875.

17. Faye, p. 77; Thorpe, i. 115; Craigie, *Blackwood's Magazine,* 1912, cxci. 304 f.

18. R. Kirk, *Secret Commonwealth of Elves, Fauns, Fairies,* ed. A. Lang, London, 1893, p. 10.

CHAPTER XXIII

1. *Am.,* 45.
2. *Heliand,* cc. 146, 66, etc., and *Codex Exon.,* 355, see Grimm [a], i. 406; *Beowulf,* 2240, 5145.
3. *Sig. en skamma,* 5.
4. O. Schade, *Altdeutsches Wörterbuch,* Halle, 1872–82, i. 657.
5. *Gylf.,* cc. 15, 16; *Faf.,* 13.
6. *Faf.,* 11, 12, 44; *HH* i. 1 ff.
7. *Sigrd.,* 17, 8.
8. *Reg.,* 2.
9. *Sig. en skamma,* 5, 7.
10. *Gud.,* ii. 39.
11. *Ghv.,* 13.
12. *HH* ii. 18.
13. *Ham.,* 28, 30.
14. *Saga Library,* iii. 126; *Egils-saga,* c. 24.
15. *Reg.,* 24.
16. Munch, p. 301; *Ham.,* 29.
17. *Vol.,* 8, 20.
18. *Vaf.,* 49.
19. *Svip.,* 47.
20. Kershaw, p. 35 f., 178 f. See MacCulloch [b], Chapter XV.
21. See MacCulloch [c], Chapter V; Bolte and Polivka, i. 434 ff.
22. Saxo, vi. 223 [181].
23. See p. 132 and MacCulloch [a], pp. 44 ff.
24. *Vol.,* 19, 20; *Hav.,* 110; *Svip.,* 7.
25. *Vol.,* 31.
26. Plato, *Repub.,* 10; Isidore of Seville, *Etymol.,* viii. 11, 92.
27. *Gylf.,* cc. 23, 35; *Fms.,* ii. 483; *Volsunga-saga,* c. 19.
28. *Yngl.-saga,* c. 33; Munch, p. 33.
29. *Hervarar-saga,* c. 1; *Egils-saga,* c. 44; *CPB* i. 405; cf. Grimm [a], i. 402.
30. Grimm, iv. 1746.

31. Burchard ('Corrector'), § 151, in H. J. Schmitz, *Die Buss-bucher*, Dusseldorf, 1898, ii. 442.

32. Golther [a], p. 107; Mogk [a], p. 283; Liebrecht, p. 329.

33. Grimm [a], i. 409, 416, iv. 1402; *KHM* no. 14; Bolte and Polivka, i. 109 f., 439; cf. Bugge [b], pp. 102 ff.

34. Adam la Bossue, in *Les classiques françaises du moyen-âge*, p. 24 f.; Keightley, p. 469; F. Jónsson, *Hist. eccles. Islandiae*, ii. 367.

35. Holinshed, *Chronicles*, 1577, p. 243; H. Boece, *Hist.*, 1683, book xii, p. 258; *Complaynt of Scotlande*, ed. J. Leyden, Edinburgh, 1801, ii. 99; Chaucer, *Troilus*, iii. 733, *Legend of Good Women*, l. 2630; Bp. Percy, *Reliques*, iii. 218 f.

36. Grimm [a], i. 403, 409.

37. *Viga-Glums-saga*, c. 12, ed. Head, p. 48.

CHAPTER XXIV

1. For *oska-synir* see *Gylf.*, c. 20, and cf. Loki as Odin's *oskmǫgr*, *Lok.*, 16. For the various titles see *Faf.*, 43, *HH* i. 56, *Vol.*, 31, *Gud.*, i. 17.

2. *Gylf.*, c. 36.

3. *Grim.*, 36; *Vol.*, 31.

4. *HHj.*, prose to 9, 5 prose, 28; *HH* i. 15, 16, 56; *HH* ii. 4 prose, 7, prose to 16; *Vol.*, 31.

5. *HH* i. 40.

6. ib., i. 56, ii. 7.

7. *Skaldsk.*, c. 47.

8. *Gylf.*, c. 49; *Skaldsk.*, c. 2 (Ulf Uggason).

9. *Volsunga-saga*, c. 2.

10. *Gylf.*, c. 24; *Skaldsk.*, cc. 17, 20.

11. *Viga-Glums-saga*, ed. Head, p. 82; *CPB* ii. 74; *Orig. Island.*, ii. 477.

12. *Sturlunga-saga*, vii. 28.

13. *Fms.*, vi. 402.

14. Metcalfe, p. 382.

15. *CPB* i. 263 f.; *Story of Hakon the Good*, c. 32, in *Saga Library*, iii. 189 f.

16. *CPB* i. 260 f.

17. *Faf.*, 42 ff.; *Sigrd.*, 1 ff.

18. ib.; *Grip.*, 15 ff.; *Odr.*, 15 f.; *Skaldsk.*, c. 41.

19. *HHj.*, prose to 9 ff.

20. *HH* i. 15 ff.

21. *HH* ii. prose to 50.

22. See *HH* ii. 44, 47; *HHj.*, 7, 26, 28; *Grip.*, 15; *Vkv.*, 1; *HH* i. 17.

23. *Islendinga Sögur,* ii. 103; Mogk [a], p. 270.
24. See pp. 46, 298.
25. Grimm [a], i. 401; R. Much in Hoops, ii. 578; Paul, *Grundriss,*[2] ii. 1. 63.
26. Grimm [a], i. 418; Kemble, i. 403–4.
27. ib., iii. 1244; ib., i. 403–4.
28. Metcalfe, p. 156.
29. Kemble, i. 404; Grimm [a], i. 431; Mogk, p. 270.
30. See p. 132.
31. *Sigrd., passim; Sigr. en skamma,* 54 f.
32. *Njals-saga,* c. 156; *Beowulf,* 697.
33. *Gud.,* i. 18; *HH* i. 17; *Skaldsk.,* 31; *Fms.,* ii. 483.
34. *Sturlunga-saga,* i. 220; *Viga-Glums-saga,* c. 21; *Fms.,* ii. 375 f.
35. See MacCulloch [a], p. 72; *Story of Hakon the Good,* c. 5, in *Saga Library,* iii. 155.
36. See MacCulloch [a], p. 71 f.
37. Vopiscus, *Vita Aurel.,* c. 34; *Dio Cassius,* lxxi. 3; *Paulus Diaconus,* i. 15. Vihansa, *CIL* xiii. 3592; Von Grienberger, *ZfDA* xxxvi. 310 f.; Hariasa, *CIL* xiii. 8185; Harimella, *CIL* vii. 1065. Cf. Helm, i. 376.
38. *Akv.,* 17, 45; *Fms.,* i. 379; Saxo, iii. 106 (87), vii. 275, 277 (229, 230), viii. 310 (257).
39. Cf. Mogk [a], p. 269.
40. Grimm, iv. 1747.
41. L. Strakkerjan, *Aberglaube und Sagen aus Oldenburg,* Oldenburg, 1909, i. 463 f.; Mogk, in Hoops, iv. 475; Golther, p. 113.

Chapter XXV

1. See MacCulloch [c], pp. 342 ff.; Hartland, pp. 255 ff.
2. Baring-Gould, p. 573; Grimm [a], i. 428.
3. *HBr.,* 7; cf. *Fms.,* i. 186.
4. *Fms.,* ii. 375 f.
5. *Nibelungenlied,* l. 1476.
6. Saxo, vi. 219 [178].
7. Baring-Gould, p. 574; Grimm [a], i. 429.
8. A. A. Afzelius, *Volkssagen aus Schweden,* ii. 301 f.
9. Thorpe, ii. 69.
10. *Gylf.,* c. 16.
11. Vincent of Beauvais, *Spec. Nat.,* ii. 127.
12. Baring-Gould, p. 579 f.
13. Grimm [a], i. 370; *Beowulf,* 1 ff.; Kemble, i. 414.
14. Bolte and Polivka, i. 432.

CHAPTER XXVI

1. *Vol.*, 9 ff.
2. *Gylf.*, c. 14.
3. ib., c. 8; *Skaldsk.*, c. 23.
4. *Heldenbuch*, pp. 1 f.
5. *Vol.*, 14; *Gylf.*, c. 14.
6. *Faf.*, 13; *Vol.*, 14; *Alviss.*, 16; *Hav.*, 143.
7. *Hav.*, 160.
8. Daenn, Nabbe, *Hynd.*, 7; Lit, *Gylf.*, c. 49; Fjalar and Gjallar, *Brag.*, 1; Sindri, *Vol.*, 37; *Gylf.*, c. 52.
9. Thorpe's *Edda*, i. 32.
10. See *Vol.*, 11, 12, 16; *Hynd.*, 7; *Hav.*, 143; *Vkv.*, 15; Grimm [a], ii. 445.
11. *Skaldsk.*, c. 35; cf. *Grim.*, 43, 44; *Hynd.*, 7.
12. *Reg.*, Introd. and 14 prose; *Faf.*, 22, 32 f.; *Skaldsk.*, c. 40.
13. *Skaldsk.*, c. 50.
14. *Egils-saga.*
15. *Vkv.*, 10 ff.
16. Thorpe, i. 88 f.
17. See p. 123.
18. *Hervarar-saga*, cc. 2, 8.
19. Cf. Herrmann, p. 222; *Skaldsk.*, c. 39; *Reg.*, prose to 5; *Islendinga Sögur*, ii. 48.
20. *Hürnen Seyfried*; *Nibelungenlied*, 87 f.; *Akv.*, 28.
21. *Reg.*, 3 f.; *Alviss.*, *passim*; *Brag.*, 1.
22. *Alviss.*, 2, 3.
23. *Yngl.-saga*, c. 15.
24. Munch, p. 309.
25. *Alviss.*, 35; *HHj.*, 30.
26. *Vol.*, 11; *Thidriks-saga*, xxi. 10.
27. *Heldenbuch*, p. 694; Grimm [a], ii. 466.
28. See Thorpe, ii. 56 f., 85, 89, 115; Craigie [b], pp. 93, 138, 161, 216 f.; Afzelius, ii. 157; *Faer. Anth.*, i. 326; *County Folk-Lore*, iii. *Orkney and Shetland*, p. 20 f.; Sir W. Scott, *The Pirate*, chap. 19 and notes 7, 10.
29. *Heldenbuch*, pp. 27 ff.
30. On this see A. Lütjens, *Der Zwerg in der deutschen Heldendichtung des Mittelalters*, Breslau, 1911.
31. Grimm [a], ii. 458 f.
32. R. Chambers, *Book of Days*, ii. 83; P. J. Hamilton-Grierson, 'Gifts,' *ERE* vi. 207.
33. Grimm [a], ii. 457, 1416.
34. Grimm [b], i. 18; Thorpe, ii. 146.

35. ib., i. 22, cf. [a], ii. 457, 872, iv. 1416; Thorpe, i. 115; Meiche, p. 320.
36. Grimm [c], nos. 91, 113, 116.
37. Grimm [b], i. 116 ff.; [a], ii. 465, note Keightley, pp. 221 f.
38. See *African Mythology* in this Series, Chapter IX.
39. MacCulloch, 'Fairy,' *ERE* v. 688.

CHAPTER XXVII

1. *Vol.*, 3; *Vaf.*, 31; *Hynd.*, 35; *Gylf.*, c. 5.
2. *Vaf.*, 28 ff.
3. *Gylf.*, c. 6.
4. ib., c. 7.
5. See p. 14.
6. *Gylf.*, cc. 1, 37, 45, *Brag.*, c. 1; *Skaldsk.*, c. 17; *Skir.*, Introd.; *Hym.*, 5, and cf. *Lok.*, 60; *Harb.*, 23, 29; *Vol.* 50.
7. Cf. *Thrym.*; *Hym.*; Saxo, vi. 214 (174), vii. 272 (225).
8. *Vol.*, 42.
9. *Vaf.*, 37; *Skir.*, 27; *Vol.*, 50.
10. Saxo, Preface, p. 12 (7), 14 (9); *Yngl.-saga,* c. 1; *Grim.*, 31; *Gylf.*, c. 15.
11. *Skir.*, prose to 10; *Thrym.*, 5 ff.; *Gylf.*, c. 45; *Fjol.*, 1.
12. *Skir.*, 31; *Vaf.*, 33; Saxo, i. 21 (16), 26 (21).
13. Saxo, vi. 224 (182); *FAS*, i. 412; *Skaldsk.*, (Vetrlidi the skald) c. 4.
14. *Skaldsk.*, c. 46; *Harb.*, 29; *Gylf.*, c. 49.
15. *HHj.*, 30; Munch, p. 307; Grimm [a], ii. 549.
16. Cf. *Vaf.* and *Hynd.*; *Skir.*, 34; *Hav.*, 103 f., 143.
17. *Gylf.*, c. 42; *Vol.* 50; *Grott.*, 23; Saxo, vii. 268 (223).
18. *Gylf.*, cc. 15, 21, 27, 42, 51; *Skaldsk.*, c. 4.; *Vol.* 50.
19. *Hav.*, 104; *Harb.*, 20; *Grim.*, 50.
20. *Gylf.*, cc. 6, 49; *Hym.*
21. See p. 181.
22. Saxo, vii. 271 (225), 268 (223), i. 26 (21); *HHj.*, 17, 24.
23. *Vol.*, 9, 37; *Sigrd.*, 14; cf. *Grim.*, 44, where one manuscript has 'Brimir, best of swords.'
24. *Skir.*, 28; *Hynd.*, 34.
25. ib., 35.
26. *HHj.*, 25.
27. *Brag.*, 1; *Harb.*, 19.
28. *Gylf.*, c. 34; *Hynd.*, 42.
29. ib., c. 12; *Grim.*, 39; *Vol.*, 40.
30. *Vaf.*, 37; *Vol.*, 50; *Skir.*, 27; *Gylf.*, c. 18.
31. *Brag.*, 1; *HHj.*, 20.

32. ib.; *Hav.*, 104; *HBr.*, 1; *Gylf.*, c. 23.
33. *Vol.*, 50; *Gylf.*, c. 51.
34. *Gylf.*, cc. 4, 51; *Vol.*, 52; *Vaf.*, 17, 18, 50; *Faf.*, 14; Mogk, in Hoops, iv. 300.
35. Saxo, vii. 264 (219); Herrmann, p. 476.
36. *Vol.*, 40; *Grim.*, 39; *Gylf.*, c. 12.
37. Grimm [a], ii. 481, 553.
38. *Beowulf*, 761, 1260, 1507, 1600; B. Symons, in Paul's *Grundriss*, iii. 646; *Grettis-saga*, p. 197.
39. *HHj.*, 18 f.
40. *FAS* ii. 3 f., 17 f. Cf. *Skaldsk.*, c. 27; *Heimskringla*, c. 16; Saxo, viii. 339 (281).
41. Grimm [a], ii. 539; cf. 'Giants,' *ERE* vi. 189 ff.
42. Golther [a], p. 190; Grimm [a], ii. 557.
43. O. Schoning, *Dódsriger i nordisk Hedentro*, Copenhagen, 1903; Helm, i. 210.
44. Grimm [a], ii. 535 f.
45. ib., ii. 545 f.
46. ib., ii. 551 f.
47. See p. 140.
48. *Beowulf*, 1558.
49. *Skaldsk.*, c. 42; Sijmons and Gering, i. 487 ff.; Munch, p. 348; Boer, ii. 370. The phrase 'mighty maidens' occurs in *Vol.*, 8, and is there used of the giantesses who brought the Golden Age of the gods to an end, as these giant maids brought the earthly Golden Age to an end. According to Saxo, ii. 61 (50), the first of the Frodis of whom he speaks sprinkled his food with pounded gold as a resource against poison. Perhaps this gold was that ground by the maidens, though this myth is not referred to by Saxo.
50. Boer, ii. 370.

CHAPTER XXVIII

1. *Gylf.*, c. 42; *Skaldsk.*, cc. 17, 33.
2. *Vol.*, 40.
3. *Land.-bók*, ii. 6. 2.
4. *Grettis-saga*, p. 38.
5. *Story of Olaf the Holy*, c. 151, *Saga Library*, iv. 380.
6. *Grettis-saga*, pp. 191, 194, 196.
7. Grimm [a], ii. 550; Munch, p. 307; Bugge, p. 329.
8. *Land.-bók*, i. 6. 4.
9. *The Banded Men*, *Saga Library*, i. 115; *Grettis-saga*, p. 8; *Harb.*, 145.
10. *Story of Olaf Trygg.*, c. 87, *Saga Library*, iii. 334 and iv. 366; K. Liestøl, *Norske Trollvisor*, Christiania, 1915, pp. 45 ff.

11. *Grettis-saga*, pp. 183, 187.
12. Giantesses, *Skaldsk.*, cc. 4, 75, cf. Rask's ed., pp. 101, 210; *Gylf.*, c. 12; Witch, *Skaldsk.*, c. 54; Fylgja, *HHj.*, prose to 30 and ff.
13. *Hynd.*, 5; *Gylf.*, c. 49; *HH* ii. 17; cf. Grimm [a], iii. 1054.
14. Cleasby and Vigfusson, p. 641; Thorpe, i. 218; Arnason, i. 114 f.
15. Thorpe, ii. 1, 11.
16. ib., ii. 115; Craigie [b], pp. 93, 94 ff., 422; Keightley, pp. 94 ff.
17. Keightley, p. 95; Thiele, i. 36.
18. Afzelius, ii. 157; Thorpe, ii. 56 f., 85, 89 f.
19. *County Folk-Lore*, iii. *Orkney and Shetland*, pp. 20 ff.; A. Edmonston, *A View of the Ancient and Present State of the Zetland Islands*, Edinburgh, 1809, ii. 75 f. Cf. for ‘Trows,’ *English Dialect Dictionary*, vi. 243.

CHAPTER XXIX

1. W. H. Roscher, *Ephialtes: Eine psych.-mythol. Abhandlung über die Alpträume und Alpdämonen des klassischen Altertums*, Leipzig, 1900, p. 48 f.; J. Wier, *De Praestigiis Dæmonum*, iii. 23; William of Paris, *Opera Omnia*, p. 1007; P. O. Gruppe, *Griechische Mythologie*, Munich, 1897–1906, i. 771; W. M. Wundt, *Völkerpsychologie,*[2] Leipzig, 1904–10, ii. 2. 118.
2. E. H. Meyer [a], p. 76; Mogk [a], pp. 266, 268, and in *ERE* iv. 631.
3. E. H. Meyer [a], p. 77; Golther [a], p. 75 f.; Roscher, *op. cit.*, pp. 13, 37; Grimm [b], i. 66, [c], p. 124.
4. Grimm [b], i. 66, [c], p. 124; Roscher, pp. 13 f.
5. Mogk [a], p. 266; Simrock, p. 437.
6. Craigie [b], p. 272; Simrock, p. 437.
7. Wundt, *op. cit.*, ii. 2. 118, cf. Psalm xci. 5.
8. *Yngl.-saga*, c. 16.
9. Munch, p. 47.

CHAPTER XXX

1. On the whole subject see MacCulloch, ‘Lycanthropy,’ in *ERE* viii. 206 ff.
2. *Volsunga-saga*, c. 5.
3. ib., c. 8.
4. *Eyrb.-saga*, c. 25.
5. *HH* i. 38.
6. *Howard the Halt*, in *Saga Library*, i. 2.
7. *Egils-saga*, 1.
8. *Eyrb.-saga*, c. 61.

9. *Land.-bók,* ii. 7. 1; iii. 22. 4; *Orig. Island.,* ii. 58; Mogk, p. 272.
10. ib., v. 7. 4. *Cf. CPB* 1. 425.
11. Sir W. Scott, *Minstrelsy of the Scottish Border,* London, 1839, p. 354.
12. R. Schmid, *Die Gesetze der Angelsachsen,* Leipzig,[2] 1858, p. 270; Metcalfe, p. 155.
13. Grimm [a], iii. 1094.
14. Boniface, *Sermo* xv, in *PL* lxxxix. 870 f.
15. Burchard, ('Corrector'), § 151, in H. J. Schmitz, *Die Buss-bucher,* Dusseldorf, 1898, ii. 442.

CHAPTER XXXI

1. *Hav.,* 143.
2. ib., 145.
3. *Egils-saga,* c. 72.
4. *Hav.,* 111, 144.
5. *Sigrd.,* 6 ff.
6. Sophus Müller, i. 359; Clarke, pp. 42, 121.
7. *Sigrd.,* 18 ff.
8. *Hav.,* 144.
9. *Sigrd.,* 5.
10. *Rig.,* 36, 44.
11. *Hav.,* 158; Saxo, iii. 96 (79); *Gud.,* ii. 22 f.
12. *Egils-saga,* cc. 44, 57.
13. Saxo, i. 27 (22).
14. *Hav.,* 146 ff. See p. 46.
15. *Svip.,* 1 ff.
16. *Hynd.,* 3.
17. So Clarke, p. 38; cf. p. 47 *supra.*
18. *Am.,* 30, cf. *HH* ii. 32; *Akv.,* 30; *Skir.,* 26 f.
19. *Yngl.-saga,* c. 4; *Vol.,* 22; *Lok.,* 24.
20. A. Lehmann, *Aberglaube und Zauberei,*[2] Stuttgart, 1908, p. 6; De la Saussaye, p. 389 f.
21. Head, *Viga-Glums-saga,* p. 48; Grimm [a], i. 403, 407.
22. *Saga Library,* iv. 491.
23. *Hav.,* 155.
24. *Harb.,* 20; *Eyrb.-saga,* c. 16.
25. *HHj.,* 15, 28 f.
26. *Skaldsk.,* c. 4; *CPB* ii. 24.
27. Mogk, in Hoops, ii. 522; Golther [a], p. 117; Grimm [a], iii. 1057.
28. *HH* i. 30 f.; *Saga of Olaf Trygg.,* c. 30, in *Saga Library,* iii. 405 and cf. iv. 385.

29. *FAS* iii. 175.
30. ib., ii. 131.
31. *Lex Salica,* ed. by J. H. Hessels, London, 1880, col. 397 f.
32. *Eyrb.-saga,* c. 34.
33. See p. 253.
34. *Gisla-saga,* p. 59.
35. *Sigrd.,* 27.
36. Golther [a], pp. 120–1.

Chapter XXXII

1. *Grim.,* 31; *Faf.,* 21; *Am.,* 51; *Svip.,* 41.
2. *BDr.,* 2 f.; *Vol.,* 43, 44, 49, 58.
3. *Gylf.,* c. 49; *Skaldsk.,* c. 5.
4. ib., c. 34.
5. Grimm [a], i. 313.
6. See p. 134; *Hrolfs-saga Kraka,* iv. 15; *Fostbrœdra-saga,* c. 4; Thorpe's *Edda,* i. 121.
7. *Beowulf,* 1698; Kemble, i. 396.
8. *Vol.,* 43; *Skir.,* 35; *Lok.,* 63; *Fjol.,* 26; *BDr.,* 4; *Gylf.,* cc. 4, 49.
9. *Grim.,* 44; *BDr.,* 3 f.; *Vol.,* 44, 49, 58; *Gylf.,* c. 51.
10. *BDr.,* 6 f.; *Gylf.,* c. 49.
11. *Gylf.,* c. 49; cf. *BDr.,* 5; *Vol.,* 52.
12. *HBr.*
13. Saxo, viii. 318 (264).
14. See references in *ERE* xi. 475–76, ' Shoes and Sandals.'
15. *Orig. Island.,* ii. 563.
16. *ERE* xi. 475–76.
17. *Gylf.,* c. 32; *HBr.,* 8; *Am.,* 38, 41, 47, 51, 91; *Ghv.,* 20; *Harb.,* 27; *Lok.,* 63; *Faf.,* 10, 34, 39; *Egils-saga,* c. 45.
18. Widukind, in *MGH Scrip.,* iii. 428.
19. Saxo, i. 37 (31).
20. *Yngl.-saga,* c. 16; *CPB* i. 244, 250.
21. Cf. MacCulloch, ' Underworld,' *ERE* xii. 516.
22. *Eyrb.-saga,* c. 11, cf. c. 23.
23. *HH* ii. 37 f.
24. *Land.-bók,* i. 7. 6; ii. 5. 10.
25. Kershaw, pp. 88 ff.
26. *Orig. Island.,* ii. 585.
27. *Njals-saga,* cc. 77, 78.
28. *Grettis-saga,* p. 46.
29. ib., p. 97.

30. *Eyrb.-saga*, cc. 34, 51 ff.   See MacCulloch, 'Vampire,' *ERE* xii. 589.

31. Saxo, v. 200 (162).   For other examples of impaling in Saxo, see i. 32 (26), viii. 333 (277).

32. Jordanes, xiii. 20; Adam of Bremen, iv. 26; *Vita S. Anskar.*, c. 26; Grimm iv. 1739.

33. *Halfdan the Black*, in *Heimskringla*, ii. 9; *Hervarar-saga*, c. 1; cf. 'Heroes (Teutonic),' *ERE* vi. 667.

34. *CPB* i. 416.

35. *Land.-bók*, ii. 5. 14, 16; *Eyrb.-saga*, c. 4; *CPB* i. 415.

36. *Heimskringla*, iv. 16.

37. Chadwick, *ERE* i. 467; *Yngl.-saga*, c. 53; *Ftb.*, ii. 7.

38. Saxo, i. 44 (36), iii. 91 (75).

39. See p. 191.

40. *Indiculus Superst.*, Grimm, iv. 1739; Burchard, *passim*.

41. See pp. 127, 198.

42. *Harb.*, 45.

43. *Ftb.*, i. 214; Metcalfe, p. 131.

44. Saxo, i. 27 (22).

45. *Hav.*, 157; *BDr.*, 4.

46. *Am.*, 25.

47. Saxo, i. 42 (35); *CPB* ii. 330.

48. *Orig. Island.*, i. 377, 409.

49. ib., ii. 84.

50. *Grim.*, 8 ff.; *Vaf.*, 41; *Vol.*, 43, 62.

51. R. M. Meyer, p. 462.

52. *Gylf.*, cc. 2, 38; *Skaldsk.*, c. 33.

53. ib., cc. 14, 20, 24; *Grim.*, 14; Munch, p. 289; Kauffmann, *ZfDA* xxxvi. 32 f.; Braune, *PBB* xiv. 369.

54. Magnusen, p. 557.

55. *Gylf.*, cc. 20, 38, 53; *CPB* i. 263; *Vol.*, 1, 27, 29; *Grim.*, 48.

56. Saxo, ii. 79 (65); *Harb.*, 24.

57. *CPB* i. 260, 263; *Story of Hakon the Good*, c. 32, in *Saga Library*, iii. 189.

58. *FAS* i. 424; Munch, p. 313.

59. *Yngl.-saga*, c. 7.

60. Mogk, in Hoops, i. 255, iv. 474; Golther [a], p. 289.

61. See p. 44; *Akv.*, 32; *Reg.*, 18; Mogk, *ERE* vi. 303.

62. Golther [a], p. 288; Ranke, *Deutsches Sagenbuch*, iv. 95 ff.

63. Hartland, pp. 207 ff.

64. Grimm [a], iii. 918 ff., 938; Mogk, in Hoops, i. 255; Golther [a], p. 289.

65. *Skaldsk.*, c. 49; *Sorla-thattr*, c. 43 f.; Saxo, v. 198 (160).   The story is also referred to in *Kudrun*, and is the subject of a Shetland bal-

lad, cf. M. Hœgstad, *Hildinakvadet*, Christiania, 1900, and, for the story generally, B. Symons, ed. of *Kudrun*,[2] Halle, 1914.

66. See p. 320.
67. *Akv.*, 2, 15.
68. M. E. Seaton, ' Life and Death (Teutonic),' *ERE* viii. 43.
69. *Yngl.-saga*, c. 52; and cf. *CPB* i. 250. ' Hvedrung,' however, may simply mean ' giant,' but still applied to Loki.
70. *HH* ii. 39 ff.; Niedner, *Zur Liederedda*, 1896, p. 29.
71. MacCulloch, ' Eschatology,' *ERE* v. 373.
72. *Gylf.*, cc. 20, 24, 34; *Skaldsk.*, c. 33.
73. ib., c. 3.
74. *Gylf.*, c. 34.
75. ib., c. 34; *Vaf.*, 43; *BDr.*, 2.
76. ib., cc. 3, 17, 52.
77. *Vol.*, 64.
78. ib., 37.
79. ib., 38 f.
80. *Grim.*, 32, 35; *Gylf.*, cc. 4, 15, 16; *Vol.*, 66.
81. See ' Chastity,' ' Crimes and Punishments,' and ' Oath ' (Teutonic sections) in *ERE; Sigrd.*, 23; *Reg.*, 4.
82. Saxo, i. 37 (31).
83. *Gud.*, ii. 23; *Vol.*, 36; *Grim.*, 28; MacCulloch [a], pp. 363 ff., [b], Chapter IX. Another Hel river is Geirvimul, ' Swarming with spears,' *Grim.*, 27.
84. Saxo, viii. 344 ff. (286 ff.).
85. Kershaw, p. 87.
86. Rydberg, p. 211; Herrmann [a], pp. 587–88; *Fms.*, iii. 174 f.
87. ib., p. 211.
88. ib., p. 208 f.
89. MacCulloch [a], pp. 378 ff.; [b], Chapter IX; ' Descent to Hades (Ethnic),' *ERE* iv. 653.
90. ib. [b], p. 119.
91. Rydberg, p. 231.

CHAPTER XXXIII

1. *Gylf.*, cc. 4 ff.
2. *Vol.*, 3 ff.
3. Boer, *in loc.*, Holmberg, *Siberian Mythology*, in this Series, Chapter II; Alexander, *North American Mythology*, p. 279.
4. *Vaf.*, 20 f.
5. *Grim.*, 40 f.
6. *Gylf.*, c. 9.
7. ib., c. 3.

8. Tacitus, *Annals*, xiii. 57.

9. *Skaldsk.*, cc. 23 ff.; *CPB* i. 277, ii. 55, 194.

10. Grimm [a], ii. 563 ff.; Kemble, i. 408.

11. *Vol.*, 7, 9 ff.

12. *Gylf.*, c. 14.

13. *Vol.*, 17, 18.

14. *Gylf.*, c. 9.

15. ib., c. 3.

16. See Clarke, p. 107 and note.

17. Tacitus, *Germ.*, c. 2.

18. *Gylf.*, c. 34; *Brag.*, c. 1; *Skaldsk.*, cc. 17, 23; *Harb.*, 19; cf. *CPB* ii. 9.

19. *Vol.*, 56.

20. *Gylf.*, cc. 35, 45, 47; *Hym.*, 23; *Vol.*, 50.

21. *Gylf.*, cc. 9, 14. Asgard is mentioned twice in the Poetic *Edda*. Loki tells Thor that, if his hammer is not recovered, the giants will dwell in Asgard, *Thrym.*, 17. Thor and Tyr go from Asgard to get the giant Hrym's kettle, *Hym.*, 7.

22. *Gylf.*, cc. 13, 15, 27, 51; *Grim.*, 29, 44; *Faf.*, 15; *HH* ii. 48.

23. *Vol.*, 2; *Vaf.*, 43; *Alviss.*, see Sijmons and Gering, i. 152.

24. So Gering, *Edda*, note to *Vaf.*, 43, p. 66.

25. Mogk, 'Neunzahl,' in Hoops, iii. 312.

26. *Gylf.*, c. 4 and see Gering's note, p. 300; cc. 5, 34, 42; *BDr.*, 2; *Vaf.*, 43; *Grim.*, 26.

27. *Vol.*, 2, 19 f.

28. ib., 27, 47; *Svip.*, 29 f.

29. Gering, *Edda*, p. 132.

30. *Grim.*, 31 f.

31. *Gylf.*, cc. 15 f.

32. R. M. Meyer, p. 477.

33. Bugge, [b], Introd., p. xxiv.

34. *Skaldsk.*, c. 34.

35. *Grim.*, 25 f.

36. Chadwick [b], p. 78.

37. ib., p. 75 f.; Müllenhoff [a], v. 103 f.

38. E. Welsford, 'Old Prussians,' *ERE* ix. 489.

39. Cf. Gering, *Edda*, p. 105.

40. *CPB* i. 246.

41. Chadwick [b], p. 75.

42. Cf. U. Holmberg, *Der Baum des Lebens*, Helsinki, 1922, pp. 67, 68.

43. ib., p. 75 and *passim;* cf. also *Siberian Mythology* in this Series, pp. 349 ff.

44. *Gylf.*, c. 16; *Grim.*, 26.

45. MacCulloch [c], pp. 442–3.
46. ib., Chapter XVI.
47. ib., p. 441; Holmberg, *Finno-Ugric and Siberian Mythology,*
pp. 222, 333 ff.
48. Holmberg, p. 337.
49. ib., pp. 221–2; *Der Baum des Lebens,* p. 17 f.
50. ib., *Der Baum,* p. 19; MacCulloch [a], pp. 228, 232.
51. Grimm [a], i. 116.
52. *MGH Scrip.,* iii. 423.
53. A. Olrik, 'Irminsul og Gudestøtter,' *Maal og Minne,* 1910,
p. 4 f.; Holmberg, *Der Baum,* p. 10.
54. E. H. Meyer [b], § 112; Golther, p. 530; Bugge, *Studien,*
pp. 421 ff.
55. *Vol.,* 44, 49, 58; *Vaf.,* 55; *BDr.,* 14; *HH* ii. 39; *Am.,* 21,
38, 42. Cf. *Vaf.,* 38, 39, 42, *tiva rok* (*tivar,* 'gods'). *Lok.,* 39.
56. *Vol.,* 8, 21 f., 32; cf. Mogk, *ERE* iv. 845, 'the golden age of
the gods came to an end when the Norns came into being.'
57. *Vol.,* 25 f.
58. ib., 39.
59. ib., 57, cf. 45, 'the world falls'; *Hynd.,* 44; *Vaf.,* 46 f. and
Vol., 40. Cf. p. 199. *Gylf.,* c. 51, speaks of the wolf swallowing the
sun, and the other wolf swallowing the moon. The stars vanish from
the Heavens. This follows the passage in *Grim.,* 39, and Snorri's own
earlier narrative in c. 12. For Eclipse myths see MacCulloch [a],
p. 178; A. Lang, *Myth, Ritual, and Religion,*[2] London, 1906, i. 132 f.;
Grimm [a], i. 244, ii. 705; *ERE* x. 368. Swedish, Danish, and
Norse folk-lore knows the sun-wolf. In Iceland an eclipse is 'Ulfa-
kreppa.' Golther, p. 524.
60. *Vaf.,* 44 f.; *Gylf.,* c. 53; *Hynd.,* 44; *Vol.,* 41, 45, cf. *Gylf.,*
c. 51.
61. *Vol.,* 52, 57; *Vaf.,* 50 f.; *Grim.,* 38; *Gylf.,* cc. 4, 17, 51.
62. In *Gylf.,* c. 51, the mighty winter precedes or is contemporary
with these evils.
63. Perhaps Mimir's sons are giants, if Mimir is to be regarded as a
giant, cf. Boer, ii. 22. Hence Heimdall blows his horn, because the
giants are in motion.
64. After the account of the mighty winter Snorri here inserts the
swallowing of the sun and moon; the trembling of earth and breaking
of all fetters; the advance of the Wolf; the sea rushing over the land
because the Serpent is stirring in giant fury; the ship Naglfar loose and
floating on the flood, steered by Hrym. In *Vol.,* 50, Hrym comes from
the East; the Midgard-serpent and the Eagle seem to be with him. The
stanza ends with 'Naglfar is loose.' Does this mean that they are on
board it? Or should this line go with the next stanza, which tells of a

vessel coming from the North steered by Loki, with the people of Hel. Is this vessel Naglfar? If the people of Hel are the dead, not giants, Naglfar would be a ship of the dead, and, by a false etymology, the ship made of dead men's nails. But why should the dead attack the gods? Snorri elsewhere assigns Naglfar to the sons of Muspell, *Gylf.*, c. 43. In c. 51 Snorri says that this ship is made of dead men's nails, wherefore men should be warned that if a man die with uncut nails he is adding material to this ship, which gods and men would fain see unfinished.

65. The 'wild hosts,' *fifl-meger*, are perhaps the people of *fifl*, a giant or monster, or 'the nameless host who follow without knowing why.'

66. *Gylf.*, c. 51.
67. *Vaf.*, 18, 39, 41 f.
68. *BDr.*, 14; *Grim.*, 4; *Vaf.*, 52.
69. *CPB* i. 261, 265, ii. 65, 197; *Skaldsk.*, c. 49; *HH* ii. 39.
70. E. W. West, *Pahlavi Texts*, in *Sacred Books of the East*, xviii. 109 f.; N. Söderblom, *La vie future d'après Mazdéisme*, Paris, 1901, p. 179 f.; Rydberg, pp. 256 ff.; L. H. Grey, *ERE* ii. 703; A. J. Carnoy, *Iranian Mythology*, in this Series, p. 307.
71. See MacCulloch [a], p. 232, [b], p. 34.
72. *Gylf.*, c. 51, cf. cc. 4, 5, 8, 11, 13, 37, 43, 51.
73. *Lok.*, 42; *Vol.*, 51.
74. *Faf.*, 15; *Grim.*, 29.
75. Grimm [a], ii. 808.
76. ib.; *Heliand*, 2591, 4358.
77. Golther, p. 541.
78. See these in W. Braune, *Althochdeutsche Lesebuch,*[7] p. 190 f.
79. Mogk, in Hoops, iii. 288.
80. *Vol.*, 59 ff.
81. *Hynd.*, 45.
82. *Vaf.*, 44 ff.
83. *Svip.*, 30; *ERE* ii. 702 f.
84. Boer, ii. 58 f.
85. *Gylf.*, c. 52. See p. 318.

BIBLIOGRAPHY

I. ABBREVIATIONS

A. In Text

AS	Anglo-Saxon.
MHG . . .	Middle High German.
OD	Old Danish.
OE	Old English.
OF	Old Frisian.
OHG . . .	Old High German.
ON	Old Norse.
OS	Old Saxon.

B. In Notes

Akv	Atlakvitha.
Alviss	Alvissmal.
Am	Atlamal.
AMA . . .	Abhandlungen der Königlich Bayerischen Akademie der Wissenschaft (Münich).
ANF	Arkiv für nordisk Filologi.
ARW . . .	Archiv für Religionswissenschaft.
BDr	Baldrs Draumar.
Brag	Bragarædur (Snorri's *Edda*).
CIL	Corpus Inscriptionum Latinorum.
CPB	Corpus Poeticum Boreale (Vigfusson and Powell).
ERE	Encyclopædia of Religion and Ethics.
Faf	Fafnismal.
FAS	Fornaldar Sögur Nordlanda.
Fjol	Fjolsvinnsmal.
Ftb	Flateyjarbók.
Fms	Fornmanna Sögur.
Fra d. Sinf . .	Fra dautha Sinfjotla
Ghv	Guthrunarvot.
Grim	Grimnismal.
Grip	Gripesspo.
Grott . . .	Grottasong.
Gud i. ii. . .	Guthrunarkvitha.
Gylf	Gylfaginning (Snorri's *Edda*).
Ham	Hamthesmal.

HBr	Helreid Brynhildar.
HH	Helgakvitha Hundingsbana.
HHj	Helgakvitha Hjorvardssonar.
Hynd . . .	Hyndluljod.
Land.-bók . .	Landnama-bók.
Lok	Lokasenna.
MGH Leg .	Monumenta Germaniæ Historiæ, Leges.
MGH Scrip .	Monumenta Germ. Hist., Scriptores.
Odr	Oddrunargratr.
PBB	Paul and Braune, Beiträge.
PG	Migne's Patrologia Græca.
PL	Migne's Patrologia Latina.
Reg	Reginsmal.
SBAW . . .	Sitzungsberichte der Berliner Akademie der Wissenschaften.
Sg	Sigurtharkvitha en skamma.
Sigdr	Sigrdrifumal.
Skaldsk . . .	Skaldskaparmal (Snorri's *Edda*).
Skir	Skirnismal.
Svip	Svipdagsmal.
SWAW . .	Sitzungsberichte der Wiener Akademie der Wissenschaften.
Thrym . . .	Thrymskvitha.
Vaf	Vafthrudnismal.
Vkv	Volundarkvitha.
Vol	Voluspa.
ZfDA . . .	Zeitschrift für deutsches Altertum.
ZfDPh . . .	Zeitschrift für deutsche Philologie.
ZVV	Zeitschrift des Vereins für Volkkunde.

II. TEXTS AND SOURCES

A. The Poetic Edda

Die Edda, mit historisch-kritischen Commentar. R. C. Boer. 2 vols. Haarlem, 1922.

Sæmundar Edda, mit einem Anhang. Herausgegeben und erklärt von F. Detter und R. Heinzel. 2 vols. (i. Text. ii. Anmerkungen). Leipzig, 1903.

Edda. Die Lieder der Codex Regius. G. Neckel. 2 vols. (i. Text. ii. Kommentierendes Glossar). Heidelberg, 1927.

Die Lieder der Edda. Herausgegeben von B. Sijmons und H. Gering. 2 vols. (i. Text. Einleitung von B. Sijmons. ii. Vollständiges Wörterbuch von H. Gering). Halle, 1903–6. (A third volume of Commentary has not yet appeared).

Die Edda. Die Lieder der sogenannter älteren Edda. Die mythischen und heroischen Erzählungen der Snorra Edda. Übersetzt und erläutert von Hugo Gering. Leipzig and Wien, 1892.

The Elder or Poetic Edda. Part i. The Mythological Poems. Translated by Olive Bray. (Viking Club). London, 1908.

The Edda of Sæmund the Learned from the Old Norse or Icelandic with a Mythological Index. 2 parts. B. Thorpe. London, 1866.

The Poetic Edda. Translated from the Icelandic with an Introduction and Notes by H. A. Bellows. 2 volumes in one. New York, 1923. (Scandinavian Classics, vols. xxi and xxii. American-Scandinavian Foundation).

Corpus Poeticum Boreale. G. Vigfusson and F. Y. Powell. 2 vols. Oxford, 1883. (Contains text and translation of the Eddic and skaldic poems).

Eddica Minora. Dichtungen eddischer Art aus den Fornaldarsögur und anderen Prosawerken. Zusammengestellt und eingeleitet von A. Heusler und W. Ranisch. Dortmund, 1903.

B. SNORRI'S EDDA

Edda Snorra Sturlusonar. Mit lateinischer Übersetzung. (The Arnamagnæan edition). 3 vols. Copenhagen, 1848–87.

Snorra-Edda. R. K. Rask. Stockholm, 1818.

Snorri Sturluson: Edda. Finnur Jónsson. Copenhagen, 1900. (Critical edition of the text).

The Prose Edda by Snorri Sturluson. Translated from the Icelandic with an Introduction by A. G. Brodeur, Ph.D. New York, 1916. (Scandinavian Classics, vol. v. American-Scandinavian Foundation).

The Prose Edda. Translated by G. W. Dasent. Stockholm, 1842.

See also Gering's edition under Poetic *Edda.*

C. THE SAGAS

Flateyjarbók. En Samling af norske Konge-Sagaer. G. Vigfusson and C. R. Unger. 3 vols. Kristiania, 1860–68.

Fornaldar Sögur Nordlanda. C. C. Rafn. 3 vols. Copenhagen, 1829–30.

——— V. Ásmundarson. 3 vols. Reykjavik, 1886–91.

Fornmanna Sögur eftir gömlum handritum. 12 vols. Copenhagen, 1825–37.

392   EDDIC MYTHOLOGY

Altnordische Saga-Bibliothek. Herausgegeben von G. Cederschiöld,
H. Gering, and E. Mogk. 14 vols. Halle, 1892–1909.
*Origines Islandicae: Sagas and other native Writings relative to the
Settlement and early History of Iceland.* Edited and translated by
G. Vigfusson and F. Y. Powell. 2 vols. Oxford, 1905.
*Icelandic Sagas and other historical Documents relative to the Settle-
ments and Descents of the Northmen on the British Isles.* Edited
by G. Vigfusson. 4 vols. (Rolls Series). London, 1887–94.
(Text and translation of Orkneyinga, Magnus, and Hakonar
Sagas).
Saga Library, The. Edited by W. Morris and G. Vigfusson. 6
vols. London, 1893–1905. i. Howard the Halt. The
Banded Men. Hen Thorir. ii. The Ere-dwellers. The
Heath-slayers. iii–vi. Stories of the Kings of Norway (Snorri's
Heimskringla).
Egils-saga Skallagrimssonar. Translated by W. C. Green. London,
1893.
Laxdæla Saga. Translated by M. A. C. Press. London, 1899.
Northern Library, The. Contains the following Sagas: i. The Saga
of King Olaf Tryggvason, translated by J. Sephton. ii. The
Tale of Thrond of Gate, commonly called Færeyinga Saga,
englished by F. York Powell. vi. The Saga of King Sverri of
Norway (Sverris-saga), translated by J. Sephton. London,
1895–99.
Orkneyinga Saga. Translated by J. A. Hjaltalin and G. Goudie.
Edinburgh, 1873.
SNORRI STURLUSON. *Heimskringla.* Translated with dissertations by
S. Laing. 3 vols. London, 1844. Second ed., revised, with notes
by R. B. Anderson. 4 vols. London, 1889. See also *Saga
Library.*
Story of Burnt Njal, The. (*Njals-saga*). Translated by G. W.
Dasent. 2 vols. Edinburgh, 1861.
Story of Gisli the Outlaw, The. (*Gisla-saga*). Translated by G. W.
Dasent. Edinburgh, 1866.
Story of Grettir the Strong, The. (*Grettis-saga*). Translated by E.
Magnússon and W. Morris. London, 1869, and in Morris's
Collected Works, vol. vii, 1911.
*Sturlunga Saga. Including the Islendinga Saga of Sturla Thordarson
and other Works.* With Prolegomena by G. Vigfusson. 2 vols.
Oxford, 1878.
Viga-Glúms Saga. Translated by Sir E. Head. London, 1866.
Völsunga Saga: the Story of the Volsungs and Niblungs. Translated by
E. Magnússon and W. Morris. London, 1888, and in Morris's
Collected Works, vol. vii, 1911.

D. POETRY OF THE SKALDS

F. JÓNSSON, *Den norsk-islandske Skjaldedigtning.* Copenhagen and Kristiania, 1908 and continuing.

T. WISÉN, *Carmina Norroena.* 2 vols. Lund, 1886–89.

E. OTHER SOURCES

ADAM OF BREMEN, *Gesta Hammaburgensis Ecclesiæ Pontificum usque ad Annum* 1072 A.D.

Beowulf. There are many editions and translations of this poem. The following may be mentioned — the editions of A. J. Wyatt, revised by R. W. Chambers, Cambridge, 1914; of W. J. Sedgefield, Manchester, 1910; the translations by W. Morris and A. J. Wyatt, Kelmcott, 1895, London, 1898; J. R. C. Hall, London, 1911.

SAXO GRAMMATICUS, *Gesta Danorum.* Herausgegeben von A. Holder. Strassburg, 1886.

——— *The First Nine Books of the Danish History of Saxo Grammaticus.* Translated by O. Elton. With some considerations on Saxo's Sources, Historical Methods, and Folk-lore, by F. York Powell. London, 1894. (In the Notes the references are to the Book and page of this edition, and to the pages of Holder's edition in brackets).

III. GENERAL WORKS

AFZELIUS, A. A., and GEIJER, E. J., *Svenske Folkevisor.* Stockholm, 1814–16.

ARNASON, J., *Icelandic Legends.* Translated by G. Powell and E. Magnússon. London, 1864–66.

BARING-GOULD, S., *Curious Myths of the Middle Ages.* London, 1888.

BLUM, I., *Die Schutzgeister in die altnordische Litteratur.* Zabern, 1912.

BOLTE, J., and POLIVKA, G., *Anmerkungen zu den Kinder- und Hausmärchen der Brüder Grimm.* 2 vols. Leipzig, 1913–15.

BUGGE, SOPHUS [a], *Studier over de nordiske Gude- og Heltesagns Oprindelse.* 2 vols. Kristiania and Copenhagen, 1881–96. Translated into German by O. Brenner, *Studien über die Enstehung der nordischen Götter- und Heldensagen.* Munich, 1889.

——— [b], *The Home of the Eddic Poems, with especial Reference to the Helgi-lays.* Translated by W. H. Schofield. London, 1899.

CELANDER, H., *Lokes mystika Ursprung.* Upsala, 1911.

CHADWICK, H. M. [a], *The Origin of the English Nation.* Cambridge, 1907.

——— [b], *The Cult of Othin.* London, 1899.

CHANTEPIE DE LA SAUSSAYE, D., *The Religion of the Teutons.* Translated by B. J. Vos. Boston, 1902.

CLARKE, D. E. MARTIN, *The Hávamál, with Selections from other Poems of the Edda, illustrating the Wisdom of the Northern Heathen Times.* Edited and translated by D. E. Martin Clarke. Cambridge, 1923.

CLEASBY, R., and VIGFUSSON, G., *Icelandic-English Dictionary.* Oxford, 1874.

CRAIGIE, W. A. [a], *The Religion of Ancient Scandinavia.* London, 1906.

——— [b], *Scandinavian Folk-lore.* London, 1896.

——— [c], *The Icelandic Sagas.* Cambridge, 1913.

DASENT, SIR G., *Wonder Tales from the Norse.*[3] London, 1903.

DU CHAILLU, PAUL B., *The Viking Age.* 2 vols. London, 1889.

FAERÖSK ANTHOLOGI, edited by V. U. Hammershaimb. Copenhagen, 1891.

FAYE, A., *Norske Folkesagn.*[2] Kristiania, 1844.

FRAZER, SIR J. G., *Balder the Beautiful.* 2 vols. (Vols. ix and x of *The Golden Bough*).[3] London, 1913.

FRIESEN, O. VON, *Runenschrift,* in Hoops, iv. 5 ff.

GERING, H., *Über Weissagung und Zauber im nordischen Altertum.* Kiel, 1902.

——— See also under ' Edda ' (Section II).

GOLTHER, W. [a], *Handbuch der germanischen Mythologie.* Leipzig, 1895.

——— [b], ' Studien zur germanischen Sagengeschichte. i. Der Valkyrien Mythus.' *AMA* i. Klasse, 18 Band, 1888, pp. 401 ff.

GREIN, C., *Bibliothek der angelsächsischen Poesie.* Neu bearbeitet von R. P. Wülker. 3 vols. Kassel, 1883–1898.

GRIMM, J. [a], *Teutonic Mythology.* Translated by J. F. Stallybrass. 4 vols. London, 1880–88.

——— [b], *Deutsche Sagen.*[3] 2 vols. Berlin, 1891. (This is edited by J. and W. Grimm).

——— [c], *Kinder- und Hausmärchen.*[9] Leipzig, 1870. (J. and W. Grimm).

——— [d], *Irische Elfenmärchen.* (This is the German translation of Croker's *Fairy Legends of the South of Ireland,* with an Introduction by J. and W. Grimm). London, 1828. Another edition of the Introduction is in J. Grimm's *Kleinere Schriften.*

GRÖNBECH, V. [a], *Vor Folkeaet i Oldtiden.* Copenhagen, 1909–12.
—— [b], *Die Germanen,* in Chantepie de la Saussaye, *Lehrbuch der Religionsgeschichte.*[4] Herausgegeben von A. Bertholet und E. Lehmann, 2 vols. Tübingen, 1925.

HARTLAND, E. S., *The Science of Fairy Tales.* London, 1891.

HELM, K., *Altgermanische Religionsgeschichte.* Erster Band. Heidelberg, 1913.

HERRMANN, P. [a], *Erlauterungen zu den ersten neun Büchern der Dänischen Geschichte des Saxo Grammaticus.* (Zweiter Teil. Kommentar). Leipzig, 1922.
—— [b], *Nordische Mythologie.* Leipzig, 1903.

HOFFORY, J., *Eddastudien.* Berlin, 1889.

HOOPS, J., *Reallexicon der Germanischen Altertumskunde.* 4 vols. Strassburg, 1911–1919. (Contains numerous articles on Religion and Mythology).

JESSEN, E., ' Über die Eddalieder, Heimat, Alter, Character,' *ZfDPh,* 1871, iii. 1 ff.

JIRICZEK, O. L. [a], *Die deutschen Heldensagen.* Stuttgart, 1897. English translation by M. Bentinck Smith, *Northern Hero Legends.*
—— [b], *Deutsche Heldensagen.* Strassburg, 1898.

JÓNSSON, F. [a], *Den oldnorske og oldislandske Literaturs Historie.* 3 vols. Copenhagen, 1894–1902.
—— [b], *Den islandske Literaturs Historie.* Copenhagen, 1907. See also under ' Skaldic Poetry ' (Section II).

KAUFFMANN, F. [a], *Deutsche Mythologie.* Stuttgart, 1890. English translation by M. Steele Smith, *Northern Mythology.* London, 1903.
—— [b], *Balder.* Strassburg, 1902.

KEIGHTLEY, T., *The Fairy Mythology.* London, 1900.

KELLETT, E. E., *The Religion of our Northern Ancestors.* London, 1914.

KEMBLE, J. M., *The Saxons in England.* 2 vols. London, 1849.

KERSHAW, N., *Stories and Ballads of the Far Past.* Translated from the Norse. Cambridge, 1921.

KOCK, A., ' Die Göttin Nerthus und der Gott Njordhr,' *ZfDPh* xxviii. 289 ff.

KÖGEL, R., *Geschichte der deutschen Litteratur bis zum Ausgange der Mittelalters.* 2 vols. Strassburg, 1894–97.

KROHN, K., *Skandinavisk Mytologi.* Helsingfors, 1922.

LEYEN, F. V. D., *Der gefesselte Unhold.* Prague, 1908.

LIEBRECHT, F., *Zur Volkskunde.* Heilbronn, 1879.

LIESTØL, K. [a], *Norske trollvisor og norrøne Sogor.* Kristiania, 1915.
───── [b], 'Jøtnarne og Joli' in *Maal og Minne,* 1911.
MacCULLOCH, J. A. [a], *The Religion of the Ancient Celts.* Edinburgh, 1911.
───── [b], *Celtic Mythology* (in this Series), Boston, 1918.
───── [c], *The Childhood of Fiction.* London, 1905.
MAGNUSEN, F., *Priscæ Veterum Borealium Mythologiæ Lexicon.*
  Havniae, 1828.
MANNHARDT, W. [a], *Wald- und Feldkulte.* 2 vols. Berlin, 1875–
  77.
───── [b], *Die Baumkultus der Germanen.* Berlin, 1875.
MAURER, K., *Die Bekehrung des norwegischen Stammes zum Chris-
  tenthume.* 2 vols. Munich, 1855–56.
MEICHE, A., *Sagenbuch des Konigreichs Sachsen.* Leipzig, 1903.
METCALFE, F., *Englishman and Scandinavian: A Comparison of
  Anglo-Saxon and Old Norse Literature.* London, 1880.
MEYER, E. H. [a], *Mythologie der Germanen.* Strassburg, 1903.
  [b], *Germanische Mythologie.* Berlin, 1891.
  [c], *Völuspa.* Berlin, 1889.
  [d], *Die eddische Kosmogonie.* Freiburg, 1891.
MEYER, R. M., *Altgermanische Mythologie.* Berlin, 1891.
MOGK, E. [a], *Mythologie.* In Paul, *Grundriss der Germanischen
  Philologie,*[2] Strassburg, 1898 ff., iii. 230–406.
───── [b], *Geschichte der norwegisch-isländischen Literatur.* In ib.
  ii. 2. 555–922.
───── [c], 'Untersuchungen über die Gylfaginning,' in *PBB* vi, vii.
MONTELIUS, O., *The Civilization of Sweden in Heathen Times.* London, 1888.
MUCH, R., *Der Germanische Himmelsgott.* (*Festgabe für Richard
  Heinzel,* pp. 189 ff.) Halle, 1898.
MÜLLENHOFF, C. V. [a], *Deutsche Altertumskunde.* 5 vols. Berlin,
  1883–1900.
───── [b], 'Frija und der Halsband-mythus,' in *ZfDA* xxx. 217 ff.
───── [c], 'Über Tuisco und seine Nachkommen,' in *Allgemeine
  Zeitschrift für Geschichte,* viii. 209 ff.
───── [d], 'Um Ragnarok,' in *ZfDA* xvi. 146 ff.
───── and SCHERER, W., *Denkmäler deutscher Poesie und Prosa
  aus dem VIII–XII Jahrhundert.*[3] 2 vols. Berlin, 1892.
MÜLLER, S., *Nordische Altertumskunde.* Translated by O. L.
  Jiriczek. 2 vols. Strassburg, 1897–98.
MÜLLER, W., *Mythologie der deutschen Heldensage.* Heilbronn,
  1886.
MUNCH, P. A., *Norse Mythology: Legends of Gods and Heroes.* Revised by M. Olsen. Translated from the Norwegian by S. B.

Hustvedt. New York, 1926 (Scandinavian Classics, vol. xxvii. American-Scandinavian Foundation).

NECKEL, G. [a], *Beiträge zur Eddaforschung.* Dortmund, 1908.

——— [b], *Walhall.* Dortmund, 1923.

——— [c], *Die Ueberlieferungen vom Gotte Balder.* Dortmund, 1920.

NIEDNER, F., ' Baldr's Tod, *ZfDA* xli. 305 ff.

OLRIK, A. [a], ' Om Ragnarok,' in *Aarboger for nordisk oldkyndighed,* 1902.

——— [b], ' Ragnarokforestillingernes udspring,' in *Danske Studier,* 1913.

——— [c], *Kilderne til Sakses Oldhistorie, en literaturhistorisk Undersögelse.* 2 vols. Copenhagen, 1892–94.

——— [d], *Kilderne . . . Norröne Sagaer og danske Sagn.* Copenhagen, 1894.

——— [e], *Danmarks Heltedigtning.* Copenhagen, 1910. English translation by L. M. Hollander, *The Heroic Legends of Denmark.* New York, 1919. (Scandinavian Monographs, vol. iv. American-Scandinavian Foundation).

OLSEN, M., ' Det gamle norske Ønavn Njardarlog,' *Kristiania Videnskabsselskabs forhandlinger,* 1905.

PAUL, H., *Grundriss der germanischen Philologie.*[2] 3 vols. Strassburg, 1898 ff.

——— and BRAUNE, W., *Beiträge zur Geschichte der deutschen Spräche und Literatur.* Halle, 1874, and continuing. Cited as *PBB.*

PETERSEN, H., *Om Nordboernes Gudedyrkelse og Gudetro i Hedenold.* Copenhagen, 1876.

PHILLPOTTS, B. S. [a], *The Elder Edda and Ancient Scandinavian Drama.* Cambridge, 1920.

——— [b], *Germanic Heathendom,* in *Cambridge Medieval History,* vol. ii, Chapter xv. Cambridge, 1913.

ROEDIGER, M., ' Der grosse Waldesgott der Germanen,' *ZfDPh* xxvii. 1 ff.

RYDBERG, V., *Undersökningar i germanisk Mythologi.* 2 vols. Kristiania, 1886–89. English translation of vol. i. by R. B. Anderson, *Teutonic Mythology,* London, 1889.

SCHOMING, O., *Dodsriger i nordisk Hedentro.* Copenhagen, 1903.

SCHRADER, O., *Reallexicon der indogermanische Altertumskunde.* Strassburg, 1901.

SCHREIBER, H. [a], *Die Feen in Europa.* Freiburg-im-Breisgau, 1842.

——— [b], *Feen und Hexen.* Freiburg-im-Breisgau, 1846.

SCHUCK, H., *Studier i Nordisk Literatur- och Religionshistoria.* 1904.

SIMROCK, C. G., *Handbuch der deutschen Mythologie.*[4] Bonn, 1874.

STORM, G. [a], ' Ginnungagap i Mythologien og i Geografien,' in *ANF* 1890, vi. 304 ff.
———— [b], ' Om Thorgerd Hølgebrud,' in *ANF* ii. 124 ff.
SYMONS, B., *Heldensage,* in Paul's *Grundriss,*[2] iii. 606 ff.
THORPE, B., *Northern Mythology.* 3 vols. London, 1851–52.
TIELE, J. M., *Danske Folkesagn.* Copenhagen, 1818–20.
UHLAND, L., *Schriften zur Geschichte der Dichtung und Sage.* 8 vols. Stuttgart, 1865–73.
UNWERTH, W. VON, *Untersuchungen über Totenkult und Odinnverehrung bei Nordgermanen und Lappen.* Breslau, 1911.
VIGFUSSON, G., see CLEASBY, R., in this section and under ' Eddas ' and ' Sagas ' (Section II).
WEINHOLD, K. [a], *Altnordisches Leben.* Berlin, 1856.
———— [b], ' Über den Mythus von Wanenkrieg,' in *SBAW* 1890, clxxxix. 611 ff.
———— [c], ' Die Sagen von Loki,' in *ZfDA* vii. 1 ff.
———— [d], ' Die Riesen der germanischen Mythus,' in *SWAW* xxvi. 225 ff.
WIGSTROM, E., *Folkditning . . . Samlad och Upptecknad i Skaane.* Copenhagen, 1880.
WISÉN, T., *Oden och Loke.* Stockholm, 1873.

IV.　PRINCIPAL ARTICLES ON TEUTONIC MYTH-OLOGY AND RELIGION IN THE ENCYCLO-PÆDIA OF RELIGION AND ETHICS (VOLS. I–XII)

CHADWICK, H. M., " Ancestor Worship (Teutonic)," i. 466–7.
———— " Calendar (Teutonic)," iii. 138–41.
CLARKE, D. E. MARTIN, " Teutonic Religion," xii. 246–54.
CRAIGIE, W. A., " State of the Dead (Teutonic)," xi. 851–53.
CRAWLEY, A. E., " Eating the God," v. 136–39.
DICKINS, T. B., " Transmigration (Teutonic)," xii. 440.
GASKELL, C. J., " Altar (Teutonic)," i. 354.
———— " Art (Teutonic)," i. 886–88.
———— " Bull," ii. 889.
———— " Divination (Teutonic)," iv. 827.
GRAY, L. H., " Names (Indo-European)," ix. 162–67.
HÄLSIG, F., " Magic ₍Teutonic)," viii. 307–11.
JÓNSSON, F., " Eddas," v. 159–62.
KEANE, A. H., " Ethnology," v. 522–32.
———— " Europe," v. 591–97.

KERSHAW, N., "Teutonic Religion," xii. 254–59.
LEHMANN, E., "Christmas Customs," iii. 608–10.
MacCULLOCH, J. A., "Blest, Abode of the (Teutonic)," ii. 707–10.
———— "Branches and Twigs," ii. 831–33.
———— "Cross-roads," iv. 330–35.
———— "Eschatology," v. 374.
———— "Fairy," v. 678–89.
———— "Landmarks and Boundaries," vii. 789–95.
———— "Lycanthropy," viii. 206–20.
———— "Mountains, Mountain Gods," viii. 863–68.
———— "Nature (Primitive and Savage)," ix. 201–7.
———— "Serpent-Worship (Introductory and Primitive)," xi. 399–411.
———— "Underworld," xii. 516–19.
———— "Vampire," xii. 589–91.
MacRITCHIE, D., "Giants," vi. 189–93.
MOGK, E., "Birth (Teutonic)," ii. 662–63.
———— "Demons and Spirits (Teutonic)," iv. 630–35.
———— "Doom, Doom Myths," iv. 845.
———— "Expiation and Atonement (Teutonic)," v. 669–71.
———— "God (Teutonic)," vi. 303–6.
———— "Hamadryads," vi. 485–86.
———— "Human Sacrifice (Teutonic)," vi. 865–67.
———— "Muspilli," ix. 62.
MUNRO, R., "Death and Disposal of the Dead (Prehistoric Europe)," iv. 464–72.
PHILLPOTTS, B. S., "Dreams and Sleep (Teutonic)," v. 37–38.
———— "Ethics and Morality (Teutonic)," v. 518–22.
———— "Festivals and Fasts (Teutonic)," v. 890–91.
———— "Inheritance (Teutonic)," vii. 311–12.
———— "Old Age (Teutonic)," ix. 480.
———— "Purification (Teutonic)," x. 503–5.
———— "Soul (Teutonic)," xi. 753–55.
ROBINSON, F. N., "Deæ Matres," iv. 406–11.
SCHRADER, O., "Aryan Religion," ii. 11–57.
———— "Chastity (Teutonic)," iii. 499–503.
———— "Family (Teutonic)," v. 749–54.
———— "King (Teutonic)," vii. 728–32.
———— "Law (Teutonic)," vii. 887–89.
SEATON, M. E., "Heroes and Hero-gods (Teutonic)," vi. 667–68.
———— "Images and Idols (Teutonic)," vii. 155–59.
———— "Life and Death (Teutonic)," viii. 42–44.
———— "Music (Teutonic)," ix. 59–61.
———— "Ordeal (Teutonic)," ix. 530–33.

———— "Swan–Maidens," xii. 125–26.

SUDHOFF, K., " Disease and Medicine (Teutonic)," iv. 759–62.

WALLIS, W. D., " Prodigies and Portents," x. 362–76.

WELSFORD, E., " Nature (Teutonic)," ix. 253–54.

———— " Prayer (Teutonic)," x. 201–2.

———— " Serpent," xi. 419–20.

———— "Sun, Moon and Stars (Teutonic)," xii. 101–3.

YOUNGERT, S., " Cosmogony (Teutonic)," iv. 176–79.

———— "Sacrifice (Teutonic)," xi. 38–39.

———— "Salvation (Teutonic)," xi. 149–51.

———— " Sin (Teutonic)," xi. 570–71.

———— " Vows (Teutonic)," xii. 659–61.

FULL PAGE ILLUSTRATIONS

PLATE II

Borg in Iceland

Borg, Iceland, the home of the poet Egil Skallagrimsson and of Snorri Sturluson, author of the Prose
Edda (see p. 4). The farm of the same name is in
the centre of the picture. In the foreground is the
family tomb, partly destroyed, where Egil in his poem
saw Hel stand and wait his coming. From W. G.
Collingwood's *Sagasteads of Iceland*.

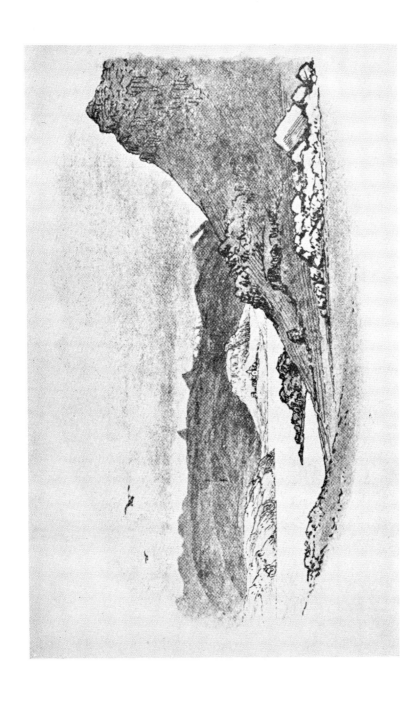

PLATE III

THE THREE ODINS AND GANGLERI

The Three Odins (Har, Jafnhar, and Thridi) questioned by Gangleri. See p. 6. From a MS of Snorri's *Edda*.

gangtan ſpiʒʒ

PLATE IV

The Golden Horns

These golden horns were found in a field on the
west coast of Slesvig, the longer in 1639, the shorter
in 1734. The surfaces of the horns are divided into
compartments with figures believed to represent deities
and mythic scenes. The date of the horns is the fifth
century A.D. If, as has been maintained by some, the
scenes depict Eddic gods and myths, including representations of Valhall and Yggdrasil, then much of the
mythology is of far earlier date than most scholars
assign to it. This interpretation of the figures and
scenes is, however, entirely hypothetical and has won
little support. The runes at the rim of the smaller
horn give the name of the artificer.

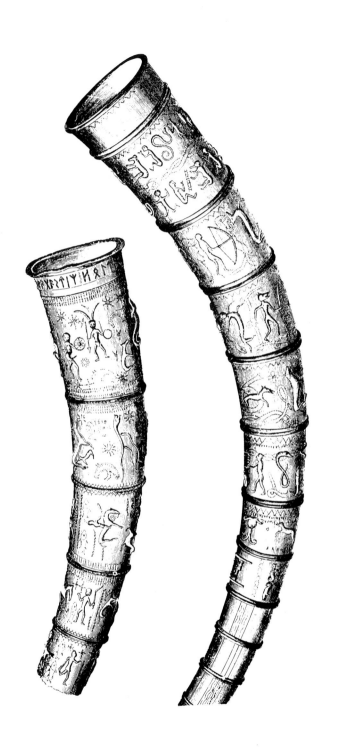

PLATE V

DETAILS OF THE LARGER HORN

The upper compartment is assumed to depict the Fenris-wolf playing with the gods, then (below) bound, while Tyr with his hand bitten off is close by (see p. 99). The next compartments show gods and animals and animal-headed monsters. In the sixth the design is interpreted as showing wolves attacking the sun (see p. 199), and, in the lowest, as the entrance to the realm of the dead.

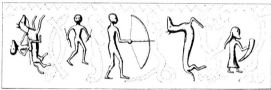

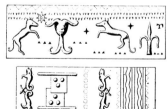

PLATE VI

DETAILS OF THE SMALLER HORN

As interpreted by J. J. A. Worsaae this horn depicts scenes from Valhall. In the upper compartment is Odin with spear, sceptre, and the ring Draupnir. Below him is the boar Sæhrimnir. To the left are two Einherjar; to the right Odin's wolves, the hart Eikthyrnir, and the goat Heidrun. Beyond these is Frey with sickle and sceptre; below him the boar Gullinbursti. The next compartment shows, to the right, a three-headed figure representing the triad of gods, Odin, Thor, and Frey (others regard the figure as that of Thor). The large serpent is Loki with Idunn's apple in his mouth. The bird attacking a fish is the giant Thjazi; the fish is Loki. To the extreme left are figures symbolizing the slaying of Balder. The third compartment represents the gate of Valhall, fish swimming in the river surrounding it, the Ash Yggdrasil with the serpent Nidhogg at its roots, Hermod on Sleipnir, etc. In the fourth is Frey, with horse and sickle. All this interpretation is purely hypothetical.

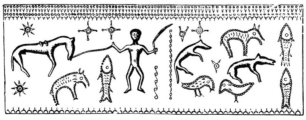

PLATE VII

Odin

Odin riding, with helmet, spear, and shield. The birds are his ravens. See p. 65. Part of a helmet found in the royal graves at Vendel, Sweden, and dating from *c.* 900 A.D. From Stolpe and Arne, *Vendel-fyndet*. See pp. 58, 217.

PLATE VIII

SWEDISH GRAVE-STONE

Grave-stone from Tjangvide, Götland, Sweden, *c.* 1000 A.D. The figure on the eight-legged horse may be Odin on Sleipnir. See p. 65.

PLATE IX

The uppermost design, from the smaller golden horn, of a three-headed deity is held by some to represent Thor with an axe and one of his goats.

The central design, of a god with an axe and a monster at his right hand, is supposed to represent Thor. From the decoration of a helmet found at Vendel in Sweden.

The two lowest designs are embossed bronze plates from the island of Öland, Sweden, representing Thor and a monster, and a god (Thor?) between two monsters.

PLATE X

THOR AND THE MIDGARD-SERPENT

The upper design shows a sculptured capital from the church of Bocherville, Normandy, eleventh century, and is supposed to represent Thor attacking the Midgard-serpent.

The lower illustration of a sculpture of Scandinavian origin in the churchyard of Gosforth, Cumberland, shows Thor fishing with the giant Hymir (p. 85).

PLATE XI

THOR'S HAMMER AMULETS

The upper, of silver, from Uppland, Sweden. The lower, of silver decorated with gold and filigree work, is from East Götland, Sweden.

PLATE XII

Altar to Mars Thingsus

This altar, dedicated to Mars Thingsus and the two Alaisiagae, Bede and Fimmilene, is one of two found at Housesteads on the line of Hadrian's wall. They were erected by Frisian soldiers from Twenthe (see p. 98).

DEO
MARTI
THINGSO
I DVABVS
AAESIAGIS
BEDE FI
MMILENE
INAVGGER
MGAESTV
I HANTI
VSLM

PLATE XIII

SCENES FROM THE LARGER GOLDEN HORN

The upper design is assumed to depict the Fenris-wolf and the gods. He is seen bound in the lower part of the design, with Tyr to the left, his hands bitten off. See p. 99.

In the lower design two wolves are supposed to be attacking the sun (the figure with a face, above which is a sun-symbol). Below this is a representation of Hel-gate with reptiles and rivers (to right); the posts are made of bones of the dead. The interpretation is doubtful.

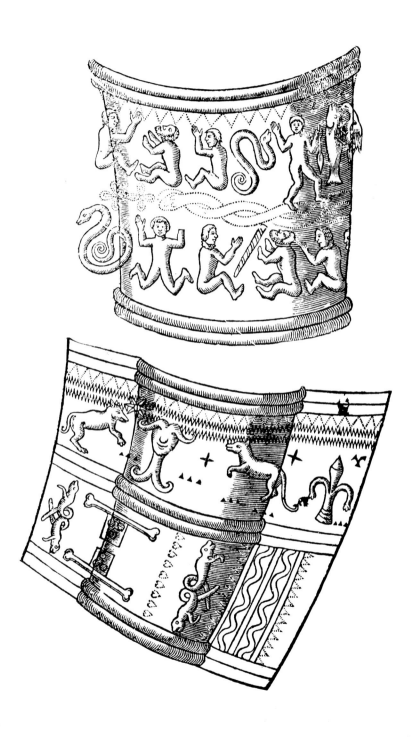

PLATE XIV

FREY

Upper figure, to right. Ithyphallic squatting image, probably of Frey, intended to be carried in its owner's purse and buried with him. From Södermanland, Sweden, tenth century.

Lower design, to right. One of several golden plates representing the sacred marriage of a god of fertility (possibly Frey) and a goddess. Found in the neighbourhood of the farm of Fröjsland ('land of Frey'), south-west Norway. See p. 116.

Design on left. The sacred marriage depicted on a tenth century runic stone, the figures represented separately because of the form of the stone. From the same district as the gold plate.

PLATE XV

ANCIENT WAGON

A wagon of the early Iron Age found in the moor of Deibjerg, Jutland, and restored. Such a wagon may have been used to carry round an image, as in the Nerthus and Frey cults (pp. 102, 115), or to transport a dead man to his grave-mound, where it was buried with him for use on the Hel-way or in the Other World.

PLATE XVI

The Oseberg Ship

The custom of interring a dead. chief or king in a funeral chamber within a ship, which was then enclosed in a tumulus, was common in Norway. Such burial sites were always near the sea, and nine royal tumuli of this type exist at Borre on the western coast of the Oslo fjord. At some distance from these, at Oseberg, another tumulus was opened and was found to contain a ship, eighty feet long, richly carved, with a funeral chamber full of all kinds of objects for the use of the dead. Within the chamber were two beds and two bodies of women. One of these is believed to be that of queen Aasa, grandmother of Harald the Fair-haired, the other that of her chief attendant. The date of the tumulus is about the middle of the ninth century. At some period unknown the tumulus had been opened and all the objects made of gold and silver abstracted, and many of the funerary objects smashed. The ship reconstructed is now preserved at Oslo. The illustration shows the elaborate carving of the wood.

The funeral of Balder points to a different method of ship-interment, viz., not burial within a tumulus but cremation (p. 130).

From a photograph, by permission of the Director of the Universitetets Oldsaksamling, Oslo.

PLATE XVII

SCULPTURED STONE FROM GÖTLAND

This stone, of the Viking period, from Tjängvide, Stenkyrka, Götland, shows ships and warriors.

PLATE XVIII

LOKI AND SIGYN

From a sculptured Cross at Gosforth, Cumberland.
The two figures within the circle are supposed to be
Loki bound and tortured by the serpent's venom, and
his wife, Sigyn, holding a vessel to catch the venom as
it drips. See p. 144.

PLATE XIX

Heimdall

From a Runic Cross at Jurby, Isle of Man. The figure blowing a horn is believed to be Heimdall (see p. 152). From *The Saga-Book of the Viking Club*, vol. i.

PLATE XX

Bronze Trumpet

Bronze trumpet or horn (*lur*), one of several found in Denmark and South Sweden, with ornamental disc at the wider end and mouth-piece. These horns were cast in several pieces, though the metal is extremely thin, save at the ends. On Midsummer Day a concert is held at Copenhagen where these instruments are used. The number of the sounds produced, their purity and force, are remarkable, and suggest a well developed artistic taste in the Scandinavian Bronze Age. Cf. the references to Heimdall's horn, pp. 154, 156, and A. Hammerich, " Les *lurs* de l'age du bronze au musée national de Copenhagen,' in *Société royale des antiquaires du Nord, Memoires*, n. s., 1892, pp. 137 ff.

PLATE XXI

Vidarr

This scene, from a sculptured Cross at Gosforth, Cumberland, is believed to represent Vidarr attacking the Fenris-Wolf (p. 159). His foot is on its lower jaw. The serpentine form of the monster's body is an ornamental design.

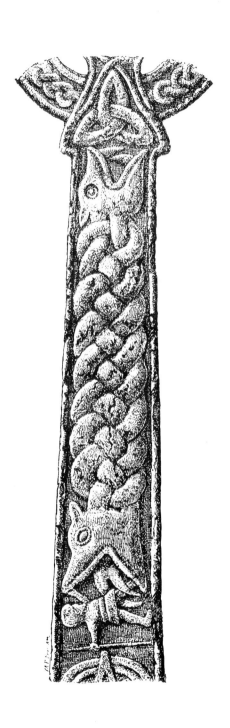

PLATE XXII

IMAGES AND GRAVE-PLATE

To left. Image of a god wearing a helmet, found in Scania. Ninth or tenth century.

To right. Bronze image of a goddess, possibly of fertility, from Scania, c. 700 B.C. Similar figures are common in the Baltic area, and the type goes back to images of the Babylonian Istar, goddess of fruitfulness.

Centre. Grave plate from Kivike, early Bronze Age. From *Mannus*, vol. vii.

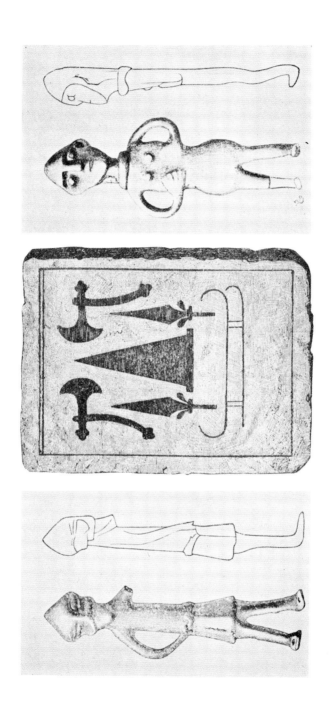

PLATE XXIII

The lower part of the plate shows the remains of
an Icelandic temple, with walls of turf, eight feet thick.
Near them are two rows of foundations for wooden
pillars. The building is oblong, but divided by a low
stone cross-wall, separating the gods' abode, in which
was an altar, from the hall. Images stood on this wall.
Along the floor of the hall hearths existed, with pits in
which meat was cooked in hot ashes. Those who
partook of the feast sat on long benches along the hall,
between the pillars.

The upper part of the plate shows the remains of a
hearth and pit.

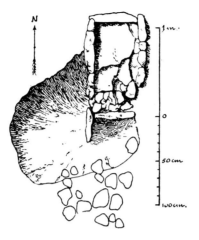

PLATE XXIV

Sun Symbols

These symbols cut on rocks and stones in Scandinavia during the Stone and Bronze Ages represent the sun as a disc or wheel rolling through the sky. See p. 198.

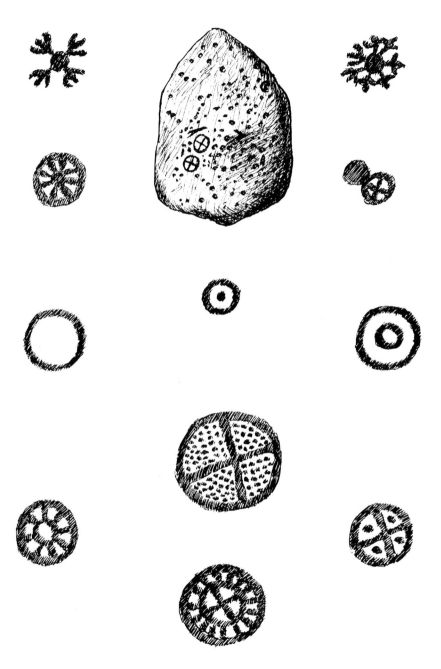

PLATE XXV

SUN CARRIAGE

Sun carriage, with horse and wheels, of bronze covered with gold. Found at Trundholm, Seeland. Described on p. 198.

PLATE XXVI

Sun Symbol

Bronze sun disc mounted on a metal ring with ten wheels. From Ystad in Schonen. See p. 199.

PLATE XXVII

Rock-carvings and Bronze Razors

The designs of boats, to the left and right, upper corner, are from rock-carvings at Bohuslan, Sweden, and date from the early Bronze Age. Some of these boats, of which there are many carvings, have a high and narrow stem, terminating in an animal's head. The stern is decorated in the same way in some examples.

The bronze razors (right) have spiral designs representing boats. These were common in Scandinavia, and the boat design is sometimes associated with circles having a cross or dot inside or lines radiating from the circumference. These may be sun symbols. Some have seen a sun symbol in the boat also, as if a myth of the sun's crossing the ocean at night in a boat had been current in Scandinavia in the Bronze Age. See p. 198 and J. Déchelette, *Manuel d' archéologie*, ii, chapter 4.

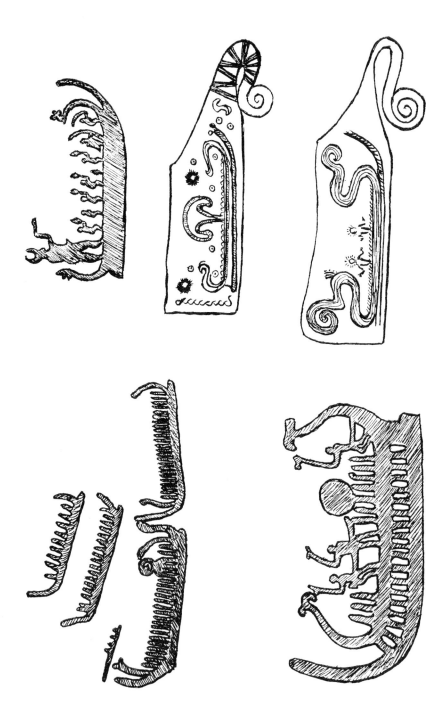

PLATE XXVIII

SEA-GIANTESS

Sea-giantess or siren attacking sailors in their boat.
From an Icelandic MS of the *Physiologus*, *c.* 1200 A.D.
See p. 190.

Sirena iartein ifegrþ raddar sinar oc setr g͛
sa þera er men hafa til felo iþeim h̄ oc ga þeſem̄
oc ſopna ſva fra goþū vkō endyret tek my oc fyr
fer þeī þa es þr ſona aftag roddo. Sva faraſe mar
ger afſeliſi ſino ef þat er vilia gera iþeim u her

Ack ſa er i babilon þa er h̄ frevefe þa leggiaſe i
akrenn flvgvr þer er kallaſe af alþyþo kleggiar
þr eta yr frecomet oc ſpilla ſva auertin ū. En br

PLATE XXIX

WOLF-HEADED MONSTER

Above.　God or demon with Wolf's head on a bronze plate found in Bavaria.

Below.　A similar wolf-being and a horned warrior, on a bronze plate found in the Island of Öland, Sweden.

PLATE XXX

PLATE XXXI

RUNIC STONE AND GUNDESTRUPP SILVER BOWL

Above. Runic stone, *c.* 800 A.D., from Seeland.
Erected for Gunwald the Thul or ' Reciter.' On the
stone are the Thor's hammer symbol (part of a
svastika), and the sign of Odin, three horns inter-
laced, with allusion to poetry as ' the mead of Odin '
(see p. 55). After Wimmer, *Danske Runemindes-
mærker.*

Below. Silver bowl from Gundestrupp, Jutland, in
the region of the Cimbri. It was used in the sacred
ritual. On the outside are heads of deities. Inside are
figures, human and animal, and scenes of cult. The
subjects are partly drawn from classical art, partly
from Celtic sources, e.g., the horned god is copied from
representations of the Celtic Cernunnos (see next
plate). Strabo records that the Cimbri sent their holiest
bowl to Augustus.

PLATE XXXII

The Gundestrupp Bowl

Above. Horned god from the Gundestrupp bowl, copied from a Celtic original of a god with horns, necklace, serpent, and stags. See Plates XVI and XXV of *Celtic Mythology* in this Series.

Below. Sacrificial scene from the inside of the Gundestrupp bowl. The priest is holding a human victim over the vessel of sacrifice for the blood to gush forth. A procession of warriors is also depicted. Among the ancient Cimbri a priestess went with the army. She cut the throat of a human victim over the rim of a cauldron, and took auspices from the blood that flowed into it.

PLATE XXXIII

This vessel, perhaps used in sacrifice or in rain-magic, or possibly for burning incense, was found at Peckatel, Schwerin. It stands sixteen inches high, and the diameter of the vessel's mouth is fourteen inches. Similar vessels have been found in Seeland and Schonen. Bronze Age.

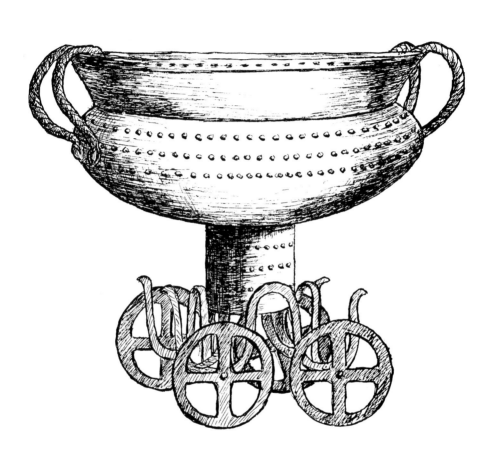

PLATE XXXIV

This Anglo-Saxon casket, presented to the British
Museum by Sir A. W. Franks, is one of whalebone
from Northumbria, and dates from the seventh or
eighth century. There are several designs carved on
it, and two of these represent incidents from the Volund
story. This story was of Saxon origin, and is referred
to in Anglo-Saxon poetry, e.g., *Deor's Lament*. It
was popular over all the Teutonic area, where it is
sometimes associated with other legendary cycles, and
in Scandinavia the *Volundarkvitha* in the *Edda* and the
Velints-saga contained in the *Thidriks-saga* show that
it had been adopted there. As told in the second part
of the *Volundarkvitha* King Nithud learned that
Volund was in Ulfdalir. He had him bound in his
sleep and hamstrung. Then the prisoner was forced
to make ornaments for the king. The king's two
sons came to see these, and Volund slew them and cut
off their heads. Then he set their skulls in silver, fashioned gems of their eyes, and made a brooch of their
teeth, presenting these to Nithud, his wife, and his
daughter Bothvild, respectively. The illustration
shows Volund holding one of the skulls with a pair of
tongs as he makes a goblet of it. The headless body
lies on the ground. Bothvild and her attendant are
also shown, and Volund's brother Egil is seen catching
birds with whose wings or feathers Volund is later to
fly off (as told in the *Velints-saga*). The design to
the right shows the Magi at the cradle of the Holy
Child. See pp. 259, 267.

From a photograph, by permission of the British
Museum authorities.

PLATE XXXV

After Volund had by craft seduced Bothvild, he apparently made himself wings, or, as in the *Thidriks-saga*, his brother Egil shot birds, out of whose plumage a feather-dress was made. Then he revealed to Nithud all he had done to his sons and to Bothvild, and now rose aloft in the air, escaping his vengeance. In the *Thidriks-saga* Egil is made to shoot at him by Nithud. A bladder full of blood was concealed under Volund's arm. When the bladder, as arranged beforehand, was pierced by the arrow, Nithud thought that the blood was Volund's, and believed that he was dead. The incident is shown in this design from the Casket. These designs form the earliest record of the Volund story.

From a photograph, by permission of the British Museum authorities.

PLATE XXXVI

RUNIC MONUMENT WITH TROLL-WIFE

Runic monument at Hunestad, Scania, Denmark,
tenth century. The figure is that of a troll-wife or
giantess riding on a wolf, bridled by a snake. See
p. 286.

PLATE XXXVII

Spear-head, Sword, and Bear's Tooth

The spear-head is from Kowel in Volhynia, Russia, and has runic markings.

The sword, of the La Téne period, has snakes engraved on its surface. See p. 216.

The bear's tooth with a hole for a cord was used as an amulet. From West Götland. See pp. 296–97.

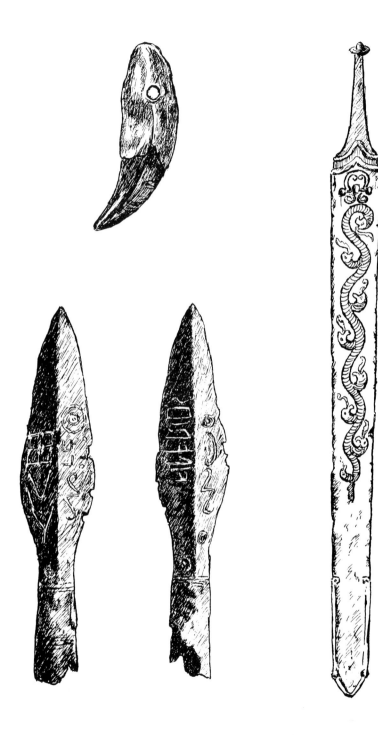

PLATE XXXVIII

ENTRANCE TO A GIANT'S CHAMBER

This double Giant's Chamber or Jættestue is on the Island of Möen in the Baltic. It is a large chambered barrow or tumulus of the Stone Age, with a double entrance and double interior chamber.

PLATE XXXIX

Bronze Age Barrow or Tumulus

Tumulus of the later Bronze Age at Refsnaes, See-land, made of stones covered with earth. It contains urns with stone cists.

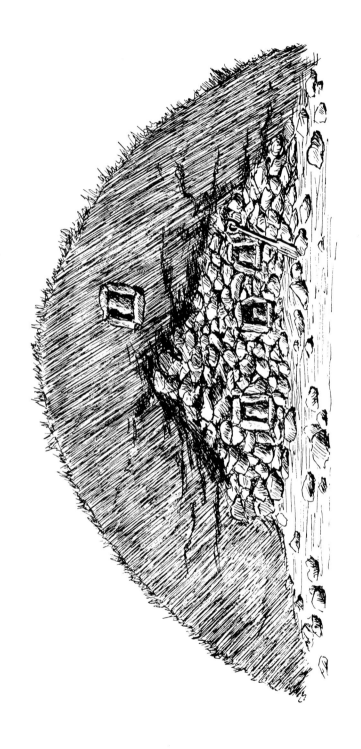

PLATE XL

The upper picture shows Helga-fell, ' Holy Fell ' or 'Holy Mountain,' in Western Iceland, with the farm of the same name beneath it to the right. The hill was that into which the dead died, and was held to be most sacred. The idea that it was the abode of the dead may have arisen from the form of the hill, like a house with a great gate. From W. G. Collingwood, *Sagasteads of Iceland*. See p. 310.

The lower picture is that of a sacred birch-tree and mound near the farm of Slinde at Sogn, West Norway. No one might cut its branches and at the Christmas festival ale was poured over its roots by every member of the family. The tree fell in 1874. From a painting by Thomas Fearnley, 1840. See p. 203.

PLATE XLI

Holy Well and Royal Barrows

The upper illustration is that of a holy well at Tisvilde, north coast of Seeland, for long the most famous
of Danish wells and still frequented for healing. It is
called S. Helen's Well, but the name Tisvilde suggests
that it may once have been sacred to Tyr. From a
photograph in the Copenhagen collection of folk-lore.

The lower illustration shows the great royal barrows at Upsala. The church in the background probably stands on the site of the temple of Upsala. There
are remains of a holy well in the churchyard. The
barrows were supposed to be those of ancient legendary
kings.

PLATE XLII

The Bewcastle Cross

On this Cross at Bewcastle, Cumberland, and on
the similar cross at Ruthwell, Dumfriesshire, there are
elaborate designs of a tree with roots, trunk, branches,
foliage, and fruit. Birds and animals are shown in
the tree, eating the fruit. On this face of the Bewcastle Cross, counting from below, there are a complete
quadruped, two fantastic animals with forelegs only,
two birds, and two squirrels. It illustrates Bugge's
theory that a Norse poet saw these designs and from
them elaborated the myth of the Ash Yggdrasil in
which were various animals, as told in *Grimnismal*.
The serpent is lacking in the design on the Cross. See
p. 332. The Cross is Anglo-Saxon and dates from
the seventh century. For a full description of these
two Crosses see Professor G. Baldwin Brown, *The
Arts in Early England*, vol. v, from which the illustration is taken.

PLATE XLIII

DETAILED CARVING ON THE BEWCASTLE CROSS

The illustration shows one of the fantastic animals and a bird. From Prof. Baldwin Brown, *The Arts in Early England*, vol. v.

PLATE XLIV

The Ruthwell Cross

The left and right sides of the Ruthwell Cross are
decorated in a similar manner to the design on the
Bewcastle Cross. The illustration shows the left side.
The long lower panel shows the tree and begins below
with a bird having a fantastic tail, an otter, two birds,
two fantastic animals. The upper panel has a bird
and possibly a squirrel. This Cross is also Anglo-
Saxon, of the seventh century, and illustrates Bugge's
theory of Ash Yggdrasil, see p. 332. The illustration
is from Prof. Baldwin Brown, *The Arts in Early
England,* vol. v.

PLATE XLV

The Dearham Cross

This illustrates the tree design as on the Ruthwell and Bewcastle Crosses, but here the tree-stem only is shown, while the branches have become a chain plait ornament. The date of this Cross at Dearham, Cumberland, is *c.* 1000 A.D. From a photograph by Prof. Baldwin Brown.

PLATE XLVI

Magic Symbols: Detail from the Smaller Golden Horn

Magic signs from later Icelandic tradition.

(1). *Ægishjalmr.* In Eddic poetry this made its possessor irresistible. In modern Icelandic custom this sign is moulded in lead, and the mould is pressed between the eyes, while the formula 'I wear the helmet of terror between my brows,' or 'I wash off from me the hates of my fiends, the anger of mighty men,' is repeated.

(2). *Ginnir,* 'the divine,' 'the demoniac,' cf. the Eddic words *ginnheilag,* 'supremely holy,' *ginnregin,* 'high or holy gods.'

(3). *Ginnfaxi,* the *ginnir* provided with a *fax,* written on the leaf of a tree, and placed by wrestlers in their shoe.

(4). *Angrgapi,* meaning uncertain.

(5). *Thorshamar,* 'the hammer of Thor.' Cf. J. Arnason, *Islenzkar Tjodsögur og æfintyre,* vol. i.

Two warriors, from the smaller golden horn. Beside each is the symbol which represents the *ægishjalmr* or 'helmet of terror,' signifying invincibility.

Ægishjálmur.   Ginfaxi.   Angurgapi   Ginnir.   Þórshamar.

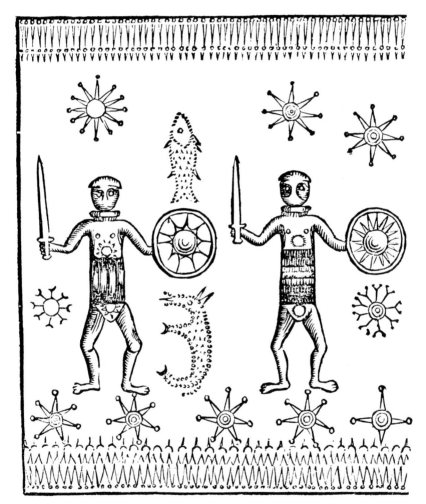

PLATE XLVII

ANGLO-SAXON DRAUGHTSMEN

Draughtsmen, of horses' teeth, beginning of seventh century. From a set of sixty-three pieces found at King's Field, Faversham, Kent, now in the British Museum.

Another set, of the same date but of more elaborate technique, found in a tumulus at Taplow, Buckinghamshire, and now in the British Museum. These illustrate the passages in *Voluspa* regarding the game of tables played by the Gods. See pp. 345–46.

From photographs, by permission of the British Museum authorities.

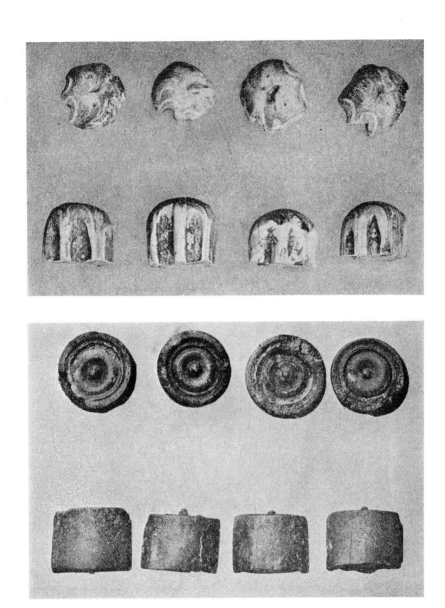